Judaism,
Christianity,
and Islam

JUDAISM, CHRISTIANITY, AND ISLAM

The Classical Texts and Their Interpretation

VOLUME 3

The Works of the Spirit

F. E. PETERS

Princeton University Press

Princeton, New Jersey

Copyright © 1990 by Princeton University Press

Published by Princeton University Press, 41 William Street,
Princeton, New Jersey 08540
In the United Kingdom: Princeton University Press,
Chichester, West Sussex

Library of Congress Cataloging-in-Publication Data
Peters, F. E. (Francis E.)
Judaism, Christianity, and Islam : the classical texts
and their interpretation / F.E. Peters.
p.   cm.
Also published in a single volume.
Includes index.
Contents: v. 1. From covenant to community — v. 2. The word
and the law and the people of God — v.3. The works
of the spirit.
ISBN 0-691-02044-2 (v. 1 : acid-free paper)
ISBN 0-691-02054-X (v. 2 : acid-free paper)
ISBN 0-691-02055-8 (v. 3 : acid-free paper)
1. Judaism. 2. Christianity. 3. Islam. I. Title.
BL80.2.P455   1990b
291—dc20   90-36670

This book has been composed in Linotron Perpetua type

Princeton University Press books are printed on acid-free paper
and meet the guidelines for permanence and durability of the
Committee on Production Guidelines for Book Longevity of the
Council on Library Resources

Printed in the United States of America

(Pbk.)   5   7   9   10   8   6   4

For

Barakat Ahmad

in whose true spirit this work was conceived,
and to whose joyfully recollected memory
it is now gratefully dedicated

Contents

CHAPTER 3

Withdrawal from the World   123

CHAPTER 4

The Mystics' Ascent to God   186

CHAPTER 5

Thinking about God   263

CHAPTER 6

The Last Things   328

Preface

"Hear, O Israel," the Lord said to His Chosen People near the beginning of their extraordinary relationship. And that is the matter of this book: what His people heard from the Lord and how they understood it. Not merely the original Israelites, but His other peoples, the Christians and Muslims: they too chosen, as they say; they too, as they claim, authentic "sons of Abraham."

What they heard when God spoke to them is not difficult to discover. Jews, Christians, and Muslims alike felt strongly and thought carefully enough about it to preserve the words of God inside the covers of a Book, or rather, three books—the Bible, the New Testament, and the Quran—which they eye somewhat uneasily in each other's hands. So it is in the first instance God's words that have been reproduced here, not in their entirety—the integral texts are readily enough available—but in extracts and, more importantly, in a manner that will make it somewhat simpler to comprehend the other element of what is undertaken in this work: How did the Jews, Christians, and Muslims understand what they had heard?

The words of God to Abraham and later to Moses on Sinai, they had all heard. The Bible is Scripture for all three religious communities, and indeed it is the basis of each's claim to be God's own people. But each group understood those words differently, whether as a basis of belief or as a directive to action. And even in each group's own, more particular and privileged communication with or from God—the Jews' Mishna, for example, or the letters of Paul, or the traditions from the Prophet Muhammad—there is little enough agreement within the community itself on what exactly God meant or what precisely was the good to be done or the evil to be avoided.

What I have attempted is to lay out the kinds of issues these three intimately related groups chiefly thought about, the questions that most interested them, and particularly such matters as might encourage comparison among the three; I have then selected standard or well-known or important texts to illustrate those matters. Jews, Christians, and Muslims all thought about the Law of God, for example, and how God ought to be worshiped, about authority and the authorities, about angels and heaven and hell; each group attempted on occasion to state what it believed and to make its members somehow conform to it; and most consequential of all perhaps, the three religious communities shared an invincible conviction that God's revelation to them was not confined to that revered and well-guarded Book we call Scripture.

This is obviously not a history of Judaism, Christianity, and Islam, and even less of the three communities of believers. The historically minded will doubtless be puzzled, and perhaps dismayed, at the sometimes odd juxtaposition of authorities or events. I have no remedy for either the puzzlement or the dismay except to refer them to histories of the faiths or the communities, of which there is certainly no lack. Here the objective is to keep the three communities of believers in one line of sight and to focus on each through a single topic that interested them all. Thus, after the first four chapters, which follow a rough time line, the presentation moves to a topical arrangement that violates the chronological order at almost every turn but has the advantage, I hope, of hearing each group out on subjects of parallel or mutual or polemical concern.

It is, in any event, the same way the sources themselves deal with the matter. Though Scripture is often cast in the form of history, not many of those who came after viewed the sacred books through the eyes of the historian. There is the Jew Josephus, yes, and the Christian Eusebius, and Muhammad's biographer Ibn Ishaq. But for the rest, the authors represented in these pages are chiefly lawyers, theologians, priests, and visionaries—Jewish, Christian, and Muslim believers who were disinterested in the past as past, since for them the past was, like the Torah in the Talmud and like the Bible in both the Gospels and the Quran, eternally present. In reading the third-century rabbis, for example, one cannot really tell that there was no longer a Temple in Jerusalem and that no priests had made sacrifice there for more than a century, much less when that catastrophic destruction took place or what merely human acts contributed to it.

Nor were those same authorities much interested in the present as present. We catch contemporary reflections, of course, but their primary concern was not to bring us up to date on the present state of the People of God, on how well or poorly the Law of God was being observed. Our authors tell us, for example, that there were rules governing the conduct of Christians and Jews living under Islam; but they do not tell us, as other kinds of sources do, which regulations were actually in force and for whom, or which were simply on the books. Since the "books" in question are likely to have been holy books or equally holy traditions, to be on them or in them was what really mattered and not how many "commoners of the land" were actually fornicating, killing their neighbors, or violating the Sabbath. We have ways of discovering, or guessing about, the latter, but not from our lawyers and divines, who had more important things to concern them.

In reproducing rather than retelling Scripture, I have allowed God speak for Himself, and I have extended the courtesy to the Jews, Christians, and Muslims as well. And those children of a voluble God have spoken, sometimes clearly and eloquently; at times obscurely, perhaps because they did not understand or perhaps because they chose not to say; sometimes gently and sometimes rudely, especially when they are speaking of each other. I have kept my own explanations to a minimum on the simple principle that all these "Peoples of the Book" are capable of and should be permitted to speak for themselves. I have supplied some factual data, provided contexts where such seemed required, and attempted some explanatory transitions across what is a somewhat discontinuous terrain. Much is missing, to be sure: saints are often more interesting than their writings and religious art more striking than tracts on iconoclasm. God's own preference for history over theology is well known.

I have made here almost no judgments about authenticity: these are the received texts, scriptural and otherwise, of each community. And I have tried, despite strong professional and personal inclinations to the contrary, not to seduce the reader into the enormous historical and textual problems that almost every one of these texts—and often every line and every single word of them—has raised over the centuries among believers and nonbelievers alike. Thus there are no traces here of the revelations of Julius Wellhausen or Ignaz Goldziher, no echoes of the prophetic voices of Rudolf Bultmann or Joseph Schacht, of Jacob Neusner or Patricia Crone, no sign of "P" or "E" or "J" or the even more celebrated "Q". And finally, I have attempted to reduce technical vocabulary, particularly of the transliterated variety, to an absolute minimum: lovers of halakha and hadith will have to be served elsewhere.

This work was originally composed as a companion for my Children of Abraham: Judaism, Christianity, Islam. It is in a sense the flesh to the latter's bone, and, in the ineluctable manner of flesh, has put on quite a bit of weight in the process. Nor is the order exactly the same as in that earlier work. Here the matter is divided into three parts: From Covenant to

Community; The Word and the Law and the People of God; The Works of the Spirit. But even though the arrangement is different, the same general topics are covered. More important, the time parameters of the earlier work are this one's as well: we begin here literally at the beginning, but break off while each religious complex is still in its "classical" or, perhaps less provocatively, its "scholastic" period. To put it another way, this collection ends before the great movements of modernism and reform touched—at different moments and in differing degrees—Judaism, Christianity, and Islam and rendered them different. Not everyone will be happy with such a peremptory leave-taking, particularly those who prefer the reformed to the traditional versions of these communities. No matter. Given the limitations of the guide, it cannot be otherwise.

The only abbreviations requiring explanation are: B.C.E. = Before the Common Era, and C.E. = the Common Era. The M prefix before a title means Mishna; BT = Babylonian Talmud and JT = Jerusalem or Palestinian Talmud.

The texts used for this work have all been published in one place or another, often in many places since, as I have said, my objective throughout is to place before the reader the "classical texts" of the three religious communities. They are not only published; most of them are very well known to the members of the community whose heritage they are. Thus they have also been translated out of their original Hebrew and Aramaic, Greek and Latin, Arabic and Persian into a variety of other languages, including English. The question is not where to find the texts but which to choose and whose version to prefer.

Of the translations used in compiling this dossier, some are mine and some, as noted in the Acknowledgments, are from other hands. Where I have used others' versions, I have generally modified them only to the extent of standardizing names—the English word "God" has replaced the translators' untranslated "Allah" throughout, for example—and of reducing all dates to those of the Common Era.

Stockport, New York

Acknowledgments

Translations of the Hebrew Bible are derived from *A New Translation of the Holy Scriptures according to the Massoretic Text*, second edition, Philadelphia: Jewish Publication Society of America, 1982.

Translations of the biblical apocrypha are derived from *The Apocryphal Old Testament*, edited by H.D.F. Sparks, Oxford: Clarendon Press, 1984.

Translations of the deutero-canonical books and the New Testament are derived from *The New English Bible with the Apocrypha*, corrected impression of the second edition, New York: Oxford University Press, 1972. Translations of the New Testament apocrypha are derived from Edgar Hennecke and Wilhelm Schneemelcher (eds.), *New Testament Apocrypha*, 2 vols., translated by R. McLean Wilson et al., Philadelphia: Westminster Press, 1963–1965.

Translations of the Quran are derived from Ahmed Ali, *Al-Qur'an*, Princeton: Princeton University Press, 1988.

A Brief Chronology

B.C.E. is an abbreviation of "Before the Common Era" and C.E. of the "Common Era." The Common Era is that of the Gregorian calendar, where time is measured before or after what was thought to be the birth year of Jesus: in Latin, *Anno Domini*, the "Year of the Lord," abbreviated A.D. In fact, Jesus' date of birth is now placed in or about 4 B.C.E.

Muslims also use a "before" and "after" system. In their case the watershed date is that of the *Hijrah* or Emigration of Muhammad from Mecca to Medina in 622 C.E., called in the West A.H., or *Anno Hegirae*.

Jewish time reckoning is only "after," that is, from the Creation of the World, normally understood to be about 4000 years B.C.E.

B.C.E.

ca. 1700	God's Covenant with Abraham
ca. 1200	The exodus from Egypt; the giving of the Torah to Moses on Mount Sinai
ca. 1000	David, king of the Israelites, captures Jerusalem and makes it his capital
ca. 970	Solomon builds the First Temple in Jerusalem
621	Josiah centralizes all Jewish worship in the Temple in Jerusalem
587	Babylonians under Nebuchadnezzar carry Israelites into exile in Babylon; the destruction of Solomon's Temple
538	Exiles return to Judea; Ezra; Nehemiah; rebuilding of Jerusalem Temple
332	Alexander the Great in the Near East; Greek dynasties rule Palestine
ca. 280	Translation of Bible in Greek: the "Septuagint"
200	The Seleucid dynasty of Syria replaces the Ptolemies as rulers of Palestine
175–164	Antiochus IV Epiphanes; profanation of the Temple
164	Maccabean revolt; Jewish independence
164–37	The Hasmonean dynasty rules Palestine

37–4	Herod the Great, king of Judea
ca. 25–45 C.E.	Philo in Alexandria
20	Herod begins restoration of the Temple
ca. 4	Birth of Jesus in Bethlehem

C.E.

6	Romans take over direct rule of Judea
26–36	Pontius Pilate, Roman prefect of Judea
ca. 30	Execution of Jesus in Jerusalem
the 50s	Letters of Paul
ca. 60–70	Composition of Mark, earliest of the Gospels
ca. 62	Death of James in Jerusalem and Peter and Paul in Rome
66	Jewish insurrection in Palestine; flight of Yohanan ben Zakkai to Jabneh (Jamnia) and of Jewish Christians to the Transjordan
70	Romans under Titus destroy Herod's Temple
ca. 80–100	Remaining three canonical Gospels written
ca. 100	Death of the Jewish historian Josephus
135	Second Jewish revolt in Palestine; Jerusalem leveled and Jews forbidden to live there
ca. 200	Widespread persecutions of Christians in the Roman Empire; redaction of the Mishna by Judah "the Prince"
ca. 250	Antony, the first hermit, withdraws to the desert of Egypt
303	Last violent persecution of Christians by Diocletian
313	Constantine, the first Christian emperor, suspends persecution of Christians
318	Pachomius founds the first monastery, or community of ascetics, in Egypt
325	First ecumenical council of the Christian Church at Nicea
330	Constantine and his mother Helena begin the conversion of Jerusalem into a Christian holy city
340	First Christian monasteries founded in the West
381	Decree establishing Christianity as the official religion of the Roman Empire
399	Death of the Christian mystic Evagrius of Pontus
410	Visigoths sack Rome
425	Office of Nasi, or Patriarch, abolished in the Roman Empire
430	Death of Augustine, Latin theologian of Hippo in North Africa
451	Ecumenical council of Chalcedon
ca. 500	Completion of the *gemaras* at Tiberias and (ca. 600) in Iraq: thus the final versions of the "Jerusalem" and "Babylonian" Talmuds
ca. 535	Benedict founds his monastery at Monte Cassino
ca. 570	Birth of Muhammad at Mecca

1134–1204	Moses Maimonides, Jewish theologian and lawyer
1187	Muslims under Saladin retake Jerusalem
1198	Death of the Muslim philosopher Ibn Rushd (Averroes)
1225–1274	Thomas Aquinas; the height of medieval Christian theology in the West
ca. 1300	Compilation of the *Zohar*, the primary work of Kabbala
1323	Pope Boniface VIII publishes the bull *Unam Sanctam*
1377	Ibn Khaldun's *Prolegomenon to History*
1453	Constantinople falls to the Turks
1492	Christian reconquest of Spain completed; Jewish migrations to Islamic lands in North Africa and the Near East
1488–1575	Joseph Caro, author of *Shulhan Aruch*
1517	Luther posts his controversial theses; beginning of the Protestant Reformation

Introduction

Judaism, Christianity, and Islam, in addition to their family affiliation, were also members of the larger community of religions in the Near East. By the time of the advent of Islam, that fellowship had been much diminished, due largely to the spread of Christianity. But at some stages of their history all three were exposed not only to the doubtless powerful attraction of each other—even Judaism, the disinterested progenitor of the other two, had to live for millennia under the political sovereignty of Christianity or Islam—but to the religious beliefs and practices of the pagans, from the theriolatry of Pharaonic Egypt to the Hindu sensibilities of medieval India.

It was not exactly a symmetrical encounter. Most of the pagan cults of the ancient and medieval worlds were officially and actually tolerant of the religious practices of others—there is room for all in a polytheistic world. The Children of Abraham, on the other hand, though grudgingly accepting of each other, were professedly and actually intolerant of all other religious systems. The One True God of Abraham was, on His own witness, a jealous deity who brooked no rivals, and his followers were as fanatic and intolerant as He in their view of the ritual acts and spiritual beliefs of those other "gentiles," "pagans," and "infidels." Conversion or death was a choice that no one of the three hesitated to impose on those unbelievers unhappy enough to be caught under their severe sovereignty.

Yet if acceptance of paganism was out of the question, adaptation was not. Novelty, exoticism, and the political power of unbelievers were all inducements to accepting other modes of worship and other ways of thinking about God. The Israelites did it in a dangerously open fashion on occasion—and paid God's price. More generally, the borrowing was dressed and veiled, not often in a conscious way, in the raiment of tradition.

It is not the purpose here to ferret out these concealed borrowings from the Gentiles. They are assuredly there, even in the oldest parts of the Bible, though in reading the Torah it is difficult to imagine how there could possibly be any room for such, so detailed are God's prescriptions as to how and where and by whom He wished to be worshiped. The rules for priesthood, tabernacle, and sacrifice were all laid out for the Israelites in Sinai, and the books of Kings show how easily and sumptuously those same settings and rituals could be transferred to a new urban setting in Jerusalem.

The Temple and the priesthoods are a source of immense self-congratulation in both the Torah and the later chronicles of Israel, and they are a source of renewed pride when reinstituted after the Exile. But there were anxieties as well, growing uneasiness as to the spiritual validity of animal sacrifice, doubts as to the authenticity of contemporary versions of the priestly line. And there were alternatives, chiefly the synagogue, a place of study and prayer that had developed perhaps during the Exile but stood ready, even if unintended as such, to serve as the center of Jewish community life in all its aspects after the destruction of the Commonwealth and its Temple in 70 C.E.

Study and prayer replaced sacrifice in post-70 Judaism—the ease and rapidity of the changeover appears nothing short of astonishing. And, the survival of the pre-Islamic pilgrimage apart, the same sensibility prevailed in Islam: the mosque is functionally identical to a synagogue as a place of community assembly and prayer. The differences are purely political. Since the Muslim community was a sovereign one, the assembly was overtly political and the prayer publicly and proudly announced by a lofty crier. Christianity, on the other hand, remained faithful to its legacy from Temple Judaism. The Christian Church was not an adaptation of a synagogue but none other than the Temple writ small, and the Christians' primary liturgical act, for all its similarities to a Passover Seder and its eventual borrowing from some synagogue practices, was read by Christians from the beginning as a form of sacrifice, wherein Jesus was both the new victim and the priest of the New Dispensation.

There is borrowing, then, and in plenty, from the cherubim in Exodus to the rites of the Muslim pilgrimage. We have ignored it, since the communities themselves either ignore or deny that any of their cult practices derive from a source other than Scripture and Tradition. But the works of religion extend far beyond ritual. Out in these farther reaches, divine prescription yields to the broader, more elastic, and so, in fact if not in intent, more permissive work of the Holy Spirit, who "listeth where He will." It was there that the Children of Abraham began to move beyond Scripture, and even beyond mere borrowing, onto that terrain which can only be described as the religious heritage of man. The great mass of the faithful, for example, continued to acknowledge God through liturgical, Scripture-sanctioned worship. But there were other paths whereby believers in the three faiths have sought, either individually or in concert, to approach their Creator. Some Jews, Christians, and Muslims chose to withdraw themselves from a society, their own or others', that they judged too devoted to the world or too distanced from God, in order to pursue their own, private visions of perfection. Flight or search, the impulse has carried them into sometimes solitary and sometimes community exercises that range from self-examination and purification to the most extreme forms of ego-abnegation—all with only the most tenuous connection with Scripture.

For many of its practitioners this ascetical regimen has been an end in itself, a form of psychic catharsis or psychic control. For as many others the denial of self is but a preliminary to a higher and more difficult enterprise: the passage of the liberated soul to the very presence of God, "the flight of the alone to the Alone," as the influential pagan Plotinus called it. Mystics too occur in almost all religious communities, though among the Children of Abraham the motifs and texts of meditation are, of course, Scripture-derived: Moses confronting God Himself on Sinai, Ezekiel in trance before his celestial chariot, Jesus transfigured on Tabor, Muhammad borne by night to Jerusalem and thence to the highest heaven. These are the traditional patterns, though the formulas are often startlingly transcended and the mystics' own expressions of what lay in the bosom of God even more startlingly, sometimes shockingly, idiosyncratic.

The legal establishments of Judaism and Islam, the rabbis on both sides of that aisle, were sometimes unhappy with the mystics' often extravagant claims to a higher and more intimate access to God, as were the more highly institutionalized, and so even less flexible, clerics of the Christian Church. For their part, the more prudent among the mystics took refuge in trope and allegory, wrote poetry, or simply put on an antic air. In the end mysticism, like its antecedent asceticism, found some home place in its community. The rabbis discovered to their occasional unease that kabbala and midrash were not antithetical, nor were sufism and hadith. Christianity built cloisters for its ascetics and welcomed into them, and into the control they implied, those who would fly farther and higher still.

To this point we have followed the Children of Abraham in disclaiming all borrowing. Here we shall likewise follow them in acknowledging the adoption, or at very least the close inspection, of the spiritual goods of the pagans—what one Christian sage called, with a nod toward a little biblically sanctioned larceny in the wake of the Exodus, the "spoliation of the Egyptians." The "Egyptians" in question were actually Greeks, the cultural Hellenes who in the wake of Alexander the Great presented to the Jews a different view of the world and its workings. We have already seen something of that encounter of Judaism with Hellenism, how the political version of the latter was repudiated in Palestine by the Maccabees at the same time that many of its intellectual premises were discovered to be both attractive and useful by Jews in Alexandria, for example. Philo found that the rationalized view of the universe that had been carefully crafted by the Greeks and acknowledged as such could be generally reconciled with what his own Scripture had to say on the subject. When Greek philosophy turned to the question of God—to theology, in short—it was found to be useful in defining, explaining, and even, as the Greeks insisted, in proving what God Himself had revealed. The Jewish experiment with Hellenism aborted at that point; political events in Palestine determined the agenda of first- and second-century Judaism. But Christians found it even more congenial; little wonder, since they were increasingly themselves Hellenes born or reared. The Christian Fathers took up with enthusiasm the discarded work of Philo—as the Jews were themselves to do, though not with quite the same enthusiasm or conviction.

Theology was a generally confident and exuberant growth within the bosom of the Christian Church and, from the fourth century onward, the prevailing mode of discourse for orthodox and heretic alike. Its supple dialectic put in the hands of the Christian teacher and the Christian polemicist a powerful instrument indeed. Eventually the polemicist found good use for the weapon against his new Muslim adversary, and the shock of that encounter may have persuaded the Muslim to train himself in the new, for him, intellectual technology. Some did, if only for counterpolemic; some few went even farther down the road where Aristotle beckoned. It was an enterprise not highly thought of in Islam, however, or in traditional Judaism, where a thoroughgoing rationalism, which the Christians thought they had tamed to their own satisfaction, was judged dangerous and, in the end, too inimical to the faith.

Reason and revelation are hoary adversaries among all the Children of Abraham, but not the only ones. Nor are they even likely the most important. Scripture and tradition, orthodoxy and orthopraxy, the rule of the lawyer and the affect of the mystic have likewise struggled for dominance or control in that same arena. But the verities remained: the fact of Creation and of our consequent dependence, and the certitude of the Judgment. The End Time haunts and colors all thought, whether the concern is personal or communal: the sinner quaking before God, the felicitous in Paradise, the apocalyptic Messiah or Mahdi, the Church Triumphant, the sad fate of "those who have no share in the Afterlife." And beyond even That Time is God Himself, the Maker of the Promise and its Fulfillment.

The Works of the Spirit

1. The Worship of God: Temple and Synagogue

1. The Cult Prescribed from Sinai

In the book of Exodus the Lord provides Moses with elaborate instructions for the veneration of His presence in the midst of the Israelites.

They shall make an ark of acacia wood, two and a half cubits long, one cubit and a half wide and one cubit and a half high. Overlay it with pure gold—overlay it inside and out—and make upon it a gold molding round about. Cast four gold rings for it, to be attached to its four feet, two rings on one of its side walls and two on the other. Make poles of acacia wood and overlay them with gold, then insert the poles into the rings at the side walls of the ark, for carrying the ark. The poles shall remain in the rings of the ark; they shall not be removed from it. And deposit in the ark the [tablets of] the Pact which I shall give you.

You shall make a cover of pure gold, two and a half cubits long and one cubit and a half wide. Make two cherubim of gold—make them of hammered work—at the two ends of the cover. Make one cherub at one end and the other cherub at the other; of one piece with the cover shall you make the cherubim at its two ends. The cherubim shall have their wings spread out above, shielding the cover with their wings. They shall confront each other, the faces of the cherubim being turned toward the cover. Place the cover on top of the ark, after depositing in the ark the Pact which I will give you. There I will meet with you, and I will impart to you—from above the cover, from between the two cherubim that are on top of the ark of the Pact—all that I will command you concerning the Israelite people. (Exodus 25:10–22)

You shall make a table of acacia wood, two cubits long, one cubit wide, and a cubit and a half high. . . . Make its bowls, ladles, jars and jugs with which to offer libations; make them of pure gold. And on the table you shall set the bread of display, to be before Me always. (Exodus 25: 23–30)

You shall take choice flour and bake it into twelve loaves, two-tenths of a measure for each loaf. Place them on a pure table before the Lord in two rows, six to a row. With each row you shall place pure frankincense, which is to be a token offering for the bread, as an offering by fire to the Lord. He [that is, Aaron] shall arrange them before the Lord regularly every sabbath day—it is a commitment for all time on the part of the Israelites. They shall belong to Aaron and his sons, who shall eat of them in the sacred precinct; for they are his as most holy things from the Lord's offering by fire, a due for all time. (Leviticus 24:5–9)

This sacred bread offered to God in the Temple later provided Jesus with a point of departure for one of his own interpretations of the Law.

Once about that time Jesus went through the wheat fields on the Sabbath; and his disciples, feeling hungry, began to pluck some ears of grain and eat them. The Pharisees noticed this and said to him, "Look, your disciples are doing something which is forbidden on the Sabbath." He answered, "Have you not read (1 Sam. 21:1–7) what David did when he and his men were hungry? He went into the house of God and ate the sacred bread, though neither he nor his men had a right to eat it, but only the priests." (Matthew 12:1–4)

We return to the text in Exodus and its description of how the Menora, or lampstand, should be constructed.

Make a lampstand of pure gold. . . . Six branches shall issue from its sides: three branches from one side of the lampstand and three branches from the other side of the lampstand. . . . Make its seven lamps—its lamps shall be so mounted as to give the light on its front side—and its tongs and fire pans of pure gold. It shall be made, with all these furnishings, out of a talent of pure gold. Note well and follow the patterns for them that are being shown you on the mountain. (Exodus 25:31–40)

2. The Tent of the Presence

As for the tabernacle, make it of ten strips of cloth; make these of fine twisted linen, of blue, purple and crimson yarns, with a design of cherubim worked into them. The length of each shall be twenty-eight cubits, and the width of each cloth shall be four cubits, all the cloths to

have the same measurements. . . . You shall make the planks for the tabernacle of acacia wood, upright. The length of each plank shall be ten
cubits and the width of each plank a cubit and a half. (Exodus 26:1–16)

It was within this tent that the Ark of the Covenant was to be preserved.

You shall make a curtain of blue, purple and crimson yarns, and fine
twisted linen; it shall have a design of cherubim worked into it. Hang it
upon four posts of acacia wood overlaid with gold, and having hooks of
gold (set) in four silver sockets. Hang the curtain under the clasps and
carry the Ark of the Pact there behind the curtain, so that the curtain
shall serve you as a partition between the Holy and the Holy of Holies.
Place the cover upon the Ark of the Pact in the Holy of Holies. Put the
table outside the curtain and the lampstand by the south wall of the
Tabernacle, opposite the table, which is placed by the north wall. (Exodus
26:31–35)

3. The Altars

*Then the Lord turns to the subject of the liturgy, His ongoing public and community
worship. First comes the matter of altars.*

You shall make the altar of acacia wood, five cubits long by five
cubits wide—the altar is to be square—and three cubits high. Make its
horns on the four corners, the horns to be of one piece with it, and
overlay it with copper. Make for it pails for removing its ashes, as well as
its scrapers, basins, flesh hooks and fire pans—make all its utensils of
copper. Make for it a grating of meshwork in copper, and on the mesh
make four copper rings at its corners. Set the mesh below, under the
ledge of the altar, so that it extends to the middle of the altar. And make
poles for the altar, poles of acacia wood, and overlay them with copper.
The poles shall be inserted into the rings, so that the poles remain on the
two sides of the altar when it is carried. Make it hollow, of boards. As you
were shown on the mountain, so shall they be made. (Exodus 27:1–8)

Now this is what you shall offer on the altar: two yearling lambs each
day, regularly. You shall offer the one lamb in the morning, you shall offer
the other lamb at twilight. There shall be a tenth of a measure of choice
flour with a quarter of a *hin* of beaten oil mixed in, and a libation of a
quarter *hin* of wine for one lamb; and you shall offer the other lamb at
twilight, repeating with it the meal offering of the morning with its libation—an offer by fire for a pleasing odor to the Lord, a regular burnt
offering through the generations, at the entrance of the Tent of Meeting

before the Lord. For there I will meet with you, and there I will speak with you, and there will I meet with the Israelites, and it shall be sanctified by My Presence.

I will sanctify the Tent of Meeting and the altar, and I will consecrate Aaron and his sons to serve Me as priests. I will abide among the Israelites and I will be their God. And they shall know that I am the Lord their God, who brought them out of the land of Egypt that I might abide among them, I the Lord their God. (Exodus 29:38–46)

There was to be a second altar as well.

And you shall make an altar for burning incense; make it of acacia wood. It shall be a cubit long and a cubit wide—it shall be a square—and two cubits high, its horns of one piece with it. . . . Put it in front of the curtain that is over the Ark of the Pact—where I will meet with you. On it Aaron shall burn aromatic incense; he shall burn it every morning when he tends the lamps, and Aaron shall burn it at twilight when he lights the lamps—a regular incense offering before the Lord throughout the ages. You shall not offer alien incense on it, or a burnt offering or a meal offering; neither shall you pour a libation over it. Once a year Aaron shall perform a purification on its horns with the blood of the sin offering of purification; purification shall be performed on it once a year throughout the ages. It is most holy to the Lord. (Exodus 30:1–10)

4. The Sacrifices

The Lord is to be worshiped by sacrifices, four of which are specified in Leviticus: (1) the whole or burnt offering, (2) the meal or grain offering, (3) the sin offering, and (4) the guilt offering.

The Lord spoke to Moses, saying: Command Aaron and his sons thus:

This is the ritual of the burnt offering. The burnt offering shall remain where it was burned upon the altar all night until morning, while the fire on the altar is kept going on it. The priest shall dress in linen raiment, with linen breeches next to his body; and he shall take up the ashes to which the fire has reduced the burnt offering on the altar and place them beside the altar. He shall then take off his vestments and put on other vestments, and carry the ashes outside the camp to a clean place. The fire on the altar shall be kept burning, not to go out: every morning the priest shall feed wood to it, lay out the burnt offering on it, and turn into smoke the fat parts of the offering of well-being. . . .

This is the ritual of the meal offering. Aaron's sons shall present it before the Lord, in front of the altar. A handful of the choice flour and oil of the meal offering shall be taken from it, with all the frankincense that is on the meal offering, and this token portion shall be turned into smoke on the altar as a pleasing odor to the Lord. What is left of it shall be eaten by Aaron and his sons; it shall be eaten as unleavened cakes, in the sacred precinct; they shall eat it in the enclosure of the Tent of Meeting. It shall not be baked with leaven; I have given it as their portion from My offerings by fire; it is most holy, like the sin offering and the penalty offering. Only the males among Aaron's descendants may eat of it, as their due, for all time throughout the ages from the Lord's offerings by fire. Anything that touches these shall become holy. (Leviticus 6: 7–11)

. . . This is the ritual of the sin offering: the sin offering shall be slaughtered before the Lord, at the spot where the burnt offering is slaughtered: it is most holy. The priest who offers it as a sin offering shall eat of it; it shall be eaten in the sacred precinct, in the enclosure of the Tent of Meeting. Anything that touches its flesh shall become holy; and if any of its blood is spattered on a garment, you shall wash the bespattered garment in the sacred precinct. . . . Only the males in the priestly line may eat of it: it is most holy. But no sin offering may be eaten from which any blood is brought into the Tent of Meeting for expiation in the sanctuary; any such shall be consumed in the fire.

This is the ritual of the guilt offering: it is most holy. The guilt offering shall be slaughtered at the spot where the burnt offering is slaughtered, and its blood shall be dashed on all sides of the altar. All its fat shall be offered: the broad tail; the fat that covers the entrails; the two kidneys and the fat that is on them at the loins; and the protuberance on the liver, which shall be removed with the kidneys. The priest shall burn them into smoke on the alter as an offering by fire to the Lord; it is a guilt offering. Only the males of the priestly line may eat it; it shall be eaten in the sacred precinct: it is most holy.

The guilt offering is like the sin offering. The same rule applies to both: it shall belong to the priest who makes expiation thereby. So, too, the priest who offers a man's burnt offering shall keep the skin of the burnt offering that he offered. Further, any meal offering that is baked in an oven, and any that is prepared in a pan or a griddle, shall belong to the priest who offers it. But every other meal offering, with oil mixed in or dry, shall go to the sons of Aaron all alike. (Leviticus 6:17–7:10)

5. The Temple of Solomon

When David first installed the Ark in his new capital of Jerusalem it was still housed in what must have been a permanent replica of the Tent of the Presence that had been moved from place to place during the long passage from Sinai to the Promised Land. But Solomon had other plans.

Solomon sent this message to King Hiram of Tyre: "In view of what you did for my father David in sending him cedars to build a palace for his residence—see, I intend to build a House for the name of the Lord my God; I will dedicate it to Him for making incense offering of sweet spices in His honor, for the regular rows of bread, and for the morning and evening burnt offerings on sabbaths, new moons, and festivals, as is Israel's eternal duty. The new House I intend to build will be great, inasmuch as our God is greater than all gods." (2 Chronicles 2:2–4)

The building of the House of the Lord began. It was to be, by our best reckoning, 90 × 30 × 45 feet in length, width, and height.

It was in the four hundred and eightieth year after the Israelites left Egypt . . . in the second month, in the fourth year of his reign over Israel [ca. 957 B.C.E.], Solomon began to build the House of the Lord. The house which King Solomon built for the Lord was sixty cubits long, twenty cubits wide and thirty cubits high. The portico in front of the Great Hall of the House was twenty cubits long—along the width of the House— and ten cubits deep to the front of the House. He made windows for the House, recessed and latticed. Against the outside wall of the House—the outside walls of the House enclosing the Great Hall and the Shrine [that is, the Holy of Holies]—he built a storied structure, and he made side chambers all around. . . .

When the House was built, only finished stones cut at the quarry were used, so that no hammer or ax or any iron tool was heard in the House while it was being built. (1 Kings 6:1–7)

At the center of the complex, shielded from the profanity without, was an inner shrine, the "Holy of Holies," which was, like its counterpart in Mecca, a ka'ba or cube. Inside it was placed the sacred Ark of the Covenant.

When Solomon had completed the construction of the House, he paneled the walls of the House on the inside with planks of cedar. . . . Twenty cubits from the rear of the House, he built (a partition) of cedar planks from the floor to the walls [or "the rafters"]; he furnished its interior to serve as a shrine, as Holy of Holies. The front part of the

House, that is, the Great Hall, measured forty cubits. . . . In the innermost part of the House he fixed a shrine in which to place the Ark of the Lord's Covenant. The interior of the shrine was twenty cubits long, twenty cubits wide and twenty cubits high. He overlaid it with solid gold; he similarly overlaid (its) cedar altar. (1 Kings 6:14–21)

Once the building was complete, there followed a ceremony similar to the one that had occurred in David's day to install the Ark of the Covenant in its holy and inviolable housing within Solomon's sanctuary.

Then Solomon convoked the elders of Israel—all the heads of the tribes and the ancestral chieftains of the Israelites—before King Solomon in Jerusalem, to bring up the Ark of the Covenant of the Lord from the City of David, which is called Sion. All the men of Israel gathered before King Solomon at the (pilgrimage) Feast (of Tabernacles) in the month of Ethanim. When all the elders of Israel had come, the priests lifted the Ark and carried up the Ark of the Lord. Then the priests and the Levites brought the Tent of Meeting and all the holy vessels that were in the Tent. Meanwhile King Solomon and the whole community of Israel, who were assembled with him before the Ark, sacrificed sheep and oxen in such abundance that they could not be numbered or counted.

The priests brought in the Ark of the Covenant of the Lord to its place underneath the wings of the cherubim, in the shrine of the House, in the Holy of Holies; for the cherubim had their wings spread over the place of the Ark, so that the cherubim shielded the Ark and its poles from above. The poles projected so that the ends of the poles were visible in the Sanctuary in front of the Shrine, but they could not be seen outside; and there they remain to this day. There was nothing inside the Ark but the two tablets of stone which Moses placed there at Horeb, when the Lord made (a covenant) with the Israelites after their departure from the land of Egypt. (1 Kings 8:1–9)

6. The Temple Liturgy

The full liturgy was then established in the splendid new House of the Lord in Jerusalem.

At that time Solomon offered burnt offerings on the altar which he had built in front of the porch. What was due for each day he sacrificed according to the commandment of Moses for the sabbaths, the new moons and the thrice yearly festivals—the (pilgrimage) Feast of Unleavened Bread [or Passover], of Weeks [or Shabuoth], and of Tabernacles [or

Sukkoth]. Following the prescription of his father David, he set up the divisions of the priests for their duties, and the Levites for their watches, to praise and serve alongside the priests, according to each day's requirement, and the gatekeepers in their watches, gate by gate, for such was the commandment of David. (2 Chronicles 8:12–14)

The element of praise confided to the Levites in the Temple service had been initiated by David himself even before the Temple was built on Mount Moriah. It included from the beginning the singing of psalms, to the accompaniment of instrumental music and dancing.

David ordered the officers of the Levites to install their kinsmen, the singers, with musical instruments, harps, lyres and cymbals, joyfully making their voices heard. (1 Chronicles 15:16)

They brought in the Ark of God and set it up inside the tent which David had pitched for it. . . . He [that is, David] appointed Levites to minister before the Ark of the Lord, to repeat the name, to invoke, to praise, and to extol the Lord God of Israel. Their leader was Asaph. . . . It was then on that day that David first commissioned Asaph and his kinsmen to give praise to the Lord:

> "Praise the Lord; call on His name;
> proclaim His deeds among the peoples.
> Sing praises to Him;
> speak of all His wondrous acts."

(1 Chronicles 16:1–9)

7. Liturgical Psalms

A number of the poems collected in the Bible's Book of Psalms were used for liturgical purposes, chiefly, it is supposed, in the Jerusalem Temple rebuilt after the return from the Babylonian Exile. Indeed, the liturgy itself is described in this passage from Psalm 68.

> Men see Your procession, O God,
> the procession of my God, my king, into the sanctuary.
> First come singers, then musicians,
> amidst maidens playing timbrels.
> In assemblies bless God,
> all Israel assembled bless God,
> the Lord, O you who are from the fountain of Israel.
> There is little Benjamin who rules them,

the princes of Judah who command them,
the princes of Zebulon and Naphtali.
(Psalm 68:24–28)

Psalm 47 is described as an "Enthronement Hymn," one of the type sung at Temple festivals like Sukkoth.

All you peoples, clap your hands,
raise a joyous shout to God.
For the Lord Most high is awesome,
great king over all the earth!
He subjects peoples to us,
sets nations at our feet.
He chose our heritage for us,
the pride of Jacob whom He loved.

God ascends amidst acclamation;
the Lord, to the blasts of the horn.
Sing, O sing to our king;
for God is king over all the earth; sing a hymn.
God reigns over the nations,
God is seated on His holy throne.
The great of the peoples are gathered together,
the retinue of Abraham's God;
for the guardians of the earth belong to God;
He is greatly exalted.
(Psalm 47)

Finally, this "Royal Psalm" is one of the songs used liturgically at the coronation ceremony of an Israelite king. Such songs later found particular favor among the Christians, who read them in a Messianic context.

Why do the nations assemble,
    and peoples plot vain things;
    kings of the earth take their stand,
    and regents intrigue together
    against the Lord and against His anointed?
"Let us break the cords of their yoke,
    shake off their ropes from us!"
He who is enthroned in heaven laughs;
    the Lord mocks at them.
Then He speaks to them in anger,
    terrifying them in His rage,

"But I have installed My king
    on Sion, My holy mountain."
Let me tell of the decree:
    the Lord said to me,
    "You are My son,
    I have fathered you this day.
Ask it of Me,
    and I will make the nations your domain;
    your estate, the limits of the earth.
You can smash them with an iron mace,
    shatter them like potter's ware."

So now, O kings, be prudent;
    accept discipline, you rulers of the earth!
Serve the Lord in awe;
    tremble with fright,
    pay homage in good faith,
    lest He be angered and your way be doomed
    in the mere flash of His anger.
Happy are those who take refuge in Him.
(Psalm 2)

8. The Daily Whole Offering

The central act of the Temple liturgy was the tamid, *or whole offering, daily slaughtered on the high altar. The details of the ritual were preserved intact in the Mishna tractate called Tamid, written down more than a century after such sacrifices had ceased being offered by Jewish priests in Jerusalem.*

The officer said to them [that is, the assembled priests], "Come and cast lots," (to decide) which of you should slaughter, which should sprinkle the blood, which should clear the inner altar of ashes, which should trim the candlestick, and which should take up the ramp the members (of the daily whole offering, namely) the head and the (right) hind leg, and the two fore legs, the rump and the (left) hind leg, the breast and the neck, and the two flanks, the innards and the fine flour, the baked cakes and the wine. They cast lots, and the lot fell upon whom it fell. . . . He said to them, "Go and bring a lamb from the Chamber of Lambs." Now the Chamber of Lambs was in the northwestern corner. Four chambers were there, one was the Chamber of the Lambs, one was the Chamber of the Seals, one the Chamber of the Hearth and one the chamber wherein they made the Bread of the Presence. . . .

He to whom it fell to slaughter the daily whole offering dragged it along to the slaughterhouse, and they to whom it fell to carry the members followed after. The slaughterhouse lay north of the Altar and there stood there eight short pillars; upon these were four-sided blocks of cedar wood into which were fixed iron hooks, three rows to each, whereon they used to hang (the slaughtered beasts). They used to flay them on marble tables between the pillars. . . .

The lamb was not (wholly) bound but only tied, and they to whom it fell to take the members laid hold on it. . . . He whose lot it was to slaughter slaughtered it; and whose lot it was to receive the blood, received the blood and came to the northeastern corner of the Altar and sprinkled it to the east and the north; and then he came to the southeastern corner and sprinkled it to the east and the south. The residue of the blood he poured out at the base (of the Altar) on the south side.

He (that slaughtered it) did not break its hind leg but pierced the knee joint and so hung it up; he flayed it downwards as far as the breast; when he reached the breast he cut off the head and gave to him whose lot it was to take it.

The slaughtering continues in a highly prescribed fashion, the limbs and liturgical paraphernalia are distributed to the priests, who take them and place them on the ramp leading up to the Altar.

And then they came down and betook themselves to the Chamber of Hewn Stone to recite the "Hear, O Lord" [that is, the *Shema*; see below]. The officer said to them, "Recite a benediction!" They recited a benediction, and recited the Ten Commandments, the *Shema* and the "And it shall come to pass if you pay heed . . . " (Deut. 11:13–21) and the "And the Lord spoke to Moses . . . " (Num. 15:37–41). They pronounced three benedictions with the people: "True and firm" and the Abodah and the Priestly Blessing (Num. 6:24–26), and on the Sabbath they pronounced a further benediction for the outgoing course of priests.

He said to them. "You that have never drawn the lot to make the incense preparations, come and cast lots," and the lot fell upon whom it fell. "Both you who have done it before and you who have not, come and cast lots, which of you shall take up the members (of the lamb) from the ramp of the Altar." . . . The other priests they delivered to the servants of the officer of the Temple. These stripped them of their raiment and left them with their drawers only. There were wall niches there whereon were written (the names of) the several articles of clothing. . . .

When the High Priest came in (to the Sanctuary) to prostrate himself, three priests held him, one by his right hand and one by his left hand and one by the precious stones; and when the officer heard the sound of the High Priest's feet as he came out (of his own chamber), he raised the curtain (of the Sanctuary) for him, and he went in and prostrated himself and came out. Then his brethren the priests went in and prostrated themselves and came out.

They came and stood on the steps of the Porch. . . . They then pronounced the Blessing (of the Priests) over the people as a single blessing; in the provinces it was pronounced as three blessings, but in the Temple as a single blessing. In the Temple they pronounced the (divine) Name as it was written, but in the provinces by a substituted word. . . . When the High Priest was minded to burn the offering, he used to ascend the ramp having the Prefect (of the priests) at his right hand. When he had reached the half way, the Prefect took him by the right hand and led him up. The first priest stretched out to him the head and the hind leg (of the lamb), and he laid his hands on them and threw them (into the Alter fire). . . . In like manner they held out to him the rest of the members (of the offering) and he laid his hands on them and threw them into the fire. When he was so minded, he only laid his hands on them and others threw them into the fire. Then he walked around the Altar. Where did he begin? From the corner on the southeast, and so to the northeast and to the northwest and to the southwest.

They (then) gave him the wine for the drink offering, and the Prefect stood by each horn of the Altar with a towel in his hands, and two priests stood at the table of the fat pieces (from the lamb) with two silver trumpets in their hands. They blew a prolonged, a quavering, and prolonged blast. Then they came and stood by Ben Arza [that is, the master of the cymbals], the one on his right and the other on his left. When he [that is, the High Priest] stooped to pour out the drink offering the Prefect waved the towel and Ben Arza clashed the cymbal and the Levites broke forth into singing. When they reached a break in the singing they blew upon the trumpets and the people prostrated themselves; at every break there was a blowing of the trumpet and at every blowing of the trumpet a prostration.

This was the rite of the daily whole offering in the service of the House of our God. May it be His will that it shall be built up again speedily, in our days. Amen. (M.Tamid 3:1–7:3)

9. The Pilgrimage Feasts

Three times a year you shall hold a festival for me. You shall observe the Feast of Unleavened Bread [Passover]—eating unleavened bread for seven days as I have commanded you—at the set time in the month of Abib, for in it you went out of the land of Egypt. . . . You shall celebrate the Feast of Harvest [Shabuoth or "Weeks"], of the firstfruits of your work, of what you sow in the field; and the Feast on the Ingathering [Sukkoth or "Tabernacles"] at the end of the year, when you gather in the results of your work from the field. These three times a year shall all your males appear before the Sovereign, the Lord. (Exodus 23:14–17)

There is another, more complete account of the holy days in Leviticus 23, again as part of the instructions imparted to Moses on Sinai.

The Lord spoke to Moses, saying: Speak to the Israelite people and say to them:

These are My fixed times, the fixed times of the Lord, which you shall proclaim as sacred occasions. [SABBATH] On six days work may be done, but on the seventh day there shall be a sabbath of complete rest, a sacred occasion. You shall do no work; it shall be a sabbath of the Lord throughout your settlements. (Leviticus 23:1–3)

. . . [PASSOVER] In the first month on the fourteenth day of the month, at twilight, there shall be a passover offering to the Lord, and on the fifteenth day of the month, the Lord's Feast of Unleavened Bread. You shall eat unleavened bread for seven days. The first day shall be for you a sacred occasion; you shall not work at your occupations. Seven days you shall make offerings by fire to the Lord. The seventh day shall be a sacred occasion: you shall not work at your occupations. (Leviticus 23:4–8)

. . . [SHABUOTH] When you enter the land which I am giving you and you reap its harvest, you shall bring the first sheaf of your harvest to the priest. He shall wave the sheaf before the Lord for acceptance on your behalf. On the day you wave the sheaf, you shall offer as a burnt offering to the Lord a yearling lamb without blemish. The meal offering with it shall be two-tenths of a measure of choice flour with oil mixed in, an offering by fire of pleasing odor to the Lord; and the libation with it shall be of wine, a quarter of a *hin*. Until that very day, until you have brought the offering of your God, you shall eat no bread or parched grain or fresh ears; it is a law for all throughout the ages in your settlements.

From the day on which you bring the sheaf or wave offering—the day after the sabbath—you shall count off seven weeks. They must be complete: you must count until the day after the seventh week—fifty days [hence, in Greek, Pentecost or "Fifty"]; then you shall bring from your settlements two loaves of bread as a wave offering. . . . They are the Lord's firstfruits. With the bread you shall present, as burnt offerings to the Lord, seven yearling lambs without blemish, one bull of the herd, and two rams, with their meal offerings, and libations, an offering by fire of pleasing odor to the Lord. You shall also sacrifice one he-goat for a sin offering and two yearling lambs as a sacrifice of well-being. . . . On that same day you shall hold a celebration; it shall be a sacred occasion for you; you shall not work at your occupations. This is a law for all time in all your settlements, throughout the ages. (Leviticus 23:10–21)

[SUKKOTH] On the fifteenth day of the seventh month, when you have gathered the yield of your land, you shall observe the Lord's festival [of Tabernacles], for seven days: a complete rest on the first day, and a complete rest on the eighth day. . . . On the first day you shall take the product of *hadar* [traditionally, citrons], branches of palm trees, boughs of leafy trees, and willows of the brook, and you shall rejoice before the Lord your God for seven days. . . . You shall live in booths for seven days, all citizens in Israel shall live in booths, in order that future generations might know that I made the Israelite people live in booths when I brought them out of the land of Egypt, I, the Lord your God. (Leviticus 23:39–43)

The Mishna tractate Sukkah elaborates.

An arbor which is more than twenty ammot in height is not valid, and one which is less than ten handbreadths in height is not valid, or which does not have three walls, or which has a larger area shaded than unshaded, is not valid. If an arbor is old, the School of Shammai consider it invalid, and the School of Hillel says it is valid. What is an old arbor? One constructed thirty days before the festival. But if it was built specifically for the festival, it is valid even if made at the beginning of the year. (M.Sukkah 1:1)

Rabbi Eleazar said: A man is required to eat fourteen meals in the arbor, one during the day and one each evening. The Sages said: there is no prescribed number, but he must eat in the arbor on the first evening of the festival. Rabbi Eleazar also said: If a man has not eaten in the arbor on the first evening of the festival, he must fulfill the obligation on the last evening of the festival. The Sages said: You cannot speak of compensating for a missed obligation, for it is written, "That which is crooked cannot

be made straight and that which is lacking cannot be counted" (Ecclesiastes 1:15). (Ibid. 2:6)

"And thus," Leviticus 23 concludes, "Moses announced to the Israelites the ap-
pointed seasons of the Lord."

10. Rosh Hashanah

In the seventh month, on the first day of the month, you shall observe a complete rest, a sacred occasion commemorated with loud blasts.
You shall not work at your occupations; and you shall bring an offering
by fire to the Lord. (Leviticus 23:23–25)

The Mishna notes this same sacred day that marked the beginning of a new year.

If Rosh Hashanah fell on the Sabbath, they blew the Shofar in the
Temple, but not elsewhere. After the Temple was destroyed, Rabbi Yohanan ben Zakkai ruled that the Shofar might be blown wherever there
was a court. Rabbi Eleazar said: Rabbi Yohanan ben Zakkai made this
ruling only for Yabneh [where the Sanhedrin sat after 70 C.E.]. They
answered him: It makes no difference whether it was Yabneh or any other
place which has a court. (M.Rosh Hashanah 4:1)

11. Yom Kippur

Mark the tenth day of the seventh month as the Day of Atonement.
It shall be a sacred occasion for you: you shall practice self-denial, and you
shall bring an offering by fire to the Lord; you shall do no work throughout that day. For it is a Day of Atonement, on which expiation is made
on your behalf before the Lord your God. Indeed, any person who does
not practice self-denial throughout that day shall be cut off from his kin,
and whoever does any work throughout that day, I will cause that person
to perish from among his people. Do no work whatever; it is a law for all
time, throughout the ages in all your settlements. It shall be a sabbath of
complete rest for you, and you shall practice self-denial; on the ninth day
of the month at evening, from evening to evening, you shall observe this
your sabbath. (Leviticus 23:27–32)

Once again the Mishna spells out the legal details of observance.

On Yom Kippur eating, drinking, washing, anointing, putting on
sandals, and sexual intercourse are forbidden. A king and a bride may
wash their faces, and a woman who has just delivered a child may put on

sandals. This was the opinion of Rabbi Eleazar. But the Sages forbade it. (M.Yoma 8:1)

Young children are not required to fast on Yom Kippur. But they should be trained a year or two in advance so that they may become accustomed to the obligation. (Ibid. 8:4)

If ravenous hunger seizes a man (who is fasting), he may be given even non-kosher things to eat until his eyes brighten. If a mad dog bites him, he may not be given a lobe of its liver to eat, but Rabbi Mattathiah ben Heresh permits it. Rabbi Mattathiah also said: If a man has a pain in his throat, they may drop medicine into his mouth (despite the fast) on the Sabbath, since it is possible his life is in danger. Whenever there is a possibility that life is in danger, this overrides the Sabbath. (Ibid. 8:6)

And Jesus on the same point:

On another occasion when he [that is, Jesus] went to synagogue, there was a a man in the congregation with a withered arm, and they were watching to see whether he would cure him on the Sabbath, so they could bring a charge against him. He said to the man with the withered arm, "Come and stand out here." Then he turned to them. "Is it permitted to do good or to do evil on the Sabbath, to save life or to kill?" They had nothing to say; and looking round at them with anger and sorrow at their obstinate stupidity, he said to the man, "Stretch out your arm." He stretched it out and his arm was restored. (Mark 3:1–5)

12. The Scapegoat

The Lord said to Moses: Tell your brother Aaron that he is not to come at will into the Shrine behind the curtain, in front of the cover that is upon the Ark, lest he die; for I appear in the cloud over the cover. Thus only shall Aaron enter the Shrine: with a bull of the herd for a sin offering and a ram for a burnt offering. . . . And from the Israelite community he shall take two he-goats for a sin offering and a ram for a burnt offering. Aaron is to offer his own bull as a sin offering and make expiation for himself and his household. Aaron shall take the two he-goats and let them stand before the Lord at the entrance of the Tent of Meeting; and he shall place lots upon the two goats, one marked for the Lord and the other marked for Azazel [possibly a demon once exorcised from the community]. Aaron shall bring forward the goat designated by lot for the Lord, which he is to offer as a sin offering, while the goat designated by lot for

Azazel shall be left standing alive before the Lord, to make expiation with it and to send it off to the wilderness for Azazel. . . .

(After sacrificing the bull) he shall take a firepan full of glowing embers scooped from the altar before the Lord, and two handfuls of finely ground aromatic incense, and bring this behind the curtain [that is, within the Holy of Holies]. He shall put the incense on the fire before the Lord, so that the cloud from the incense screens the cover over the [Ark of the] Pact lest he die. He shall take some of the bull's blood and sprinkle it with his finger over the cover on the east side; and in front of the cover he shall sprinkle some of the blood with his finger seven times.

There follows a ritual of purification for both the Tent of the Meeting and of the inner shrine, which was the prototype of the later Holy of Holies in Solomon's Temple.

When Aaron has finished purging the Shrine, the Tent of Meeting, and the altar, the live goat shall be brought forward. Aaron shall lay both his hands on the head of the live goat and confess over it all the iniquities and transgressions of the Israelites, whatever their sins, putting them on the head of the goat; and it shall be sent off into the wilderness through a designated man. Thus the goat shall carry on it all their iniquities to an inaccessible region; and the goat shall be set free in the wilderness. (Leviticus 16:3–22)

In most of the Mishnaic texts cited on Leviticus to this point the elaboration has been legal. Here the recollection—the ceremony had not been performed for over a century when these passages were edited—is liturgical.

He [the High Priest] then went to the scapegoat, placed both his hands on it, and confessed. He said: "O God, Thy people, the House of Israel, have committed iniquities, have transgressed, and have sinned before Thee. O God, forgive, I pray, the iniquities, transgressions and sins which Thy people Israel have committed and transgressed and sinned before Thee, as it is written in the Torah of Thy servant Moses: 'For on this day He shall atone for you to cleanse you; from all your sins you shall be clean before the Lord.' " When the priests and the people standing in the Temple court heard the Ineffable Name out of the mouth of the High Priest, they knelt and bowed down and fell on their faces and said: "Blessed by Thy Name, the glory of whose kingdom is forever and ever." (M. Yoma 6:2)

The High Priest was told: "The he-goat has reached the wilderness." How did they know that the he-goat had reached the wilderness? They set up sentinel posts and from these cloths were waved. Thus they knew that the he-goat had reached the wilderness. Rabbi Judah said: Did they not have a better sign? It was three miles from Jerusalem to Beth Ha-roro. Someone could walk a mile, return a mile, wait enough time to go another mile, and then they would know that the he-goat had reached the wilderness. Rabbi Ishmael said: Did they have another sign? A crimson thread was tied to the door of the Sanctuary. When the he-goat reached the wilderness, the thread turned white, as it is written: "Though your sins be as scarlet, they shall be as white as snow" (Isa. 1:18). (M. Yoma 6:8)

13. The Passover Commandment

Inserted in the description of the historical events surrounding the Israelites' departure from Egypt (Exodus 23ff.), the following instructions are found.

This day shall be to you one of remembrance: you shall celebrate it as a festival of the Lord throughout the ages; you shall celebrate it as an institution for all time. Seven days you shall eat unleavened bread; on the very first day you shall remove leaven from your houses, for whoever eats leavened bread from the first day to the seventh day, that person shall be cut off from Israel.

On the first day you shall hold a sacred convocation, and on the seventh day there shall be a sacred convocation; no work at all shall be done on them; only what every person is to eat, that alone may be prepared for you. You shall observe the [Feast of] Unleavened Bread because this was the very day on which I brought your ranks out of the land of Egypt; you shall observe this day throughout the ages as an institution for all time.

In the first month from the evening which begins the fourteenth day you shall eat unleavened bread until the evening which begins the twenty-first day of the month. No leaven shall be found in your houses for seven days. For whoever eats what is leavened, that person shall be cut off from the assembly of Israel, whether he is a stranger or a citizen of the country. . . . When you enter the land which the Lord will give you, as He promised, you shall observe this rite. And when your children ask you, "What do you mean by this rite?" you shall say, "It is the passover sacrifice to the Lord, because He passed over the houses of the Israelites in Egypt when He smote the Egyptians but saved our houses." (Exodus 12:14–20, 24–27)

14. The Figurative Interpretation of Passover

In the third book of his Guide of the Perplexed *the Torah scholar and philosopher Maimonides (d. 1204 C.E.) lays out what he regards as the reasons for the ceremonial prescriptions of the Torah—the feast days, the appointments of the sanctuary, the priestly vestments, and so on. The exercise is repeated in Questions 101–102 of the* Summa Theologica *of the Christian theologian Thomas Aquinas (d. 1274). In his literal interpretation of these same ceremonies Aquinas follows closely, and even explicitly, the reasons adduced by Maimonides. But for Aquinas, as for most of the Christian tradition, the liturgical prescriptions of the Mosaic Law had, in addition to their principal literal purpose of the suppression of idolatry, a further intent: to figure or foreshadow the New Covenant signaled by the incarnation of Jesus. Thus Aquinas on the literal and figurative cause of Passover.*

The literal reason for the Passover banquet was to commemorate the blessing of being led by God out of Egypt. Hence, by celebrating this banquet, they declared that they belonged to that people which God Himself had taken out of Egypt. For when they were delivered from Egypt they were commanded to sprinkle the lamb's blood on the lintels of their house doors, as though declaring that they were departing from the rites of the Egyptians who worshiped the ram. Hence, by sprinkling or rubbing the blood of the lamb on the doorposts, they were delivered from the danger of extermination which threatened the Egyptians. . . .

The figurative reason is evident, for the sacrifice of the Passover lamb signified the sacrifice of Christ, according to 1 Cor. 5:7, "Christ our Passover is sacrificed." The blood of the lamb, which ensured deliverance from the destroyer, by being sprinkled on the doorposts, signified faith in Christ's Passion in the hearts and on the lips of the faithful, by which same Passion we are delivered from sin and death, according to 1 Pet. 1:18: "You were . . . redeemed . . . with the precious blood . . . of a lamb unspotted." The partaking of its flesh signified the eating of Christ's body in the Sacrament (of the Eucharist); and the flesh was roasted in the fire to signify Christ's passion or charity. And it was eaten with unleavened bread to signify the blameless life of the faithful who partake of Christ's body, according to 1 Cor. 5:8: "Let us feast . . . with the unleavened bread of sincerity and truth." The wild lettuces were added to denote repentance for sins, which is required of those who receive the body of Christ. Their loins were girt in sign of chastity, and the shoes of their feet are the examples of our dead ancestors. The staves they held in their hands denoted pastoral authority; and it was commanded that the Passover lamb should be eaten in one house, that is, in the Catholic Church, and not in the conventicles of heretics. (Aquinas, *Summa Theologica* I/2, ques. 102, art. 5, ad 2) [AQUINAS 1945: 2:886–887]

15. The Upkeep of the Temple

The legislation on Sinai made elaborate and even generous provision, as we have seen, for the support of the priests and Levites dedicated to the service of the Lord. What changed over the centuries was the architectural institutionalization of that service in the Jerusalem Temple, which, with its altar, courts, and outbuildings, constituted an immense liturgical and commercial "industry." The Mosaic Law never envisioned such a permanent complex and had made no provisions for its upkeep or expenses; thus it fell to a later generation of Israelites to address the problem. Solomon himself may have done so, but our first detailed account comes a century and a half later, from the reign of Joash, king of Judah from 837 to 798 B.C.E.

Joash said to the priests, "All the money, current money, which is brought into the House of the Lord as sacred donations, any money a man may pay as the money equivalent of persons [cf. Leviticus 27:2–7] or any other money a man may be minded to bring to the House of the Lord, let the priests receive it, each from his benefactor; they, in turn, shall make repairs on the House, wherever damage may be found." But in the twenty-third year of the reign of Joash (it was found that) the priests had still not carried out repairs to the House. King Joash summoned the priest Jehoiada and the other priests and said to them, "Why have you not kept the House in repair? Henceforth do not accept money from your benefactors any more, but have it donated (directly) to the repair of the House." The priests agreed that they would neither accept money from the people nor undertake repairs on the House.

And the priest Jehoiada took a chest and bored a hole in its lid. He placed it at the right side of the altar as one entered the House of the Lord, and the priestly guards of the threshold deposited there all the money that was brought into the House of the Lord. Whenever they saw that there was much money in the chest, the royal scribe and the High Priest would come up and put the money accumulated in the House of the Lord into bags, and they would count it. Then they would deliver the money that was weighed out to overseers of the work, who were in charge of the House of the Lord. These in turn used it to pay the carpenters and the laborers who worked in the House of the Lord, and the masons and stonecutters. They also paid for the wood and the quarried stone with which to make repairs on the House of the Lord, and for every other expenditure that had to be made in repairing the house. However, no silver bowls and no snuffers, basins or trumpets—no vessels of gold or silver—were made at the House of the Lord from the money brought into the House of the Lord; this was given only to the overseers of the work for the repair of the House of the Lord. No check was kept on the men to whom the money was delivered to pay the workers; for they dealt honestly. Money brought as a guilt offering or a sin offering was not deposited in the House of the Lord; it went to the priests. (2 Kings 12:4–16)

16. Temple Finances after the Exile

After the Exile, in a now impoverished Judea, the question of Temple finances presented itself in a new and urgent form. One rather visionary solution was proposed by Ezekiel.

The burnt offerings, the meal offerings, and the libations on festivals, new moons, sabbaths—all fixed occasions—of the House of Israel shall be the obligation of the prince; he shall provide the sin offerings, the meal offerings, the burnt offerings and the offerings of well-being, to make expiation for Israel. (Ezekiel 45:17)

No Jewish prince arrived, however, to fulfill Ezekiel's vision, and the Temple, without endowed lands or estates, had to make shift as it could. One resource was a new tax voluntarily undertaken by the people at the time of Nehemiah and specifically earmarked for the Temple sacrifices.

We have laid upon ourselves obligations: To charge ourselves one-third of a shekel yearly for the service of the House of our God—for the rows of bread, for the regular meal offering, for the regular burnt offering, (for those of) the sabbaths, the new moons, festivals, for consecrations, for sin offerings to atone for Israel and for all the work in the House of the Lord.

We have cast lots among the priests, the Levites and the people, to bring the wood offering to the House of our God by clans annually at set times in order to provide fuel for the altar of the Lord our God, as is written in the Teaching [that is, the Torah].

We undertake to bring to the House of the Lord annually the first-fruits of our soil and of every fruit tree, also the firstborn of our sons and our beasts, as is written in the Teaching, and to bring the firstlings of our cattle and flocks to the House of our God for the priests who minister in the House of God.

We will bring to the storerooms in the House of our God the first pat of our dough, and our gifts [of grain] and of the fruit of every tree, wine and oil for the priests, and the tithes of our land for the Levites— the Levites who collect the tithes in all our towns subject to royal service. An Aaronite priest must be with the Levites when they collect the tithe; and the Levites must bring up a tithe of the tithes to the House of our God, to the storerooms of the treasury. For it is to the storerooms that the Israelites and the Levites must bring the gifts of grain, wine and oil. The equipment of the sanctuary and of the ministering priests and gate-keepers and the singers is also there. (Nehemiah 10:32–40)

17. Gentile Sacrifice

Gentiles too could offer certain freewill sacrifices in the Temple (M.Shekalim 1:5), but more consequential to the politics of the Temple was the principle that the ruler, Jew or Gentile, could and should contribute to the support of the Temple liturgy. We have explicit testimony in a decree of Antiochus III from about 200 B.C.E., preserved by Josephus.

First we have decided by reasons of piety to furnish for the sacrifices a contribution of sacrificial offerings and wine and oil and incense to the value of 20,000 (drachmas) of silver, and of flour of grain in sacred artabas according to the measure of the country, 1,460 mediamni of wheat and 375 mediamni of salt. I wish all these contributions be furnished them as I have commanded and that the work on the Temple be achieved, the stoas and whatever else needs be built. Let wood be provided from both Judea itself and from among the other peoples and from the Lebanon, without being taxed. Likewise for the other things required to make the restoration of the Temple outstanding. (Josephus, *Antiquities* 12.3.3)

The same point is made somewhat later in Maccabees, with some illuminating comments on the mischief inherent in the system.

During the rule of the High Priest Onias, the holy city (of Jerusalem) enjoyed complete peace and prosperity, and the laws were still observed most scrupulously, because he was a pious man and hated wickedness. The (Greek) kings themselves held the sanctuary in honor and used to embellish the Temple with the most splendid gifts; even Seleucus, king of Asia [Seleucus IV, 187–175 B.C.E.], bore all the expenses of the sacrificial worship from his own revenues.

But a certain Simon, of the clan of Bilgah, who had been appointed administrator of the Temple, quarreled with the High Priest about the regulations of the city market (of Jerusalem). Unable to get the better of Onias, he went to Apollonius son of Thraseus, then governor of Coele-Syria and Phoenicia, and alleged that the treasury at Jerusalem was full of untold riches, indeed the total of the accumulated balances was incalculable and did not correspond to the account of the sacrifices; he suggested that these balances might be brought under the control of the king. When Apollonius met the king, he reported what he had been told about the riches. The king selected Heliodorus, his chief minister, and sent him (to Jerusalem) with orders to remove those treasures. (2 Maccabees 3:1–7)

When the Romans exercised sovereignty over Palestine, they assumed in turn the responsibility of paying for the Temple sacrifices and the honor of having them offered on their behalf. And in 66 C.E., with rebellion brewing in Palestine, that became precisely the issue and, in the sequel, the casus belli *of one of the greatest debacles in Jewish history.*

Some of those most anxious for war made a concerted assault on a fort called Masada, captured it by stealth and exterminated the Roman garrison, installing a garrison of their own in its place. At that same time in the Temple courts Eleazar, son of Ananias the High Priest and a very confident young man, who was Temple Captain, persuaded the ministers of the Temple to accept no gift or offering from a foreigner. And it was this act that made war with Rome inevitable; for they abolished the sacrifices offered for Rome and Caesar himself, and in spite of the earnest appeals of the chief priests and prominent citizens not to cancel the customary offerings for the government, they would not give in.

Among those prominent citizens were the Pharisees, who, if they were unyielding in their punctiliousness in the case of the Jewish king Herod, showed themselves somewhat more pragmatic and accommodating in the case of the Gentile Romans.

Thereupon the principal citizens assembled with the chief priests and the most notable Pharisees to deliberate on the state of affairs, now that they were faced with what seemed like inevitable disaster. . . . They began by expressing their keenest indignation at the audacity of this revolt and their country being threatened with so serious a war. They then proceeded to expose the absurdity of the alleged pretext. Their forefathers, they said, had adorned the sanctuary mainly at the expense of aliens and had always accepted the gifts of foreign nations; not only had they never taken the sacrilegious course of forbidding anyone to offer sacrifices, but they had set up around the Temple the dedicatory offerings that were still to be seen and had remained there for so long a time. But now here were these men, who were provoking the arms of the Romans and courting a war with them, introducing a strange innovation into their religion, and besides endangering the city, laying it open to the charge of impiety, if henceforth it was the Jews alone who allowed no alien the right to sacrifice or worship.

Should such a law be introduced in the case of any private individual, [they continued,] they would be indignant at so inhuman a decree; yet they made light of putting the Romans and Caesar outside the pale. It was to be feared, moreover, that once they rejected the sacrifices for the Romans, they might not be allowed to offer sacrifices even for themselves, and that their city might be placed outside the pale of the empire, unless, with a quick return to discretion, they restored the sacrifices and made amends for the insult before the report reached the ears of those whom they had insulted.

In the course of these pleas, they produced priestly experts on the traditions, who declared that all their ancestors had accepted the sacrifices of aliens. But not one of the revolutionary party would listen to them; even the Temple ministers failed to come to their support and were thus instrumental in bringing about the war. (Josephus, *War* 2.17.1–4)

18. Changing Attitudes toward Sacrifice

Hear the word of the Lord, you chieftains of Sodom;
Give ear to the Lord's instruction,
> You folk of Gomorrah!
"What need have I of all your sacrifices?"
> says the Lord.
"I am sated with the burnt offerings of rams,
> and the suet of fatlings;
> And blood of bulls;
> I have no delight in lambs and he-goats.
That you come to appear before Me—
Who asked that of you?
Trample my courts no more;
> Bringing oblations is futile.
> Incense is offensive to Me.
New moons and sabbaths, proclaiming of solemnities,
> Assemblies with iniquity,
> I cannot abide.
Your new moons and fixed seasons

Fill Me with loathing;
   they are become a burden to Me,
   I cannot endure them.
And when you lift up your hands,
   I will turn my eyes away from you.
Though you pray at length,
I will not listen.
Your hands are stained with crime—
Wash yourselves clean;
Put your evil doings
   Away from My sight.
Cease to do evil;
   Learn to do good.
Devote yourselves to justice;
   Aid the wronged.
Uphold the rights of the orphan;
Defend the cause of the widow."
(Isaiah 1:10–17)

What can I do for you, Ephraim,
What can I do for you, Judah?
When your goodness is like morning clouds
Like dew so early gone?
That is why I have hewn down the prophets,
Have slain them with the words of My mouth:
And the day that dawned brought on your punishment.
For I desire goodness, not sacrifice,
Obedience to God rather than burnt offerings.
(Hosea 6:4–6)

I loathe, I spurn your festivals;
I am not appeased by your solemn assemblies.
If you offer Me burnt offerings—or your meal offerings,
I will not accept them,
I will pay no heed to your gifts of fatlings.
Spare Me the sound of your songs;
And let Me not hear the music of your lutes.
But let justice well up like a river
And righteousness like an unfailing stream.
Did you offer sacrifices and oblations to Me

Those forty years in the wilderness,
O House of Israel?

And you shall carry off your "king"—
Sikkuth and Kiyyun
The images you have made for yourselves
Of your astral deity—
As I drive you into exile beyond Damascus.
(Amos 5:21–27)

19. The Herodian Temple

These late prophetic sentiments did not signal any diminution of popular or official approval of the Temple cult. Zerubbabel's restored Second Temple may have been a relatively modest affair in the wretched circumstances under which it was constructed; but when the resources were available, as they were under Herod (37–4 B.C.E.), a new and more magnificent structure was built upon Mount Moriah in Jerusalem. Josephus is our guide to the inside of the new Jerusalem Temple, which he himself had seen.

Within it [that is, the unrestricted Court of the Gentiles] and not far distant was a second court, accessible by a few steps and surrounded by a stone balustrade with an inscription prohibiting the entry of a foreigner under threat of penalty of death. On its southern and northern side the inner court had three-chambered gateways, equally distant from one another, and on the side where the sun rises it had one great gateway [that is, Nicanor's Gate], through which those of us who were ritually clean used to pass with our wives. Within this court was the sacred court where women were forbidden to enter, and still further within was a third court into which only priests were permitted to go. In this (priests' court) was the Temple (proper), and before it was an altar on which we used to sacrifice whole burnt offerings to God. Into none of these courts did King Herod enter since he was not a priest and was therefore prevented from so doing. But with the construction of the porticoes and the outer courts he did busy himself, and these he finished building in eight years. The Temple (proper) itself was built by the priests in a year and six months, and all the people were filled with joy and offered thanks to God, first of all for the speed (of the work) and next for the king's zeal, and as they celebrated they acclaimed the restoration. (Josephus, *Antiquities* 15.11.5–7)

The Mishna treatise Middoth, which has an elaborate treatment of the chambers of the Temple, also supplies some additional information on the courts.

The Temple Mount measured five hundred cubits by five hundred cubits. Its largest open space was to the south, the next largest to the east, the third largest to the north, and its smallest (open space) was to the west; the place where its measure was greatest was where its use was greatest.

Inside the Temple Mount was a latticed railing, ten handbreadths high. It had thirteen breaches which the Grecian kings had made; they were fenced up again and over against them thirteen prostrations were decreed. Inside this was the Rampart, ten cubits broad. . . .

All the walls there were high, save only the eastern wall, because the (High) Priest that burns the (Red) Heifer and stands on the top of the Mount of Olives should be able to look directly into the entrance of the Sanctuary when the blood is sprinkled. (M.Middoth 2:1, 3, 4)

The careful distinction of the courts, even to the posting of a public warning in Greek and Latin threatening death to intruders beyond the stone balustrade, is the working out in architectural terms of the degrees of holiness focused in that place. The Mishna treatise Kelim sets them out, beginning with the Land of Israel and ending in the inner courts of the Temple.

The Temple Mount is still more holy (than the city of Jerusalem), for no man or woman that has the flux, no menstruant, and no woman after childbirth may enter therein. The Rampart is still more holy, for no Gentiles and none that have contracted uncleanness from a corpse may enter therein. The Court of the Women is still more holy, for none that has immersed himself the selfsame day (because of uncleanness) may enter therein, yet none would thereby become liable to a sin offering. The Court of the Israelites is still more holy, for none whose atonement is yet incomplete may enter therein, and they would thereby become liable to a sin offering. The Court of the Priests is still more holy, for Israelites may not enter therein, save only when they must perform the laying on of hands, slaughtering and waving.

Between the Porch and the Altar is still more holy, for none that has a blemish or whose hair is unloosed may enter there. The Sanctuary is still more holy, for none may enter therein with hands or feet unwashed. The Holy of Holies is still more holy, for none may enter therein save only the High Priest on the Day of Atonement at the time of the (Temple) service. Rabbi Yosi said: In five things is the space between the Porch and the

Altar equal to the Sanctuary: for they may not enter there that have a blemish, or that have drunk wine, or that have hands or feet unwashed, and men must keep far from between the Porch and the Altar at the time of the burning of incense. (M.Kelim 1:8–9)

20. The Sanctuary

And finally, there was the Temple proper, the sanctuary building that housed the Holy of Holies, where the presence of God still dwelled among His people.

Passing within one found oneself in the ground floor of the Sanctuary. This was sixty cubits in height, the same in length, and twenty cubits in breadth. But the sixty cubits of its length were again divided. The front portion, partitioned off at forty cubits, contained within it three most wonderful works of art, universally renowned: a lampstand, a table and and an altar of incense. The seven lamps (such being the number of the branches of the lampstand) represented the planets; the loaves on the table, twelve in number, the circle of the Zodiac and the year; while the altar of incense, by the thirteen fragrant spices from sea and from land, both desert and inhabited, with which it was replenished, signified that all things are of God and for God.

The innermost recess measured twenty cubits, and was screened in like manner from the outer portion by a veil. In this stood nothing whatever; unapproachable, inviolable, invisible to all, it was called the Holy of Holies.

In front of it (the Sanctuary) stood the altar, fifteen cubits high, and with a breadth and length extending alike to fifty cubits, in shape a square with hornlike projections at the corners, and approached from the south by a gently sloping acclivity. No iron was used in its construction, nor did iron ever touch it. (Josephus, *War* 5.5.5–6)

21. The Qumran Community as the Temple of God

There may have been misgivings about Herod both as as a ruler and as a Jew, but the main body of Jews accepted his Temple as a legitimate successor to the Houses of the Lord built by Solomon and Zerubbabel. But not so the priesthoods that served in it. The problem of the legitimacy of the post-Exilic priesthood has nothing to do with Herod but goes back to an earlier era, the Hasmonean monarchy, when a number of Jews refused to accept the validity of the Temple priesthood in the restored

Jewish state and so the validity of the very sacrifices performed by them in the Jerusalem Temple. That, at any rate, is how we read the somewhat opaque allusions that occur in the writings of a body of Jews who withdrew into a separatist community at Qumran at the northwest corner of the Dead Sea. Both the "Community Rule" that formed part of their library, the famous "Dead Sea Scrolls," and another, related document called the "Damascus Rule" make reference to a profanation of the Temple in their day, that is, sometime in the first or second century B.C.E. *The Qumran Community Rule describes the consequences in terms of Temple ritual.*

In the Council of the Community there shall be twelve men and three Priests, perfectly versed in all that is revealed of the Law, whose works shall be truth, righteousness, justice, loving kindness and humility. They shall preserve the faith in the Land with steadfastness and meekness, and shall atone for sin by the practice of justice and by suffering the sorrows of affliction. They shall walk with all men according to the standard of truth and the rule of time.

When these are in Israel, the Council of the Community shall be established in truth. It shall be an everlasting plantation, a House of Holiness for Israel, an Assembly of Supreme Holiness for Aaron. They shall be witnesses to the truth at the Judgment, and shall be the Elect of Goodwill who shall atone for the Land and pay to the wicked their reward. It shall be that tried wall, that "precious cornerstone" whose foundations shall neither rock nor sway in their place (Isa. 28:16). It shall be a Most Holy Dwelling for Aaron, with everlasting knowledge of the Covenant of justice, and shall offer up a sweet fragrance. It shall be a House of Perfection and Truth in Israel that they may establish a Covenant according to the everlasting precepts. And they shall be an agreeable offering, atoning for the Land and determining the judgment of wickedness, and there shall be no more iniquity. (*The Community Rule* 8)
[VERMES 1968: 85]

When these (initiates) become members of the Community in Israel according to all these rules, they shall establish the spirit of holiness according to everlasting truth. They shall atone for guilty rebellion and for sins of unfaithfulness that they may obtain loving kindness for the Land without the flesh of holocausts and the fat of sacrifice. And prayer rightly offered shall be as an acceptable fragrance of righteousness, and perfection of way as a delectable freewill offering. At that time the men of the community shall set apart a House of Holiness in order that it may be united to the most holy things and a House of Community for Israel,

for those who walk in perfection. The sons of Aaron alone shall command
in matters of justice and property, and every rule concerning the men of
the Community shall be determined according to their word. (Ibid. 9)
[VERMES 1968: 87]

22. "Mercy Not Sacrifice Is My Desire"

*The tractate Middoth, from which the following reflections upon the Temple and its
sacrifices are drawn, was collected into the Mishna sometime about 200 C.E., or 130
years after the physical building of the Temple was utterly destroyed in 70 C.E., so
that the Christians could say of it, as Jesus had predicted, "not a stone stood upon
a stone." In some sense, on a spiritual or an ideal plane, the Jerusalem Temple still
existed for those rabbis. But the ritual conservatism implicit in those carefully
preserved details of Temple and courts and now defunct rituals masks a deeper
adjustment to a new reality. Those rabbinic sages had also reflected on the prophetic
wisdom of Hosea and Amos and begun the painful revision of their thinking. And
according to one account, that process was begun almost immediately after the event
by Yohanan ben Zakkai himself, the very sage who escaped the city on the eve of
its destruction and who gave shape and form to much of the rabbinic thinking that
followed.*

Once, as Rabban Yohanan ben Zakkai was coming forth from Jerusalem, Rabbi Joshua followed him and saw the Temple in ruins. "Woe
unto us," Rabbi Joshua cried, "that this, the place where the iniquities of
Israel were atoned for, is laid waste."

"My son," Rabban Yohanan said to him, "be not grieved. We have
another atonement as effective as this." "And what is it?" "It is acts of
loving kindness, as it is said, 'For mercy not sacrifice is My desire' (Hos.
6:6)." [ABOTH RABBI NATHAN 1955: 4:3]

*"Acts of loving kindness" are not further specified in the text. Perhaps there was no
need, since another, more practical and concrete theme was soon woven into the
meditation: Torah study.*

Simeon the Just [perhaps the same High Priest celebrated by Jesus
ben Sira in the passage from Ecclesiasticus 50 already cited] was among
the last of the men of the Great Assembly. He used to say: By three things
is the world sustained: by the Law, by the Temple service and by deeds
of loving kindness. (M.Aboth 1:2)

How so the Torah? Behold, it says, "Mercy is my desire and not sacrifice, not whole offerings but the knowledge of God" (Hos. 6:6). Hence
we see that the whole offering is the most beloved of sacrifices, for the

whole offering is entirely consumed by the flames. . . . But the study of the Torah is more beloved by God than whole offerings. For if a man studies Torah, he comes to know the will of God, as it is said, "Then shall you understand the fear of the Lord and find the will of God" (Prov. 2:5). Hence, when a sage sits and expounds to his congregation, Scripture accounts it to him as though he had offered up fat and blood on the altar. [ABOTH RABBI NATHAN 1955: 4:1]

23. The Nature of Ritual Acts According to Judah Halevi

Freed of the literal obligation to perform a sacrificial liturgy, an even later genera-
tion of Jews was also free to contemplate the deeper significance of those acts, as
Judah Halevi does in this passage.

All these ceremonies, the remission of sins on the Day of Atonement, the cleansing of the sanctuary from impurities by means of the he-goat of Azazel, with all the accompanying ceremonies; the blessing of Israel through Aaron's uplifted hands, and the reciting of the verse "The Lord bless you"; upon every one of these ceremonies the Divine Influence rested. Religious ceremonies are, like the works of nature, composed of accurately measured proportions of the four elements. A trifle renders them perfect and gives them their proper animal or plant form. Every mixture receives the shape proper to it but can also lose it through a trifle. . . . Who, then, can calculate actions upon which the Divine Influence rests, save God alone? This is the mistake made by alchemists and necromancers [that is, those who sought to duplicate nature]. The former thought, indeed, that they could weigh the elementary fire on their scales and produce what they wished, and thus alter the nature of materials, as is done in living beings by natural heat which transforms food into blood, flesh, bones and other organs. . . .

When these necromancers heard that the appearance of the Deity from Adam down to the Children of Israel was gained by sacrifices, they thought it was the result of meditation and research; that the prophets were but deeply learned persons who accomplished their wonders by means of calculations. Then they, for their part, were anxious to fix sacrifices to be offered up at certain times and astrological opportunities, accompanied by ceremonies and burning of incense which their calculations prescribed. . . . The artificial is not like the natural, however, and religious acts are like nature. Being ignorant of their designs, one thinks

of it as nothing but play until the results become apparent. Then one
praises their guide and mover and professes belief in Him.

Suppose you heard nothing about intercourse and its consequences,
but you feel yourself attracted by the lowest of female organs. If you
thought only about the degradation of woman's surrender to you, or the
ignominy of surrendering yourself to a woman, you would say wonder-
ingly, this is as vain as it is absurd! But when you see a being like yourself
born of a woman, then you marvel and take note that you are one of the
preservers of mankind created by God to inhabit the earth. It is the same
with religious actions fixed by God. You slaughter a lamb and smear
yourself with its blood in skinning it, cleaning its entrails, washing, dis-
membering it and sprinkling its blood. Then you arrange the wood, kindle
the fire, place the body upon it. If this were not done in consequence of
a divine command, you would think little of all these actions and think
that they estranged you from God rather than bringing you nearer to
Him. But as soon as the whole is properly accomplished, and you see the
divine fire, or notice in yourself a new spirit, unknown before, or see true
visions and great apparitions, you are aware that this is the fruit of the
preceding acts, as well as of the great influence with which you have come
in contact. (Judah Halevi, *The Khazar King*) [HALEVI 1905: 181–183]

24. Maimonides and Aquinas
on Prayer and Sacrifice

Maimonides distinguished between the primary intention of the Law—the inculca-
tion of true opinions about the existence and nature of God—and a secondary
intention: the gradual abolition of idolatry. The same distinction may be observed
with regard to the specific prescriptions of the Law, and here he applies it to Torah
commands to prayer and sacrifice and supplies as well a gloss on the kinds of
prophetic texts already cited.

I return to my subject and I say, as this kind of worship—I mean the
sacrifices—pertains to a second intention [that is, the abolition of idola-
try], whereas invocation, prayer and similar modes of worship come
closer to the first intention and are necessary for its achievement, He [that
is, God] made a great difference between the two kinds. For one kind of
worship, I mean the offering of sacrifices, even though it was done in His
name, may He be exalted, was not prescribed to us in the way it existed
at first; I mean to say in such a way that sacrifices could be offered in
every place and at every time. Nor could a temple be set up in any

fortuitous place nor could any fortuitous man offer the sacrifice: "Who-soever would, he consecrated him" (1 Kgs. 13:33). On the contrary, He forbade all this and established one single house (as the Temple), "Unto the place which the Lord shall chose" (Deut. 12:26), so that the sacrifices should not be offered elsewhere: "That you offer not your burnt offerings in every place you see" (Deut. 12:13). Also only the offspring of one particular family can be priests. All this was intended to restrict this kind of worship, so that only the portion of it should subsist whose abolition is not required by His wisdom. On the other hand, invocations and prayers are made in every place and by anyone whoever he may be. This also applies to the fringes, the (prayers on) doorposts, and the phylacter-ies and other similar modes of worship.

Because of this notion I have revealed to you, people are frequently blamed in the books of the Prophets because of their zeal for sacrifices, and it is explained to them that they are not the object of a purpose sought for its own sake and that God can dispense with them. Thus Samuel says: "Has the Lord as great delight in burnt offerings and sacrifices as in hearkening to the voice of the Lord . . . " (1 Sam. 15:22). And Isaiah says: " 'To what purpose is your multitude of sacrifices to me?' says the Lord . . . " (Isa. 1:11) And Jeremiah says: "For I spoke not to your fathers, nor commanded them in the day I brought them out of the land of Egypt, concerning burnt offerings or sacrifices; but this thing I com-manded them, saying: Hearken to My voice and I will be your God and you will be My people" (Jer. 7:22–23). This dictum has been regarded as difficult by everyone whose words I have seen or heard. They say: How can Jeremiah say of God that He has given us no injunctions concerning burnt offerings and sacrifices, seeing that the great part of the command-ments are concerned with these things? However, the purpose of the dictum is as I have explained to you. For He says that the first intention consists only in your apprehending Me and not worshiping someone other than Me: "And I will be your God and you will be My people." These laws concerning sacrifices and going to the Temple were given for the sake of the realizing of this fundamental principle. It is for the sake of that principle that I transferred these modes of worship to My name, so that the trace of idolatry be effaced and the fundamental principle of My unity be established. . . .

I have another way of interpreting this verse; it too leads to the very same purpose that we have mentioned. It has been made clear in both the (scriptural) text and in the tradition that in the first legislation given to us there was nothing at all concerning burnt offerings and sacrifices. You ought not to occupy your mind with the passover of Egypt [that is, the sacrifice of the lamb already prescribed in Egypt] for the reason for this is clear and evident, as we shall set forth. . . . The first command given after the exodus from Egypt was the one given us in Marah, namely His saying to us there: "If you will diligently hearken to the voice of the Lord etc." (Exod. 15:26). "There He made them a statute and a judgment etc." (Exod. 15:25). And the correct tradition says: "The Sabbath and the civil laws were prescribed at Marah" (B.Shabbat 87b; B.Sanhedrin 56b). Accordingly, the statute referred to is the Sabbath and the judgment consists in the civil laws, that is, the abolition of mutual wrongdoing. And this is, as we have explained, the first intention: I mean the belief in correct opinions, namely, in the creation of the world in time. For you already know that the foundation of the law addressed to us concerning the Sabbath is its contribution to fortifying this principle, as we have explained in this treatise. Besides the correctness of the beliefs, the intention also included the abolition of wrongdoing among men. (Maimonides, *Guide* 3.32) [MAIMONIDES 1963: 529–531]

Aquinas (d. 1274 C.E.) took Maimonides' argument to its conclusion, driven not so much by logic as by his own Christian reading of God's sacred purpose.

The New Law does not void the observance of the Old Law except in the matter of the ceremonial precepts. Now the latter were figurative of things to come. Therefore, from the very fact that the ceremonial precepts were fulfilled when those things were accomplished which they foreshadowed, it follows that they were no longer to be observed; for if they were to be observed, this would mean that something was still to be accomplished and is not yet fulfilled. Thus the promise of a future gift holds no longer when it has been fulfilled by the presentation of the gift. In this way the legal ceremonies are abolished by being fulfilled. (Aquinas, *Summa Theologica* I/2, ques. 107, art. 2, ad 1) [AQUINAS 1945: 2:961–962]

25. The Synagogue Liturgy

We cannot trace the exact origins of the synagogue, though the existence of some kind of institution combining prayer and Torah study may well go back to the time of the Exile, when the Jews in Iraq had to make do without a Temple and sacrifice. Whatever the case, there were synagogues in Palestine and the Diaspora by the first century. Philo, an eminent Jewish scholar of that era in Alexandria, appears to refer to a service in one such in the following passages.

Innumerable schools of practical wisdom and self-control are opened every seventh day in all cities. In these schools the people sit decorously, keeping silence and listening with the utmost attention out of a thirst for refreshing discourse, while one of the best qualified stands up and instructs them in what is best and most conducive to well-being, things by which their whole life may be made better. (Philo, *On the Special Laws* 2.15)

He [Moses] required them to assemble at the same place on these seventh days, and sitting together in a respectful and orderly manner, hear the laws read so that none should be ignorant of them. And indeed they always assemble and sit together, most of them in silence except when it is the practice to add something to signify their approval of what is read. But some priest who is present or one of the elders reads the holy laws to them and expounds them point by point until about the late afternoon, when they depart, having gained expert knowledge of the holy laws and considerable advance in piety. (Philo in Eusebius, *Evangelical Preparation* 8.7)

This latter passage appears to refer to the homiletic part of a synagogue service. In our earliest accounts from Palestine, which occur in the Gospels, the emphasis is likewise on the guest preacher's discourse on the Scriptures.

They came to Capernaum, and on the Sabbath he [that is, Jesus] went to synagogue and began to teach. The people were astounded at his teaching, for, unlike the doctors of the Law, he taught with a note of authority. (Mark 1:21–22)

Then Jesus, armed with the power of the Spirit, returned to Galilee; and reports about him spread through the whole countryside. He taught in their synagogues and all men sang his praises.

So he came to Nazareth, where he had been brought up, and went to synagogue on the Sabbath day as he regularly did. He stood up to read the lesson and was handed the scroll of the prophet Isaiah. He opened the scroll and found the passage that says, "The spirit of the Lord is upon me because He has anointed me; He has sent me to announce good news to the poor, to proclaim the release for prisoners and recovery of sight for the blind, to let the broken victims go free, to proclaim the year of the Lord's favor" (Isa. 61:1–2).

He rolled up the scroll, gave it back to the attendant, and sat down. And all eyes in the synagogue were fixed on him. He began to speak. "Today," he said, "in your very hearing this text has come true." There was a general stir of admiration; they were surprised that words of such grace should fall from his lips. "Is not this Joseph's son?" they asked. (Luke 4:14–22)

26. The *Shema* ("Hear!")

From these brief texts we cannot conclude what prayers were said as part of the service or even whether the reading from Isaiah was part of the regular cycle of biblical passages that was later characteristic of the synagogue liturgy. That there were standardized prayers from the beginning and that they derived in the main from Scripture seems almost certain. One prayer taken over intact from the earlier Temple liturgy and whose recitation was obligatory, morning and evening, upon every Jew was the Shema, "Hear!" so called from its opening phrase. The whole was derived directly from the Torah.

Hear, O Israel! The Lord is our God, the Lord alone. You shall love the Lord your God with all your heart and with all your soul and with all your might. Take to heart these instructions with which I charge you this day. Impress them upon your children. Recite them when you stay at home and when you are away, when you lie down and when you get up. Bind them as a sign on your hand and let them serve as a symbol [or "frontlet"] between your eyes; inscribe them on the doorposts of your house and your gates. (Deuteronomy 6:4–9)

The Lord spoke to Moses as follows: Speak to the Israelite people and instruct them to make for themselves fringes on the corners of their garments throughout the ages; let them attach a cord of blue to the fringe at each corner. That shall be your fringe; look at it and recall all the commandments of the Lord and observe them, so that you do not follow your heart and eyes in your lustful urge. Thus you will be reminded to observe all My commandments and to be holy to your God. I am the Lord your God who brought you out of the land of Egypt to be your God. I, the Lord your God. (Numbers 15:37–41)

The Mishna provides additional details on the recitation of these scriptural prayers.

If a man recites the "O Hear" so softly that he himself cannot hear, he has nevertheless fulfilled the obligation. Rabbi Yosi says: He has not fulfilled it. If he recites it without pronouncing the words distinctly, Rabbi Yosi says he has fulfilled the obligation; Rabbi Judah says he has not. If a man recites the paragraphs in the wrong order, he has not fulfilled the obligation. If he recites it and makes a mistake, he must go back and recite it again. (M.Berakoth 2:3)

Women, slaves and minors are exempt from reciting the "O Hear" and from putting on phylacteries [that is, the "frontlets" of Deuteronomy 6:8]. But they are obliged to say "the Prayer" [that is, the *tefilla*; see below], to perform the obligation of affixing and kissing a mezuza (next to the doorpost) and to say the blessing after meals. (Ibid. 3:3)

27. "The Prayer" (*Tefilla*)

The liturgical "prayer" (tefilla) par excellence was the Amida, said thrice daily while standing. Attested to from about 100 C.E. onward, it comprised the Shemoneh esreh, the "eighteen" benedictions that lay at the heart of the daily synagogue services, and, in a slightly reduced version, those of the Sabbath and other festivals.

God, open my lips, and my mouth shall pronounce Thy praise.

1. Blessed be You, O God, the God of our fathers, the God of Abraham, Isaac and Jacob, the great God, strong and terrible, most exalted One, Creator of heaven and earth, our shield and the shield of our fathers, our trust in every generation. Blessed be You, O God, the shield of Abraham.

2. You are strong, humiliating those who exalt themselves and pronouncing judgment against the oppressors. You live forever, bringing the dead back to life. You cause the wind to blow and the dew to fall. You support the living and revive the dead, and on a sudden You will bring us salvation. Blessed be You, O God, who brings the dead back to life.

3. You are holy and Your name is awe-inspiring. There is no god besides You. Blessed be You, O God, the Holy God.

4. Favor us with the knowledge which comes from You, and with the intelligence and understanding which comes from Your Torah. Blessed be You, O God, who favors us with knowledge.

5. Cause us to return unto You, O God, and we shall return. Renew our days as before. Blessed be You, O God, who delights in our conversion.

6. Forgive us, O Father, for we have sinned against You; wipe out and remove our iniquities from before Your eyes, for great is Your mercy. Blessed be You, O God, who forgives abundantly.

7 Look upon our distress and fight for us; redeem us because of Your Name. Blessed by You, O God, Redeemer of Israel.

8. Cure us, O God, of the wounds of our hearts, of sorrow and longing. Remove them from us and heal our sickness. Blessed be You, who heals the sicknesses of Your people Israel.

9. Bless this year, O our God, on our behalf, so that it shall be good for all kinds of harvests, and let us see soon the time of our redemption. Send dew and rain to the earth, and feed the earth with the treasures of Your goodness and blessings. Blessed be You, O God, who blesses the years.

10. Sound the great trumpet for our freedom, and raise the standard for the calling together of our exiles. Blessed be You, O God, who gathers the scattered members of Your people Israel.

11. Restore our judges and our counselors as at the beginning. And be You alone ruler over us. Blessed be You, O God, who loves justice.

12. Let there be no hope for renegades, and wipe out the kingdom of pride speedily in our days, and may all Nazarenes and heretics perish instantly, may their names be erased from the Book of Life and not be inscribed with those of the righteous. Blessed be You, O God, who humbles the proud.

13. May You have mercy on those who are converted to justice, and give us ample reward together with those who do Your will. Blessed be You, O God, the trust of the righteous.

14. Have mercy on Your people Israel, on Your city of Jerusalem, on Sion the dwelling place of Your glory, on Your Temple, and on the kingship of the house of David, Your truly anointed one. Blessed be You, O God, the God of David, who builds Jerusalem.

15. Hear, O God, the voice of our prayer and have pity on us, because You are a God full of grace and mercy. Blessed be You, O God, who hears prayer.

16. Be gracious to us and dwell in Sion, and may Your servants serve You in Jerusalem. Blessed be You, O God, whom we serve in reverence.

17. We thank You, our God and the God of our fathers, for all Your kindnesses, for Your love and mercy which You have bestowed on us and upon our fathers. When we stumble, Your love supports us. Blessed be You, O God, who loves to be gracious.

18. Send Your peace to Your people Israel and to Your city and Your portion, and bless us all together. Blessed be You, O God, who makes peace.

Certain rabbis attempted to push the origin of these prayers as far back as patriarchal times, though another tradition connected them directly with the destruction of the Temple in 70 C.E.

It has been stated: Rabbi Yosi son of Rabbi Hanina said: The Tefillas were instituted by the Patriarchs. Rabbi Joshua ben Levi says: The Tefillas were instituted (by the men of the Great Assembly) to replace the daily sacrifices. It has been taught in accordance with Rabbi Yosi ben Hanina and it has (likewise) been taught in accordance with Rabbi Joshua ben Levi. According to Rabbi Yosi ben Hanina Abraham instituted the morning Tefilla, as it says, "And Abraham got up early in the morning to the place where he had stood" (Gen. 19:27), and "standing" means only prayer, as it says, "Then stood up Phineas and prayed" (Ps. 106:30). Isaac instituted the afternoon Tefilla, as it says, "And Isaac went out to meditate in the field at eventide" (Gen. 24:63), and "meditation" means only prayer, as it says, "A prayer of the afflicted when he faints and pours out his meditation before the Lord" (Ps. 102:1). Jacob instituted the evening prayer, as it says, "And he lighted upon the place." (BT.Berakoth 26b)

As the same text in the Babylonian Talmud continues, it becomes unmistakable that the thrice-daily prayer in the synagogue was in fact set down next to, in time if not in place, the prescribed Temple rituals.

Why did they say that the morning "Prayer" could be said until midday? Because the regular morning sacrifice could be brought up to midday. . . . And why did they say that the afternoon "Prayer" can be said up to the evening? Because the regular afternoon offering can be brought up to evening. . . . And why did they say that for the evening "Prayer" there is no limit? Because the members and the fat (of the whole offering) which were not consumed (on the altar) by the evening could be brought for the whole of the night. (Ibid.)

28. The Synagogue Cycle of Scriptural Readings

As we saw in the vignette of Jesus in the synagogue of Nazareth, the service in his day included a reading from Scripture, in his case Isaiah, and perhaps some instruction as well, as appears from this example from a Christian source, in this instance concerning Paul and companions in a Diaspora synagogue at Antioch in Pisidia.

On the Sabbath they went to synagogue and took their seats; and after the reading from the Law and the Prophets, the official of the synagogue sent this message to them: "Friends, if you have anything to say to the people by way of exhortation, let us hear it." Paul rose, made a gesture with his hand, and began. (Acts 13:14–16)

As with the synagogue "prayers," the public and liturgical reading of the Law goes back to Temple times—if not to Moses, as some authors claimed, then at least from the time that Ezra stood in the Temple and supervised the reading of the Torah.

Ezra opened the scroll in the sight of all the people, for he was (standing) above the people; as he opened it, all the people stood up. Ezra blessed the Lord, the great God, and all the people answered, "Amen, Amen," with hands upraised. Then they bowed their heads and prostrated themselves before the Lord with their faces to the ground . . . and the Levites explained the Teaching [that is, the Torah] to the people while the people stood in their places. They read from the scroll of the Law of God, translating it and giving it sense; so they understood the reading. (Nehemiah 8:5–8)

And again, at that very Feast of Tabernacles or Sukkoth:

He read from the scroll of the Torah of God each day, from the first to the last day. They celebrated the festival seven days, and there was a solemn gathering on the eighth, as prescribed. (Nehemiah 8:18)

By the middle of the first Christian century, then, the formal reading of the Law was taking place in synagogues on the Sabbath, and presumably on other festivals as well, now accompanied by selections from the Prophets. How formal or structured this practice was we cannot say, but by the time we reach our next witness, the Mishnaic tractate Megillah, the process is formal indeed.

And in the beginnings of the months and during the mid-festival [that is, in the days intervening before the opening and closing days of Passover and Sukkoth] the Law is read by four (readers); they may not take from them or add to them, and they do close with a reading from the Prophets. He that begins the reading of the Law and he that completes it say a Benediction, the one at the beginning and the other at the end. . . . On a festival day it is read by five, on the Day of Atonement by six and on the Sabbath by seven (readers). They may not take from them but they may add to them and they close with a reading from the Prophets. . . .

He that reads in the Law may not read than less than three verses; he may not read to the interpreter [that is, the translator from Hebrew in to Aramaic] more than one verse (at a time), or in (a reading from the Prophets), three verses, but if these three are three separate paragraphs, he must read them out singly. They may leave out verses in the Prophets, but not in the Law. How much may they leave out? Only so much that he leaves no time for the interpreter to make a pause. (M.Megilla 4:2, 4)

All the essentials of the standard synagogue reading practice are here. The Law was to be read continuously from Sabbath to Sabbath—the starting point was celebrated as the feast of Simhat Torah—with no omissions and with a verse-by-verse translation into Aramaic. The minimum was twenty-one verses each Sabbath (three for each of seven readers), but in fact the average number of verses included in each Sabbath's section (a parashah or seder) was far higher. The entire "Palestinian" cycle, divided into 154 sections, probably took somewhat longer than three and a half years to complete. There later arose in Babylonia a different custom, that of distributing the Torah readings in 53 or 54 parashiyot across the single year, and this annual cycle later became the synagogue norm everywhere in the Jewish world.

Each Torah reading, whether in the Palestinian or the Babylonian division, was accompanied by a haftarah, or reading from the Prophets, done not sequentially but by choice, thus providing a kind of exegesis of each Sabbath's Torah text. What precisely composed the haftarah long remained an open question. Often the connection was manifestly verbal. For example, when Genesis 8:1 on Noah was read, the haftarah was Isaiah 54:9: "For it is like in the days of Noah. . . ." Far more often the connection was eschatological and even messianic, particularly in the original Palestinian cycle. Thus the annual reading of the Torah, which began naturally with Genesis 1:1 ("In the beginning of creation, when God created heaven and earth . . . "), was accompanied in the synagogues by a reading of Isaiah 65:17: "For behold, I create new heavens and a new earth. Former things shall no longer be remembered, nor shall they be called to mind." Indeed, almost half of all the haftaroth selected for public reading in the synagogues on the Sabbath were originally taken from Isaiah, and of these more than two-thirds from the deeply messianic chapters 40–66.

29. Jesus' Passover Seder

According to the Synoptics, on the night before his execution Jesus gathered with his disciples in Jerusalem on the fourteenth of Nisan to celebrate the ritual prescribed in Exodus.

The Lord said to Moses and Aaron in the land of Egypt: This month [that is, Nisan] shall mark for you the beginning of the months; it shall be the first of months of the year for you. Speak to the whole community of Israel and say that on the tenth day of this month each of them shall take a lamb to a family, a lamb to a household. . . . Your lamb shall be without blemish, a yearling male. You may equally take a sheep or a goat. You shall keep watch over it until the fourteenth day of this month; and all the aggregate community of the Israelites shall slaughter it at twilight. They shall take some of the blood and put it on the two doorposts and the lintels of the house in which they are to eat it. They shall eat the flesh that same night; they shall eat it roasted over the fire, with unleavened bread and with bitter herbs. Do not eat any of it raw, or cooked in any way with

water, but roasted—head, legs and entrails—over the fire. You shall not
leave any of it over until morning; if any of it is left until morning, you
shall burn it. This is how you shall eat it: your loins girded, your sandals
on your feet, and your staff in your hand and you shall eat it hurriedly;
it is a passover offering to the Lord. (Exodus 12:1–11)

*Just before the Passover that was to mark his own death, Jesus celebrated some kind
of ritual—whether the actual Passover meal or some kind of preparatory repast is
not entirely clear—with the inner circle of his disciples.*

Now on the first day of Unleavened Bread, when the Passover lambs
were being slaughtered, his disciples said to him [that is, Jesus]: "Where
would you like us to go and prepare for your Passover supper?" So he sent
out two of his disciples with these instructions: "Go into the city, and a
man will meet you carrying a jar of water. Follow him, and when he
enters a house give this message to the owner: 'The Master says, where
is the room reserved for me to eat the Passover with my disciples?' He
will show you a large room upstairs, set out in readiness. Make the preparations for us there." Then the disciples went off, and when they came
into the city they found everything just as he had told them. So they
prepared for Passover.

In the evening he came to the house with the Twelve. As they sat at
supper Jesus said, "I tell you this: one of you will betray me—one who
is eating with me." At this they were dismayed; and one by one they said
to him, "Not I, surely?" "It is one of the Twelve," he said, "who is dipping
in the same bowl with me. The Son of Man is going the way appointed
for him in Scriptures, but alas for that man by whom the Son of Man is
betrayed. It would be better for that man if he had never been born."

During the supper, he took bread and having said the blessing, he
broke it and gave it to them, with the words, "Take this; this is my body."
Then he took a cup, and having offered thanks to God, he gave it to them;
and they all drank from it. And he said, "This is my blood, the blood of
the Covenant, shed for many. I tell you this, never again shall I drink from
the fruit of the vine until that day when I drink it new in the kingdom of
God."

After singing the Passover hymn, they went out to the Mount of
Olives. (Mark 14:12–26)

30. Paul on the Eucharistic Meal

The account in Mark is not our earliest information on this event. It was already recorded by Paul, though without the Passover context, since it was the central act of that evening that chiefly concerned him.

For the tradition which I handed on to you came to me from the Lord himself: that the Lord Jesus, on the night of his arrest, took bread and, after having given thanks to God, broke it and said, "This is my body, which is for you; do this as a memorial of me." In the same way, he took the cup after supper, and said, "This is the cup of the New Covenant sealed by my blood. Whenever you drink it, do this as a memorial of me." For every time you eat this bread and drink the cup, you proclaim the death of the Lord, until he comes.

It follows that anyone who eats the bread or drinks the cup of the Lord unworthily will be guilty of desecrating the body and blood of the Lord. A man must test himself before eating his share of the bread and drinking from the cup. For he who eats and drinks eats and drinks judgment on himself if he does not discern the Body. (Paul, *To the Corinthians* 1.11:23–29)

31. Jesus as the New High Priest

The following text appears somewhat abruptly in the account of Abraham in Genesis.

Then Melchizedek, king of Salem, brought food and wine. He was a priest of God Most High and pronounced this blessing on Abram: "Blessed be Abram by God Most High, creator of heaven and earth. And blessed be God Most High, who has delivered your enemies into your power." Abram gave him a tithe of all the booty. (Genesis 14:18–20)

The existence of a High Priest of the One True God in the age before Moses and so outside of the line of Aaron was of course known to the early Jewish Christians, particularly since Melchizedek had already been used in a messianic context in Psalm 110. They were quick to make capital of it, as here in the letter to the Hebrews.

Every High Priest is taken from among men and appointed their representative before God, to offer gifts and sacrifices for sins. He is able to bear patiently with the ignorant and the erring, since he too is beset by weakness; and because of this he is bound to make sin offerings for himself no less than for the people. And nobody arrogates the honor to himself: he is called by God, as indeed Aaron was. So it is with Christ: he did not confer upon himself the glory of becoming High Priest; it was granted by God, who said to him, "Thou art my Son; this day have I begotten thee" (Ps. 2:7); and also in another place he says, "Thou art a priest forever, in the succession of Melchizedek" (Ps. 110:4). In the days of his earthly life he offered up prayers and petitions, with loud cries and tears, to God who was able to deliver him from the grave. Because of this humble submission his prayer was heard: son though he was, he learned obedience in the school of suffering, and, once perfected, became the source of eternal salvation for all who obey him, named by God High Priest in the succession of Melchizedek. (Hebrews 5:1–11)

Now if perfection had been attainable through the Levitical priesthood—for it was on this basis that the people were given the Law—what further need would there have been to speak of another priest arising in the succession of Melchizedek, instead of the succession of Aaron? For a change of priesthood must mean a change of law. And the one spoken of here belongs to a different tribe, no member of which has ever had anything to do with the altar. For it is very evident that our Lord is sprung from the tribe of Judah, a tribe to which Moses made no reference in speaking of priests. The argument becomes still clearer if the new priest who arises is one like Melchizedek, owing his priesthood not to a system of earth-bound rules but to the power of a life that cannot be destroyed. For here is the testimony: "Thou art a priest forever, in the succession of Melchizedek." The earlier rules are canceled as impotent and useless, since the Law brought nothing to perfection; and a better hope is introduced, through which we draw near to God. (Hebrews 7:11–19)

32. Christian Readings: New Sacrifices, a New Temple

Paul had begun to work out the effects of Jesus' redemptive death on the legal provisions of the Torah, while the author of the Letter to the Hebrews took up the complementary question of biblical ritual and its conversion into the matter of the New Covenant.

The first covenant indeed had its ordinances of divine service and its sanctuary, but a material sanctuary. For a tent was prepared—the first tent—in which was the lampstand and the table with the bread of the Presence; this is called the Holy Place. Beyond the second curtain was the tent called the Most Holy Place. Here was a golden altar of incense and the Ark of the Covenant plated all over with gold, in which were a golden jar containing the manna, and Aaron's staff which once budded, and the Tablets of the Covenant; and above it the cherubim of God's glory, over-shadowing the place of expiation. On these we cannot now enlarge.

Under this arrangement, the priests are always entering the first tent in the discharge of their duties; but the second is entered only once a year, and by the High Priest alone, and even then he must take with him the blood which he offers on his own behalf and for the people's sins of ignorance. By this the Holy Spirit signifies that so long as the earlier tent still stands, the way into the sanctuary remains unrevealed. All this is symbolic, pointing to the present time. The offerings and worship there prescribed cannot give the worshiper inward perfection. It is only a mat-ter of food and drink and various rites of cleansing—outward ordinances in force until the time of reformation.

But now Christ has come, High Priest of good things already in being. The tent of his priesthood is a greater and more perfect one, not made by men's hands, that is, not belonging to this created world. The blood of his sacrifice is his own blood, not the blood of goats and calves. And thus he has entered the sanctuary once and for all and secured eternal deliverance. For if the blood of goats and bulls and the sprinkled ashes of a heifer have power to hallow those who have been defiled and restore their external purity, how much greater is the power of the blood of Christ. He offered himself without blemish to God, a spiritual and eternal sacrifice; and his blood will cleanse our conscience from the dead-ness of our former ways and fit us for the service of the living God. (Hebrews 9:1–14)

33. "A Chosen Race, a Royal Priesthood"

The Letter to the Hebrews chooses to dwell on the Temple of the Old Law as prefiguring that of the New, but there was another set of images surrounding Temple and priesthood, derived in the first instance from a striking messianic figure in Psalm 118:22–23. These images are echoed first by Jesus himself in the Gospels and then enlarged and developed in the first letter of Peter, who may have been thinking of his own Jesus-bestowed name of "stone" or "rock."

> The stone which the builders rejected,
>> has become the chief cornerstone.
> This is the Lord's doing;
>> it is marvelous in our sight.
> (Psalm 118:22–23)

Jesus said to them [that is, the "chief priests and elders of the nation"], "Have you never read in the Scriptures: 'The stone which the builders rejected has become the chief cornerstone. This is the Lord's doing and it is marvelous in our eyes'? Therefore I tell you, the kingdom of God will be taken away from you and given to a nation which yields the proper fruit." (Matthew 21:42–43)

Come to him our living Stone, the stone rejected by men but choice and precious in the sight of God. Come and let yourselves be built, as living stones, into a spiritual temple, become a holy priesthood, to offer spiritual sacrifices acceptable to God through Jesus Christ. For it stands written [Isa. 28:16]:

"I lay in Sion a choice cornerstone of great worth.
The man who has faith in it will not be put to shame."

The great worth of which it speaks is for you to have faith. For those who have no faith, the stone which the builders rejected has become not only the cornerstone but a stone to trip over, a rock to stumble against. They fall when they disbelieve the Word. Such was their appointed lot!

But you are a chosen race, a royal priesthood, a dedicated nation and a people claimed by God for His own, to proclaim the triumph of him who called you out of the darkness into his own marvelous light. You are now the people of God, who were once not His people; outside His mercy once, you have now received His mercy. (Peter, *Letter* 1.2:4–10)

34. The New Christian Temple

The same question of a new, spiritual Temple, and a criticism of the old, is taken up less than a century later in the Letter of Barnabas *in still another manner.*

We now come to the matter of the Temple; and I will show you how mistaken those miserable folk were in pinning their hopes to the building itself, as if that were the home of God, instead of to God, their own Creator. Indeed, they were scarcely less misguided than the heathen in the way they ascribed divine holiness to their Temple. For mark how completely the words of the Lord Himself dispense with it: "Who is it who can span the whole heaven with the breadth of one hand, or the earth with the flat of his palm? Is it not I, says the Lord. The heaven is a throne for me, and the earth a stool for my feet. What sort of house then will you build for Me, and where is the spot on earth that can serve Me for a resting place?" (Isa. 66:1). You can see that their hope was the purest folly. Besides, He also says, "Behold, those who pulled the Temple down will not rebuild it" (Isa. 49:17), the very thing which is in process of fulfillment now; for after their armed rebellion it was demolished by their enemies, and now they themselves are about to build it up again, as subjects of their foemen. All the same, it has been revealed that city, Temple and Jewish people are all alike doomed to perish one day; for Scripture says, "it will come to pass in the last days that the Lord will deliver up to destruction the sheep of the pasture, with their sheepfold and their watchtower" (Enoch 89:56). And for the Lord to say such a thing is for that thing to come about.

But what we have to ask next is, Can there be any such thing as a temple to God at all? To be sure there can, but where He Himself tells us that He is building it and perfecting it. For it is written, "when the Week draws near its close, then a temple of God will be built gloriously in the Name of the Lord" [source unknown]. And from this I must infer that there is indeed such a thing as a temple. Only, mark that it is to be "built in the Name of the Lord"; for in the days before we believed in God, our hearts were a rotten, shaky abode, and a temple only too truly built with hands, since by our persistent opposition to God we had made them into a chamber of idolatry and a home for demons. . . . But when we were granted remission for our sins and came to put our hopes in His Name, we were made new men, created all over again from the beginning; and as a consequence of that, God is actually dwelling within us in that poor habitation of ours. . . . It is in these ways that He admits us, the bondsmen of mortality, into the Temple that is immortal. (*Letter of Barnabas*)

[STANIFORTH 1968: 215–216]

Augustine's understanding of the new Temple is likewise based on his reading of Scripture, in this case a passage in Haggai. He analyzes it not in the allegorizing moral sense of the Letter of Barnabas *but according to the typological exegesis that he wielded with such sophistication.*

The prophecy of Haggai, in which he said that the glory of the house of God would be greater than the first had been (Hag. 2:9), was not fulfilled in the rebuilding of that (second Temple). For it can never be shown to have had so much glory after it was rebuilt as it had in the time of Solomon; rather, the glory of that house is shown to have diminished, first by the cessation of prophecy and then by the nation itself suffering so great calamities, even to the final destruction made by the Romans. . . . But this house which pertains to the New Testament is just as much more glorious as the living stones, I mean believing, renewed men, of which it is constructed, are better. But it was typified by the rebuilding of that (second) Temple for this reason, because the very renovation of that edifice typifies in the prophetic oracle another testament which is called new. When, therefore, God said to the prophet just named, "And I will give peace in this place" (Hag. 2:9), he is to be understood who is typified by that place; for by that place is typified the Church which was to be built by Christ, nothing else can be accepted as the meaning of the saying "I will give peace in this place" except I will give peace in the place which that place signifies. For all typical things seem in some way to personate those whom they typify, as is said by the Apostle (Paul), "that Rock was Christ" (1 Cor. 10:4).

Therefore the glory of this New Testament house is greater than the glory of the Old Testament house; and it will show itself as greater when it shall be dedicated. For then "shall come the desired of all nations" (Hag. 2:7), as we read in the Hebrew. For before his coming he had not yet been desired by all nations. For they knew not him whom they ought to desire, in whom they had not believed. Then, also, according to the Septuagint version—for it also is a prophetic meaning—"shall come those who are elected of the Lord out of all nations." For then indeed there shall come only those who are elected, whereof the Apostle says, "According as He has chosen us before the foundations of the world" (Eph. 1:4). For the Master Builder who said, "Many are called but few are chosen" (Matt. 22:11–14), did not say this of those, who, on being called, came in such a way as to be cast out of the feast, but would point out the house built up of the elect, which henceforth shall dread no ruin. (Augustine, City of God 18.48) [AUGUSTINE 1948: 2:457–458]

35. Idols and Images

You shall not make for yourself a sculpted image, or any likeness of what is in the heavens above, or on the earth below, or in the waters under the earth. (Exodus 20:4–5)

This charge is given to Moses in Deuteronomy:

These are the laws and the rules which you must carefully observe in the land that the Lord, the God of your fathers, is giving to you to possess, as long as you live on earth. You must destroy all the sites at which the nations you are to dispossess worshiped their gods, whether on lofty mountains and on hills or under any luxuriant tree. Tear down their altars, smash their pillars, put their sacred posts to the fire, and cut down the images of their gods, obliterating their name from that site. (Deuteronomy 12:1–3)

Throughout most of their history down to the Exile, the problem of idol worship plagued the Israelites. The Bible makes no effort to dissemble their attraction, from the golden calf set up during Moses' absence on Sinai to the official policy of idol worship established by Jeroboam and his successors as kings of Israel. How seriously the problem was taken emerges clearly from this witheringly sarcastic attack on idols that occurs in chapter 44 of Isaiah.

The makers of idols all work to no purpose;
And the things they treasure can do no good,
As they themselves can testify.
They neither look nor think,
And so shall they be shamed.
Who would fashion a god or cast a statue
That can do no good?
Lo, all its adherents shall be shamed;
They are craftsmen, are merely human.
Let them assemble and all stand up!
They shall be cowed and they shall be shamed. . . .

The craftsman in wood measures with a line.
And marks out a shape with a stylus;
He forms it with scraping tools,
Marking it out with a compass.
He gives it a human form,
The beauty of a man, to dwell in a shrine.
For his use he cuts down cedars;
He chooses plane trees and oaks.
He sets aside trees of the forest;
Or plants firs, and the rain makes them grow.
All this serves man for fuel:
He takes some to warm himself,
And he builds a fire and bakes bread.
He also makes a god of it and worships it,
Fashions an idol and bows down to it!
Part of it he burns in a fire:
On that part he roasts meat.
He eats the roast and is sated.
He also warms himself and cries, "Ah,
I am warm! I can feel the heat!"

Of the rest he makes a god—his own carving!
He bows down to it, worships it;
He prays to it and cries,
"Save me for you are my god!"

They have no wit or judgment:
Their eyes are besmeared, and they see not;
Their minds, and they cannot think.
They do not give thought,
They lack the wit to say:
"Part of it I burned in a fire;
I also baked bread on the coals,
I roasted meat and I ate it—
Should I make the rest an abhorrence?
Should I bow to a block of wood?"
He pursues ashes!
A deluded mind has led him astray,
And he cannot save himself,
"The thing in my hand is a fraud!"
(Isaiah 44:9–20)

After the Exile, and with the Jews' exposure to another, Greek form of paganism, the problem appears to have shifted focus from simply idols to the cult of the ruler, the practice of the Greeks and the Romans of deifying their rulers and encouraging, and occasionally requiring, their veneration as an act of political and cultural solidarity. The Jews understood it as no such thing of course, and the Mishnaic tract devoted to idolatry, Abodah Zarah, or "Alien Cult," is quite specific on the matter of what constituted "idols" in the second century C.E.

All images are forbidden, because they are worshiped once a year. So Rabbi Meir. But the Sages say: Only that is forbidden which bears in its hand a staff or a bird or a sphere. Rabbi Simeon ben Gamaliel says: That which bears anything in its hand.

If a man found fragments of images, these are permitted. If he found (a fragment in) the shape of a hand or the shape of a foot, these are forbidden, since an object the like of these is worshiped.

If a man found objects on which is a figure of the sun, a figure of the moon, or a figure of a serpent, he must throw them into the Dead Sea. Rabbi Simeon ben Gamaliel says: If the figures are found on objects of value, these are forbidden, but if on worthless objects, these are permitted. Rabbi Yosi says: One should break them into pieces and scatter them to the winds or throw them into the sea. They said to him: Even so, (in the first case) they would become manure, and it is written, "Let nothing out of all that had been laid under the ban be found in your possession" (Deut. 13:17). (M.Abodah Zarah 3:1–3)

On the face of it, both the stricter and the broader ruling in the first passage appear to be directed against emperor worship. As the Palestinian Gemara on this passage explains, it is primarily regalia from the imperial iconography that is mentioned in 3:1.

A staff because he ruled the world with it, a bird, as it is written, "My hand has found like a nest the wealth of the peoples," a sphere because the world is made in the shape of a sphere. (JT.Abodah Zarah 3.1)

"It refers," as the Babylonian Gemara flatly states, "to the statues of kings." As a matter of fact, synagogue decoration appears to have gone much further, and floor mosaics from Palestinian synagogues depict not only biblical scenes like the "binding of Isaac" but even the sun god riding in his chariot in the center of a zodiacal circle or standing in majesty with a globe and a whip in his hand. Sentiments obviously changed over the years, and the Palestinian Gemara on this same Mishnaic passage reveals two rabbis who took an obviously more lenient view. The "walls" in question would appear to be those of synagogues.

In the days of Rabbi Yohanan [third century C.E.] they began to paint on walls, and he did not prevent them. . . . In the days of Rabbi Abun [fourth century C.E.] they began to make designs on mosaics, and he did not prevent them. (JT.Abodah Zarah 42b)

And there was, finally, an attempt to distinguish act from intent, idolatry from mere decoration. The point of departure is a text in Leviticus.

You shall not make idols for yourselves, or set up for yourselves carved images or pillars or place figured stones in your land to worship upon, for I am the Lord your God. You shall keep My sabbaths and venerate My sanctuary, Mine, the Lord's. (Leviticus 26:1)

One of the Targums paraphrases this passage.

You shall not set up a figured stone in your land, to bow down to it, but a mosaic pavement of designs and forms you may set in the floor of your places of worship, so long as you do not do obeisance [or "prostrate yourselves"] to it. (Targum Pseudo-Jonathan *ad loc.*)

One of the motives for this relative, and by no means universal, leniency was that the Jews were at ease on the issue of idolatry and that image worship was no longer a major problem or concern. Already in the second century B.C.E. the book called Judith was suggesting that:

There is not one of our tribes or clans, districts or towns, that worships man-made gods today. This did happen in days gone by, and that was why our ancestors were abandoned to their enemies to be slaughtered and pillaged, and great was their downfall. But we acknowledge no God but the Lord. (Judith 8:18–19)

The rabbis remained vigilant, however, and the Talmud found it difficult to resist a good, moralizing story on the subject of idolatry.

Our rabbis taught: Sabta, a townsman of Avlas [in Cilicia] once hired out an ass to a Gentile woman. When she came to Peor, she said to him: "Wait till I enter and come out again." When she came out, he said to her, "Now you wait for me until I go in and come out again." "But," she said, "are you not a Jew?" He replied, "What does that concern you?" He then entered (the shrine), uncovered himself before the idol and then wiped himself on the idol's nose, while the shrine attendants praised him, saying, "No man has ever served this idol this way before."

The pleasantry over, the rabbis register their disapproval, since the ways of the Gentiles are inscrutable in this matter of idols.

He who uncovers himself before Baal Peor thereby serves it, even if his intention was to degrade it.

This story, in the associative manner of the Talmud, recalls a similar point and ruling, this one reminiscent of the pre-Islamic ritual of "stoning of the devils," which was incorporated into the Islamic pilgrimage ceremony.

And he who cast a stone at Merculis thereby serves it, even if his intention was to bruise it. Thus, Rabbi Manasseh was going to Be Toratha [a town in Babylonia]. On his way he was told, "An idol stands in that place." He took up a stone and cast it at the idol's statue. Thereupon they said to him, "It is Merculis." . . . So he went and inquired at the House of Study (whether he had done wrong). They informed him, "We have learned, 'He who casts a stone at Merculis thereby serves it,' that is to say, even if it was merely to bruise it." He said to them, "Then I will go and remove it." But they replied, "Whether one casts a stone or removes it, he incurs guilt, because every stone thus removed leaves room for another." (BT.Sanhedrin 64a)

36. Christian Images

It must have taken the Christians some time to adjust their attitudes toward images that depicted some religious subject matter and so might fairly be thought of as either idolatrous or at the very least unseemly. One such image was an imperial portrait. Christians had once been executed for refusing to worship such, and already the New Testament Apocalypse (Revelation 20:4) refers to the fact. But when it was a Christian emperor who was the subject of the portraiture, there appeared to be few misgivings. Far from being scandalized, the Church historian and Constantine's biographer Eusebius took theological comfort in this particular type of image.

One may ascertain the power of that godly faith which sustained his [that is, Constantine's] soul by this consideration, namely that he had his image portrayed on gold coins in such a manner that he appeared to be gazing upward, as if praying to God. These effigies of his circulated throughout the Roman world. Furthermore, at the palaces the statues placed high over the entrance represented him standing upright, gazing up to heaven, and stretching out his arms in the manner of a man praying. (Eusebius, *Life of Constantine* 4.15) [MANGO 1972: 15]

There were limits, however, as appears in this letter addressed by Eusebius, now speaking as a bishop and not as a historian, to Constantine's sister Constantia. She is immediately plunged into the theological dilemma of the two natures of Jesus Christ, one of which, the divine, could obviously not be portrayed, while the other, the human, seemed almost to invite such portraiture.

You also wrote to me concerning a supposed image of Christ, which image you wished me to send you. Now what kind of thing is this that you call the image of Christ? I do not know what impelled you to request that an image of our Savior be delineated. What sort of image of Christ are you seeking? Is it the true and unalterable one which bears his essential characteristics, or the one which he took up for our sake when he assumed the form of a servant (Phil. 2:7)? . . . Granted, he had two forms, even I do not think that your request has to do with the divine form. . . . Surely, then, you are seeking his image as a servant, that of the flesh which he put on for our sake. But that too, we have been taught, was mingled with the glory of his divinity, so that the mortal part was swallowed up by Life. . . . He showed on the mount (Tabor) that nature which surpasses the human one—when his face shone like the sun and his garments like light. Who, then, would be able to represent by means of dead colors and inanimate delineations the glistening, flashing radiance of such dignity and glory, when even his superhuman disciples could not

bear to behold him in this guise and fell on their faces (Matt. 17:1–8). . . .
How can one paint an image of so wondrous and unattainable a form—if
the term "form" is at all applicable to the divine and spiritual essence—
unless, like the unbelieving pagans, one is to represent things that bear no
possible resemblance to anything? . . . For they too make such idols when
they wish to mold the likeness of what they consider to be a god or, as
they might say, one of the heroes or anything else of the kind, yet are
unable even to approach a resemblance and so delineate and represent
some strange human shapes. Surely, even you will agree that such practices are not lawful for us.

*But Jesus was, after all, a man, and as such subject to portraiture. And he was being
portrayed in Eusebius' day. The bishop is constrained in the end to resort to the
biblical argument.*

But if you mean to ask of me the image not of his form transformed
into that of God but that of the mortal flesh before its transformation, can
it be that you have forgotten that passage in which God lays down the law
that no likeness can be made either of what is in heaven or what is in the
earth beneath? Have you ever heard anything of the kind either yourself
in church or from another person? Are not such things banished and
excluded from churches all over the world, and is it not common knowledge that such practices are not permitted to us alone? (Eusebius, *Letter
to Constantia*) [MANGO 1972: 16–17]

*Eusebius' scruples were overwhelmed by events, chiefly, it would appear, by the
growing popularity of the cult of the saints and martyrs and of their relics. Opposition to the cult did not entirely disappear in the East, however. This is a letter sent
by Epiphanius, bishop of Salamis (d. 403 C.E.), to Emperor Theodosius.*

Which of the ancient Fathers ever painted an image of Christ and
deposited it in a church or a private house? Which ancient bishop ever
dishonored Christ by painting him on door curtains? Which one of them
ever made a spectacle of Abraham, Isaac, Jacob, Moses and the other
prophets and patriarchs, of Peter, Andrew, James, John, Paul and the
other Apostles by painting them on curtains or walls? . . . Furthermore,
they lie by representing the appearance of saints in different forms according to their own whim, sometimes delineating the same persons as
old men, sometimes as youths, and so intruding into things they have not
seen. For they paint the Savior with long hair, and this by conjecture
because he is called a Nazarene, and Nazarenes [that is, a sect of Judeo-
Christians called by that name] wear long hair. They are in error, those

who try to attach stereotypes to him; for the Savior drank wine, whereas the Nazarenes did not. . . .

See you not, O most God-loving emperor, that this state of things is not agreeable to God? Wherefore I entreat you . . . that the curtains which may be found to bear in a spurious manner—and yet they do bear—images of the Apostles or prophets or of the Lord Christ himself should be collected from churches, baptisteries, houses and martyria and that you should give them over for the burial of the poor, and as for the images on the walls, they should be whitewashed. As concerns those that have already been represented in mosaic, seeing that their removal is difficult, you know what to ordain in the wisdom that has been granted you by God: if it is possible to remove them, well and good; but if it proves impossible, let that which has already been done suffice and let no one paint in this manner henceforth. For our fathers delineated nothing except the salutary sign of Christ [that is, the cross] both on their doors and everywhere else. (Epiphanius, *Letter to Theodosius*)   [MANGO 1972: 41–42]

Christians had earlier been called upon to defend their veneration of images, against pagans whose own spiritual view of the deity had already made them remote from the idolatry of their ancestors, and particularly against Jews, whose own position, though fluid, could hardly countenance the Christians' practice. Eventually there were no more pagans, but the argument with the Jews went on, here taken up by the Christian theologian Leontius. The time is early in the seventh century, not long before the arrival of the first Muslims. Earlier in his tract Leontius points out that the Bible itself shows that the Jews had little reluctance to surround themselves with images, and in the most sacred of places, in the Tent of the Presence—witness the golden cherubim—and in the Temple in Jerusalem. He then takes another course.

You do obeisance to the book of the Law, but you do not make obeisance to the parchments and ink but to the words contained in them. And it is thus that I do obeisance to the icon of God, for when I hold the lifeless representation of Christ in my hands, through it I seem to hold and do obeisance to the Christ. As Jacob kissed the bloody coat of Joseph and felt that he held him in his arms, so Christians think that in holding the image they hold Christ or his Apostles and martyrs. . . . As I have often said, in every greeting and obeisance it is the purpose of the action which is in question. And if you accuse me of doing obeisance to the wood of the cross as though it were God, why do you not say the same of the staff of Joseph? Abraham did obeisance to infamous men who sold a sepulcher, and went on his knees before them, but not as though they were gods. Jacob blessed the idolater Pharaoh and did obeisance to Esau,

but not as though they were gods. Do you not see how many salutations and obeisances I have adduced out of the Scriptures, and all without blame? You call us idolaters when it was Christian saints and martyrs who destroyed the temples of the idolaters. (Leontius, *Against the Jews*)
[BAYNES 1955: 233]

37. Christian Iconoclasm

In 787 C.E. an ecumenical council was convened at Nicea, the site of the first general council of the Church, to settle the matter of image worship, which had been troubling the Eastern Church for more than half a century. As part of their deliberations, the bishops sitting there requested a report from a certain John, a Jerusalem presbyter, who described for them the events earlier in that century that had led to an outbreak of image smashing in the Byzantine Empire.

When Umar [Umar II, Caliph 717–720 C.E.] had died, he was succeeded by Yazid [Yazid II, Caliph 720–724 C.E.], a frivolous and fickle man. Now there was in Tiberias a certain leader of the lawless Jews, who was a sorcerer and the instrument of soul-destroying demons, called "Forty Cubits High." . . . Being informed of the frivolity of the ruler Yazid, this wicked Jew went up to him and attempted to make some prophecies. Having in this manner gained the tyrant's favor, he said: "I wish, O Caliph, in the light of the good will which I have toward you, to suggest a certain method, easy to accomplish, by which you will gain an extension of your life and will remain here to rule for thirty years, if you put what I say into effect." Won over by the promise of longevity . . . the senseless tyrant replied: "Anything you suggest to me I shall readily do. . . ." Whereupon the Jewish sorcerer said to him: "Give an order without delay or postponement that an encyclical letter be issued throughout your dominions to the effect that every kind of pictorial representation, be it on boards or on wall mosaics or on holy vessels or altar cloths, or anything else of the sort that is found in Christian churches should be obliterated and utterly destroyed; not only these, but also all the effigies that are set up as decoration in the marketplaces of cities." It was a devilish plot on the part of the false prophet to have added "all effigies" because he tried to avoid the suspicion of being hostile to us (Christians).

The wicked tyrant was easily persuaded by him and sent out emissaries throughout his dominions to pull down the holy icons and other images. And in this fashion he denuded God's churches . . . before this plague had reached our country [that is, the Byzantine Empire]. And since the God-loving Christians took to flight (across the frontier) so as not to destroy the icons with their own hands, the Amirs who had been charged with this task imposed it on accursed Jews and miserable Arabs. And so they burnt the holy icons, and some churches they whitewashed, while others they scraped down.

When the unworthy bishop of Nacolia [a see in Anatolia] and his followers heard of this, they imitated the lawless Jews and infidel Arabs and set about insulting the churches of God. . . . And when after doing this, the Caliph Yazid died, no more than two and a half years later, and went into the eternal fire, the images were restored to their original position and honor. And his son Walid [Walid II, Caliph 743–744 C.E.; Yazid's immediate successor was Hisham, Caliph 724–743] was very angry and ordered the magician to be put to death for his father's murder, as just punishment for his false prophecy. (Acts of II Nicea)

[MANGO 1972: 151]

John's report received an immediate confirmation from an eyewitness who was present at the council and said: "I was a young boy living in Syria when the Caliph of the Saracens destroyed the images." This story appears, in one version or another, in most of the Byzantine accounts of the beginning of a reaction to the veneration of images in the Christian Roman Empire. According to it, Byzantine iconoclasm, "image destruction," was inspired by a Jew living under Islam who convinced the Muslim Caliph Yazid to ban images and image worship in his realms. This probably occurred in 721 C.E. Not long afterward the "infection" spread across the frontier, where a number of bishops succumbed, and they in turn caught the ear of Emperor Leo III (717–741 C.E.), who was himself a native of the Syrian frontier region and, as one Byzantine historian had it, a notorious "Saracen sympathizer." A number of edicts against images were issued beginning in 726 C.E., and the effects are described in the life of a contemporary holy man, Stephen.

In every village and town one could witness the weeping and lamentation of the pious, whereas, on the part of the impious, one saw sacred things trodden upon, (liturgical) vessels turned to other use, churches scraped down and smeared with ashes because they contained holy images. And wherever there were venerable images of Christ or the Mother of God or the saints, these were consigned to the flames or were gouged out or smeared over. If, on the other hand, there were pictures of trees or birds or senseless beasts, and in particular of satanic horse races, hunts, theatrical and hippodrome scenes, these were preserved with honor and given greater lustre.

Somewhat later, under Leo's son and successor, Constantine V (741–775 C.E.):

The tyrant [Constantine V] scraped down the venerable church of the all-pure Mother of God at the Blachernae (in Constantinople), whose walls had previously been decorated with pictures of God's coming down to us, and going on to His various miracles as far as His Ascension and the Descent of the Holy Spirit. Having thus suppressed all Christ's mysteries, he converted the church into a storehouse of fruit and an aviary: for he covered it with mosaics (representing) all kinds of birds and beasts, and certain swirls of ivy leaves (enclosing) cranes, crows and peacocks, thus making the church, if I may say so, altogether unadorned. (*Life of Saint Stephen the Younger*) [MANGO 1972: 152]

It was Constantine V who in 754 convened a council to make the prohibition of images part of the official teaching of the Church. This is part of its Definition of Faith on that occasion.

We have considered it proper to demonstrate in detail by the present Definition the error of those who make and reverence images. . . . How senseless is the notion that the painter, who from sordid love of gain pursues the unattainable, namely to fashion with his impure hands things that are believed by the heart and confessed by the mouth. This man makes an image and calls it Christ. Now the name "Christ" means both God and man. Hence he has either included, according to his vain fancy, the uncircumscribable Godhead in the circumscription of created flesh, or he has confused that unconfusable union . . . and in so doing has applied two blasphemies to the Godhead, namely through the circumscription and the confusion. So also, he who reveres images is guilty of the same blasphemies.

The same argument does not pertain to images of the Virgin and the saints, it might be argued. The Council replies:

How indeed do they dare depict through the gross art of the pagans the all-praised Mother of God who was overshadowed by the plenitude of divinity, through whom an unapproachable light did shine for us, who is higher than the heaven and holier than the cherubim? Or the saints who will reign with Christ, and sit beside Him to judge the world, and share in His glory . . . are they not ashamed to depict them through pagan art? For it is not lawful for Christians who believe in the resurrection to adopt the customs of demon-worshiping Gentiles, and to insult by means of inglorious and dead matter the saints who will be adorned with much glory.

The Definition *concludes:*

Let no man dare to pursue henceforth this impious and unholy practice. Anyone who presumes from now on to manufacture an icon, or to worship it, or to set it up in a church or a private house, or to hide it, if he is a bishop or a presbyter or deacon, he shall be deposed; if he is a monk or a layman, he shall be anathematized and deemed guilty under imperial law as a foe of God's commands and an enemy of the doctrines of the Fathers. (*Definition of Faith of the Council of 754*) [MANGO 1972: 166–168]

Among those who rallied to the defense of the veneration of images was John of Damascus, scion of a Christian family that had long served in the Muslim civil service in Damascus. John followed another course, however; he retired to a monastery near Jerusalem, where he wrote tirelessly in defense of Christian orthodoxy. For him that included the veneration of images of Jesus, his mother, and the saints.

Since some find fault with us for showing reverence and honoring the image of our Savior and that of our Lady, and also of the rest of the saints and servants of Christ, let them hear that from the beginning God made man after His own image. On what other grounds, then, do we show reverence to each other than that we are made after God's image? For as Basil, that most learned expounder of things divine, says, "The honor given to the image passes over to the prototype." Now a prototype is that which is imaged, from which the form is derived. Why was it that Moses' people showed reverence round about the tabernacle which bore an image and type of heavenly things, or rather the whole of creation? God indeed said to Moses, "See that you make all things after the pattern that We showed you on the mountain" (Exod. 33:10). The cherubim also, which overshadowed the seat of mercy, are they not the work of men's hands? What is the renowned Temple at Jerusalem? Is it not made by hands and fashioned by the skill of men?

The veneration that the Christians pay to their images is different from that given by the pagans to idols: witness the fact that God permitted the sacrifices of the Jews but banned those of the Greeks.

The divine Scriptures, however, blame those who show reverence to graven images, but also those who sacrifice to demons. The Greeks sacrificed and the Jews also sacrificed; but the Greeks to demons; the Jews, however, to God. And the sacrifice of the Greeks was rejected and condemned, but the sacrifice of the just was acceptable to God. For Noah sacrificed, and God smelled a sweet savor of a good purpose, receiving also the fragrance the right choice and goodwill toward Him. And so the graven images of the Greeks, since they were the images of demon deities, were rejected and forbidden. But besides this, who can make an imitation of the invisible, incorporeal, uncircumscribed and formless God? Therefore to give form to the Deity is the height of folly and iniquity. And therefore in the Old Testament the use of images was repressed.

What has changed from the biblical circumstances is the enfleshing of God in the person of Jesus Christ.

But after God, in the depths of His mercy, became for our salvation in truth man, not as He was seen by Abraham in the semblance of man, or by the Prophets, but He became in truth man, according to substance, and after He lived upon earth and dwelt among men, worked miracles, suffered and was crucified, He rose again and was received up into heaven; since all these things actually took place and were seen by men, they were written for the remembrance and instruction of us who were not present at that time in order that, though we saw not, we may still, hearing and believing, obtain the blessing of the Lord.

John passes to a new argument, the educational value of images, which serve the same purpose for the illiterate as books do for the educated.

But since all have not a knowledge of letters or time for reading, it appeared good to the Fathers, that these events, as acts of heroism, should be depicted on images to be a brief memorial of them. Often, doubtless, when we have not the Lord's Passion in mind and see the image of Christ's crucifixion, we remember the Passion and fall down and show reverence not to the material but to that which is imaged; just as we do not show reverence for the material of the Gospel, or to the material of the cross, but that which these typify. For wherein does the cross that typifies the Lord differ from a cross that does not do so? It is the same also in the case of the Mother of God. For the honor which is given her is referred to Him who was incarnate of her. And similarly also the brave acts of holy men stir us to bravery and to emulation and imitation of their valor and to the glory of God.

Finally, there is an appeal to the unwritten tradition of the Church, with a considerable debt to Basil's On the Holy Spirit.

The honor rendered the image passes over to the prototype. But this is an unwritten tradition, just as is also the demonstration of reverence toward the East and to the cross and very many similar things. Moreover, that the Apostles handed down much that was unwritten, Paul the Apostle of the Gentiles writes: "Therefore, brethren, stand fast and hold the traditions which you have been taught by us, whether by word or by letters" (2 Thess. 2:14). And to the Corinthians he writes, "Now I praise you, brethren, that you remembered me in all things and keep the traditions as I have delivered them to you" (1 Cor. 2:2). (John of Damascus, *On the Orthodox Faith* 4.16)

The issue of image worship was apparently settled by the seventh ecumenical council, that held in Nicea in 787 C.E. It rejected the policy of Leo III and the theology of Constantine V. This is the pertinent part of its Confession of Faith.

To make our confession short, we keep unchanged all the ecclesiastical traditions handed down to us, written or unwritten, and of these one is the making of pictorial representations, agreeable to the history of the preaching of the Gospel, a tradition useful in many respects, but especially in this, that so the incarnation of the Word is shown forth as real and not merely fantastic, for these have mutual indications, and without doubt also have mutual significations.

We, therefore, following the royal pathway and the divinely inspired authority of our holy Fathers and the traditions of the Catholic Church for, as we all know, the Holy Spirit dwells in her, define with all certitude and accuracy, that just as the figure of the precious and life-giving cross, so also the venerable and holy images, as well in painting and mosaic, as of other fit materials, should be set forth in the holy churches of God, and on the sacred vessels and on the vestments and on hangings and in tablets both in houses and by the wayside, to wit, the figure of our Lord God and Savior Jesus Christ, of our spotless lady, the Mother of God, and of all pious people. For by so much the more frequently as they are seen in artistic representation, by so much the more readily are men lifted up to the memory of their prototypes, and to a longing after them; and to these should be given due salutation and honorable reverence (*proskynesis*), not indeed the true worship (*latreia*) which pertains to the divine nature alone; but to these, as to the figure of the precious and life-giving cross, and to the book of the Gospels and to other holy objects, incense and lights may be offered according to ancient pious custom. For the honor which is paid to the image passes on to that which the image represents, and he who shows reverence to the image shows reverence to the subject represented in it. (Acts of II Nicea, *Confession of Faith*) [MANGO 1972: 166–168]

This was by no means the end of the controversy over images, neither in the Eastern Church, where it first arose and was to arise again shortly after this council, nor in the Western, where the Roman Church's veneration of images became part of the agenda of the reformers.

38. Islam and the Graven Image

Ibn Ishaq's biography of the Prophet provides an account of both the origins and some of the modalities of idol worship among the pagan Arabs of Mecca and its vicinity in the days before Islam.

They say that the beginning of stone worship among the sons of Ishmael was when Mecca became too small for them and they wanted more room in the country. Everyone who left town took with him a stone from the sacred area to do honor to it. Wherever they settled they set it up and walked around it as they had around the Ka'ba. This led them to worship what stones they pleased and those which made an impression on them. Thus as generations passed they forgot their primitive faith and adopted another religion for that of Abraham and Ishmael. They worshiped idols and adopted the same errors as the people before them. Yet they retained and held fast practices going back to the time of Abraham, such as honoring the temple [that is, the Ka'ba] and going round it, the great and the little pilgrimage [that is, the *hajj* and the *'umra*], and the standing on Arafat and Muzdalifa, sacrificing the victims, and the pilgrim cry at the great and little pilgrimage, while introducing elements which had no place in the religion of Abraham. . . .

Every household had an idol in their house which they used to worship. When a man was about to set out on a journey he used to rub himself against it as he was about to ride off; indeed, that was the last thing he used to do before his journey; and when he returned from his journey the first thing he did was to rub himself against it before he went to his family. . . .

Now along with the Ka'ba the Arabs had adopted Tawaghit, which were temples which they venerated as they venerated the Ka'ba. They had their guardians and their overseers and they used to make offerings to them as they did to the Ka'ba and to circumambulate them and sacrifice at them. Yet they recognized the superiority of the Ka'ba because it was the temple and mosque of Abraham the friend of God. (Ibn Ishaq, *Life*) [IBN ISHAQ 1955: 35–38]

The Prophet made no secret of his intentions regarding these idols of the Arabs. When he finally entered Mecca after his long emigration to Medina, he put his intentions into action, as described in a passage in Ibn Ishaq's Life.

The Messenger after arriving in Mecca, once the populace had settled down, went to the shrine and went round it seven times on his camel, touching the black stone with a stick which he had in his hand. This done, he summoned Uthman ibn Talha and took the keys of the Ka'ba from him, and when the door was opened for him, he went in. There he found a dove made of wood. He broke it in his hands and threw it away. . . . (According to another account) the Messenger entered Mecca on the day of the conquest and it contained 360 idols which Iblis [or Satan] had strengthened with lead. The Messenger was standing by them with a stick in his hand saying, "The truth has come and falsehood has passed away" (Quran 17:81). Then he pointed at them with his stick and they collapsed on their backs one after another.

When the Messenger had prayed the noon prayer on the day of the conquest (of Mecca) he ordered that all the idols which were around the Ka'ba should be collected and burned with fire and broken up. . . . The Quraysh had put pictures in the Ka'ba including two of Jesus son of Mary and Mary, on both of whom be peace. Ibn Shihab said: Asma the daughter of Shaqr said that a woman of the Banu Ghassan had joined in the pilgrimage of the Arabs and when she saw a picture of Mary in the Ka'ba she said: "My father and my mother be your ransom! (Mary), you are surely an Arab woman!" The Messenger ordered that the pictures be erased, except those of Jesus and Mary. (Ibn Ishaq, *Life*) [IBN ISHAQ 1955: 552]

We know little of what to make of that last curious event. What we can say, on the basis of the Quran, is that, for all Muhammad's opposition to idolatry, there is no sign in that Book of any preoccupation, no open approval or disapproval even, of pictures or images. But conditions must soon have changed. The collections of Prophetic traditions are filled with condemnations of images and image making.

Abu Talha reported the Prophet as saying, "The angels do not enter a house which contains dogs or pictures." Bukhari and Muslim transmit this tradition.

Aisha told that she had screened a storeroom of hers with a curtain on which there were figures and the Prophet tore it down; so she made two cushions out of it and had them in the house for sitting on. Bukhari and Muslim transmit this.

She also reported the Prophet as saying, "Those who will receive the severest punishment on the Day of Resurrection will be those who imitate what God has created."

Sa'id ibn Abi Hasan said: "When I was with Ibn Abbas a man came to him and said, 'Ibn Abbas, I am a man whose livelihood comes only from the work of my hands, and I make these representations of things.' Ibn Abbas replied that he would tell him only what he had heard from

God's Messenger. He had heard him say, 'If anyone makes a representation of anything, God will punish him until he blows a spirit into it, and he will never be able to do that.' Then when the man gasped and became pale, he said to him, 'Out upon you! If you must do so, make representations of these trees or of anything which does not possess a soul.' " Bukhari transmitted this tradition.

Ibn Abbas reported God's Messenger as saying, "The one who receives the severest punishment on the Day of Resurrection will be he who kills a prophet, or who is killed by a prophet, or kills one of his parents, or who makes representations of things, and a learned man who derives no benefit from his learning." (Baghawi, *Mishkat al-Masabih* 21.5.1–3)

We do not know when those traditions were put into circulation. If they are authentic, we are faced with the same kind of dilemma that the figuratively decorated synagogues of Palestine posed to a supposedly aniconic Jewish tradition: Muslim coinage bore representations of the Caliph down to the reign of Abd al-Malik (685–705 C.E.), and even after that date Muslim sovereigns continued to build Syrian steppe palaces decorated in a style that was not merely figurative but even aggressively and suggestively secular. It is perhaps safer to conclude that Islam came to its iconophobia gradually and that the Prophetic traditions reflect a later and not a primary stage in that evolution. The later official Islamic sentiment on images is clear enough, however. This is how it is expressed in one of the standard Islamic law books, that written by the Syrian jurist al-Nawawi (d. 1377 C.E.). Now all fear of idolatry is gone, and the reasons for the prohibition are overtly theological.

The learned authorities of our (Shafiʿite) school and others hold that painting a picture of any living thing is strictly forbidden, because it is threatened with grievous punishment as mentioned in the Prophetic traditions, whether it is intended for common domestic use or not. So the making of it is forbidden under every circumstance, because it implies a likeness to the creative activity of God. . . . On the other hand, the painting of a tree or of camel saddles and other things that have no life is not forbidden. Such is the decision on the actual making of a picture.

Similarly, it is forbidden to make use of any object on which a living thing is pictured, whether it is to be hung on a wall or worn as a dress or a turban or on any other object of common domestic use. But if it is on a carpet trampled underfoot, or on a pillow or cushion . . . then it is not forbidden. Whether such an object will prevent the angels of God from entering the house in which it is found is quite another matter.

In all this there is no difference between what casts a shadow and what does not cast a shadow. This is the decision of our school on the question, and the majority of the Companions of the Prophet and their immediate followers and the learned of succeeding generations accepted it. . . . Some later authorities make the prohibition refer only to objects that cast a shadow, and see no harm in objects that have no shadow. But this view is quite wrong, for the curtain to which the Prophet objected was certainly condemned, as everyone admits, yet the picture on it cast no shadow; and the other traditions make no distinction between one picture and another. Al-Zuhri holds that the prohibition refers to pictures in general, and similarly to the use of them and to entrance into a house in which they are found, whether it is a case of design on a dress or any other design, whether the picture hangs on a wall or is on a robe or a carpet, whether in common domestic use or not, as is the clear meaning of the Prophetic traditions. (Nawawi, *Guide to an Understanding of Muslim* 8.398) [Cited by ARNOLD 1928: 9–10]

2. The Worship of God: Church and Mosque

1. Early Christian Worship

For our first glimpse of the Christians at worship we must return to Paul.

To sum up, my friends: when you meet for worship, each of you contributes a hymn, some instruction, a revelation, an ecstatic utterance, or the interpretation of such an utterance. All of these must aim at one thing: to build up the Church. If it is a matter of ecstatic utterance, only two should speak, or at most three, one at a time, and someone must interpret. If there is no interpreter, the speaker had better not address the meeting at all but speak to himself and to God. Of the prophets, two or three may speak, while the rest exercise their judgment upon what is said. If someone else, sitting in his place receives a revelation, let the first speaker stop. You can all prophesy, one at a time, so that the whole congregation may receive instruction and encouragement. It is for prophets to control prophetic inspiration, for the God who inspires them is a God not of disorder but of peace.

As in all congregations of God's people, women should not address the meeting. They have no license to speak, but should keep their place as the law directs. If there is something they want to know, they can ask their husbands at home. It is a shocking thing that a woman should address the congregation. (Paul, *To the Corinthians* 1.14:26–35)

Early community worship is also discussed in the letter Paul sent to Timothy.

First of all, then, I urge that petitions, prayers, intercessions and thanksgivings be offered for all men, for sovereigns and all in high office, that we may lead a tranquil and quiet life in full observance of religion and high standards of morality. Such prayer is right and approved by God our Savior, whose will it is that all men should find salvation and come to know the truth. . . . It is my desire, therefore, that everywhere prayers be said by the men of the congregation, who shall lift up their hands with pure intention, excluding angry and quarrelsome thoughts. . . . A woman must be a learner, listening quietly and with due submission. I do not permit a woman to be a teacher, nor must woman domineer over man; she should be quiet. (Paul, *To Timothy* 1.2:1–12)

Earlier in the same letter to the Corinthians just cited, Paul touched upon one of the problems that had arisen in the still rather spontaneous Christian liturgy: the role of the ecstatic in community worship.

I say, then, that the man who falls into ecstatic utterance should pray for the ability to interpret. If I use such language in my prayer, the Spirit in me prays, but my intellect lies fallow. What then? I will pray as I am inspired to pray, but I will also pray intelligently. I will sing hymns as I am inspired to sing, but I will sing intelligently too. Suppose you are praising God in the language of inspiration; how will the plain man who is present be able to say "Amen" to your thanksgiving when he does not know what you are saying? Your prayer of thanksgiving may be all that could be desired, but it is of no help to the other man. Thank God I am more gifted in ecstatic utterance than any of you, but in the congregation I would rather speak five intelligible words, for the benefit of others as well as myself, than thousands of words in the language of ecstasy. (Paul, *To the Corinthians* 1.14:13–19)

2. How Christians Worship: An Explanation to the Gentiles

Sometime about 150 C.E. the former philosopher Justin, now converted to the Christian faith, wrote an open letter to Emperor Antoninus Pius explaining and defending Christianity and its practices. This is how he set forth the Christians' manner of worship.

After washing [that is, baptizing] him who has been convinced and has given his assent, we bring him to those who are called the brethren, where they are assembled, to offer prayers in common, both for ourselves and for him who has been enlightened as well as for all men everywhere, with all our hearts, that, just as we have learned the truth, so we may be counted worthy to be found good citizens and guardians of the commandments to the end that we find eternal salvation.

When we have finished our prayers we salute one another with a kiss. Then there is brought to the president of the brethren bread and a cup of water and wine. And he takes them and offers up praise and glory to the Father of all things, through the name of the Son and the Holy Spirit, and gives thanks at length that we are deemed worthy of these things at His hand. When we have finished the prayers and thanksgiving, all those present assent by saying *Amen*, which in the Hebrew tongue means "So be it." When the president has given thanks and all the people have assented, those who are called deacons among us give to those present a portion of the Eucharistic bread and wine and water, and carry it away to those who are absent.

This food is called among us the Eucharist, and none is allowed to partake of it except he believe that our teachings are true, and has been washed with the washing for the remission of sins and for regeneration, and who lives as Christ directed. For we do not receive them as ordinary food or ordinary drink, but as the Word of God, Jesus Christ, our Savior; as he took flesh and blood for our salvation, so too, we are taught, the food blessed by the prayer of the word which we received from him, by which, through its transformation, our blood and flesh are nourished, this food is the flesh and blood of Jesus who was made flesh. For the Apostles in the memoirs made by them, which are called Gospels, have thus narrated that the command was given: that Jesus took bread, gave thanks, and said, "Do this in remembrance of me; this is my body." And he took the cup in like manner and said, "This is my blood," and gave it to them alone. This very thing the evil demons imitated in the mysteries of Mithras, and commanded to be done. For, as you know or can discover, bread and a cup of water are set out in the rites of initiation with the repetition of certain words.

And on the matter of the "Lord's Day," formerly the "Sun's Day":

. . . On the day which is called the day of the sun there is an assembly of all those who live in the towns or in the country; and the memoirs of the Apostles or the writings of the prophets are read, as long as time permits. Then the reader ceases and the president speaks, admonishing us and exhorting us to imitate these excellent examples. Then all arise together and offer prayers; and, as we have said before, when we have concluded our prayer, bread is brought and wine and water, and the president in like manner offers up prayers and thanksgivings with all his might; and the people assent with *Amen*. And there is the distribution and partaking by all of the Eucharistic elements; and to them who are not present they are sent by the hand of the deacons. And they that are prosperous and wish to do so give what they will, each as he wishes.

Whatever is collected is deposited with the president, who gives aid to the orphans and widows and such as are in want because of sickness or some other cause; and to those also who are in prison, and to strangers from abroad; he is in fact a protector to all who are in need.

We hold our common assembly on the day of the sun because it is the first day, on which God put to flight darkness and chaos and made the world, and on the same day Jesus Christ our Savior rose from the dead; for on the day before that of Saturn they crucified him; and on the day after Saturn's day, the day of the sun, he appeared to his Apostles and disciples and taught them these things, which we have also handed on to you for your consideration. (Justin, *Apology* 1.65–67)

3. The Christian Celebration of the Sabbath

Although the first day of the week, the "Lord's day," was early marked as a peculiarly Christian holy day, the Sabbath continued to be observed in Christian circles, as this prayer from the Apostolic Constitutions *bears witness.*

O Almighty Lord, who did create the world through Christ, and did ordain the Sabbath as a memorial of creation, because on it You rested from Your work . . . You, O Lord, brought our fathers out of Egypt . . . (and) commanded them to keep the Sabbath, not providing thereby an excuse for idleness but an occasion for godliness. (*Apostolic Constitutions* 7.36)

Or again in Origen's somewhat idealized vision, with its reminiscence of synagogue attendance:

Leaving on one side the Jewish observance of the Sabbath, let us see of what kind the observance of the Sabbath ought to be for the Christian. On the Sabbath no worldly affairs ought to be undertaken. If, then, you abstain from all secular works and do nothing worldly, but employ yourself in spiritual works, and come to church and give ear to the Scripture readings and to sermons, if you think on heavenly things and are concerned with your future hope, if you have before your eyes the coming judgment, and do not look to the present and the visible, but to the invisible and the future, this is the observance of the Sabbath for the Christians. (Origen, *Sermon on Numbers* 23.4)

By the fourth century the Sabbath was everywhere yielding place to Sunday as the Christians' holy day; but its attraction, and the letter of the Law, still operated on Augustine.

"Observe the Sabbath day": This commandment concerns us even more than it concerns them [that is, the Jews]. The Jews observe the Sabbath in a servile fashion, spending it in riotousness and drunkenness. How much better could their women be employed at the spinning wheel than in dancing on that day in the balconies of their houses. Let us not concede for a moment, my brothers, that they observe the Sabbath. The Christian observes the Sabbath spiritually, by abstaining from servile work. For what is "from servile work"? From sin. How do we prove this? Ask the Lord: "Whoever commits sin is the servant of sin" (John 8:34). So that on us likewise is enjoined spiritually the observance of the Sabbath. (Augustine, *On the Gospel of John* 3.19)

The consecration of Sunday as the Christians' holy day was finally sealed by the Roman state's own recognition.

[7 March 321 C.E.]: Constantine to Elpidius. All judges, city people and craftsmen shall rest on the venerable day of the Sun. But countrymen may without hindrance attend to agriculture, since it often happens that this is the most suitable day for sowing grain or planting vines, so that the opportunity offered by divine providence may not be lost, for the right season is of short duration. (Code of Justinian 3.12.3)

[3 July 321 C.E.]: The Emperor Constantine to Elpidius. Just as we thought it most unfitting that the day of the Sun, with its venerable rights, should be given over to swearing and counter-swearing of litigants and their unseemly brawls, so it is a pleasant and a joyful thing to fulfill petitions of special urgency on that day. Therefore on the festal day let all be allowed to perform manumission and emancipation (of slaves); and let nothing that concerns this be forbidden. (Theodosian Code 2.8.1)

4. Two Eucharistic Liturgies

The Teaching of the Apostles *is an anonymous Christian tract, perhaps from the second century, that already has a developed Eucharistic liturgy between its lines.*

Concerning the Eucharist, give thanks in this way. First for the cup: "We give thanks to You, our Father, for the holy vine of David Your servant, which You have made known to us through Your servant Jesus. To You be the glory forever." And for the broken bread: "We give thanks to You, our Father, for the life and knowledge which You have made known to us through Your servant Jesus. To You be the glory forever. As this broken bread was scattered upon the hills, and was gathered together

and made one, so let Your Church be gathered together into Your kingdom from the ends of the earth; for Yours is the glory and the power
through Christ Jesus forever."

Let none eat or drink Your Eucharist, save such as are baptized into
the name of the Lord. For concerning this the Lord has said: "Give not
that which is holy to the dogs."

And after you are filled, give thanks as follows: "We give thanks,
Holy Father, for Your holy name, which You have made a tabernacle in
our hearts, and for the knowledge, faith and immortality which You have
made known to us through Your servant Jesus. To You be the glory
forever. You, Lord Almighty, created all things for Your name's sake and
gave food and drink to men for their enjoyment, that they might give You
thanks; and to us You granted spiritual food and drink and life eternal,
through Your servant. Above all we thank You that You are mighty. To
You be glory forever. Remember, Lord, Your Church, to deliver us from
all evil and to make her perfect in Your love, and to gather from the four
winds her that is sanctified into Your kingdom which You have prepared
for her; for Yours is the power and the glory forever. Let grace come, and
let this world pass away. Hosanna to the God of David. If any is holy, let
him approach; if any be not holy, let him repent. *Maranatha* Amen."
(*Teaching of the Apostles* 9–10)

The following liturgy, drawn from the Apostolic Tradition *of Hippolytus and
dating from about 225* C.E., *is more explicit and more formal than that in the*
Teaching.

THE BISHOP: The Lord be with you.
PEOPLE: And with your spirit.
BISHOP: Lift up your hearts.
PEOPLE: We lift them up to the Lord.
BISHOP: Let us give thanks to the Lord.
PEOPLE: It is right and just.
BISHOP: We give You thanks, O God, through Your beloved Son
Jesus Christ, whom You sent to us in the last times to be a savior and a
redeemer and a messenger of Your will; who is Your inseparable Word,
through whom You made all things and in whom You were well pleased.
You did send him from heaven into the Virgin's womb; he was conceived
and became incarnate and was shown to be Your Son, born of the Holy
Spirit and the Virgin; who, fulfilling Your will and preparing for You a
holy people, stretched out his hands in suffering, that he might free from
suffering all who believed in You.

When he was being betrayed to his voluntary suffering, that he might destroy death, break the chains of the devil, tread Hell underfoot, bring forth the righteous from it, and set a boundary to it, and that he might show forth his Resurrection, Our Lord took bread and gave thanks to You and said: "Take, eat: This is my body which is broken for you." So too the cup, saying: "This is my blood which is shed for you. As often as you do this, you shall do it in remembrance of me."

And so we, who are mindful of his death and resurrection, offer You this bread and this cup, giving thanks to You that You considered us worthy to stand before You and minister as Your priest. And we beseech You that You should send Your Holy Spirit upon the offering of the Holy Church; and that You should grant it to all the saints who partake, making them one, for fulfillment of the Holy Spirit and for the confirmation of their faith in truth; that we may praise and glorify You through Your Son Jesus Christ, through whom be honor and glory to You, to the Father and to the Son with the Holy Spirit in Your Holy Church, both now and forever. Amen. (Hippolytus, *The Apostolic Tradition* 8:4)

5. The Service of the Word of God

In its developed form, the Eucharistic liturgy was a composite ceremony, and the Eucharist proper, of the type described in the Teaching of the Twelve Apostles *and the* Apostolic Tradition, *was preceded by a service of prayer and worship and followed by a communion or the distribution of the consecrated bread and wine to the faithful. The opening prayers, sometimes called "the Service of the Word of God" or, in its Western form, "the Mass of the Catechumens," was open to all Christians—those under instruction for baptism (that is, the "catechumens"), as well as the baptized—and it owed much of its form and conduct to the synagogue service from which it doubtless derived. This description of such a service is from a work entitled* The Apostolic Constitutions *and dates from the fourth century* C.E. *It is addressed to the bishop of a community.*

When you call an assembly of the church as one that is the commander of a great ship, appoint the assemblies to be made with all possible skill, charging the deacons as sailors to prepare places for the brethren as passengers, with all due care and decency. First, let the building be long, with its head [that is, the apse] toward the east end, so that it will be like a ship. In the middle let the bishop's throne be placed, and on each side of him let the presbyters sit down; and let the deacons stand near, in close and girt garments, for they are like the sailors and managers of the ship. Let the laity sit on the other side, with all quietness and good order. And let the women sit by themselves, they also keeping silence.

In the middle let the reader stand upon some raised place: let him read the book of Moses, of Joshua son of Nun, of the Judges and of the Kings and Chronicles, and those written after the return from the captivity; and besides these, the books of Job and of Solomon, and of the sixteen prophets. When there have been two lessons severally read, let some other person sing the hymns of David, and let the people join at the conclusion of the verses. Afterwards let our Acts be read, and the Letters of Paul our fellow worker, which he sent to the churches under the conduct of the Holy Spirit; and afterwards let a deacon or presbyter read the Gospel, both those which I [that is, Peter], Matthew and John have directed to you and those which the fellow workers of Paul received and handed on to you, Luke and Mark. And while the Gospel is read, let all the presbyters and deacons and all the people, stand up in great silence; for it is written: "Be silent and hear, O Israel" (Deut. 27:9), and again, "Stand there and hear" (Deut. 5:31).

In the next place, let the presbyters one by one, not all together, exhort the people, and the bishop last of all, since he is the commander. Let the doorkeepers stand at the entries of the men and observe them. Let the deaconesses also stand at those of the women, as sailors. For the same description and pattern was in both the Tent of the Witnessing and in the Temple of God (Deut. 23:1). But if anyone is out of his place, let him be rebuked by the deacon . . . and removed into the place proper for him; for the church is not only like a ship, but also like a sheepfold. For as the shepherds place all the animals distinctly, I mean goats and sheep, according to their age and kind, and still every one runs together, like with like; so it is to be in the church. Let the young persons sit by themselves, if there is a place for them; if not, let them stand up. But let those that are already advanced in years sit in order. . . . Let the younger women also sit by themselves, if there is a place for them; if there is not, let them stand behind the other women. Let those women who are married and have children be placed by themselves, but let the virgins and the widows and the older women stand or sit before all the rest; and let the deacon be the assigner of places, that every one who comes in may go to his proper place and may not sit around the entrance. In like manner, let the deacon oversee the people, that nobody may whisper, or sleep, or laugh, or nod; for all ought to stand wisely and soberly and attentively in church, with all his attention on the word of the Lord.

This marks the end of the Service of the Word of God. Then, after the departure of some lay persons, the offertory ceremony preparatory to the Eucharist begins.

After this let all arise as one, and looking toward the east, after the catechumens and penitents [that is, those under a temporary ban] have left, pray toward the east to God, who ascended up to the heaven of heavens to the east, from the same direction that the first humans, when they had yielded to the persuasion of the serpent and disobeyed the command of God, were expelled. As for the deacons, after the prayer is over, let some of them attend upon the offering of the Eucharist, ministering to the Lord's body with fear. Let others of them watch the multitude and keep them quiet. But let the deacon who is at the High Priest's side say to the people, "Let no one have any quarrel with another; let no one come in hypocrisy." Then let the deacon pray for the whole Church, for the whole world and the several parts of it, and the fruits of it; for the priests and the rulers, for the High Priest and the king, and the peace of the universe. After this, let the High Priest pray for peace upon the people, and bless them, as Moses commanded the priests to bless the people, in these words: "The Lord bless you and keep you; the Lord make His face to shine upon you and give you peace." Let the bishop also pray for the people and say: "Save Your people, O Lord, and bless Your inheritance, which You have obtained with the precious blood of Your Christ, and have called a royal priesthood and a holy people."

After this let the sacrifice [that is, the Eucharist proper] follow; and when the offering has been made, let every rank by itself partake of the Lord's body and precious blood in order, and approach in reverence and holy fear, as toward the body of their king. Let the women approach with their heads covered, as is becoming the order of women; but let the door be watched, lest any unbeliever, or one not initiated, come in. (*Apostolic Constitutions 57*)

6. Pentecost in Jerusalem

The Constitutions' *presentation of the liturgy was intended to be instructional and normative. How the Christians actually conducted their liturgical life is better learned from eyewitnesses. Here the witness is Egeria, a Western visitor to Jerusalem in 380 C.E. The occasion is Pentecost, as Egeria herself explains.*

And finally, Pentecost, fifty days after Easter, the day on which the Holy Spirit descended on Jesus' disciples who were patiently and fearfully collected in an upper room, as it was believed, on Mount Sion.

When it is the morning (of Pentecost Sunday) all the people assemble in their usual way in the Great Church, the Martyrium [that is, what was later called the Church of the Holy Sepulcher], and have sermons from the presbyters and then the bishop, and the offering is duly made in the way that is usual on the Lord's day, except that the dismissal at the Martyrium is hurried, so that it is over before nine o'clock. And soon after the dismissal at the Martyrium all the people escort the bishop with singing to Sion, where they arrive in time for nine o'clock. When they arrive, they have a reading of the passage from the Acts of the Apostles where the Spirit descends so that all nations might understand the things that were spoken, after which the Mass proceeds as usual.

The presbyters read this passage from the Acts of the Apostles because this place on Sion, though it has now been altered into a church, is the very spot where what I have mentioned was done by the multitude who were assembled with the Apostles after the Lord's Passion.

After that the service proceeds as usual, and they make the offering there. Then as the people are dismissed the archdeacon makes this announcement: "Let us all be ready today on the Mount of Eleona at the Imbomon immediately after midday."

So all the people return home for a rest. And as soon as they have had their meal, they go up to Eleona, the Mount of Olives, each at his own pace, till there is not a Christian left in the city. Once they have climbed Eleona, the Mount of Olives, they go to first to the Imbomon, the place from which the Lord ascended into heaven, where the bishop and the presbyters take their seats, and likewise all the people. They have readings, and between them hymns and antiphons suitable to this day and to the place. . . . When this has been done, the catechumens are blessed, and also the faithful.

It is now already three o'clock, and they go down singing hymns from there to another church, also on Olivet, and in it is the cave where the Lord used to sit and teach the Apostles. By the time they get there it is after four, and they have vespers. The prayer is said, the catechumens are blessed, and then the faithful.

From there all the people go down with their bishop, singing hymns and antiphons suitable to the day, and so, very slowly and gently, they make their way to the Martyrium. When they arrive at the city gate it is already night, and the people have brought hundreds of church candles to help them. But since it is quite a way from the gate to the Great Church, the Martyrium, they arrive there at about eight at night, going very slowly all the way so that the walk does not weary the people. The great doors which face the market street are opened, and the bishop and all the people enter the Martyrium with hymns.

Once inside the church they have hymns and a prayer, and the catechumens are blessed, and also the faithful. Then they set off once more with hymns to the Anastasis. Again in the Anastasis [or "Resurrection"] they have more hymns and antiphons and a prayer, and the catechumens are blessed, and also the faithful. Then the same is done again at the Cross. And once more all the Christian community conducts the bishop with hymns to Sion. Once there, they have suitable readings, psalms and antiphons, a prayer, the blessing of the catechumens and the faithful, and so they are dismissed. After the dismissal everyone goes to have the bishop's hand laid on him, and about midnight everybody returns to his home. Thus this is a very tiring day for them, for they have never stopped all day since they kept vigil in the Anastasis at cock-crow, and the services have taken so long that it is midnight by the time they are dismissed at Sion and all return to their homes. (Egeria, *Pilgrimage* 70–71)

7. An Eastern Eucharistic Liturgy

Egeria gives us a glimpse of the liturgical life of the Church while still in its formative period. Although its central element, the re-enactment of Jesus' "Last Supper," did not much vary, there grew up around this act different combinations of readings, prayers, commemorations, and petitions, depending on local tradition and practice. Eucharistic liturgies in Rome or Milan, for example, or Alexandria, Edessa, or Constantinople all displayed an elemental similarity with considerable local variants of language and style.

Eventually the growing power of the great ecclesiastical centers and the concentration of authority and prestige there led to the decline, and in some instances the disappearance, of local liturgical traditions. The "Mass" of the Roman Church replaced many of the Western variants, while the liturgies called after St. Basil and St. John Chrysostom, the preferred forms in Constantinople, had a similar, though perhaps not so thoroughgoing effect in the East.

The "John Chrysostom" is the form celebrated in the daily Eucharistic liturgy of the Eastern Church; the "St. Basil" is used on feast days. The former is divided, like its Western counterparts, into two sections: a "Eucharistic liturgy"—the "canon" of the Western "Mass"—preceded by a "liturgy of the catechumens" open to those undergoing "catechesis," the instruction prior to baptism, and to the excommunicated cut off from full participation in the life of the Church. This "liturgy of the catechumens," composed chiefly of prayers, hymns, and the daily prescribed readings from Scripture, has a distinct Hellenic nuance. The emphasis on knowledge as light and on membership in the Kingdom as citizenship can be heard in this prayer, said between the reading of Paul and the Gospel.

O Merciful Master, cause the pure light of the knowledge of you to shine into our hearts, and open the eyes of our mind to discern your message of Good Tidings; fill us with the fear of your blessed commandments, that in treading under foot our fleshly desires, we may seek a heavenly citizenship, and may do and consider all those things that are pleasing to you. For you, Christ our Lord, are the source of light to our souls and bodies, and to you we ascribe glory, together with your Eternal Father, and your All-Holy, Righteous and Life-Giving Spirit, now and forever, and from all ages to all ages.

There follows, as in the West, a series of prayers for the living—the emperor and the imperial family prominently to the fore—and a commemoration for the dead. Then comes another of the remarkable hymns that typify the Eastern liturgy, in this instance the "Cherubic Hymn," traditionally attributed to the eighth-century theologian John of Damascus.

> Let us, the mystic counterparts of the Cherubim,
> Who sing the thrice-holy hymn to the life-creating Trinity
> Now put aside all earthly cares,
> That we may welcome the King of all,
> Invisibly escorted by the Angelic Hosts.
> Alleluia, Alleluia, Alleluia.

Although the basic structure is one in both East and West—the Creed and the Offertory, for example, which now follow—there are distinguishing emphases. Thus at the Eastern offering of the bread and the wine, they are wafted by a gold or silver fan representing the wings of the Cherubim: the presence of the invisible angelic host is strongly felt and often expressed in word and in symbol in the Eastern liturgies.

The liturgy of the catechumens is completed, and the celebrant, priest or bishop, performs the central eucharistic act, first with the bread, then with the wine.

Take, eat: this is my body, which is broken for you, for the remission of sins. . . . Drink you all of this; this is my blood of the New Covenant, which is shed for you and for many for the remission of sins.

There then occurs in the Eastern liturgy a prayer that is undoubtedly the theological crux between East and West, a "summoning" of the Holy Spirit to transform the bread and wine into the body and blood of Christ—the "transubstantiation" of the Western theologians—a miracle that occurs, according to the Latin Church, at the simple pronouncing of the words, "This is my body . . . This is my blood. . . ." The "summoning" is something more as well: a prayer for the communion of all the faithful, the Old Testament knit into the New.

Unite us all [prays the priest], as many as are partakers of the one bread and cup, each with the other, in the participation of the one Holy Spirit; allow no one of us to share in the holy Body and Blood of Your Christ to our judgment or our condemnation, but to the end that we may all find in it mercy and grace, together with all the saints who have been well pleasing to You ever since the world began, our forefathers and fathers, the patriarchs, prophets, apostles, preachers, evangelists, martyrs, confessors, teachers, and with all the spirits of the saints who have been made perfect in faith.

At the completion of this and other prayers, first the priest and then the deacon shares in the Eucharistic bread and wine. Then, before he distributes them likewise to the congregation, the priest prays on the communicants' behalf.

I believe, O Lord, and I confess that you are truly the Christ, the Son of the Living God, who came into the world to save sinners, of whom I am the chief. I also believe that this is indeed your most precious blood. Wherefore, I pray you, have mercy on me, forgive me my offenses, voluntary and involuntary, whether in word or in deed . . . and account me worthy to partake without condemnation in your most pure mysteries, for the remission of my sins and the attainment of everlasting life.

Each member of the congregation approaches the sanctuary of the temple-church of the New Dispensation and receives the bread and wine, now transformed into the Body and Blood of Christ. And although there are additional prayers and hymns, the liturgy, whether Eastern or Western, is in effect completed. "Go," the Latin worshiper is told, "the Mass is over."

8. Worship Compared

According to a story told in the Russian Primary Chronicle, *Prince Vladimir of Kiev, who was about to declare an official religion for his princedom, wished to inform himself about the forms of worship in use among his neighbors of different faiths. In 987 C.E. he sent envoys to the Muslim Bulgars, the Western Christian Germans, and the Eastern Christian Greeks at Constantinople to observe and compare. The envoys' reactions, which may have had as much to do with cultural differences and political considerations as with prescribed manners of worship, are reported by the same* Chronicle.

Thus they returned to their own country, and the prince [that is, Vladimir] called together his vassals and elders. Vladimir then announced the return of the envoys, and suggested that their report be heard. He thus commanded them to speak out before his vassals. The envoys reported: "When we journeyed among the (Muslim) Bulgarians, we beheld how they worship in their temple, called a mosque, while they stand ungirt. The Bulgarian bows, sits down, looks hither and thither like one possessed, and there is no happiness among them, only sorrow and a dreadful stench. Their religion is not good. Then we went among the (Roman Catholic) Germans, and saw them performing many ceremonies in their temples; but we beheld no glory there. Then we went on to Greece, and the (Byzantine) Greeks led us to the edifices where they worship their God, and we knew not whether we were in heaven or on earth. For on earth there is no such splendor or such beauty, and we are at a loss how to describe it. We know only that God dwells there among men, and their service is fairer than the ceremonies of other nations. For we cannot forget that beauty. . . ."

Then the vassals spoke and said: "If the Greek faith were evil, it would not have been adopted by your grandmother Olga, who was wiser than all other men." Vladimir then inquired whether they should all accept baptism, and they replied that the decision rested with him. (*Russian Primary Chronicle*) [ZENKOVSKY 1963: 68]

9. "When You Pray . . . "

The Eucharist is the chief form of liturgical worship among Christians; but in common with Jews and Muslims, they petition and thank God through a great variety of private prayers. Although there is no liturgical instruction in the Gospels, Jesus not only advised his followers on how they should pray but also gave them the very words they should use.

When you pray, do not be like the hypocrites; they love to say their prayers standing up in the synagogue and at the street corners, for everyone to see them. I tell you this: they have their reward already. But when you pray, go into a room by yourself, shut the door, and pray to your Father who is there in the secret place; and your Father, who sees what is secret, will reward you.

In your prayers do not go babbling on like the heathen, who imagine that the more they say the more likely they are to be heard. Do not imitate them. Your Father knows what your needs are before you ask Him.

This is how you should pray:

Our Father in heaven,
thy name be hallowed;
thy kingdom come,
on earth as in heaven.
Give us this day our daily bread.
Forgive us the wrong we have done,
as we have forgiven those who have wronged us.
And do not bring us to the test,
but save us from the evil one.
(Matthew 6:5–13)

Those words continued to be used, of course, and others as well—some taken directly from the Gospels or the Greek or Latin version of the Bible, some the products of private piety or individual inspiration, in prose and poetry, in all the languages in use among Christians, now recited, now chanted or sung. Again, some of these prayers were inserted in the Eucharistic and other liturgies and so became "public" or "official" prayers of the Church; others remained the subject of private devotion.

All Christian preaching and instruction urges prayer on the faithful, but only rarely has the exhortation been accompanied by formal instruction. In the sixteenth century the degeneration, and the revival, of private devotion and popular forms of piety was a source of growing concern in Church circles. As a consequence, there arose a concerted effort to revitalize Christian piety and particularly the practice of prayer. Two influential figures in that movement were the Spaniards Ignatius of Loyola (1491–1556 C.E.) and Teresa of Avila (1515–1582). The latter, who spent nearly fifty years of her life in a Carmelite convent, explains in direct and comprehensible terms the difference between the simple recitation of words and what she calls "mental prayer."

You must understand that the mere opening or closing of the mouth does not determine whether a prayer is vocal or mental. If, while I am praying vocally, I am entirely absorbed in God to whom I am speaking, and if I concentrate my attention more on Him than on the words I am uttering, I am combining therein both vocal and mental prayer. (Teresa of Avila, *The Way of Perfection*)

One of the more popular forms of religious instruction in the sixteenth-century Catholic revival was that found in the Spiritual Exercises *written by Ignatius of Loyola, the religious innovator who founded the Society of Jesus, or Jesuits, in 1534. The "spiritual exercises" were precisely that, a set of exercises to be administered by his followers to the Christian faithful to raise their spiritual consciousness and so their devotion to Jesus and their dedication to the Roman Church. The carefully structured and detailed exercises, which are nothing less than a clinical course on prayer carried out under the supervision of a skilled practitioner—the Christian was intended to "make" the exercises, not merely study them—are filled with practical instruction, a great deal of it on prayer, including what Loyola called "Three Methods of Prayer." The first is a kind of examination of conscience with regard to the Ten Commandments and so on; the second is what Teresa of Avila called "mental prayer," a thoughtful reflection, an interior realization of the words of a well-known prayer like the "Our Father."*

The second method of prayer is that the person, kneeling or seated, according to the greater disposition in which he finds himself, and as more devotion accompanies him, keeping the eyes closed or fixed on one place, without going wandering with them, says "Father" [that is, the first word of the prayer], and remains on the consideration of this word as long as he finds meanings, comparisons, relish and consolation in considerations pertaining to such a word. At let him do likewise with each word of the "Our Father" or of any other prayer he wishes to say in this way.

First Rule: The first rule is that he will be an hour on the whole "Our Father" in the manner just mentioned. If he finishes, he will say a "Hail Mary," "Creed," "Soul of Christ" and "Hail, Holy Queen," vocally or mentally, according to the usual way.

Second Rule: The second rule is that, should the person who is contemplating the "Our Father" find in one word, or in two, matter so good to think over, and relish and consolation, let him not concern himself to pass on, even though the hour ends on what he finds there. The hour ended, he will say the rest of the "Our Father" in the usual way.

Third Rule: The third is that if one has lingered for a whole hour on one word or two of the "Our Father," when he will want to come back on another day to the prayer, let him say the above-mentioned word or two as he is accustomed, and on the word which immediately follows, let him begin to contemplate according to what was said in the second rule. (Ignatius of Loyola, *Spiritual Exercises*, "The Fourth Week")

10. The Recollection of the Name of God

It is uncertain which Eastern Christian composed the following text, whether Symeon the New Theologian in the eleventh century or somebody else somewhat later. It gives rather explicit directions for the type of rhythmic prayer just described.

One must acquire, above all else, three things: death to everything, a pure conscience which preserves you from every self-accusation, and freedom from every passion that might incline you toward the present age, or even toward your own body. Then, seated in a peaceful cell, apart, in a corner, do as I instruct you: close the door and raise your spirit above every vain and temporal object; then, resting your beard on your breast, and turning your physical eye and your entire spirit toward the middle of your belly, also called the navel, restrain the air that passes through your nose in such a way as to render your breathing difficult, and mentally explore within your entrails to find there the heart where it pleases all the faculties of the soul to abide.

In the beginning you will find darkness and a stubborn dullness, but if you persevere and carry out this exercise day and night, you will discover, O wonder! a happiness without limit. As soon, in fact, as the spirit discovers the place of the heart, it will suddenly perceive what it has never known: it will perceive the air that exists at the center of the heart, and it will perceive itself whole and full of discernment, and henceforward, as soon as a thought issues forth, even before it is completely formed, by the invocation of Jesus Christ the spirit tracks it down and destroys it. . . . The rest you will understand with the help of God by keeping guard over your spirit and holding Jesus in your heart.

[Cited by HAUSHERR 1927: 68–69]

The "invocation of Jesus," here associated with rhythmic breathing techniques, is doubtless the "Jesus prayer," or "single-word prayer," favored by Eastern Christian masters of the spirituality of stillness. John Climacus was already using it familiarly in the seventh century.

Let the remembrance of death and the concise Jesus Prayer go to sleep with you and get up with you, for nothing helps you as these do when you are asleep. (John Climacus, *The Ladder of Divine Ascent*, Step 15)

[JOHN CLIMACUS 1982: 178]

*In a definition of stillness (*hesychia*), the "remembrance of Jesus" is connected with breathing.*

Stillness is worshiping God unceasingly and waiting on Him. Let the remembrance of Jesus be present with your every breath. Then indeed you will appreciate the value of stillness. (Ibid., Step 27)

[JOHN CLIMACUS 1982: 269–270]

The "Jesus prayer" is, then, formulaic, repetitive, and rhythmically connected with breathing. It occurs in a number of similar formulas, of which "Lord Jesus Christ, have mercy on me" is one of the more common.

A parallel phenomenon occurs in Islam, and mutual borrowings between Eastern Christians and Muslims are by no means to be ruled out. In Muslim circles this type of prayer is called "remembrance" or "recollection" of the name of God.

"Recollect God often," the Quran commands (Quran 33:40), for "the recollection of God makes the heart calm" (Quran 13:28). The Quran does not say what form that recollection is to take, but it eventually became centered, as it did in Christianity, upon the divine Name; and one or another form of such recollection was built into the liturgy of every Sufi fraternity in Islam. "Recollection" is, quite simply, the most common form of noncanonical Muslim piety and perhaps the best known in non-Muslim circles, since its practice as a communal and public devotion from the twelfth century down to modern times has drawn the attention of Western pilgrims and travelers in the Near East. How closely the Muslim "recollection" resembles its Christian counterpart is clear from this very early testimony to the practice by Sahl al-Tustari (d. 896 C.E.).

Sahl said to one of his disciples: Strive to say continuously for one day "O God! O God! O God!" and do the same the next day and the day after that—until he became habituated to saying those words. Then he bade him repeat them at night also, until they became so familiar that he uttered them even during his sleep. Then he said: Do not repeat them any more but let all your faculties be engrossed in remembering God. The disciple did this, until he became absorbed in the thought of God. One day, when he was in his house, a piece of wood fell on his head and broke it. The drops of blood which trickled to the ground bore the legend "O God!" (Hujwiri, *The Unveiling of the Hidden*) [HUJWIRI 1911: 195]

In this text directions do not go much beyond urging the continuous repetition of the formula, here simply the divine name "Allah, Allah, Allah." But with the passage of time both the physical directions and the formulas become more complex. Thus Ibn Iyad in the mid-thirteenth century provides recitation instructions on the very common prayer formula drawn from the first part of the profession of faith: La illaha ill'Allah, *"There is no god but The God."*

Its recitation is begun from the left side of the breast, which is like the niche enclosing the lamp of the heart, the center of spiritual brightness. It continues going down and around the base of the breast, up the right side to its top. Continue until you reach the starting position. (Ibn Iyad, *Lofty Deeds*) [Cited by ANAWATI & GARDET 1961: 202]

Ibn Iyad belonged to a Sufi group called the Shadhilis, and he is describing their characteristic method of "recollection." Another account of the same method comes from Muhammad al-Sanusi (d. 1859 C.E.), a collector of Sufi traditions and himself the founder of one the last two great Sufi fraternities, the Sanusis.

The positions to be taken in a Shadhili "recollection" consist in squatting down on the ground, legs crossed, knees raised, arms around the legs, head lowered between the two knees, eyes closed. The head is then raised while reciting *la ilaha* during the interval between the arrival of the head at the height of the heart from its (starting) position on the right shoulder. One should be careful to banish from the soul whatever is alien to God. When the head reaches the level of the heart, the *illa* should be enunciated with vigor so that it makes its impression there and its effect spreads thence to all the members of the body. That is what one calls the prayer of compassion and expulsion. . . . One then says the *Allah* directly into the heart in a manner even more energetic: the formula then has the effect of compressing there the principles of the fear of God and of affirming His Oneness. (Sanusi, *The Gushing Spring*)

[Cited by ANAWATI & GARDET 1961: 202–203]

The Muslim's private "recollection" has, then, its obvious resemblances to the East-ern Christian practice of the single-phrase "Jesus prayer." The Muslim manifesta-tion, however, was often enlarged to embrace a litany of the "Ninety-nine Beautiful Names of God," whose recitation was commonly assisted by a chaplet of thirty-three or ninety-nine beads, an obvious ancestor to the Western Christian's "rosary beads."

11. Spiritual Concerts

Equally characteristic of Islamic piety was the performance of the "recollection" ritual in unison by groups of Sufis, often accompanied by music and even dancing. Such a devotion, called an "audition" and perhaps best understood as a kind of spiritual concert, was widespread—though by no means universally approved of—across the entire Islamic world down to modern times. One of the earliest apprecia-tions we have of the spiritual concert comes from Ahmad Ghazali (d. 1126 C.E.), the brother of the more famous lawyer and theologian. The Sufis gather, and their master gives them a spiritual exegesis of some passage from the Quran. Then a singer begins the chanting of Sufi poetry.

When they [that is, the assembled Sufis] experience within them a stirring which affects them like the commotion of one who is called to the service of a mighty king and to appear before God, he who falls into ecstasy does not rise until he is overpowered, and the rest do as he does. The dance is not to be affected or feigned; no, their movements must be in accordance with the state, like one who is overcome by terror or unavoidable trepidation. Then when their spirits receive a mystical appre-hension of the unseen states, and their hearts are softened by the lights of the Divine Essence and are established in purity and the spiritual lights, they sit down, and the chanter chants a light chant to bring them forth by degrees from the internal to the external. . . . Then they get up from the place of the audition and go to their dwellings and sit watching for the revelation of what appeared to them in the state of their absorption in ecstasy. After the audition some of them dispense with food for days on account of the nourishment of their spirits and hearts with unseen mystical experiences. (Ahmad Ghazali, *On the Audition*) [TRIMINGHAM 1971: 196]

"Things went on that way," Ghazali continues, fully aware that he is describing a devotion undergoing rapid changes, "till the common people imitated them, and the good was mingled with the corrupt and the system was disordered." What may have disordered the system was the transformation of these "spiritual concerts" into celebrations that seemed little different from a party or a carouse. One who was notorious for the lavish entertainments of his "concerts" at Nishapur was Abu Sa`id ibn Abi al-Khayr (d. 1049 C.E.). Once approached by another Sufi who questioned him about this innovation of "permitting the young men to dance and sing," Abu Sa`id responded with this lesson in sublimation.

As for the young men's dancing in the spiritual "audition," the souls of young men are yet purged of lust—indeed it may be the prevailing element—and lust takes possession of all the limbs. Now if a young dervish claps his hands, the lust of his hands will be dissipated, and if he tosses his feet, the lust of his feet will be lessened. When by this means the lust fails in their limbs, they can preserve themselves from great sins, but when all lusts are united—which my God forfend—they will sin mortally. It is better that the fire of their lust should be dissipated in the "audition" than in something else. (Abu Sa`id, *The Secrets of Holiness* 269) [NICHOLSON 1921: 58]

The answer is undoubtedly orthodox and may have been calculated to appease, unlike another response reported to a similar objection.

There was at Qa'in a venerable Prayer Leader, whose name was Khwaja Muhammad Qa'ini. When Abu Sa`id arrived at Qa'in, Khwaja Muhammad spent most of his time in waiting upon him, and he used to attend all the parties to which Abu Sa`id was invited. On one of these occasions, during the "audition" which followed the feast, Abu Sa`id and all the company had fallen into transports of ecstasy. The muezzin gave the call to noonday prayers, but Abu Sa`id remained in the same rapture and the dervishes continued to dance and shout. "Prayers! Prayers!" cried the Prayer Leader Muhammad Qa'ini. "We *are* at prayers," said Abu Sa`id, whereupon the Prayer Leader left them in order to take part in the prayer service. When Abu Sa`id came out of his trance, he said, "Between its rising and its setting the sun does not shine upon a more venerable and learned man than Khwaja Muhammad. But his knowledge

of Sufism is less than the tip of a hair." (Abu Sa'id, *The Secrets of Holiness*
293) [NICHOLSON 1921: 60–61]

*Ghazali may have had Abu Sa'id's practices in mind when he expressed some
reservations about "spiritual concerts." He would certainly not have approved of the
late medieval form of the devotion that Edward Lane witnessed in Cairo in 1836.
Here the Sufis belonged to the Mawliyya or Mevlana order, the famous "whirling
dervishes" founded by Jalal al-Din Rumi (d. 1273 C.E.) at Konya in Turkey.*

Most of the dervishes [*darwish* is the Persian word to describe the
Arabic *Sufi*, the Muslim ascetic/mystic; see Chapter 3 below] were Egyptians, but there were among them many Turks and Persians. I had not
waited many minutes before they began their exercises. . . . The dervishes
who formed the large ring (which enclosed four of the marble columns
of the portico) now commenced their *zikr* [Arabic *dhikr*: "recollection"],
exclaiming over and over again "Allah" and, at each exclamation, bowing
the head and the body and taking a step to the right, so that the whole
ring moved rapidly round. As soon as they commenced this exercise,
another dervish, a Turk of the order of Mowlawees, in the middle of the
circle, began to whirl, using both his feet to effect this motion, and
extending his arms; the motion increased in velocity until his dress spread
out like an umbrella. He continued whirling thus for about ten minutes;
after which he bowed to his superior, who stood within the great ring,
and then, without showing any signs of fatigue or giddiness, joined the
dervishes in the great ring; who had now begun to ejaculate the name of
God with great vehemence, and to jump to the right instead of stepping.

After whirling, six other dervishes, within the great ring, formed
another ring, but a very small one, each placing his arms on the shoulders
of those next to him; and thus disposed they performed a revolution
similar to that of the larger ring, except in being more rapid; repeating
also the same exclamation of "Allah!" but with a rapidity proportionately
greater. This motion they maintained for about the same length of time
that the whirling of the single dervish before had occupied; after which
the whole party sat down to rest. They rose again after the lapse of about
a quarter of an hour and performed the same exercise a second time.
[LANE 1836: 172–174]

12. The Sacraments

*To return to Christian worship, the Eucharist and baptism were but two, albeit the
most important, of a number of acts and ceremonies that took on a special religious*

significance for Christians. These were called, from the fourth century onward, mysteria by the Greeks and sacramenta by the Latins. Their distinguishing characteristic was that they were exterior signs of the operation of an invisible, interior grace. Or, as Augustine put it, speaking expressly of the bread and wine of the Eucharist: "They are called sacraments because one thing is seen in them, another understood. What is seen is a bodily appearance, but what is understood has a spiritual fruit."

The definition of a sacrament was sufficiently elastic—"an indication, by means of signs and symbols, of invisible and ineffable realities," according to one— that the number of them seems to have fluctuated in the early Church. Where there was agreement was that Christ was the principal agent in working that invisible grace; the priest was simply an instrument, whence it followed that the virtue or spiritual condition of the officiating cleric had no effect on the operation of that grace. There was dispute, however, over how that connection between the realm of spirit and that of matter was effected. That it came about through the words of the officiating priest serving as Jesus' deputy was the general view in the West; in the Eastern churches the prevailing sentiment was for a more direct divine intervention in the form of a descent of the Holy Spirit. That difference in viewpoints long separated the Eastern and Western churches.

Eventually the number of sacraments became stabilized at seven: Baptism, Confirmation, Unction, Penance, Eucharist, Holy Orders, and Matrimony. Reflection on each of them became more complex, particularly as it became more theological. Here, for example, is the treatment of the sacraments in what became one of the classic textbooks of the Middle Ages, the Four Books of Sentences *of Peter Lombard, written sometime about 1150 C.E. Further, it bears the unmistakable signs of the method characteristic of Hellenically derived theology: a carefully systematic presentation and reliance on what had already become the Church's authorities, the "Fathers."*

ON SACRAMENTS

The Samaritan who tended the wounded man (Luke 10:30–37) applied to his wounds the dressings of the sacraments, just as God instituted the remedies of the sacraments against the wounds of original and actual sin. Concerning the sacraments, four questions first present themselves for consideration: what a sacrament is, why it was instituted, wherein it consists, and how it is performed; and what the difference is between the sacraments of the Old and New Covenant.

WHAT A SACRAMENT IS

"A sacrament is the sign of a sacred thing" (as Augustine says). However, a sacred mystery is also called a sacrament, so that a sacrament may be (both) the sign of something sacred and the sacred thing signified.

So (as Berengar of Tours says) "a sacrament is the visible form of an invisible grace." . . .

HOW A SIGN AND A SACRAMENT DIFFER

Furthermore, "some signs are natural, as smoke which signifies fire; others conventional" (as Augustine says); of those which are conventional, some are sacraments and some are not. For every sacrament is a sign, but the converse is not true. A sacrament bears a resemblance to the thing of which it is the sign. "For if sacraments did not bear a resemblance to things of which they are the sacraments, they could not be properly called sacraments." For a sacrament is properly so called because it is a sign of the grace of God and the expression of invisible grace, so that it bears its image and its cause. Sacraments, therefore, were not instituted merely to signify something, but also as a means of sanctification. For things which were instituted only to signify are signs only, and not sacraments; such were the sacrifices of the flesh and the ceremonial observances of the Old Law, which could never justify those who offered them, because, as the Apostle (Paul) says: "The blood of goats and of oxen and the ashes of a heifer being sprinkled sanctify such as are defiled, to the cleansing of the flesh" (Heb. 9:13), but not of the spirit. Now this uncleanness (referred to in the Old Law) was the touching of a dead body. . . . These legal observances also cleansed sometimes from bodily leprosy; but no one was ever justified by the works of the Law, as the Apostle says (Rom. 3:20; Gal. 2:16), even if he performed them in faith and charity. Why? Because God has ordained them for servitude, not for justification, so that they might be the types of things to come, wishing that these offerings should be made to Him rather than to idols. They therefore were signs, yet also sacraments, although they are often called so incorrectly in the Scriptures, because they were rather signs of a sacred thing than availing anything themselves. These moreover the Apostle calls "works of the Law," which were instituted only to signify something, or as a yoke.

Peter Lombard shortly returns to this question of the "sacraments" of the Old Law, which in turn leads him to those of the New.

OF THE DIFFERENCE BETWEEN
THE OLD AND THE NEW SACRAMENTS

Now it remains to note the difference between the old and the new sacraments, since we call sacraments what anciently they called sacred things, such as sacrifices and oblations and the like. The differences be-

tween these Augustine indicated briefly when he said, "because the former only promised and signified salvation, while the latter gave it."

Let us now come to the sacraments of the New Covenant, which
are baptism, confirmation, the blessing of bread, that is, the eucharist,
penance, extreme unction, ordination, marriage. Of these some offer a
remedy for sin and confer a helping grace, like baptism; others are merely
a remedy, like marriage; others strengthen us with grace and virtue, such
as the eucharist and ordination. If indeed we are asked why these sacraments were not instituted immediately after the fall of man (through
Adam's sin), since in them are justification and salvation, we say that
before the coming of Christ, who brought grace, the sacraments of grace
could not be granted, for they have derived their virtue from his death
and passion. Now Christ was unwilling to come (into this world) before man was convinced that he could find help in neither natural nor
written law. (Peter Lombard, *Sentences* 4.1.1–2)

[PETER LOMBARD 1917: 79–82]

13. A Famous Relic

*This Christian sanctification of matter, whose theoretical ground rested in the
Incarnation and which is so systematically apparent in the doctrine of the sacraments, was another potent element in kindling Christian piety. The veneration of
relics, for example, both in the cult of the martyrs and saints and in the question
of images and icons was a popular and widespread form of devotion among Christians, and one that profoundly separated them, in theory if not always in fact, from
Jews and Muslims. The matter of relics arose early in the history of the Church, in
a quite spectacular fashion.*

When the business at Nicea [that is, the ecumenical council there in
325 C.E.] was finished, the priests returned home. The Emperor (Constantine) rejoiced greatly at the restoration of unity of opinion in the
Catholic Church, and in his desire to express, on behalf of himself, his
children and the empire, the gratitude toward God which the unanimity
of the bishops inspired, he directed that a house of prayer should be
erected to God at Jerusalem near the place called Calvary. At the same
time his mother Helena went to the city for the purpose of offering up
prayer and of visiting the sacred places. Her zeal for Christianity made her
anxious to find the wood which formed the adorable Cross. But it was no
easy matter to discover either this relic or the Lord's sepulcher; for the

pagans, who in former times had persecuted the Church and who, at the first promulgation of Christianity, had had recourse to every artifice to exterminate it, had concealed that spot under much heaped-up earth and built up what before had been a depression, the way it appears now, and the more effectively to conceal them had enclosed the entire place of the Resurrection and Mount Calvary within a wall and had moreover ornamented the whole area and paved it with stone. . . .

At length, however, the place was discovered, and the fraud about it that had been so zealously maintained was detected; some say that the facts were first disclosed by a Hebrew who dwelt in the East and who derived his information from some documents which had come to him by paternal inheritance; but it seems more likely to suppose that God revealed the fact by means of signs and dreams. . . . When by command of the emperor the place was excavated deeply, the cave whence our Lord arose from the dead was discovered; and at no great distance three crosses were found and another separate piece of wood on which were inscribed in white letters in Hebrew, Greek and Latin the following words: "Jesus of Nazareth, the king of the Jews." These words, as the sacred book of the Gospels relates, were placed by command of Pilate, governor of Judea, over the head of Christ.

There remained a difficulty, however, in distinguishing the Divine Cross from the others, for the inscription had been wrenched from it and thrown aside and the cross itself had been cast aside with the others, without any distinction, when the bodies of the crucified were taken down. . . . It was no concern of theirs [that is, the Roman executioners] to deposit the crosses in their original order, since it was growing late, and as the men were dead they did not think it worthwhile to remain to attend to the crosses. A more divine indication than could be furnished by man was therefore necessary in order to distinguish the Divine Cross from the others and this revelation was given in the following manner. There was a certain lady of rank in Jerusalem who was afflicted with a most grievous and incurable disease. Macarius, bishop of Jerusalem, accompanied by the mother of the emperor and her attendants, went to her bedside. After engaging in prayer, Macarius signaled the spectators that the Divine Cross would be the one which, on being brought in contact with the invalid, would cure the disease. He approached her with each of the three crosses in turn, but when two of the crosses were laid upon her, it seemed but folly and mockery to her for she was at the gates of death. When, however, the third cross was in like manner brought to her, she

suddenly opened her eyes, regained her strength, and immediately sprang
from her bed well. It is said that a dead person was, in the same way,
restored to life. The venerated wood having thus been identified, the
greater portion of it was deposited in a silver case, in which it is still
preserved in Jerusalem; but the empress sent part of it to her son Constantine, together with the nails by which the body of Christ had been
fastened. (Sozomen, *Church History* 2.1)

*Thus were discovered the remains of the "True Cross," the premier relic of Christen-
dom. When Egeria visited Jerusalem about fifty years after Helena, she found the
cross already the subject of a considerable cult. The time is Easter week, and the
place is Constantine's shrine at Golgotha, the site of Jesus' crucifixion.*

The people are dismissed at the Cross (after the dawn service) even
before the sun is up, and those who are more ardent go to Mount Sion
to pray at the pillar at which the Lord was scourged. They then go home
for a short rest, but it is not long before everyone is assembled for the
next service. The bishop's chair is placed on Golgotha behind the cross
which stands there now. He takes his seat and a table is placed before him
with a linen cloth on it. The deacons stand round, and there is brought
to him a gold and silver box in which is the Holy Wood of the Cross. It
is opened and the Wood of the Cross and the Title are taken out and
placed on the table.

As long as the Holy Wood is on the table, the bishop sits with his
hands resting on either end of it and holds it down, and the deacons
round him keep watch over it. They guard it like this because the custom
is that all the people, catechumens as well as the faithful, come up one by
one to the table. They lean down over it, kiss the Wood and move on.
And it is said that on one occasion one of them bit off a piece of the Holy
Wood and stole it away, and for this reason the deacons stand round and
keep watch in case anyone dares to do the same again.

Nor are the remains of the cross the only relic displayed and venerated.

Thus all the people go past one by one. They stoop down, touch the
Holy Wood and the inscription with their forehead and then their eyes,
then kiss it, but no one dares put out his hand to touch it. When they
have kissed the Cross they go to a deacon who stands holding the Ring
of Solomon, and the Horn with which the kings of Israel were anointed.
These they venerate by kissing them, and they start around about eight
o'clock, with everyone going by, entering by one door and going out by
the other, until midday. (Egeria, *Pilgrimage* 67)

14. The Christian Cult of Martyrs

Jews, Christians, and Muslims all reverenced their holy men, dead as well as alive, but what sets Christianity apart from the other two religions is the development of an approved and official cult of the saints, and particularly the martyrs for the faith. If there were such cults among Jews and Muslims, as there certainly were, they remained on the level of popular practice and were viewed with suspicion and even hostility by the guardians of orthodoxy. The following is Augustine's defense of the Christian practice, not in the face of a Jewish objection but against a pagan one.

We do not build temples and ordain priests, rites and sacrifices to the martyrs; for they are not our gods, but their God is our God. Certainly we honor their reliquaries, as the memorials of holy men of God who strove for the truth even to the death of their bodies, that the true religion might be made known, and false and fictitious religions exposed. For if there were some before them who thought that these religions were really false and fictitious, they were afraid to give expression to their convictions. But who ever heard of a priest of the faithful, standing at an altar built for the honor and worship of God over the body of some holy martyr, say in his prayers, "I offer to you a sacrifice, O Peter, or O Paul, or O Cyprian"? It is to God that sacrifices are offered at their tombs, the God who made them both men and martyrs, and associated them with the angels in celestial honor.

And the reason why we pay such honors to their memory is that by so doing we may both give thanks to the true God for their victories, and by recalling them afresh to remembrance, may stir ourselves to imitate them by seeking to obtain like crowns and palms, calling to our help the same God on whom they called. Therefore, whatever honors the religious may pay in the places of the martyrs, they are but honors rendered to their memory, not sacred rites or sacrifices offered to dead men as to gods. And even such as bring thither food—which indeed is not done by the better Christians, and in most places in the world is not done at all—do so in order that it may be sanctified to them through the merits of the martyrs, in the name of the Lord of the martyrs, first presenting the food and offering prayer, and thereafter taking it away to be eaten, or to be in part bestowed upon the needy. But he who knows the one sacrifice of Christians, which is the sacrifice offered in those places, also knows that these are not sacrifices offered to the martyrs. It is, then, neither with divine honors nor with human crimes, by which they [that is, the pagans] worship their gods, that we honor our martyrs; neither do we offer sacrifices to them or convert the crimes of the gods into their sacred rights. (Augustine, *City of God* 8.27) [AUGUSTINE 1948: 2:134–135]

15. Muslim Canonical Prayer

Another visitor from the Christian West to the Muslim East was Ricoldo di Monte Croce, who was there not simply to make pilgrimage but rather to confute and convert the Muslims. Ricoldo was not, then, a disinterested visitor, but he nonetheless found something in Islamic practice to admire.

What can I say of their prayers? For they have such great care and devotion in their prayers that I was amazed when I saw and experienced it firsthand. For I spent three and a half months with the camel nomads in the deserts of Arabia and Persia and never for any reason did I ever see these camel Arabs neglect to pray at the prescribed hours of the day or night, and particularly in the morning and the evening. They manifest such a devotion in their prayers that they put all other things from them. (Ricoldo, *Itinerarium*) [LAURENT 1873: 131–132]

What Ricoldo found so impressive was the performance of the liturgical prayers obligatory upon all Muslims, male and female, who have attained the use of reason. They had to be performed facing the direction of Mecca five prescribed times daily. According to the classic Letter on the Roots of Jurisprudence of al-Shafi̔i, the Egyptian legal scholar who died ca. 820 C.E., the obligations imposed by God on men can be derived (1) explicitly from the Quran, though with progressive abrogations; (2) in general terms from the Quran and explicitly regarding its modalities from the Prophet; (3) from the Prophet's teachings alone, which are also binding; and (4) deductively from the Quran or the teachings of the Prophet, the famous "personal initiative" of Islamic jurisprudence. How the first two operated in the question of liturgical prayer is made clear in the following passage from the same Letter.

Shafi̔i said: I have heard some scholars who related that God had imposed a certain duty for prayer before He laid down that for the five prayers. For He said:

> O you wrapped in your mantle,
> Stay up the night, except a little,
> Half of it, or a little less
> Or a little more,
> And chant the Quran distinctly.
> (Quran 73:1–4)

God abrogated this duty by another, which may be found in the same Sura, and it reads as follows:

"The Lord knows that you stay up nearly two-thirds of the night, or half of it, or a third of it, and a party of those with you likewise, and God determines the night and the day. He knows that you will never count it up, so He has turned toward you in mercy. So recite what may be convenient for you of the Quran; He knows that some of you will be sick and others journeying about in the land, seeking the bounty of God, and others fighting in the path of God. So recite what is convenient of it, and observe the prayer and pay the alms." (Quran 73:20)

Even these latter modifications are not entirely clear, Shafiʿi argues, and so it is necessary to turn to the Prophetic tradition for clarification.

Shafiʿi said: In such a case it is obligatory to seek the evidence of the Prophetic tradition for determining which of the meanings is valid. Thus the Prophetic tradition has indicated that no duty other than that of the five prayers is obligatory and that any earlier prayers have been abrogated by that tradition. (Shafiʿi, *Risala*) [SHAFIʿI 1961: 128–129]

Shafiʿi resumes the standard teaching.

God, Blessed and Most High, said: "Truly prayer has become for the believers a thing prescribed at stipulated times" (Quran 4:103). And He said, "Observe the prayer and pay the alms tax" (Quran 2:43 etc.). And He said to His Prophet, "Take of their wealth an alms tax to cleanse and purify them thereby and pray for them" (Quran 9:103). And He said: "Pilgrimage to the House [that is, the Kaʿba] is a duty to God from the people, whoever is able to make his way there" (Quran 3:97).

Thus God has laid down in the Quran the duties of prayer, alms tax and pilgrimage and specified the modes of their performance through His Prophet's tongue.

So the Apostle specified that (each day) prayers shall number five, that the number of the cycles in the noon, afternoon and evening prayers shall number four repeated twice in the towns, and the cycles at the sunset prayer shall number three and at the dawn prayer two.

He decreed that in all (the prayers) there should be recitals (from the Quran), audible at the sunset, evening and dawn prayers, and silent recitals at the noon and afternoon prayers.

He specified that at the beginning of each prayer there shall be the declaration "God is great" and at the ending salutations on the Prophet and his house, and that each prayer consists of the "God is great," the recital (from the Quran), the bowing and two prostrations after each inclination, but that beyond these nothing is obligatory.

He decreed that prayer while one is on a journey can be shorter, if
the traveler so desires, in the three occasions that have four cycles, but
he made no change in the sunset and dawn prayers when those prayers
are performed in town. However, all prayers must be (performed) in the
direction of Mecca, whether one is in town or on a journey. (Shafiʿi,
Risala) [SHAFIʿI 1961: 158–159]

*The turning toward Mecca in prayer provides Shafiʿi with an illustrative example
of the use of "personal initiative" in a matter of law.*

Shafiʿi said: (God ordered the performance of prayer) in the direction of the Sacred Mosque [in Mecca; that is, the Kaʿba] and said to His
Prophet: "Sometimes We see you turning your face about toward the
heaven. So We will turn you in a direction that will satisfy you. Turn your
face in the direction of the Sacred Mosque, and wherever you are, turn
your faces in that direction" (Quran: 2:144). And He said: "And from
whatever place you have gone forth, turn your face in the direction of the
Sacred Mosque; and wherever you may be, turn your faces in its direction" (Quran 2:149).

Thus God, glorified be His praise, guided men, should they be at a
distance from the Sacred Mosque, by using the reasoning powers which
He has implanted in men and which discriminate between things and
their opposites and the landmarks which He set up for them when the
Sacred Mosque, to which He commanded them to turn their faces, is out
of sight. For God said, "For it is He who made for you the stars, that you
might be guided by them in the darkness of land and sea" (Quran 6:98).
And He said, "And by the landmarks and by the stars they are guided"
(Quran 16:16).

Shafiʿi said: Such landmarks may be the mountains, the nights and
the days, which have winds of known names though they blow from
different directions, and the sun and the moon and the stars whose risings
and settings and whose places in the sky are known.

Thus God prescribed to men the use of personal reasoning in turning
in the direction of the Sacred Mosque by means of guidance to them,
which I have described; so long as men use their personal reasoning they
will not deviate from His command, glorious be His praise; but He did
not permit them to pray in any direction they wished if the Sacred
Mosque were out of sight. And He also instructed them about His will
and providence and said, "Does man think that he will be left roaming at
will?" (Quran 75:36). "Left roaming at will" means one who is neither
commanded nor prohibited. (Shafiʿi, *Risala*) [SHAFIʿI 1961: 69–70]

Shafiʿi's is the voice of the lawyer, a powerful one in Islam, but by no means the only accent heard in religious circles. There was also the voice of the mystic, in this case the Spaniard Ibn al-Arabi (1165–1240 C.E.). He read the matter of the direction of prayer in a very different way indeed.

Consider this matter, for as men know God (in this world), so they will see Him on the Day of Resurrection. . . . So beware lest you restrict yourself to a particular tenet (concerning the Reality) and so deny any other tenet (equally reflecting Him), for you would forfeit much good; indeed, you would forfeit the true knowledge of what is. Therefore, be completely and utterly receptive to all doctrinal forms, for God Most High is too All-embracing and Great to be confined within one creed rather than another, for He has said, "Wheresoever you turn, there is the face of God" (Quran 2:115), without mentioning any particular direction. He states that there [that is, "wheresoever you turn"] is the face of God, the face of a thing being its reality.

. . . The perfect servant, despite his knowledge of this [that is, the omnipresence of God], nevertheless maintains himself, in his outer and limited form, in prayer, his face turned toward the Sacred Mosque (in Mecca), believing God to be in that direction when he prays; the Sacred Mosque is in truth representative of a facet of the Reality, as in the verse, "Wheresoever you turn, there is the face of God," and in facing it one is face to face with God in it. However, do not tell yourself that He is in that direction only, but rather maintain both your attitude (of prayer) in facing the Sacred Mosque and your attitude (of understanding) the impossibility of confining His face to that particular direction, it being merely one of the points toward which men turn. (Ibn al-Arabi, *The Bezels of Wisdom*, "Hud") [IBN AL-ARABI 1980: 137–138]

If these sentiments of the mystic seem to undermine the uniqueness and absoluteness not only of Mecca but even of Islam itself, Ibn al-Arabi apparently had little hesitation in making his views on worship even clearer.

> My heart is capable of every form,
> a cloister of the monk, a temple for idols,
> a pasture for gazelles, the votary's Kaʿba,
> the tables of the Torah, the Quran.
> Love is the creed I hold: Wherever turn
> His camels, love is still my creed and faith.
> (Ibn al-Arabi, *Tarjuman* 11.13–15)

16. Prophetic Traditions on Prayer

When Shafi'i speaks of Muhammad "decreeing" the specifics of the obligation to prayer set down in general terms in the Quran, he is referring to the "traditions" or reports originally transmitted by Muhammad's contemporaries and professing to recount the Prophet's teachings or conduct. Even in Shafi'i's own lifetime these were beginning to be collected for legal purposes. In the end they provided, together with the Quran, the chief foundation of Islamic law. The following are some typical and widely circulated Prophetic traditions on the subject of prayer. First, as to its times:

Burayda told of a man asking the Apostle of God about the time of prayer, to which he [Muhammad] replied: "Pray with us these two," meaning two days. When the sun passed the meridian he summoned Bilal, who uttered the call to prayer, then he commanded him and he made the announcement declaring that the time to begin the afternoon prayer had come when the sun was high, white and clear. Then he gave him command and he made the announcement declaring that the time to begin the sunset prayer had come when the sun had set. Then he gave command and he made the announcement declaring that the time to begin the night prayer had come when the twilight had ended. Then he gave command and he made the announcement declaring that the time to begin the dawn prayer had come when the dawn appeared.

The next day he commanded him to delay the (summons to the) noon prayer until the extreme heat had passed and he did so, and he allowed it to be delayed until the extreme heat had passed. He observed the afternoon prayer when the sun was high, delaying it beyond the time when he had previously observed it. He observed the sunset prayer before the twilight had ended; he observed the night prayer when a third of the night had passed; and he observed the dawn prayer when there was clear daylight. Then asking where the man was who had inquired about the time of prayer and receiving from him a reply that he was present, he said, "The time for your prayer is within the limits of what you have seen." Muslim has transmitted this report. (Baghawi, *Mishkat al-Masabih* 4.2.1)

Ibn Mas'ud said that the extent of the shadow when the Apostle of God prayed the noon prayer was three to five feet in summer and five to seven feet in winter. Abu Dawud and Nasa'i have both transmitted this report. (Ibid. 4.2.3)

Abu Hurayra reported the Apostle of God as saying, "No prayer is more burdensome to the hypocrites than the dawn and the evening prayer; but if they knew what blessings lie in them, they would come to them even if they had to crawl to do so." Muslim transmits this report. (Ibid. 4.4.1)

Amr ibn Shuᶜayb on his father's authority reported his grandfather as saying that God's Messenger prohibited the recitation of poems in a mosque, buying and selling in it, and sitting in a circle in a mosque on Friday before the prayer. Abu Dawud and Tirmidhi transmitted this report.

Ibn Umar said that there were seven places where the Apostle of God forbade men to pray: a dunghill, a slaughterhouse, a graveyard, the middle of the road, a bath, places where camels kneel to drink, and the roof of God's House. Tirmidhi and al-Maja have transmitted this report. (Ibid. 4.8.2)

Anas ibn Malik reported the Apostle of God as saying, "A man's prayer in his house is equivalent to a single observance of prayer, his prayer in a tribal mosque is worth twenty-five, his prayer in a Friday mosque is equivalent to five hundred, his prayer in the Aqsa mosque (in Jerusalem) is equivalent to fifty thousand, his prayer in my mosque (in Medina) is (also) equivalent to fifty thousand, and his prayer in the Sacred Mosque [that is, the Haram at Mecca] is equivalent to a hundred thousand." Ibn Maja has transmitted this report. (Ibid. 4.8.3)

Ibn Umar reported the Apostle of God as saying, "Do not prevent your women from coming into mosques, but their houses are better for them." Abu Dawud transmitted this report.

Ibn Masᶜud reported the Prophet as saying, "It is more excellent for a woman to pray in her house than in her courtyard, and more excellent for her to pray in her own room than (elsewhere) in the house." Abu Dawud transmitted this report. (Ibid. 4.24.2)

Jabir ibn Samura said: The Apostle of God came out to us . . . and said, "Why do you not draw yourselves up in rows (for prayer) as the angels do in the presence of the Lord?" We asked, "Apostle of God, how do the angels draw themselves up in rows in the presence of the Lord?" He replied, "They make the first rows complete and keep close together in the row." Muslim transmitted this report.

Anas reported the Apostle of God as saying, "Complete the front row, then the one that comes next, and if there is any incompleteness, let it be in the last row." Abu Dawud transmitted this report.

Abu Hurayra reported the Apostle of God as saying, "The best of the men's rows (in prayer) is the first and worst is the last, but the best of the women's rows is the last and the worst is the first." Muslim transmitted this report. (Ibid. 4.25.1–2)

Abu Saʿid reported the Apostle of God as saying, "When there are three people (praying together), one of them should lead them. The one among them most worthy to act as prayer leader is the one most versed in the Quran." Muslim transmitted this report. (Ibid. 4.27.1)

Abu Hurayra reported the Apostle of God as saying, "When one of you leads the people in prayer he should be brief, for among them are the sick, the weak and the aged. But when one of you prays by himself, he may be as long as he likes." This report has been transmitted by Bukhari and Muslim. (Ibid. 4.28.1)

Tariq ibn Shihab reported the Apostle of God as saying, "The Friday prayer in congregation is a necessary duty for every Muslim, with four exceptions: a slave, a woman, a boy and an invalid." Abu Dawud transmitted this report. (Ibid. 4.44.2)

Salman reported the Apostle of God as saying, "If any man bathes on Friday, purifies himself as much as he can with ablution, anoints himself with oil or puts on a touch of perfume which he has in his house, then goes out and, without squeezing between two men, prays what is prescribed for him, then remains silent when the prayer leader preaches, his sins between that time and the next Friday will be forgiven him." Bukhari has transmitted this tradition. (Ibid. 4.45.1)

17. The Institution of the Call to Prayer

The standard Life of Muhammad *provides the setting for the institution of many of the practices that became standard in the devotional life of the Muslim community, among them the public call to prayer.*

When the Apostle was firmly settled in Medina and his brethren the "Emigrants" were gathered to him and the affairs of the "Helpers" were arranged, Islam became firmly established. Prayer was instituted, the alms tax and fasting were prescribed, legal punishments fixed, the forbidden and the permitted prescribed, and Islam took up its abode with them. . . . When the Apostle first came (to Medina), the people gathered about him for prayer at the appointed times without being summoned. At first the Apostle thought of using a trumpet like that of the Jews who used it to summon to prayer. Afterwards he disliked the idea and ordered a clapper to be made [like the Christians'], so that it was duly fashioned to be beaten when the Muslims should pray.

Meanwhile Abdullah ibn Zayd ibn Tha'laba . . . heard a voice in a dream and came to the Apostle saying: "A phantom visited me at night. There passed by me a man wearing two green garments carrying a clapper in his hand, and I asked him to sell it to me. When he asked me what I wanted it for I told him that it was to summon people to prayer, whereupon he offered to show me a better way: it was to say thrice: 'God is great. I bear witness that there is no god but the God. I bear witness that Muhammad is the Apostle of God. Come to prayer. Come to prayer. Come to success. Come to success. God is great. God is great. There is no god but the God.' " When the Apostle of God was told of this he said that it was a true vision if God so willed it, and that he should go to Bilal and communicate it to him so that he might call to prayer thus, for he had a more penetrating voice. When Bilal acted as muezzin Umar heard him in his house and came to the Apostle dragging his cloak on the ground and saying he had seen precisely the same vision. The Apostle said, "God be praised for that!" (Ibn Ishaq, *Life* 346–347) [IBN ISHAQ 1955: 235–236]

18. On the Sublimity of Ritual Prayer

One of the great Muslim reformers was the lawyer and theologian Ghazali (d. 1111 C.E.). In many of his works, and most notably in his Revivification of the Sciences of Religion, *Ghazali attempted to breathe a deeper spirituality into the practice of ordinary Muslims by heightening their awareness in the performance of ritually prescribed actions. It was necessary to prepare the soul for ritual acts, Ghazali insisted, and to perform them with proper and explicit intention. Here, for example, is the appropriate way to fulfill the obligation of washing before prayer, with all the lawyer's attention to detail but accompanied by the spiritual awareness of the saint.*

Make the intention of removing filth from the body or of fulfilling the ceremonial preparation for worship. The making of the intention must not be omitted before the washing of the face, for otherwise the ablution is invalid. Then take a handful of water for your mouth and rinse your mouth three times, making sure that the water reaches the back of it—unless you are fasting, in which case, act gently—and say: "O God, I am purposing to read Your Book and to have Your name many times on my lips; through the steadfast word make me steadfast in this life and the world to come." Then take a handful of water for your nose, draw it in three times and blow out the moisture in your nose; while drawing it in say, "O God, make me breathe in the fragrance of Paradise, and may I be pleasing to You," and while blowing it out, "O God, I take refuge with You from the odors of Hell and from the evil abode." Then take a handful for your face, and with it wash from the beginning of the flattening of the forehead to the end of the protuberance of the chin, up and down and from ear to ear across. . . . Make the water reach the four places where hair grows: the eyebrows, the moustache, the eyelashes and the cheeks. . . . As you wash your face say, "O God, make my face white through Your light on the day when You whiten the faces of Your elect, and do not blacken my face with darkness on the day when You blacken the faces of your enemies." Do not omit wetting the thick part of the beard.

Then wash your right hand, and after that the left, together with the elbow and half the upper arm; for the adornment in Paradise reaches to the places touched in ablution. As you wash your right hand say, "O God, give me my book (of accounting) in my right hand and grant me an easy reckoning." As you wash your left say, "O God, I take refuge with You from being given my book in my left hand or behind my back." Then, moistening the fingers, rub all over your head, keeping the fingertips of right and left hands close together, placing them on the fore part of the head and moving them back to the nape of the neck and forward again. Do this three times—and similarly with the other parts of the body— saying, "O God, cover me with Your mercy, send down Your blessing upon me, shelter me beneath the shadow of Your Throne on the day when there is no shadow save Yours; O God, make my hair and my flesh forbidden things to the Fire."

Then run your ears outside and inside with clean water; place your fingers in your earholes and rub the outside of your ears with the ball of your thumbs and say, "O God, make me one of those who hear the word and follow the good in it; O God, make me hear the crier of Paradise along with the righteous in Paradise." Then rub your neck and say, "O God, deliver my neck from the Fire; O God, I take refuge with You from the chains and fetters."

Then wash your right foot and after that the left, together with the ankles. With the little finger of your left hand wash between your toes, beginning with the little toe on the right foot and finishing with the little toe on the left. Approach the toes from below and say, "O God, establish my feet on the straight path along with the feet of Your righteous servants." Similarly, when you wash the left say, "O God, I take refuge with

You that You may not cause my feet to slip from the path into the Fire on the day when You cause the feet of the hypocrites and idolaters to slip."

If a man says all these prayers during his ablution, his sins will have departed from all parts of his body, a seal has been set upon his ablution, it has been raised to beneath the Throne of God and unceasingly praises and hallows God, while the reward of that ablution is recorded for him to the Day of Resurrection. (Ghazali, *The Beginning of Guidance* 8–9)
[GHAZALI 1953: 95–97]

Although Ghazali was a mystic of considerable stature in Islam, he was here writing for the Muslim layman, converting, so to speak, the religious sensibilities of the "spiritual" Muslim into common practice. The mystics' own characteristic view of the deeper significance of ritual practices like daily prayer—and how remote it is from mere compliance—is on more explicit display in this page from a book by the Sufi al-Kharraz (d. 890 C.E.) on the etiquette of prescribed prayer.

When entering on prayer you should come into the Presence of God as you would on the Day of Resurrection, when you will stand before Him with no mediator between, for He welcomes you and you are in confidential talk with Him, and you know in whose presence you are standing, for he is the King of kings. When you have lifted your hands and said "God is most great," then let nothing remain in your heart save glorification and let nothing be in your mind in the time of glorification than the glory of God Most High, so you forget this world and the next when glorifying Him.

When a man bows in prayer, then it is fitting he should afterwards raise himself, then bow again and make intercession, until every joint of his body is directed toward the throne of God Most High, until there is nothing in his heart greater than God Most Glorious and he thinks so little of himself that he feels himself to be less than a mote of dust.
[SMITH 1950: no. 26]

19. A Muslim Philosopher on the "Uses" of Prayer and Ceremonial Observances

Both the theologian and the mystic were well within what the Muslim tradition understood as orthodoxy. Philosophers too prayed in Islam, and perhaps with the same fervor as a Ghazali or a Kharraz. But they had access to another, non-Muslim strain of thought that affected their attitudes even on prayer and ritual observance.

In the course of his account of the role of the prophet, Avicenna offers his coolly detached reflections, somewhat in the manner of Plato, on the "uses" of religion, specifically of prayer and other acts of worship.

Now this person, the prophet, is not of the kind that often comes into this world, or in every age: the gross (human) matter able to receive his sort of perfection occurs in but few temperaments. It follows from this that the prophet must devise means of securing the survival of his code and laws in all the spheres of human welfare. . . . He must therefore prescribe certain acts which men should repeat at close intervals, so that if the time for the performance of one is missed, there may soon be an opportunity for performing the next like act while the memory is still fresh and has not yet been obliterated. These acts must of course be linked up with some means of calling God and the afterlife to mind, else they will be useless: this mnemonic can only consist of set words to be uttered, or set resolves to be intended in the imagination. Men must be told that these acts are means of winning God's favor and of qualifying for great and generous reward. . . . In a word, these acts should be reminders; and these reminders must be either certain motions, or the denial of certain motions resulting in other motions. The former category may be illustrated by the instance of formal prayers, the latter by fasting. . . .

He should also if possible mix in with these observances other interests, in order to strengthen and extend the code, and to make their practice generally advantageous in a material sense also. Examples of this are Holy War and pilgrimage. He should specify certain places in the world as the most suitable for worship, stating that they belong exclusively to God; certain obligatory acts must also be specified as being done for God's sake only—as for instance the offering of sacrifices, which are a great help in this connection. The place which is advantageous in this context, if it be the town where the lawgiver took refuge and dwelt, will also serve the purpose of bringing him to mind, an advantage second only to that of remembering God and the Angels. . . .

The noblest of these observances from a certain point of view is that one in which the performer assumes that he is addressing God in private converse, that he is turning to God and standing before Him. This observance is prayer. Certain steps preparatory to prayer must also be prescribed, similar to those which a man customarily undertakes of his own accord before entering the presence of a human ruler; namely, purification and cleansing. The regulations laid down for these should be effective and impressive. The act of prayer should further be accompanied by those attitudes and rules of conduct usually observed in the presence of kings: humility, quietness, lowering the eyes, keeping the hands and feet withdrawn, not turning about and fidgeting. For every moment of the act of worship appropriate and seemly rules should be prescribed. All these conditions of religious observance serve the useful purpose of keeping the people's thoughts fixed firmly upon the recollection of God, and in this way they will continue in their close attachment to the laws and ordinances of the Faith. (Avicenna, *Book of Deliverance*) [AVICENNA 1951: 45–47]

20. The Friday Service

The noon prayer on Friday, "when the sun passes over the meridian," was the congregational prayer obligatory on all Muslims. As might be expected, a number of Prophetic traditions are reported on the subject.

Abu Hurayra reported the Messenger of God, may peace be upon him, as saying: The best day on which the sun has risen is Friday: on it Adam was created, on it he was made to enter Paradise, on it he was expelled from it. And the Last Hour will take place on no other day but Friday.

Abu Hurayra reported God's Messenger, may peace be upon him, as saying: We are the last (religious community) but we would be the first on the day of Resurrection and we would be the first to enter Paradise except that they [that is, the Jews and Christians] were given the Book before us and we were given it after them. They disagreed regarding the truth. And it was this day of theirs about which they disagreed, but God guided us to it, and that day is Friday for us; the next day is for the Jews and the day following for the Christians. (Muslim, *Sahih* 4.302, 1857, 1860)

Ghazali, as we have just seen, took as his goal the revivification of religious practices in Islam, which he hoped to accomplish by emphasizing both their spiritual content and the intent of the worshiper. This, for example, is his treatment of the Friday prayer.

Friday is the festival of the believers. It is an excellent day, ordained specially for this community by God, may He be magnified and exalted. In the course of it there is a period, the exact time of which is unknown; and if any Muslim, making request to God Most High for what he needs, chances to do so in this period, God grants his request. Prepare then for it [Friday] on Thursday by cleansing of the clothes, by many acts of praise and by asking forgiveness on Thursday evening, for that is an hour equal in merit to the (unknown) hour of the Friday. Make the intention of fasting on Friday, but do so on Saturday or Thursday as well, since there is no prohibition on fasting on Friday alone.

When the morning breaks, wash, since Friday washing is obligatory on every adult, that is, it is "established" and "confirmed." Then array yourself in white clothes, for these are the most pleasing to God. Use the best perfume you have. Cleanse your body thoroughly by shaving, cutting your hair and nails, using the toothpick and practicing other forms of cleanliness, as well as by employing fragrant perfumes. Then go early to the mosque, walking quietly and calmly. . . . It is said that, in respect to nearness to the beholding of the face of God, people come in the order of their early arrival for the Friday observance.

When you have entered the mosque, take your place in the first [that is, the nearest] row. If the congregation has assembled, do not step between their necks and do not pass in front of them while they are praying. Place yourself near a wall or pillar so that the people do not pass in front of you. Before sitting say the prayer of "greeting." Best of all, however, is to perform four prostrations, in each of which you recite the Sura of Purity (Sura 112). There is a tradition to the effect that whoever does that will not die until he has seen, or, in a variant reading, has been shown, his place in Paradise. . . .

When the leader has come out to commence the worship, break off your private worship and conversation and occupy yourself with responding to the muezzin, and then by listening to the sermon and taking it to heart. Do not speak at all during the sermon. It is related in a Prophetic tradition that "whoever says 'Hush!' to his neighbor while the leader is giving the sermon, has spoken idly, and whoever speaks idly has no Friday observance (credited to him)." The point is that in saying "Hush" he was speaking, whereas he ought to have checked the other man by a sign, not by a word. . . .

After the Friday observance perform two prostrations, or else four or six in pairs. All this is traditionally related of the Messenger of God, God bless him and preserve him, in various circumstances. Then remain in the mosque until the sunset worship, or at least until the late afternoon service. Watch carefully for the "excellent hour," for it may occur in any part of the day, and perhaps you will light upon it while making humble supplication to God. In the mosque do not go to the circle of people or the circle of storytellers, but to the circle of profitable knowledge, that is, the knowledge that increases your fear of God Most High and decreases your desire for this world; ignorance is better for you than all the knowledge which does not draw you away from this world toward the next.

Take refuge with God from unprofitable knowledge. Pray much at the rising, declining and setting of the sun (on Fridays), at the formal institution of worship, at the preacher's ascending the pulpit, and at the rising of the congregation for worship; the likelihood is that the "excellent hour" will be at one of those times. Endeavor on this day to give such alms as you can manage, even if it is little. Divide your time between the worship, fasting, almsgiving, reciting the Quran, recollection of God, solitary devotions, and "waiting for prayer." Let this one day of the week be devoted to what pertains to the future life, and perhaps it will be an atonement for the rest of the week. (Ghazali, *The Beginning of Guidance* 26) [GHAZALI 1953: 127–128]

21. The Two Liturgical Festival Days

In addition to Friday, other days liturgically commemorated by Muslims are the Feast of the Immolation, or Great Festival, celebrated during the pilgrimage month in honor of Abraham's sacrifice of Isaac—an event re-enacted on the pilgrimage itself—and the Feast of Breaking the Fast, or Lesser Festival, at the end of Ramadan. Both have their social and popular aspects in Muslim societies, as they do in the following traditions, but liturgically they resemble the Friday service with sermon.

Jabir ibn Abdullah reported: The Messenger of God, may peace be upon him, stood up on the day of the Breaking of the Fast and observed prayer. And he began the prayer before the sermon. He then delivered the sermon. When the Messenger of God, may peace be upon him, had finished the sermon, he came down from the pulpit and made his way to the women and exhorted them (to do good acts), and he was leaning on the arm of (his muezzin) Bilal. Bilal had stretched out his cloth into which women were throwing alms. (Muslim *Sahih*, 4.313, 1925)

Another tradition specifies:

He then walked on till he came to the women (in the mosque) and preached to them and admonished them and asked them to give alms, for most of them are the fuel for Hell. A woman having a dark spot on her cheek stood up and said: Why is it so, O Messenger of God? He said: For you grumble often and show ingratitude to your spouses. And then they began to give alms out of their ornaments such as their earrings and rings which they threw onto the cloth of Bilal. (Ibid. 4.313, 1926)

Umm Atiya reported: We were commanded to bring out on the feast days sequestered women and those unmarried. Menstruating women (also) came out but remained behind people and pronounced the "God is Great!" along with them. (Ibid. 4.314, 1933)

Aisha reported: Abu Bakr came to see me (at the Prophet's house) and I had two girls with me from among the girls of the Helpers; they were singing what the Helpers recited to one another at the Battle of Bu'ath. They were not, however, (professional) singing girls. Abu Bakr said: What, the playing of this wind instrument of Satan in the house of the Messenger of God, may peace be upon him, and this too on the Festival Day? Upon this the Messenger of God, may peace be upon him, said: Abu Bakr, every people have a festival and this is ours. (Ibid. 4.317, 1938)

22. A Muslim Holy Day: The Tenth of Muharram

Like the religious calendars of the Jews and the Christians, the Muslims' was filled with days commemorating past events of special significance to the community. One of the most important, on a scale similar to Passover for the Jews or Easter for the Christians, was the tenth day of the lunar month of Muharram. Biruni (d. 1048 C.E.) explains its significance in his Traces of the Past.

The tenth (of Muharram) is called Ashura, a most distinguished day. The Prophet is reported to have said: "O men, hasten to do good works on this day for it is a grand and blessed day, on which God had mercy on Adam."

The day was, and is, of special significance to Shi'ite Muslims, since it marked the martyrdom of Husayn, the son of Ali and the grandson of the Prophet, at Karbala in Iraq in 680 C.E.

People marked this day with celebration until the murder of Husayn ibn Ali ibn Abi Talib occurred on it, when he and his adherents were treated in such a way as never in the whole world the worst criminals have been treated. They were killed by hunger and thirst, through the sword; they were burned and their heads roasted, and horses were made to trample over their bodies. Therefore people came to consider this day as an unlucky one.

On the contrary, the Umayyads [that is, the Muslim dynasty in power that engineered the slaughter] dressed themselves on this day in new garments, with various kinds of ornaments, and painted their eyes with kohl; they celebrated a feast, and gave banquets and parties, eating sweetmeats and pastries. Such was the custom in the nation during the rule of the Umayyads, and so it remained also after the downfall of the dynasty [in 750 C.E.].

The Shi'ite people, however, lament and weep on this day, mourning over the protomartyr Husayn in public, in Baghdad, for example, and in other cities and villages; and they make a pilgrimage to the blessed soil [that is, the burial site of Husayn] in Karbala. As this is a mourning day, their common people have an aversion to renewing the vessels and utensils of the household on this day.

And as with most of the other sacred days in the three religions, there was an attempt to connect Ashura back to biblical prototypes, and here with Gospel ones as well.

People say that on this day (of Ashura) God took compassion on Adam, that the Ark of Noah stood still on the mountain, that Jesus was born, that Moses was saved (from the Pharaoh). . . . Further, on this day Jacob regained his eyesight, Joseph was drawn out of the well, Solomon was invested with the royal power, the punishment was taken away from the people of Jonah, Job was freed from his plague, the prayer of Zachariah was granted and John (the Baptist) was given to him. . . .

Though it is possible that all these events should have occurred on this day, we must state that all this rests on the authority of popular storytellers, who do not draw upon learned sources or upon the consensus among the Peoples of the Book.

Some people say that Ashura is an Arabicized Hebrew word, to wit, Ashur, that is, the tenth of the Jewish month of Tishri, in which falls the fasting of (Yom) Kippur; that the date of this fasting was compared with the months of the Arabs, and that it was fixed on the tenth day of the Arabs' first month, as it falls with the Jews on the tenth day of their first month.

The Prophet gave order to fast on this day in the first year of the Hijra, but afterwards this fast was abrogated by the other law, to fast during the month of Ramadan, which falls later in the year. People relate that the Prophet of God, on arriving in Medina, saw the Jews fasting on Ashura. On inquiring of them, he was told that this was the day on which God had drowned Pharaoh and his people and had saved Moses and the Israelites. Then the Prophet said, "We have a nearer claim on Moses than they." In consequence he fasted on that day and ordered his followers to do the same. But when he afterwards issued the law regarding the fasting of Ramadan, he no longer ordered them to fast on Ashura, but neither did he forbid them.

This tradition is not correct, however, since scientific examination proves against it. . . . You could not maintain that the Prophet fasted on Ashura on account of its coincidence with the tenth of Tishri in this year, unless you transfer it from the first of the Jewish months to the first of the Arab months so as to make them fall together. Also in the second year of the Hijra the Jewish Ashura and the day of Muhammad's arrival cannot have coincided. (Biruni, *Traces of the Past*) [BIRUNI 1879: 326–328]

23. Adam at Mecca

All three religions possess a rich haggadic store of legend concerning the events described, or imagined, in the Book of Genesis, and Adam is not unnaturally the focus of many of those stories. In this one a Promethean Adam is connected with an antediluvian pilgrimage to Mecca.

Hashim ibn Muhammad has informed us, relating from Ubayy, from Abu Salih, from Ibn Abbas, who said: Adam departed from (the heavenly) Paradise between the time of noon prayers and the time of afternoon prayers, and was sent down to the earth. He had been dwelling in Paradise for half a day of the days of the Other World, that is, five hundred years of those days whose measure is twelve hours, for a day there is a thousand years as people count them in this world. Adam was cast down on a mountain in India called Nawdh [traditionally identified on Ceylon], and Eve fell at Jedda [the Red Sea port of Mecca]. Adam brought down with him some of the scented air of Paradise, which clung to the trees and valleys and filled all that place with perfume. It is thus that the perfumes known to us are derived from that scented air of Adam, upon whom be God's blessing and peace.

It is said that there was sent down along with Adam some of the myrtle of Paradise, also the Black Stone, which was then whiter than snow, and Moses' rod, which was of celestial myrtle wood, ten cubits long, that is, the height of Moses, upon whom be God's blessing and peace, as well as some myrrh and frankincense. Afterwards there was sent down to him the anvil, the blacksmith's hammer and pinchers. Then, from where he had fallen on the mountain, Adam looked and saw an iron shoot growing out of the mountainside, and he said: "This [the anvil] is from this [the iron shoot]." So he began to break down with the hammer trees that had grown old and had dried up, and upon them he heated that shoot till it melted. The first thing that he hammered out of it was a long knife with which he might work. Then he fashioned an earthen oven, the same one that Noah later inherited and the one that boiled over in India, bringing the punishment (of the Flood).

When (presently) Adam went on pilgrimage (to Mecca), he placed the Black Stone on (the mountain there called) Abu Qubays, where it gave light to the inhabitants of Mecca on dark nights, just the moon gives light (on clear nights). About four years before Islam the Quraysh brought it down from Abu Qubays, but meanwhile it had become black because of menstruating women and polluted persons mounting up to it and rubbing it with their hands. Adam made the pilgrimage from India to Mecca forty times. (Ibn Saᶜd, *The Great Classes* 1.11–12) [JEFFERY 1962: 189–191]

24. Abraham as the Founder of the Cult at Mecca

Stories of Adam's connection with Mecca are pervasive in Muslim religious legend. The Quran, however, knows only Abraham's role there, and it is a major one.

Remember, We made the House (at Mecca) a place of congregation and safe retreat, and said: "Make the spot where Abraham stood a place of worship"; and enjoined upon Abraham and Ishmael to keep Our House immaculate for those who shall walk around it and stay in it for contemplation and prayer, and for bowing in adoration. . . .

And when Abraham was raising the foundations of the house with Ishmael, (he prayed): "Accept this from us, O Lord, for You hear and know every thing." (Quran 2:125, 127)

What then of all the haggadic traditions in Islam that connect the House of God or the Kaᶜba at Mecca with Adam, the first prophet? The two strains of tradition are harmonized in the following commentary by Zamakhshari (d. 1144 C.E.) on these verses.

God sent down the House, which was one of the rubies of Paradise, with two emerald doors, one on the eastern and one on the western side. Then God said to Adam: "I have sent down for you that which must be circumambulated just as My Throne is circumambulated." Adam then set out on foot for the House (at Mecca) from the Land of India. Angels met him on the way, saying, "Blessed be your pilgrimage, O Adam; we too have made pilgrimage to the House of God, two thousand years before you." Adam subsequently performed the pilgrimage forty times on foot to the House of God from India. The House remained as it was until God took it up to the fourth heaven during the Flood. This was what was known as the "populous house." God later ordered Abraham to rebuild it, and Gabriel showed him the location. It is said that he built it from materials taken from five mountains: Mount Sinai, Mount Olivet, Mount Lebanon, Mount Ararat and Mount Hira, from which he took its foundation stone. Gabriel brought him the Black Stone from heaven. (Zamakhshari, *The Unveiler of the Realities, ad loc.*)

A more forthrightly "spiritualizing" reading of the Adam-Abraham-Ka'ba stories is given by the Spanish Sufi master Ibn al-Arabi (d. 1240 C.E.), who begins his account with a brief summary of traditions concerning the early history of the Ka'ba.

"And when Abraham was raising the foundations of the House" (Quran 2:127): It is said that the Ka'ba was brought down from Heaven during the time of Adam. It had an eastern and a western door. Adam made the pilgrimage from the land of India. The angels turned toward it (from a distance of) 40 parasangs. He circumambulated the House and entered it. Then, it was raised up (to heaven) during the time of the Flood of Noah. It was brought down a second time during the time of Abraham. He visited it and raised up its foundations. He made its two doors into one. It is said that (Mount) Abu Qubays shook violently, and split off from the Black Stone, which was a white sapphire from the Garden that Gabriel had brought down and had hidden in it [that is, Mount Abu Qubays] at the time of the Flood until the time of Abraham. Abraham put it in its place. Then it turned black from the fingering of menstruating women.

Then Ibn al-Arabi begins to spell out the interpretation, item by item.

Its [that is, the Ka'ba's] descent during the time of Adam signifies the appearance of the heart [that is, the spiritual faculty] during his time and its presence within him. Its having two doors—the east and the west—signifies knowledge of Creation and the Afterlife and the gnosis of the knowledge of light and the knowledge of darkness during his time, though without the knowledge of the Oneness of God. His setting out to visit it from the land of India signifies his turning toward creation and moderation, from knowing the physicality of dark natural things to the place of the heart. The turning of the angels signifies the dependence of the animal and vegetable powers upon the body, and the appearance of their traces upon it before the traces of the heart in the forty that were created in it by intention and its substance became fermented. Or its turning away, through conduct and behavior, from knowing the darkened self toward the place of the heart. . . .

Its being raised up in the time of the Flood to Heaven signifies the concealment of people in the victory of whim and caprice. The Flood is folly and ignorance in the time of Noah rather than the place of the heart.

Its remaining in the Fourth Heaven, is The Inhabited House [that is, the heavenly archetype of the Ka‘ba] which is the heart of the world. Its coming down again during the time of Abraham signifies leading the people to the place of the heart during his time through his guidance. Abraham's raising the foundations and his making one door signifies accepting the heart through his conduct from his place to the place of the spirit, which is the secret. (It is also a sign of) the raising up of his high stations and his arrival to the place of proclaiming the unity of God. For he is the first who had the idea of the Oneness of God, as he said: "As for me, I have turned my face as a hanif to Him Who cleaved the heavens and the earth. I am not a polytheist!" (Quran 6:79).

The Black Stone signifies the spirit. The violent shaking of (Mount) Abu Qubays and its splitting off from it signifies its appearance as a spiritual exercise and the setting in motion the instruments of the body for meditation in the search for its appearance. Because of that it is said: it is hidden within it. That means, it has disappeared within the body. Its turning black from the touching of menstruating women signifies its disappearance and its becoming troubled and angry by reason of the idle chatter of the mental faculty in preference to the heart and its becoming the master over it. Its blackening is the spiritually luminous way that the spirit draws near to it. (Ibn al-Arabi, Commentary, 86–87 [translated by Reuven Firestone])

25. The Pilgrimage of Islam

This mix of local and biblical traditions surrounding the boxlike building called "the Ka‘ba" in Muhammad's Mecca was the result of an attempt to link what was patently a very old, and in Muhammad's day a pagan, religious tradition in Mecca with the past age of the "religion of Abraham." The process begins, as we have just seen, in the Quran, where first Abraham and then, as a post-Quranic reflex, Adam are identified as the builders of the Ka‘ba. The linkage goes further, however, and the chief pilgrimage rituals of both Mecca and its immediate environs are confirmed as Muslim rituals.

When We chose the site of the House for Abraham (We said): Associate no one with Me and clean My House for those who will circum-ambulate it, stand (in reverence), and bow in homage.

Announce the Pilgrimage to the people. They will come to you on foot and riding along distant roads on lean and slender beasts, in order to reach the place of advantage for them, and to pronounce the name of God on appointed days over cattle He has given them as food; then eat the food and feed the needy and the poor.

Let them attend to their persons and complete the rites of pilgrimage, fulfill their vows and circuit around the ancient House. . . .

There are advantages for you in these (animals to be sacrificed) up to a time, then their place is in the ancient House for sacrifice.

For every community We have ordained certain rites that they may commemorate the name of God by reciting it over the cattle We have given them for sacrifice. Your God is One God, so be obedient to Him. (Quran 22:26–34)

Known are the months of pilgrimage. If one resolves to perform the pilgrimage in these months, let him not indulge in concupiscence, sin or quarrel. And the good you do shall be known to God. Provide for the journey, and the best of provisions is piety. O men of understanding, obey Me.

It is no sin to seek the favors of your Lord (by trading). When you start from Arafat in a concourse, remember God at the monument that is sacred, and remember Him as He has shown you the way, for in the olden days you were a people astray. Then move with the crowd impetuously, and pray God to forgive you your sins. God is surely forgiving and kind.

When you have finished the rites and ceremonies, remember God as you do your fathers, in fact with greater devotion. (Quran 2:197–200)

26. Muhammad's Farewell Pilgrimage

Since the pilgrimage was a known and ongoing rite in Muhammad's day, the Quran has no need of prescribing its rituals in inclusive detail: what was done before will continue to be done, though now under Islamic auspices. But when another, later generation of Muslims needed more guidance, they could find it in the circumstantial account of the Prophet's farewell pilgrimage in the year of his death. Not unnaturally it became the model for the performance of this obligation, incumbent on all competent Muslims, to at least once in a lifetime to go to Mecca and perform the ceremonies described here.

Ja'far ibn Muhammad [the sixth Shi'ite Imam, d. 765 C.E.] reported on the authority of his father [Muhammad al-Baqir, the fifth Imam, d. 732 C.E.]: We went to Jabir ibn Abdullah [one of the last surviving Companions of the Prophet, d. 693 C.E., aged ninety-four] and he had begun inquiring about the people till it was my turn. I said: I am Muhammad ibn

Ali ibn Husayn [that is, the grandson of Husayn, Muhammad's own grandson]. Jabir placed his hand upon my head and opened my upper button and then my lower one and then placed his palm on my chest (to bless me), and I was, during those days a young boy, and he said: You are welcome, my nephew. Ask whatever you want to ask. . . .

I said to him: Tell me about the Pilgrimage of God's Messenger, may peace be upon him. He held up nine fingers and then stated: The Messenger of God, may peace be upon him, stayed at Medina for nine years but did not perform the Pilgrimage; then he made public announcement in the tenth year to the effect that God's Messenger, may peace be upon him, was about to perform the Pilgrimage. A large number of persons came to Medina, and all of them were anxious to follow the Messenger of God, may peace be upon him, and do according to his doing. We set out till we reached Dhu al-Hulayfa [in the vicinity of Mecca]. Asma daughter of Umays gave birth (there) to Muhammad ibn Abi Bakr. She sent a message to the Messenger of God, may peace be upon him, asking him: What should I do (in my present state of ritual impurity)? He said: Take a bath, wrap up your private parts and put on the (pilgrim's) garment of purification. The Messenger of God, may peace be upon him, then prayed in the mosque (there) and after that mounted al-Qaswa [his she-camel] and it stood up with him on its back at al-Bayda.

And I saw as far as I could see in front of me nothing but riders and pedestrians, and also on my right and my left and behind me. And the Messenger of God, may peace be upon him, was prominent among us, and the (revelation) of the Quran was descending upon him, and it is he who knows its (true) significance. And whatever he did, we also did that. He pronounced the Oneness of God, saying: "At Your service, O Lord, at Your service, at Your service. You have no partner. Praise and Grace is Yours, and Sovereignty too. You have no partner." And the people also pronounced this invocation, which they (still) pronounce today. . . .

We had no intention but that of making the (formal) Pilgrimage, being unaware of the Lesser Pilgrimage, but when we came with him to the House [that is, the Ka'ba], he touched the pillar [that is, the black stone] and made (seven) circuits, running three of them and walking four. And then going to the Place of Abraham (in the Haram), he recited: "And adopt the Place of Abraham as a place of prayer" (Quran 2:125). And this place was between him and the House. . . . He recited in two prostrations "Say: He is God, One" (Sura 112) and "Say: O unbelievers . . . " (Sura 109). He then returned to the pillar and kissed it. He then went out the gate to al-Safa [a place adjoining the Haram], and as he reached it he said: "Al-Safa and al-Marwa are among the signs appointed by God" (Quran 2:158), (adding) I begin with what God has commanded me to begin. He first mounted al-Safa until he saw the House, and facing in the direction of the Ka'ba, he declared the Oneness of God and glorified Him, and said: "There is no god but the God, One; there is no partner with Him. His is the Sovereignty, to Him praise is due, and He is powerful over everything. There is no god but the God alone, who fulfilled His promise, helped His servant and routed the confederates alone." He then made supplication in the course of that, saying such words three times. He then descended and walked toward al-Marwa, and when his feet came down in the bottom of the valley, he ran, and when he began to ascend he walked until he reached al-Marwa. There he did as he had done at al-Safa.

And when it was his last running at al-Marwa, he said: If I had known beforehand what I have come to know afterwards, I would not have brought sacrificial animals and would have performed a Lesser Pilgrimage. So he who among you has not the sacrificial animals with him should put off the (pilgrim's) garment of purification and treat it as Lesser Pilgrimage. Suraqa ibn Malik ibn Ju'sham got up and said: Messenger of God, does it apply to the present year or does it apply forever? Thereupon the Messenger of God, may peace be upon him, intertwined his fingers and said twice: The Lesser Pilgrimage has become incorporated in the (formal) Pilgrimage, adding: "No, but forever and ever." . . . Then all the people, except the Messenger, may peace be upon him, and those who had with them sacrificial animals, put off the garment of purification and got their hair clipped.

When it was the eighth day of the Pilgrimage Month they went to Mina and put on the garment of purification for the Pilgrimage, and the Messenger of God, may peace be upon him, rode forth and led the noon, afternoon, sunset, evening and dawn prayers. He then waited a little till the sun rose, and commanded that a tent should be pitched at Namira [a place at the limits of the territory of Mecca]. The Messenger of God, may peace be upon him, then set out, and the Quraysh did not doubt that he would halt at the (hillock called) "the sacred site" as they used to do in the pre-Islamic period. The Messenger of God, may peace be upon him, passed on, however, until he reached (the hill of) Arafat and he found that the tent had been pitched for him at Namira. There he halted until the sun had passed the meridian; he commanded that his camel be brought and saddled for him. Then he came to the bottom of the valley (there) and addressed the people.

There follows Muhammad's farewell discourse to the Muslims, after which the narrative continues:

The Messenger of God, may peace be upon him, then mounted his camel and came to the halting place, making his camel turn toward the side where there were rocks, with the path taken by those on foot in front of him, and faced toward the Ka'ba. He kept standing there (from the time of the noonday prayer) till the sun set, and the yellow light had somewhat gone and the disk of the sun had disappeared. He made Usama sit behind him, and he pulled the nosestring of the camel so forcefully that its head touched the saddle, and he pointed out to the people on his right hand to be moderate (in their pace) . . . and this is how he reached al-Muzdalifa.

There he led the evening and sunset prayers. . . . The Messenger of God, may peace be upon him, then lay down till dawn and then offered the dawn prayer . . . when the morning light was clear. He again mounted his camel, and when he came to "the holy site" he faced toward the Ka'ba, supplicated God, glorified Him, and pronounced His Uniqueness and Oneness, and kept standing until the daylight was very clear. He then went quickly before the sun rose . . . till he came to the bottom of Muhassir [between Muzdalifa and Mina]. He urged his camel a little, and following the middle road, which comes out at the greatest pile of stones, he came to the pile near the tree. At this he threw seven small pebbles, saying "God is Great" while throwing each one of them in the manner in which small pebbles are thrown (with the fingers), and this he did at the bottom of the valley.

He then went to the place of sacrifice, and sacrificed sixty-three camels with his own hand. Then he gave the remaining ones to Ali, who sacrificed them, and he made him share in his sacrifice. He then commanded that a piece of flesh from each animal sacrificed should be put in a pot, and when it was cooked, both of them [that is, Muhammad and Ali] took some meat of it and drank its broth. The Messenger of God, may peace be upon him, again rode and came to the House (of God) and offered the sunset prayer at Mecca. He came to the tribe of Abd al-Muttalib, who were supplying (pilgrims) the water of the (sacred spring) Zamzam, and said: Draw water, O tribesmen of Abd al-Muttalib; were it not that people would usurp this right of supplying themselves with water from you (if I did so), I would have drawn it along with you. So they handed him a container and he drank from it. (Muslim, *Sahih* 7.462, 2803)

There were, then, as the text reveals, two distinct rituals: the hajj, or pilgrimage properly so called; and another set of practices called the ʿumra, or so-called lesser pilgrimage, which, as it turns out, was the genuine Meccan pilgrimage. This latter fell during a different sacred month and was celebrated in and around the Meccan Haram and not, as was the case with the hajj, at various sites in the neighborhood of but outside Mecca. But the two were formally combined on the occasion of Muhammad's first and only pilgrimage as a Muslim: "The ʿumra has become incorporated in the hajj," as he reportedly said on that occasion.

27. Pagan Survivals and Muslim Misgivings

Although the Quran was reassuring on the point that the "greater" and the "lesser" pilgrimage were both part of God's original revelation to Abraham, there was a common sense at Mecca that the associated rituals were remnants of a pagan past. We can read the source of the concern between the lines of Quran 2:158 and even more clearly in the anecdotes prompted by clarifications of that verse.

Surely Safa and Marwa are among the signs of God. Whoever goes on Pilgrimage to the House (of God), or performs the Lesser Pilgrimage, is not guilty if he walks around [or "circumambulates"] them; and he who does good of his own accord will find appreciation with God who knows everything. (Quran 2:158)

Thus, as appears from the texts themselves ("is not guilty . . . "), Muhammad's Muslim contemporaries felt some uneasiness about these pilgrimage rituals, and the Quranic commentators scanned the Prophetic traditions for evidence of it.

Wahidi [d. 1076 C.E.] relates that when asked about al-Safa and al-Marwa, Anas ibn Malik said: "We were of the opinion that they belonged to the era of heathenism. Thus when Islam came we ceased running between them. God therefore sent down this verse (2:158)."

Qurtubi the jurist [d. 1273] relates that Urwah ibn al-Zubayr said to (Muhammad's wife) Aisha: "I see nothing against anyone who does not run between al-Safa and al-Marwa, nor would I be concerned if I myself did not run between them." She answered: "Ill is that which you speak, O son of my sister! The Messenger of God ran between them and so did the Muslims. It was rather those who sacrificed to Manat, the idol that was in the Mushlal who did not run between them. Thus God sent down (2:158). Had it been as you say, the verse would have read 'in him there is no blame if he does not run between them.' "

Al-Shaʿbi said: "During the era of heathenism there was an idol on al-Safa called Isaf and another on al-Marwa called Naʾilah. People used to touch them when they ran (between the two hills). The Muslims did not wish to run between them on that account; hence God sent down this verse." [AYOUB 1984: 177]

Somewhat in the same vein is this tradition concerning the kissing of the black stone embedded in the corner of the Ka'ba.

Abdullah ibn Sarjis reported: I saw the bald one, that is, Umar ibn al-Khattab, may God be pleased with him, kissing the stone and saying: By God, I am kissing with the full knowledge that you are a stone and that you can do neither harm nor good; if I had not seen the Messenger of God, upon whom be peace, kissing you, I would not have kissed you. (Muslim, *Sahih* 7.434, 2914)

28. Substitution, Surrogation, and Sublimation

There is a long and well-established tradition in Islam that in those cases where ritual obligations cannot be fulfilled, other pious acts may be substituted for them— feeding a poor person in lieu of fasting during Ramadan, for example. Even in the case of the pilgrimage, which was site-determined rather than merely time-fixed, some degree of substitution was permissible, as the Quran itself explains.

Perform Pilgrimage (*hajj*) and the Lesser Pilgrimage ('*umra*) in the service of God. But if you are prevented, send an offering which you can afford as sacrifice, and do not shave your heads until the offering has reached the place of sacrifice. But if you are sick or have an ailment of the scalp (preventing the shaving of the head), then offer expiation by fasting or else give alms or a sacrificial offering. When you have security, then those of you who wish to perform the Lesser Pilgrimage along with the Hajj, should make a sacrifice according to your means. But he who has nothing should fast for three days during the Pilgrimage and seven on return, completing ten. This applies to him whose family does not live near the Holy Mosque. (Quran 2:196)

The circumstances envisioned for the commutation or substitution of one pious act for another, ritually required one are inevitably those where it is impossible to perform the required prayer, fasting, and so on. Here just such a case is made for pilgrimage commutation by a Sufi master of the early tenth century. The setting, however, is a juridical process presided over by the Caliphal Grand Vizier and reported by the son of one of the clerks at the hearing.

Each day the Vizier Hamid was brought a few of the notebooks found in the homes of Hallaj's disciples; they were put before him, and he handed them to my father to read them to him. Now it so happened

that on one of those days my father read to him, in the presence of the
justices Abu Umar and Abu Husayn ibn al-Ushnani, from one of Hallaj's
writings in which it was reported that "when a man wants to carry out
the legally required pilgrimage and has no way of doing it, he must set
aside a room in his home that no impurity touches, where no one goes,
and which no one may pass through; then, at the time of the pilgrimage,
he must walk around in a circle, as one does at the Sacred House; once
that is done he must perform the rituals as at Mecca. After that he will
gather together thirty orphans, prepare them the best possible meal, invite them into this place and serve them this meal himself. When they
have finished their meal and washed their hands, he will dress each one
of them in a (new) shirt and give each seven drachmas. . . . And all of that,
when it is carried out, will take the place of the hajj for him."
[MASSIGNON 1982: 1:546]

*The "Hallaj" of the text is the celebrated mystic and martyr Husayn ibn Mansur
al-Hallaj, whose life will be regarded more closely in Chapter 4 below. The doctrinal
position cited from his notebooks, which Hallaj claimed had precedent in the writings of the earlier master Hasan al-Basri and which the justice Abu Umar insisted
did not (there is in fact none such in any of Hasan's preserved texts), led quickly
to Hallaj's death sentence—"it is lawful to shed his blood"—a sentence signed, not
without hesitation, by the same Abu Umar and with a great deal of pressure from
the Grand Vizier Hamid. After some delays the sentence was confirmed by the
Caliph and carried out, with extreme cruelty, on 26 March 922 C.E.*

*There was obviously more at stake in Baghdad in 922 C.E. than a mere case
of substitution of one pious act for another. What Hallaj was suggesting was an
alternative setting for the pilgrimage, an approach that struck many of his contemporaries as usurpation rather than substitution. And indeed, such may have been his
intent, carried out in the name of that same interior spiritualization already witnessed in Ghazali. For Ghazali, however, the spiritualization of a ritual act did not
lead to the latter's destruction, as it inevitably did for Hallaj.*

God prescribed two kinds of religious duties: one concerning intermediate things [that is, religious rituals] and the other concerning the
Realities [that is, the transcendental truths of God]. Now duties to the
Realities involve knowledge that flows from God and returns to Him.
Whereas duties respecting intermediate things involve knowledge that,
flowing from objects below Him, is able to rejoin Him only by transcending them and destroying them. Now one must include the building of the
Haram and of the Ka'ba among duties to "intermediate things," just as
it is said: "the first sacred enclosure established for the people was that
at Bakka [Mecca], a blessed enclosure . . . " (Quran 3:96). As long as you

remain attached to this enclosure, you will remain separated from God. But when you have really detached yourself from it, then you will reach the One who built and established it; then meditating on the temple (destroyed) in yourself, you will possess the real presence of its Founder.

. . . Shaykh Husayn ibn Mansur Hallaj, may God be merciful to him, recited the following to me:

O you who censure me for loving Him, how much you crush me;
If only you could see the One I mean, you would no longer censure me.
People make the pilgrimage; I am going on a (spiritual) pilgrimage to
    my Host;
While they offer animals in sacrifice, I offer my heart and my blood.
Some of them walk in procession around the Temple, without their
    bodies,
For they walk in procession in God, and He has exempted them from
    the Haram.

[MASSIGNON 1982: 1:543]

3. Withdrawal from the World

1. Judah Halevi on Jewish Asceticism

For the benefit of a fictional king who was conducting an inquiry into the claims of different religions, Judah Halevi put in the mouth of his own alter ego, a traditionalist rabbi, some remarks on the subject of Jewish asceticism. Halevi's work, entitled The King of the Khazars, *was composed between 1130 and 1140 C.E.*

The divine law imposes no asceticism on us. It rather desires that we should keep the equilibrium and grant to every mental and physical faculty its due, as much as it can bear, without overburdening one faculty at the expense of another. If a person gives way to licentiousness, he blunts his mental faculty; he who is inclined to violence injures some other faculty. Prolonged fasting is no act of piety for a weak person who, having succeeded in checking his desires, is not greedy. For him feasting is a burden and self-denial. Neither is diminution of wealth an act of piety, if it is gained in a lawful way, and if its acquisition does not interfere with study and good works, especially for him who has a household and children. He may spend part of it in almsgiving, which would not be displeasing to God; but to increase it would be better for himself.

Our Law, as a whole, is divided between fear, love and joy, by each of which one can approach God. Your contribution on a fast day does nothing nearer to God than your joy on the Sabbath and the holy days, if it is the outcome of a devout heart. . . . The observance of the Sabbath is itself an acknowledgment of His omnipotence (in its recollection of the Exodus), and at the same time an acknowledgment of the creation by the divine Word. . . . The observance of the Sabbath is therefore nearer to God than monastic retirement and asceticism. (Judah Halevi, *The King of the Khazars*) [HALEVI 1905: 113–114]

2. Jewish Monasticism

Judah Halevi was reflecting on the Jewish tradition as he knew and understood it from the perspective of the twelfth century. That tradition had already forgotten, or had chosen to ignore, many of the forms of Jewish piety and observance that our sources reveal in the centuries immediately preceding and following the beginning of the Christian era. We do not always know what to make of some of them, whether they are constructs, idealizations, or reality, but they are described in great detail, particularly the two examples of what can only be called "Jewish monasticism" that we find in the pages of Philo and Josephus. The first group, called the Therapeutae, or "Healers," had their "houses" around Lake Mereotis near Alexandria.

The houses of the society are exceedingly simple, providing protection against two of the most pressing dangers of the site, the fiery heat of the sun and the icy cold of the air. They are neither near together, as in towns, since living at close quarters is troublesome and displeasing to people who are seeking to satisfy their desire for solitude, nor yet at a great distance, because of the sense of friendship they cherish and to render help to each other if robbers attack them. . . . Twice each day they pray, at dawn and at eventide: at dawn they pray for a fine bright day in the true sense of heavenly daylight which they pray may fill their minds. At sunset they ask that the soul may be wholly relieved from the burden of the senses and the objects of sense, and sitting in a place where she is both consistory and council chamber to herself, she may pursue the quest of truth. The interval between each morning and evening is spent entirely in spiritual exercises. They read the Holy Scriptures and seek wisdom from their ancestral philosophy by taking it as an allegory, since they think that the words of the literal text are symbols of something whose hidden nature is revealed by studying the underlying meaning. They have also the writings of men of old, the founders of their way of thinking, who left many memorials of the form used in allegorical interpretation, and these they take as a kind of archetype and imitate the method in which this principle is carried out. And so they do not confine themselves to contemplation, but also compose hymns and psalms to God in all sorts of meters and melodies, which they write down with the rhythms made necessarily more solemn. (Philo, *The Contemplative Life* 24–30)

Philo then describes how the Therapeutae meet together each seventh day in assembly, where the senior man among them, "who also has the fullest knowledge of the doctrines which they profess," delivers a discourse. Women too attend the general assembly, though they are separated by a head-high partition.

They lay self-control to be, as it were, the foundation of their soul and on it build the other virtues. None of them would put food or drink to his lips before sunset, since they hold that philosophy finds its right place in the light, the needs of the body in darkness and therefore they assign the day to one and a small part of the night to the other. Some in whom the desire of studying wisdom is even more deeply implanted remember to take food only after three days. . . . But on the seventh day [that is, the Sabbath], as they consider it to be sacred and festal in the highest degree, they have awarded special privileges as its due; and on it, after providing for the soul, refresh the body also, which they do as a matter of course with the cattle too, by releasing them from their continuous labor. (Ibid. 34–36)

On every seventh Sabbath there is a special feast, a banquet, which Philo compares favorably with the licentious symposia of the Greeks and Romans. Here too women are present.

. . . [M]ost of them are aged virgins, who have kept their chastity not under compulsion, like some of the Greek priestesses, but of their own free will in their ardent yearning for wisdom. Eager to have her for their life mate, they have spurned the pleasures of the body; and they desire no mortal offspring but those immortal children which only the soul that is dear to God can bring to birth unaided because the Father has sown in her spiritual rays enabling her to behold the truths of wisdom. (Ibid. 68)

At this banquet—I know some will laugh at this, but only those whose actions call for tears and lamentation—no wine is served . . . but only water of the brightest and clearest, cold for most of the guests but warm for such of the older men as live delicately. The table too is kept pure from flesh of animals; the food that is laid on it is loaves of bread with salt as a seasoning, sometimes also flavored with hyssop as a relish for the daintier appetites. Abstinence from wine is enjoined by right reason, as for the priest when sacrificing, so for these for their lifetime. For wine acts like a drug, producing folly, and costly dishes stir up that most insatiable of animals, desire. (Ibid. 73–74)

After the supper they hold the sacred vigil, which is conducted in the following way. They rise up all together and standing in the middle of the refectory, form themselves first into two choirs, one of men and one of women, the leader and preceptor chosen from each being the most honored among them and also the most musical. Then they sing hymns to God composed of many measures and set to many melodies, sometimes chanting together, sometimes taking up the harmony antiphonally, hands and feet keeping time in accompaniment and, rapt with enthusiasm, reproduce sometimes the lyrics of the procession, sometimes of the halt and of the wheeling and counterwheeling of a choral dance. (Ibid. 83–84)

If there is something utopian in this portrait of Platonic sages interrupting their contemplation of wisdom to celebrate the Sabbath with a spiritual symposium, there is something more authentically Jewish perhaps about the group Josephus calls the Essenes, who were also known to Philo under the same name.

There are three philosophical sects among the Jews. The followers of the first are the Pharisees, of the second the Sadducees, and the third sect, which pretends to a severer discipline, are called Essenes.

These Essenes are Jews by birth and seem to have a greater affection for one another than the other sects have. They reject pleasures as evil, but esteem continence and the conquest over our passions as a virtue. They neglect wedlock, but choose out other persons' children while they are still pliable and docile, and esteem them as their own kindred, and form them according to their own way of life. They do not absolutely deny the the propriety of marriage and the succession of mankind that flows therefrom, but they guard against the lewd behavior of women and are persuaded that none of them preserve their fidelity to one man.

These men are despisers of riches ... nor is anyone to be found among them who possesses more than any other, since it is a law of theirs that those who come to them must allow whatever they have to become the common property of the entire group, so that among them there is no appearance of poverty or superabundance of riches, but everyone's possessions are mixed in with everyone else's and there is, so to say, one inheritance among all the brothers. . . .

As for their piety toward God, it is very extraordinary. Before sunrise they speak not a word on profane matters but offer up certain prayers, which they have received from their forefathers, as if beseeching the sun to rise. After this each is sent off by their curators to exercise one of the skills they possess. They work hard at this until the fifth hour, when they assemble once again in one place. Then, when they have put on white veils, they bathe in cold water. After this purification, they all meet in a chamber of their own, into which no one of any other sect is admitted. They go thus purified into a refectory, as if entering a temple, and quietly seat themselves. The baker lays out loaves in order and the cook brings a single plate of one kind of food and sets it before each one of them. A priest says a blessing before the meal and it is forbidden for anyone to taste of the food until the blessing has been said. The same priest says a blessing again after the meal. . . . Afterwards they put off their white garments and return to their labors until evening, when they return home to a supper in the same fashion. . . .

In other things, they do only what they are enjoined by their curators, and there are only two things that are done according to each's free will, namely, to assist those in need and to show mercy, since they are permitted of their own accord to give assistance to deserving cases when they need it and to give food to those in want; they cannot, however, give anything to their kin without permission of the curators. . . . They take great pains in studying the writings of the ancients and select from them what is most helpful for their souls and bodies, and they inquire after such roots and stones as may cure their ills. . . .

The Essenes are stricter than any other Jews in resting from their labors on the Sabbath, for they not only get their food ready on the day previous, that they may not have to kindle a fire on the Sabbath itself, nor will they remove any vessel from its place or use it for defecation. Even on days other than the Sabbath they dig a small pit a foot deep with a scoop, a kind of hatchet that is given them when they are first admitted in that company, and covering themselves round about with their garments, that they may not affront the divine rays of light, they defecate in that pit, after which they pile the earth back in again; and even this they do in remote places, which they select for this purpose. And even though emptying the bowels is a natural act, yet it is their rule to wash themselves afterward, as if it defiled them. . . .

There is another community of Essenes who agree with the rest in their manner of life and customs and laws, but who differ from them on the subject of marriage, since they consider that in not marrying they are cutting off the principal part of human life, which is the hope of succession; indeed, they maintain, if all men were of the same mind (as the celibates), the whole human race would fail. They do, however, make trial of their spouses for three years, and if they find that they have their menstrual periods three times, as a test of their likely fertility, then they actually marry them. But they do not cohabit with their wives during pregnancy to demonstrate that they do not marry for pleasure but for the purpose of procreation. (Josephus, *War* 2.8.2–13)

3. The Monks of Qumran

The Essenes of Philo and Josephus long remained purely a literary phenomenon. Then some forty years ago the well-preserved traces of a very similar community were discovered at Qumran, at the northwest corner of the Dead Sea. Those traces included not only a community complex of buildings but also, hidden away in nearby caves, the writings of the sect, including their "Community Rule." It is by no means certain that this Jewish community at Qumran, which was occupied from the second century B.C.E. down to the destruction of the Temple in 70 C.E., is identical with Josephus' Essenes, but the similarities are such to suggest that we are dealing with, if not the same, then a very similar example of believers who had withdrawn from the mainstream of Jewish life in Palestine and had adopted a regimen of purity and of unquestioning obedience in a rigorously hierarchical community.

Every man, born of Israel, who freely pledges himself to join the Council of the Community shall be examined by the Guardian at the head of the Congregation concerning his understanding and his deeds. If he is fitted to the discipline, he shall admit him into the Covenant that he may be converted to the truth and depart from all falsehood; and he shall instruct him in all the rules of the Community. And later, when he comes to stand before the Congregation, they shall all deliberate his case, and according to the decision of the Council of the Congregation, he shall either enter or depart.

After he has entered the Council of the Congregation he shall not touch the pure Meal of the Congregation until one full year is completed, and until he has been examined concerning his spirit and his deeds; nor shall he have any share in the property of the Congregation. Then when he has completed one year within the Community, the Congregation shall deliberate his case with regard to his understanding and his observance of the Law. And if it be his destiny, according to the judgment of the Priests and the multitude of the men of the Covenant, to enter the Community, his property and earnings shall be handed over to the Bursar of the Congregation who shall register it to his account and shall not spend it for the Congregation. He shall not touch the Drink of the Congregation until he has completed a second year among the men of the Community. But when the second year has passed, he shall be examined, and if it is his destiny, according to the judgment of the Congregation, to enter the Community, then he shall be inscribed among his brethren according to his rank for the Law, and for justice, and for the pure Meal; his property shall be merged and he shall offer his counsel and judgment to the Community. (*The Community Rule* 6) [VERMES 1968: 81–82]

And this is the Rule for the men of the Community who have freely pledged themselves to be converted from all evil and to cling to all His commandments according to His will.

They shall separate from the congregation of men of falsehood and shall unite, with respect to the Law and possessions, under the authority of the sons of Zadok [the High Priest of the era of David; cf. 2 Sam. 8:17], the Priests who keep the Covenant, and of the multitude of the men of the Community, who hold fast to the Covenant. Every decision concerning doctrine, property and justice shall be determined by them.

They shall practice truth and humility in common, and justice and uprightness and charity and modesty in all their ways. No man shall walk in the stubbornness of his heart so that he strays after his heart and eyes and evil inclination, but he shall circumcise in the Community the foreskin of his evil inclination and of stiffness of neck that they may lay a foundation of truth for Israel, for the community of the everlasting Covenant. They shall atone for all of those in Aaron who have freely pledged themselves to holiness, and for those in Israel who have freely pledged themselves to the House of Truth, and for those who join them to live in community and to take part in the trial and the judgment and condemnation of all those who transgress the precepts.

On joining the Community, this shall be their code of behavior with respect to all these precepts. Whoever approaches the Council of the Community shall enter the Covenant of God in the presence of all who have pledged themselves. He shall undertake by a binding oath to return with all his heart and soul to every commandment of the Law of Moses in accordance with all that has been revealed to the sons of Zadok, the Keepers of the Covenant and the seekers of His will and to the multitude of the men of their Covenant who together have freely pledged themselves to His truth and to walking in the way of His delight. And he shall undertake by the Covenant to separate from all men of falsehood who walk in the way of wickedness. (*The Community Rule* 5) [VERMES 1968: 78–79]

They shall eat in common and pray in common and deliberate in common.

Whenever there are ten men of the Council of the Community they shall not lack a priest among them. And they shall sit before him according to their rank and shall be asked their counsel in all things in that order. And when the table has been prepared for eating, and the new wine for drinking, the Priest shall be the first to stretch out his hand to bless the firstfruits of the bread and the new wine.

And where the ten are, there shall never lack a man among them who will study the Law continually, day and night, concerning the right conduct of a man with his companion. And the Congregation shall watch in community for a third of every night of the year, to read the Book and study and Law and pray together. (Ibid., no. 6) [VERMES 1968: 80–81]

What's Jesus solve?

4. The Following of Christ

At about the same time, we read this in the Gospels, which incidentally make no mention of either the Essenes or Qumran.

Jesus then said to his disciples, "If anyone wishes to be a follower of mine, he must leave self behind; he must take up his cross and come with me. Whoever cares for his own safety is lost; but if a man will let himself be lost for my sake, he will find his own true self. What will a man gain by winning the whole world at the cost of his true self? Or what can he give that will buy that self back?" (Matthew 16:24–26)

And now a man came up and asked him, "Master, what good must I do to gain eternal life?" "Good?" said Jesus, "Why do you ask me that? One alone is good. But if you wish to enter into life, keep the commandments." "Which commandments?" he asked. Jesus answered, "Do not commit murder; do not commit adultery; do not steal; do not give false evidence; honor your father and your mother; and love your neighbor as yourself." The young man answered, "I have kept all these. Where do I still fall short?" Jesus said to him, "If you wish to go the whole way, go, sell all your possessions and give to the poor, and then you will have riches in heaven; and come, follow me." When the young man heard this, he went away with a heavy heart, for he was a man of great wealth. (Matthew 19:16–22)

These two passages from Matthew constitute in an exemplary way the Christians' invitation to a special piety and a special vocation, to "go the whole way": a call, in the first example, to the peculiarly Christian task of "taking up the cross," if not in fact, then, even more terribly, in spirit. The commentator is Thomas à Kempis (d. 1471 C.E.), the author of one of the most influential works of spirituality in the long Christian tradition.

Why are you afraid to take up the Cross, which is the road to the Kingdom? In the Cross is salvation; in the Cross is life; in the Cross is protection against our enemies; in the Cross is the infusion of heavenly sweetness; in the Cross is strength of mind; in the Cross is joy of spirit; in the Cross is the height of virtue; in the Cross is perfection of sanctity.

There is no salvation of soul, no hope of eternal life, but in the Cross. Take up the Cross, therefore, and follow Jesus, and go forward into eternal life. Christ has gone before you bearing His Cross, and He died for you on the Cross, that you also may bear your cross and desire to die on the Cross. Because if you die with Him, you shall also live with Him; And if you share His sufferings, you will also share His glory.

See how in the Cross all things consist, and all things depend on dying on it. There is no other way to life, and to true inner peace, than the way of the Cross, and of daily self-denial. Go wherever you will, seek whatever you will, you will find no higher way above or safer way below than the road of the Holy Cross. Arrange and order things to your own ideas and wishes, yet you will find suffering to endure, whether you will or not; so you will always find the Cross. For you will either endure bodily pain or suffer anguish of mind and spirit.

At times God will withdraw from you; at times you will be troubled by your neighbor, and, what is more, you will often be a burden to yourself. Neither can any comfort or remedy bring you any relief, but you must bear it as long as God wills. For God desires that you learn to bear trials without comfort, that you may yield yourself wholly to Him, and grow more humble through tribulation. No man feels so deeply in his heart the Passion of Christ as he who has to suffer in like manner. The Cross always stands ready, and everywhere awaits you. You cannot escape it, wherever you flee; for wherever you go, you bear yourself, and always find yourself. Look up or down, without you and within, and everywhere you will find the Cross. (Thomas à Kempis, *The Imitation of Christ* 2:12)

Although Thomas à Kempis was himself a monk, his preaching—and the passage just cited is a good illustration—was on behalf of a kind of populist piety, a spirituality for all Christians. But Jesus' remarks just cited from Matthew were generally read not as a populist manifesto but as a distinction drawn by Jesus himself between the Christian in search of "mere" salvation—for him the observance of the Law will bring life—and someone searching for a higher level of perfection. We are at the starting point of Christianity's double life, salvation or perfection, prescriptions or counsels, observance or asceticism, the secular or the religious vocation?

5. Celibacy: The Gospels and Paul

The cited passages in Matthew's Gospel are quite explicit: Jesus makes poverty the barrier that distinguishes the Christian seeker after perfection from the mere observer of what came to be understood as Christian morality. But poverty, not only of the spirit but actual poverty, soon had a companion along this high road to perfection: celibacy. Jesus' remarks on divorce in Mark are followed in the parallel version in Matthew 19 by a more general discussion of marriage.

The disciples said to him [Jesus], "If that is the position with husband and wife, it is better not to marry." To this he replied, "That is something which everyone cannot accept, but only those for whom God has appointed it. For while some are incapable of marriage because they were born so, or were made so by men, there are others who have themselves renounced marriage for the sake of the kingdom of Heaven. Let those accept it who can." (Matthew 19:10–12)

The early Christians of Corinth, the site of a major cult center of Aphrodite, may already have been debating this question. Such at any rate seems to be the implication behind Paul's letter to them.

You say that it is a good thing for a man to have nothing to do with women; but because there is so much immorality, let each man have his own wife and each woman her own husband. . . . Do not deny yourselves to one another, except when you agree upon a temporary abstinence in order to devote yourselves to prayer; afterwards you may come together again; otherwise, for lack of self-control, you may be tempted by Satan.

All this I say by way of concession, not command. I should like you all to be as I am myself; but everyone has the gift God has granted him, one this gift and another that.

To the unmarried and the widows I say this: it is a good thing if they stay as I am myself; but if they cannot control themselves, they should marry. Better be married than burn with vain desire. . . .

On the question of celibacy, I have no instructions from the Lord, but I give my judgment as one who by God's mercy is fit to be trusted. It is my opinion, then, that in a time of stress like the present this is the best way for a man to live—it is best for a man to be as he is. Are you bound to a marriage? Do not seek a dissolution. Has your marriage been dissolved? Do not seek a wife. If, however, you do marry, there is nothing wrong with it. . . .

I want you to be free from anxious care. The unmarried man cares for the Lord's business: his aim is to please the Lord. But the married man cares for worldly things: his aim is to please his wife; and he has a divided mind. The unmarried or celibate woman cares for the Lord's business; her aim is to be dedicated to him in body as in spirit; but the married woman cares for worldly things; her aim is to please her husband.

In saying this I have no wish to keep you on a tight rein. I am thinking simply of your own good, of what is seemly, and of your freedom to wait upon the Lord without distraction. (Paul, *To the Corinthians* 1.7:1–35)

I asked him again, saying, "Sir, since you have been so patient with me, will you explain this also?" "Speak," he said. And I said, "If a wife or husband die, and the widow or widower marry again, does he or she commit sin?" "There is no sin in marrying again," he said, "but if they remain unmarried, they gain greater honor and glory with the Lord; but if they marry, they do not sin. Guard therefore your chastity and purity, and you will live to God." (Hermas, *The Pastor* 4.4)

The ambiguity about celibacy and marriage that runs unresolved through these early texts left a lasting mark on Christian moral teaching. Not merely was the permanently vowed celibate state the Christian ideal; temporary celibacy was advocated within the married state. "Do not deny yourselves to one another, except when you agree upon a temporary abstinence in order to devote yourselves to prayer," Paul had said in the letter cited above. The progress of the idea may be seen in this example from a manual for confessors from about 525–550 C.E.

We advise and exhort that there be continence in marriage, since marriage without continence is not lawful but sin, and [marriage] is permitted by the authority of God not for lust but for the sake of children, as it is written, "And the two shall be in one flesh" [Matt 19: 5], that is, in unity of the flesh for the generation of children, not for the lustful concupiscence of the flesh. Married people, then, must mutually abstain during three forty-day periods in each single year [possibly the three "quarantines," the forty-day fasts before Christmas and Easter and following Pentecost] by consent for a time that they may be able to have time for prayer for the salvation of their souls; and on Sunday night or Saturday night they shall mutually abstain, and after the wife has conceived he shall not have intercourse until she has borne her child, and they shall come together again for this purpose, as the Apostle (Paul) says [1 Cor. 7:5]. (*Penitential of Finnian*) [MCNEILL & GAMER 1938: 96]

6. Clerical Celibacy

In the case of Christian clerics, the connection with celibacy was present from a very early date, though its application varied considerably from one jurisdiction to another.

Those who have been made deacons, declaring when they were ordained that they must marry because they were not able to continue as they were (in the celibate state), and who afterwards did marry, shall continue in the ministry because it was conceded to them by the bishop. But if they were silent on the matter, undertaking at their ordination to abide as they were, and then afterwards proceeded to marry, they shall cease from the diaconate. (Council of Ancyra [314 C.E.], Canon 10)

If any shall maintain concerning a married presbyter [or priest], that it is not lawful to partake of the oblation that he offers, let him be anathema. (Council of Gangra [355–381 C.E.], Canon 4)

Since it is declared in the Apostolic Canons that of those who are advanced to the clergy unmarried, only lectors and cantors are able to marry, we also, maintaining this, determine that henceforth it is nowise lawful for any subdeacon, deacon or presbyter after his ordination to contract matrimony; but if he shall have dared to do so, let him be deposed. And if any of those who enter the clergy wishes to be joined to a wife before he is ordained subdeacon, deacon or presbyter, let it be done.

Moreover it has come to our knowledge that in Africa and Libya and in other places the most God-beloved bishops in those parts do not refuse to live with their wives, even after consecration, thereby giving scandal and offense to the people. Since therefore it is our particular care that all things tend to the good of the flock placed in our hands and committed to us, it has seemed good that no such thing shall in any way occur. . . . But if any shall have been observed to do such a thing, let him be deposed.

Since we know it to be handed down as a rule of the Roman Church that those who are deemed worthy to be advanced to the diaconate and presbyterate should promise no longer to cohabit with their wives, we, preserving the ancient rule and apostolic perfection and order, will that lawful marriage of men who are in holy orders be from this time forward firm, by no means dissolving their union with their wives or depriving them of their mutual intercourse at a convenient season. . . . For it is meet that they who assist at the divine altar should be absolutely continent when they are handling holy things, in order that they may be able to obtain from God what they ask in sincerity. (Quinquisext Council [692 C.E.], Canons 6, 12–13)

If deacons and priests might continue, in despite of Roman practice, in the married state contracted before ordination, the same was not true of bishops.

The wife of him who is advanced to the episcopal dignity shall be separated from her husband by mutual consent, and after his ordination and consecration to the episcopate she shall enter a monastery situated at a distance from the abode of the bishop, and there let her enjoy the bishop's support. And if she is deemed worthy, she may be advanced to the dignity of deaconess. (Ibid., Canon 48)

The first Western legislation prohibiting the cohabitation of the Christian clergy with the wives they took before ordination—and this pertained to all the clergy, from deacon to bishop—appears to have been promulgated by the Council of Elvira in Spain in 306 C.E. An even clearer expression is found in a Papal decretal of 385 C.E. that connects clerical celibacy directly with the Jewish priesthoods. These decretals had the force of law in the Western Church.

Why did He admonish them to whom the Holy of Holies was committed, "Be you holy, because I the Lord your God am holy" (Lev. 20:7)? Why were they commanded to dwell in the Temple during the year of their turn to officiate, far from their own homes? Obviously it was for the reason that they might not be able to continue to have marital relations with their wives, so that, adorned with a pure conscience, they might offer to God an acceptable sacrifice. After the time of their service was completed they were permitted to resume their marital relations for the sake of continuing the (priestly) succession, because only from the tribe of Levi was it ordained that anyone should be admitted to the priesthood. . . . Wherefore also our Lord Jesus, when by his coming he brought us light, solemnly affirmed in the Gospel that he had come not to destroy but to fulfill the Law. And therefore, he who is the bridegroom of the Church wished that its form be resplendent with chastity, so that on the Day of Judgment, when he should come again, he might find it without a spot or blemish, as he taught by his Apostle. And by the rule of its ordinances which may not be denied, we who are priests and Levites are bound from the day of our ordination to keep our bodies in soberness and modesty, so that in those sacrifices which we offer daily to our God we may please Him in all things. (Pope Siricius, *Decretal*, Chapter 7)

The final and abiding position of the Western Church on clerical celibacy, now including its extension to the grade of subdeacon, is set forth in two letters of Pope Leo (440–461 C.E.), called "the Great."

Although they who are not within the ranks of the clergy are free to take pleasure in the companionship of wedlock and the procreation of children, yet, for the sake of exhibiting the purity of complete continence, even subdeacons are not allowed carnal marriage; that "both they that have wives be as though they had none" (1 Cor. 7:29) and they that have not may remain single. But if in this order (of the subdiaconate), which is the fourth from the head, this is worthy to be observed, how much more is it to be kept in the first [the episcopate], the second [the presbyterate or priesthood], and the third [the diaconate], lest anyone be reckoned fit for the deacon's duties, or the presbyter's honorable position, or the bishop's pre-eminence, who is discovered as not yet having bridled his uxorious desires. (Leo, *To Athanasius*, 5)

The same law of continence is for the ministers of the altar as for the bishops and priests, who, when they were laymen, could lawfully marry and procreate children. But when they had attained to the said ranks, what was before lawful became unlawful for them. And thus, in order that their wedlock may become spiritual instead of carnal, it is necessary that they do not put away their wives but have them "as though they had them not," whereby both the affection of their married life may be retained and the marriage function cease. (Leo, *Rusticus* 3)

7. Radical Celibacy in the Early Church

We return to early Christian discussions about celibacy. Some Christians went very far indeed in their interpretation of Jesus and Paul and simply rejected the institution of marriage, a position that found no support in the Church as a whole.

Others who style themselves Encratites [or the "Self-Controlled"] acknowledge some things concerning God and Christ in accordance with the Church, but in respect to their mode of life they pass their time inflated with pride; thinking that by meat they might glorify themselves, they abstain from all animal food, drink water, and, forbidden to marry, they devote the rest of their lives to asceticism. (Hippolytus, *Refutation of All Heresies* 8.13)

There are those who spring from Saturninus and Marcion and who are called Encratites. They preach the unmarried state, thus setting aside the original creation of God, and indirectly condemn Him who made male and female for the propagation of the human race. Some reckoned as among their number have also introduced abstention from animal food, thus showing their ingratitude to God who created all things. (Ireneus, *Against the Heresies* 1.28)

8. A Christian Holy Man

Although the Encratites had their successors and later imitators here or there in the Christian world, these remain for us obscure and marginal movements. Christian self-denial found its champion elsewhere, in the simple Egyptian named Antony who died in 356 C.E., aged 105. His life was written, and widely disseminated, shortly thereafter.

The blessed Antony was a native Egyptian, and he was descended from a noble family, and in fact he owned slaves. His ancestors were (Christian) believers, and from his earliest days he was brought up in the fear of our Lord, and when he was a child and was being reared among his own relatives, he knew nothing of his father or of what went on among his own family: he was so naturally silent and his mind was so humble that he did not even trouble his parents by questioning them. He was exceedingly modest, modest beyond measure. He was unable to read or write because he could not bear the rough behavior of the boys in the school; his whole desire was to be nothing more than what was written of Jacob, "a simple man, a dweller in tents." He clung closely to his parents, and when they came to church he would run before them in the flow of his affection. He was not like an ordinary child, whose usual routine is broken by the childish amusements. He never neglected the observance of any of the seasons of the Church. . . .

After the death of his parents, Antony was left alone with one little sister. He was about eighteen or twenty years old, and on him rested the responsibility of caring for both the household and his sister. Six months after the death of his parents, when he was going, as usual, into the Lord's house, and was reflecting within himself, he thought as he walked how the Apostles had left all and followed the Savior, and how in Acts, men sold their possessions and brought and laid them at the Apostles' feet for distribution to the needy, and what and how great a hope was laid up for them in heaven. While he was thinking of these matters he went into the church just as the Gospel was being read, and he heard the Lord say to the rich man: "If you would be perfect, go and sell what you have and give to the poor; and come and follow me and you shall have treasure in heaven." Antony, as though God had put him in mind of the saints and the passage had been read for his benefit, immediately left the Lord's house and gave the possessions which he had from his ancestors to the villagers—they were three hundred acres, productive and rich—that they should no more be a burden upon himself and his sister. And all the

rest that was unmovable he sold, and the considerable money thus collected he gave to the poor, saving a little, however, for his sister's sake.
He went back to the Lord's house, and hearing the Lord say in the
Gospel, "Be not anxious for the morrow," he could remain no longer, but
went and gave even that to the poor.

Antony committed his sister to known and faithful virgins, installing
her in a maidens' house for upbringing, and henceforth he devoted himself outside his own house to ascetic discipline, paying attention to himself and patiently training himself. For there were not as yet many monasteries in Egypt, and no monk at all had experience of the remote desert;
but every one of those who wished to have a care for himself practiced
the ascetic discipline in solitude near his own village.

There was in the next village to Antony an old man who had lived
from his youth the life of a hermit. Antony, after he had seen this man,
imitated him in piety and at first he began to live in places outside the
village. Then, if he heard of any good man anywhere else, like the prudent
bee he went forth and sought him out and did not return to his own place
until he had seen him; and he returned only after he had gotten from the
good man provisions, as it were, for his journey on the road to virtue. So
at first he lived thus and steadfastly held to his purpose not to return to
the home of his parents or to the remembrance of his family, but to
devote all his desire and energy to the perfection of his discipline. He
worked, however, with his hands, having heard that "he who is idle, let
him not eat," and part (of his wages) he spent on bread and part he gave
to the needy. And he prayed constantly, because he had learned that a
man ought to pray unceasingly in private. For he had given such heed to
what was read that none of those things that were written fell from him
to the ground; he remembered everything, and afterwards his memory
served him as Scripture. . . .

Now Saint Antony was a storehouse of fasting, and of prayer, and of
ascetic labors, and of patient endurance, and of love and of righteousness,
which is the mother of them all, but he did not compete with those others
who were young monks like himself, except in one matter only, that is to
say, he would not suffer himself to be second to any of them in good
works. . . . And when the Enemy, that hater of the virtues and the lover
of evil things, saw all this great perfection in the young man, he could not
endure it, and he surrounded himself with his slaves, as is his custom, and
began to work on Antony. At the beginnings of his tempting of the saint,
he [that is, Satan] approached him with flattery and caused him to feel
anxiety about his possessions, and solicitude and love for his sister, and

for his family, and to experience the love of money and lusts of various kinds, and to think of the rest of the things of the life of this world, and finally of the hard and laborious life that he lived, and the weakness of body which would come upon him in the course of time. . . .

Now when the Enemy saw that his craftiness in this matter was without profit, and that the more he tempted Saint Antony, the more strenuous the saint was in protecting himself with the armor of righteousness, he attacked him by means of the (sexual) vigor of early manhood which is bound up in the nature of our humanity. He used to trouble him at night with the goadings of passion, and in the daytime as well he tried him and pained him with the same desires, and to such an extent that even those who just looked upon him knew from his appearance that he was waging war against the Adversary. But the more the Evil One plagued him with filthy and maddening thoughts, the more Saint Antony took refuge in prayer and in abundant supplication, and amidst them all he remained wholly chaste. And the Evil One was working upon him every shameful deed according to his custom, and at length he even appeared to Saint Antony in the form of a woman—other similar feats he performed with ease, for such things are a subject of boasting for him.

None of these temptations are of any avail, however. Antony perseveres in virtue and soon begins to pay the price of fame.

It happened that in the course of time Antony's fame reached all the monks who were in Egypt and even all the others there who did not live the life of the ascetic and the recluse, and men of distinction and monks in Egypt began to come to him in large numbers. The Egyptian monks came to him that they might copy the manner of his life and deeds, and the laity came that he might pray over them, and might heal certain of them of their illnesses. One day, when a crowd of people had come there in a body to see him and they had besought him repeatedly to speak to them, and he had answered them not a word, they lifted the door out of its socket, and threw themselves down on their faces before him, and implored him, and then each man among them stood up and made known his request to him. And when he had gone out to them, like a man who issues from the bowels of the earth, they saw that his appearance was like that of an angel of light, and they marveled that his body had not been weakened by all his confinement and why it was that his understanding had not become feeble, and rather, on the contrary, in appearance, physique and countenance he was exactly as they had known him in the past. (Athanasius, *Life of Antony*)

9. Antony Goes into the Desert

ego

When Antony saw the great crowds of people who had collected about him and realized that the trouble which those men and women caused him was increasing, he began to fear that he should become unduly puffed up in his mind because of the things that God had accomplished through him, or that others might esteem him beyond proper bounds and more than he deserved. And so he determined to go away from that place and enter the Thebaid [that is, the desert area around Egyptian Thebes]. So he took a little bread and sat down on the river bank and waited for a boat going to the district that was his destination. And as he was reflecting there, he suddenly heard a voice from heaven: "Antony, where are you going? Why are you leaving this place?" Now he was not frightened by this voice but spoke to it like a man doing what was customary. "Because, my Lord," he replied, "the people will not allow me a little silent contemplation here. And so I intend to go to the Thebaid, and I am particularly eager to go because the people here are asking me for things which are totally beyond my powers."

God instead counseled going not to the Thebaid but into the "innermost desert" and showed Antony the way. On his journey he was assisted by the only inhabitants of the place, the local bedouin, who supplied him with bread and water.

Then the Blessed Antony was alone in that wilderness, for the place where he chose to live was desolate in the extreme. But he was thus able to reflect the more on exalted things, and he was content. And the brothers who used to visit him earlier now begged him to allow them to bring to him there every month some garden greens and olives and oil, and though he opposed them, they overcame him with their entreaties and forced him to receive them. Thus they began to pay him visits, one at a time. And the blessed man grew exceedingly elderly and advanced in years. And even there in the desert the blessed man was engaged in struggle, not with flesh and blood, but with the demons and impure spirits, as we have learned from those who visited him. They used to hear there the sounds of cries and tumult, to see flashing spears, and at night the whole mountain was filled with fiery demons and his visitors were filled with fear. . . . But he encouraged the brethren who were with him not to be frightened or tremble at such apparitions. For, he told them, "They are only empty phantoms which at the name of the Cross perish as if they had never existed." (Athanasius, *Life of Antony*)

10. Cells in the Wilderness

There were many who followed where Antony led, and for spiritual motives as varied as those traced by the seventh-century master of Eastern monasticism, John Climacus.

Some enter this harbor, this sea, or indeed the abyss of solitary life because they cannot control their tongues or because of some previous bad habit of the flesh. Others do so because they have a bad temper, which they cannot restrain in company, or because they arrogantly think it better to sail on their own rather than under the guidance of someone else. Others do so because if they live amid material things they cannot do without them. Some think a life of solitude will enhance their zeal, and some wish to punish themselves in secret for their faults. Some think of the glory a solitary life will earn them. And there are some—may the Son of Man find them on earth when He returns—who undertake this holy way of life because of a delight in, a thirst for the love and sweetness of God. (John Climacus, *The Ladder of Divine Ascent*, Step 27)
[JOHN CLIMACUS 1982: 265]

Like Antony, these seekers after solitary perfection took themselves in the first instance to the desert and wildernesses of Egypt.

Beyond Nitria there is another place in the inner desert, about nine miles distant; and this place is called, by reason of the great number of monastic dwellings scattered through the wilderness, "The Cells." To this place those who have already had their first initiation, and who desire to live a more remote life, stripped of all its trappings, withdraw themselves: for the desert is vast, and the cells are separated one from another by so wide a space that no one is in sight of his neighbor, nor can any voice be heard.

The monks abide singly in their cells, and there is a great silence and a great tranquillity among them: they come together at the church only on Saturdays and Sundays, where they see each other face to face like people restored in heaven. If anyone happens to be absent from that gathering, they immediately understand that he has been detained by some bodily ailment, and so they all go to visit him, not indeed all of them together but at different times, and each carries with him whatever he may have with him at his abode that might be appreciated by the ill person. But for no other reason does any dare disturb the silence of his neighbor, unless occasionally to strengthen someone with a good word, or, it might be, to anoint with the comfort of counsel the athletes set for the struggle. Many of them go three and four miles to church, and the distance separating one cell from another is no less great. But so great is the love that is in them . . . that if anyone should wish to dwell with them, as soon as they are aware of it, each man offers his own cell. (Rufinus, *History of the Monks of Egypt*)

Rufinus is writing history, or at least collecting anecdotes, at second hand. One who had the immediate experience and left us his own rather rhetorical account—he was also the translator of the Bible into Latin—was Jerome, who took up the monastic life in Palestine in the fourth century.

I dwelt in the desert, in the vast solitude which gives the hermit his savage home, parched by the burning sun. . . . Sackcloth disfigured my unshapely limbs, and my skin from long neglect became as black as the Ethiopian's. Tears and groans were every day my portion; if drowsiness chanced to overcome my struggle against it, my bare bones, which hardly held together, crashed against the ground. Of my food and drink I say nothing; for even in sickness the solitaries have nothing but cold water, and to eat one's food cooked is looked upon as an indulgence. . . . My face is pale and my frame chilled with fasting. (Jerome, *Letter* 22.7)

11. Pirke Aboth, Christian Style

The growth of Christian monasticism produced a parallel body of literature to instruct and edify monks and laymen alike with accounts of the struggles and the triumphs of these "athletes of God." One popular form of this literature was "the sayings of the Fathers," aphorisms on the life of self-denial by those engaged in trying to lead it.

A certain man asked the abbot Antony, "What shall I observe, that I may please God?" And the old man answered him: "Observe what I tell you. Wherever you go, have God ever before your eyes. Whatever you do, hold by the example of the Holy Scriptures. And wherever you are staying, do not be quick to leave it. These three things observe and you shall be saved."

They said of the abbot Pambo, that in the hour of his departing this life, he said to the holy men who stood about him: "From the time I came into this place of solitude and built my cell and dwelt in it, I do not recall that I have eaten bread save what my hands have toiled for, or repented of any word I have spoken to this hour. And so I go to the Lord as one who has not yet made a beginning of serving God."

The abbot Antony said: "Fish out of water die; even so monks out-side their cells or who stay with men of the world fall away from their vow of quiet. As a fish must return to the sea, so must we to our cells, lest in being out, we forget the watch within."

A certain brother came to the abbot Moses in Scete, seeking a word from him. And the old man said to him: "Go and sit in your cell, and your cell will teach you everything."

An old man saw someone laughing and said to him: "In the presence of heaven and earth we have to give an account of our whole life to God, and you laugh?"

At one time the abbot Achilles came into the cell of the abbot Isaiah in Scete and found him eating. For he had put salt and water in the pot. And seeing that he hid it behind the plaits of palm leaves, Achilles said to him, "Tell me what you were eating?" Isaiah answered, "Forgive me, father, but I was cutting palm leaves and I grew warm. And so I dipped a morsel of bread in salt and put it in my mouth; and my throat was parched and the morsel did not go down, and so I was compelled to pour a little water on the salt so that I could swallow it. But forgive me." And thereafter the abbot Achilles used to say, "Come and see Isaiah supping consommé in Scete! If you really want consommé, go down into Egypt."

A monk met certain handmaidens of God upon the road, and at the sight of them he turned aside. But the abbess said to him, "If you were a perfect monk, you would not have looked so closely as to notice that we were women."

The abbot Cyrus of Alexandria was questioned about lustful fanta-sies. He answered: "If you have not the fantasies, you are without hope, because you have either the fantasies or the deed. . . . He who sins in the flesh has no trouble with sexual fantasies."

The abbot Daniel used to say, "Even as the body flourishes, the soul grows withered; and when the body is withered, then does the soul put forth leaves."

There came to the abbot Lucius in Enna certain monks of the type called "Pray-ers," and the old man asked them: "What kind of handwork do you do?" They said: "We touch no kind of handwork, but as the Apostle says, we pray without ceasing." The old man said to them: "So you do not eat?" They said: "Yes, we eat." And the old man asked: "And while you are eating, who prays for you?" And again he questioned them: "You do not sleep either?" And they said: "We sleep." And the old man said: "And when you sleep, who prays for you?" And he said to them: "Forgive me, my brothers, but you do not do as you said; but I shall now show you how in working with my hands, I pray without ceasing. For I sit, with the help of God, steeping my few palm leaves and from them I weave a mat, and I say all the while, 'Have mercy on me, O God . . . ' Is this not a prayer?" And they said: "Yes." And he said: "And when I stay all day long working and praying with heart and mouth, I make sixteen denarii more or less (from my work), and out of that sum I leave two at the door and spend the rest on food. And whoever finds the two denarii prays for me while I eat and sleep. And thus by God's grace there is fulfilled in me what Scripture says, 'Pray without ceasing.' "

Thieves once came into an old monk's cell and said to him: "We have come to take whatever you have in this cell." And he said: "Take whatever you see, my sons." So they took whatever they could find in the cell and went away. But they overlooked a little bag that was hidden in the cell. So the old man went chasing after them, shouting, "My sons, you have overlooked this. Take it." But they marveled at the patience of the old man and brought everything back, saying to one another, "Truly, this is a man of God." (*The Sayings of the Fathers*)

12. States of the Soul

If the earliest literature produced by the monastic movement appears largely anecdotal, it quickly came of age. A notable effect of the monastic preoccupation with conscience and recollection was a new awareness of the interior states of the soul, of how the affective and volitional life worked. Here the general psychological landscape is laid out by John Climacus in his Ladder of Divine Ascent, *a work written for an early-seventh-century monastic audience in the Near East. In it he gives his own version of the catalogue of the "seven deadly sins" and contrasts them with their virtuous extremes.*

If the height of gluttony is that you force yourself to eat even when you are not hungary, then the height of temperance in a hungry man is that he restrains even the justifiable urges of nature. If the height of lechery is that one raves even over animals and inanimate things, then the height of purity is to look on everyone in the same way that one would regard inanimate objects. If the ultimate stage of cupidity is to gather without ever being satisfied, the ultimate stage of poverty is the willingness to dispense with one's own body. If the final point of despondency is to have no patience even while living in total peace, the final point of patience is to consider oneself to be at rest even in the midst of affliction. If to be furious even in solitude is talked of as a sea of wrath, then calmness, whether your slanderer be present or not, will be a sea of long-suffering. If the high point of vainglory is for a person to put on airs even when no one is present to praise him, the sure proof of its absence is that you keep your thoughts under control when someone is praising you to your face. If it is a sign of perdition, that is, pride, to be arrogant even when poorly dressed, then surely among high doings and great success lowly thoughts betoken saving humility. (John Climacus, *The Ladder of Divine Ascent*, Step 29) [JOHN CLIMACUS 1982: 283–284]

Since they dealt with extreme psychological states, the analyses of the religious writers are often graphic and arresting, as illustrated in this sophisticated fourth-century description of what John called "despondency" and what we might term monastic depression.

Our sixth struggle is with what the Greeks call accidie (*akedia*), and which we may describe as tedium or perturbation of heart. It is akin to dejection and is particularly experienced by wandering monks and solitaries, a persistent and obnoxious enemy to such as dwell in the desert, disturbing the monk especially about midday, like a fever mounting at a regular time, and bringing its highest tide of inflammation at definite accustomed hours to the sick soul. And so some of the Fathers declare it to be the demon of noontide which is spoken of in the 90th Psalm.

When this besieges the unhappy mind, it begets aversion to the place, boredom with one's cell, and scorn and contempt for one's brethren, whether they are dwelling with one or some way off, as careless and unspiritually minded persons. Also, toward any work which must be done within the enclosure of our own place, we become listless and inert. It will not permit us to stay in our cell, or to attend to our reading: we lament that in all this while, living in the same spot, we have made no progress; we sigh and complain that bereft of sympathetic fellowship we have no spiritual fruit; and bewail ourselves as empty of all spiritual profit, abiding vacant and useless in this place. . . . We praise other and far distant monasteries, describing them as more helpful to one's progress, more congenial to the health of the soul. We paint the fellowship of the brethren there, its suavity, its richness in spiritual conversation, contrasting it with the harshness of all that is at hand, where not only is there no edification to be had from any of the brethren who dwell here, but where one cannot even procure one's victuals without enormous toil. Finally, we conclude that there is no health for us so long as we stay in this place. . . .

Toward eleven o'clock or midday it induces such lassitude of body and craving for food as one might feel after the exhaustion of a long journey and hard toil, or the postponing of a meal throughout a two- or three-day fast. Finally, one gazes anxiously here and there, and sighs that no one brother of any description is seen approaching: one is forever in and out of one's cell, gazing at the sun as though it were tarrying at its setting. One's mind is an irrational confusion, like the earth befogged in a mist, one is slothful and vacant in every spiritual activity, and no remedy, it seems, can be found in this state of siege except a visit from some brother or the solace of sleep. Finally, our malady suggests that in common courtesy one should salute the brethren, and visit the sick, near or far. It dictates such offices of duty and piety as seeking out this relative or that and making haste to visit them; or there is that religious and devout lady, destitute of any support from her family, whom it is pious to visit now and again and supply in holy fashion with the necessary comforts, neglected and despised as she is by her own relations.

The directors of souls could not only diagnose such spiritual ills; they also had at hand the cure.

And so the wise Fathers in Egypt would in no way suffer the monks, especially the younger, to be idle, measuring the state of their heart and their progress in patience and humility by their steadiness at work; and not only might they accept nothing from anyone toward their own support, but out of their own toil they supplied such brethren as came by, or were from foreign parts, and sent huge stores of victuals and provisions throughout Libya, a barren and hungry land, and to those who pined in the squalor of the prisons in the towns.

The preceding is amply confirmed by example.

So the abbot Paul, so revered among the Fathers, was living in the vast desert of Porphyrio secure in his daily sustenance from the date palms there and from his small garden. Though he had no other way of keeping himself—his dwelling in the desert was seven day's journey and more from any town or human habitation, so that the cost of carrying the produce to market would be more than the work he had sweated over would fetch—he nevertheless collected palm leaves (for plaiting into mats) and every day he exacted from himself just such a measure of work that would be required to earn a living (if he sold them). And when his cave was filled with his handiwork of an entire year, he would then set fire to it and burn each year the work he had so carefully done. And thus he proved that a monk cannot endure to remain in his place without doing some manual work, nor can he climb any nearer the summit of holiness. And even though the necessity of earning a living in no way

demands it, the work should nonetheless be done for the sole purging of
the heart, the steadying of thought, perseverance in the cell, and the
conquest and final overthrow of accidie itself. (Cassian, *Collations*)

13. The Cenobites

*Antony is the archetype of the hermit monk, the Christian who has withdrawn from
the world to pursue perfection in solitude. But as was apparent in his own life, the
charismatic power of holy men was such that they were only rarely unaccompanied
by others who pursued them even into the "inner deserts" in order to sit at their feet
and imitate their ascetical style of life. It was, then, a natural development that
individuals who shared this common goal should begin to live not in the scattered
cells already described but in genuine communities, koinobia. In 420 C.E. the monk
Palladius wrote his Paradise of the Holy Fathers, which includes this version of the
beginning of the cenobitic movement among Christian ascetics.*

In the country of (Egyptian) Thebes, and in the district there called
Tabenna, there was a certain blessed man whose name was Pachomius
[ca. 292–346 C.E.], and this man led a beautiful life of ascetic excellence,
and he was crowned with the love of God and of man. Now as this man
was sitting in his cell, an angel appeared to him who said: "Since you have
completed your apprenticeship it is unnecessary for you to dwell here; go
and gather together to you all those who are wandering and make your
dwelling with them, and lay down for them such laws as I shall tell you."
And the angel gave him a book wherein was written the following.

*So came into existence the Rule of Pachomius, the first collection of ordinances
regulating the common life of Christian monks and the forerunner of the better-
known rules of Basil in the Eastern and Benedict in the Western Church. The rules
are not complex, but they are unmistakably regulatory; and they instituted practices
that were to last from that day to this. The monks, for example, were instructed to
take their meals in common.*

And he [that is, the angel] commanded that "a monk who was a
stranger and had a different garb from theirs should not enter in with
them to the table; the man who sought to be accepted as a monk in that
monastery was obliged to labor there for three years, after which he
should receive the tonsure [that is, a ritual cutting of the hair]. When the
monks were eating together they were to cover up their faces with their
cowls so that they might not see each other eating and not hold converse
together over the table, and not gaze about from one side to the other."
And he further commanded that during the course of each day they

should repeat twelve sections of the Book of Psalms, and during each evening twelve additional sections of the Book of Psalms, and that when they came to eat they should repeat the Great Psalm.

And the blessed Pachomius said to the angel: "The sections of the Book of Psalms which you have appointed for us for repetition are far too few." And the angel said to him, "The sections of the Book of Psalms which I have appointed are indeed few, so that even the monks who are weak may be able to fulfill the rules, and may not be distressed thereby. For there is no law laid down for the perfect, because their mind is at all seasons occupied with God, but this law which I have laid down is for those who have not a perfect mind, so that, though they fulfill only such things as are prescribed by the rules, they can thereby acquire openness of face." . . .

And there were living in that mountain [that is, at Tabennesi] about 7,000 brethren, and in the monastery in which the blessed Pachomius himself lived, there were living 1,300 brethren; and besides these there were also other monasteries, each containing about 300 or 200 or 100 monks, who lived in common; and they all worked with their hands and lived by that toil; and their superfluities they gave to the nunneries there. Each day those monks whose week of service it was rose up and attended to their work; others attended to the cooking, and others set out the tables and laid upon them bread and cheese, and vessels of vinegar and water. And there were some monks who went in to partake of food at the third hour of the day, and others at the sixth, and others at the ninth hour, and others in the evening, and others who ate once a day only; and there were some who ate only once a week. . . . Some worked in the orchard, some in the garden, some in the blacksmith's shop, some in the baker's shop, the carpenter's shop or the laundry; some wove baskets and mats of palm leaves, and one was a maker of nets, and one was a maker of sandals, and one was a scribe. Now all these men as they were performing their work were repeating the Psalms and the Scriptures in order.

And there were large numbers of women who were nuns, and who closely followed this same rule of life, and they came from the other side of the river [that is, the Nile] and beyond it, and there were also married women who came from the other side of the river close by. And whenever any one of them died, the other women would bring her and lay her down on the bank of the river and go away. Then certain of the brethren would cross over in a boat and bring her over with the singing of psalms and with lighted candles, and with great ceremony and honor. And when they had brought her over they would bury her in their cemetery. Without priest or deacon no man would go to that nunnery, however, and then only on Sundays. (Palladius, *Paradise of the Holy Fathers*)

14. Basis on the Superiority of Community Life — *against solitary life*

The standards of Eastern monasticism were set by Basil of Caesarea in Cappadocia (330–379 C.E.). His Rule discusses, among other topics, whether the ascetic life of the solitary or the cenobite is preferable. For Basil, the second is the better, and he starts with the most pragmatic of all reasons.

I think that the life of several persons in the same place is preferable (to that of the solitary). First, because for bodily wants no one is sufficient for himself, but we need each other in providing what is necessary. But just as the foot has one ability, but is wanting another, and without the help of the other members it would find its own power neither strong nor sufficient of itself to continue, nor any supply for what it lacks, so too in the solitary life: what is of use to us and what is wanting we cannot provide for ourselves, for God who created the world has so ordered all things that we are dependent upon each other, as it is written that we may join ourselves to one another (Wisdom 13:20). } *interdepend*

But in addition to this, reverence for the love of Christ does not permit each one to have regard only for his own affairs, for love, he says, seeks not her own (1 Cor. 13:5). The solitary has only one goal, the service of his own interests. That clearly is opposed to the law of love, which the Apostle (Paul) fulfilled when he did not in his own eyes seek his own advantage but the advantage of many, that they might be saved (1 Cor. 10:33).

Further, no one in solitude recognizes his own defects, since he has no one to correct him and in gentleness and mercy direct him on his way. For even if correction is from an enemy, it may often, in the case of those who are well disposed, rouse the desire for healing. . . . Also the commandments may be better fulfilled by a larger community and not by one alone. For while this thing is being done, another is neglected; for example, by attendance upon the sick the reception of strangers is neglected; and in the bestowal and distribution of the necessities of life, especially when they are time-consuming, the care of the work is neglected. . . .

There are dangers that we say accompany the solitary life, but the first and foremost is that of self-satisfaction. For he who has no one to test his work easily believes that he has completely fulfilled the commandments. . . . For how shall he manifest his humility, when he has no one to whom he can show himself the inferior. (Basil, *Shorter Rule*, ques. 7)

15. The Monks and the Great Church

So long as the monks remained in remote wildernesses it was their reputation rather than their actual presence that impressed itself on Christian consciences. But the monastic life, if inimical to the pagan cities of the third and fourth centuries, found the climate of the fifth-century Christian city and its environs somewhat more agreeable. It was also in the fifth century that the monks, rural or urban, began to intervene more directly in Church affairs. A single charismatic wonder-worker like Simeon Stylites, the famous pillar-saint of northern Syria, or that other Syrian monk Barsauma, the destroyer of synagogues, might influence members of the imperial house; more troublesome in both principle and practice were the hordes of monks who descended, like a fourth estate, upon the deliberations of synods and councils to demonstrate in the council chambers and on the streets outside. The Council of Chalcedon in 451 C.E. addressed this new problem and attempted to bring the monks under the control of the Church by placing them and their monasteries directly under the jurisdiction of the local bishops.

They who lead a true and worthy monastic life shall enjoy the honor that belongs to them. But since there are some who assume the monastic condition only as a pretense, and will upset the ecclesiastical regulations and affairs, and run about without distinction [or identification] in the cities and want to found monasteries for themselves, the synod therefore has decreed that no one shall build a monastery or a house of prayer or erect anything without the consent of the bishop of the city; and further, that also the monks of every district and city shall be subject to the bishop, that they shall love peace and quiet and observe the fasts and prayers in the places where they are assigned continually; that they shall not encumber themselves with ecclesiastical and secular business and shall not take part in such; that they shall not leave their monasteries except when, in cases of necessity, they may be commissioned by the bishop of the city with such; that no slave shall be admitted into the cloister in order to become a monk without the permission of his master. Whoever violates this our order shall be excommunicated, that the name of God be not blasphemed. The bishop of the city must keep a careful oversight of the monasteries. (Acts of the Council of Chalcedon, Canon 4)

16. Monasticism Comes to the West

The Church in the West was kept well informed about the development of Christian asceticism in the Near East through frequent visits of Westerners to Egypt and Palestine and the presence in Rome of the Alexandrian bishop Athanasius, the author of the Life of the Blessed Antony, *as well as by the rapid translation of the classics of the desert into Latin by Jerome and Rufinus among others. Jerome, in particular, was strenuous in encouraging on his Italian correspondents the ascetic life style, the "way of perfection" that he himself had embraced in Palestine. It is not necessary, in fact, to go to the desert; the ascetic's virtues of self-denial, of voluntary celibacy and poverty, are equally at home in the city, even, as he counsels the celibate maiden Eustochium (Letter 27), in one's mother's house: "you avoid wine as you would poison. . . . An empty stomach and fevered lungs are indispensable for the preservation of chastity. . . . Let your companions be women pale and thin from fasting; rarely go out of the house. . . . Give away your property; it is now no longer yours."*

The formal life style of the monk was introduced into the West, where Augustine, not yet a Christian but interested in the new faith, encountered it in Milan, as he describes in a famous and critical passage in his Confessions. *In August 386 C.E. he had a visitor, a certain Ponticianus, an imperial agent and himself a converted Christian, who discovered Augustine reading Paul and was both surprised and delighted. Augustine continues.*

When, then, I told him that I bestowed much pains upon these writings, a conversation ensued on his speaking of Antony, the Egyptian monk, whose name was in high repute among God's servants, though up to that time unfamiliar to us. When he came to know this he lingered on the topic, imparting to us who were ignorant a knowledge of this so eminent and marveling at our ignorance. But we were amazed, hearing God's wonderful works most fully manifested in such recent times, indeed almost in our own day [Antony had died only about thirty years earlier], wrought in the true faith and the Catholic Church. We all wondered—we that they were so great, and Ponticianus that we had never heard of them.

From this his conversation turned to the companies in the monasteries, and their way of life so fragrant to God, and of the fruitful deserts of the wilderness, of which we knew nothing. And there was a monastery at Milan full of good brethren, outside the walls of the city, under the care of Ambrose [bishop of Milan, 373–397 C.E.], and we were ignorant of it.

Augustine relates a story told by Ponticianus, how one day at the imperial court at Trier, when a number of officials went out for a walk, two of his companions strolled off by themselves.

In their ramblings they came upon a certain cottage where lived some of God's servants [that is, Christians], "poor in spirit" to whom "belongs the Kingdom of Heaven," and they found there a book in which was written the life of Antony. This one of them began to read, then marvel at, and be inflamed by it; and in reading to think about embracing such a life, and giving up his worldly employments to serve God. . . . Then Ponticianus and the other who was walking with him through other parts of the garden, came searching for the two in the same place, and when they found them, they advised them to return as the sun was setting. . . . But the other two, with their thoughts on heavenly things, remained in the cottage. And both of them were affianced to brides who also, when they heard of this, dedicated their virginity to God. (Augustine, *Confessions* 8.6)

17. Benedict on the Monastic Life

The position held by Basil in the annals of Eastern monasticism was occupied in the Latin Church by Benedict of Nursia (ca. 480–544 C.E.), whose Rule became the model for most of the others that followed down to the Counter-Reformation. Benedict's work opens with a review of the various forms of Christian monasticism.

It is manifest that there are four kinds of monks. The first is that of the cenobites, that is the monastic, serving under a rule and an abbot. The second kind is that of the anchorites, that is the hermits, those who have learned to fight against the devil not by the new fervor of a conversion but by a long probation in a monastery, having been taught already by association with many; and having been well prepared in the army of the brethren for the solitary fight of the hermit, and secure now without the encouragement of another, they are able, God helping them, to fight with their own hand or arm against the vices of the flesh or their own thoughts. But a third and very bad kind of monk is that of the sarabites, not tried as gold in a furnace by a rule, experience being their teacher, but softened after the manner of lead; keeping faith with the world by their works, they are known by their tonsure to lie to God. Being shut up by twos and threes alone and without a shepherd, in their own and not in the Lord's sheepfold, they have their own desires for a law. For whatever they think good and choose, that they deem holy; and what they do not wish, that they consider unlawful. But the fourth kind of monk is the kind called the "wanderers around" (*gyrovagi*), who during their whole life are guests for three or four days at a time in the cells of various monasteries throughout the various provinces; they are always wandering and never stationary, serving their own pleasures and the allurements of the palate, and in every way worse than the sarabites. (Benedict, *Rule*, Chapter 1)

According to Benedict, then, the two besetting vices of the ascetical way of life are self-indulgence and that tendency to roam already noted with disapproval in the

Sayings of the Fathers. *The cure for self-indulgence was, as already discussed by Basil, the life in a community under both a rule and a monastic superior. In Benedict the matter is set out with great clarity: the superior, or abbot, is Christ's representative, and the primary monastic virtue is obedience to the rule and to the abbot who is its embodiment.*

The first degree of humility is prompt obedience. This is required of all who, whether by reason of the holy servitude to which they are pledged, or through fear of hell, or to attain to the glory of eternal life, hold nothing more dear than Christ. Such disciples delay not in doing what is ordered by their superior, just as if the command had come from God. Of such our Lord says, "At the hearing of the ear he has obeyed Me" (Ps. 17:45). And to the teachers he likewise says, "He that hears you, hears me" (Luke 10:16).

For this reason such disciples, surrendering forthwith all they possess, and giving up their own will, leave unfinished what they were working at, and with the ready foot of obedience in their acts follow the word of command. Thus, as it were, at the same moment comes the order of the master and the finished work of the disciple: with the speed of the fear of God both go jointly forward and are quickly effected by such as ardently desire to walk in the way of eternal life. These take the narrow way, of which the Lord says, "Narrow is the way which leads to life" (Matt. 7:14). That is, they live not as they themselves will, neither do they obey their own desires and pleasures, but following the command and direction of another, and abiding in their monasteries, their desire is to be ruled by an abbot. (Benedict, *Rule,* Chapter 5)

18. The Ladder of Perfection

The ladder of perfection was the favorite image of Christian writers on progress in the spiritual life. And if John Climacus did not invent the image, as he surely did not, it was widely popularized by his Ladder of Divine Ascent, *a book read aloud and often in Eastern and Western monasteries for the instruction of the brethren.*

I have put together a ladder of ascent, though my meager knowledge makes me something of a second-rate architect. Still, let each one take note of the step on which he is standing. (John Climacus, *The Ladder of Divine Ascent*, Step 27) [JOHN CLIMACUS 1982: 265]

There are perhaps as many ladders as there are writers on the spiritual life, and with almost as many steps. Benedict's rule for his monks arranges the steps in terms of ascending grades of humility.

Brothers, if we would scale the summit of humility and swiftly gain the heavenly height which is reached by our lowliness in this present life, we must set up a ladder of climbing deeds like that which Jacob saw in his dream, whereon angels were descending and ascending. Without doubt that descending and ascending is to be understood by us as signifying that we descend by exalting ourselves and ascend by humbling ourselves. But the ladder itself thus set up is our life in this world, which by humility of heart is lifted by our Lord to heaven. Our body and soul we may indeed call the sides of the ladder in which our divine vocation has set up the divers steps of humility and discipline we have to ascend.

The first step of humility, then, is reached when a man, with the fear of God always before his eyes, does not allow himself to forget but is ever mindful of all of God's commandments. He remembers, moreover, that such as contemn God fall into hell for their sins, and that life eternal awaits such as fear Him. And warding off at each moment all sin and defect in thought and word, of eye, hand and foot, of self-will, let such a one bestir himself to prune away the lusts of the flesh.

If this is the degree of perfection incumbent upon all Christians, the ladder quickly mounts to higher and more difficult levels of self-control.

The second step of humility is reached when any one not loving self-will takes no heed to satisfy his own desires but copies in his life what our Lord said, "I came not to do my own will, but the will of Him who sent me" (John 6:3–8). Scripture likewise proclaims that self-will engenders punishment and necessity purchases a crown.

The third step of humility is reached when a man, for the love of God, submits himself with all obedience to a superior, imitating our Lord, of whom the Apostle (Paul) says, "He was made obedient, even to death" (Phil. 2:8).

The fourth step in humility is reached when any one in the exercise of his obedience patiently and with a quiet mind bears all that is inflicted on him, things contrary to nature, and even at times unjust, and in suffering all these he neither wearies nor gives up the work. . . .

The fifth stage of humility is reached when a monk manifests to his abbot, by humble confession, all the evil thoughts of his heart and his secret faults. . . .

The sixth step of humility is reached when a monk is content with all that is mean and vile, and with regard to everything enjoined him accounts himself a poor and worthless workman. . . .

The seventh step is reached when a man not only confesses with his tongue that he is most lowly and inferior, but in his innermost heart believes so. . . .

The eighth step of humility is reached when a monk does nothing but what is the common rule of the monastery, or what the example of his seniors enforces.

The ninth step in humility is reached when a monk restrains his tongue from talking, and practicing silence, speaks not until a question is asked of him. . . .

The tenth step of humility is attained when one is not easily and quickly moved to laughter. . . .

The eleventh step of humility is reached when a monk, in speaking, does so quietly and without laughter, humbly, gravely, and in a few words and not with a loud voice. . . .

The twelfth step of humility is reached when a monk not only has humility in his heart, but even shows it on his exterior to all who behold him. Thus, whether he be in the oratory at the "Work of God" in the monastery, or in the garden, on a journey, or in the fields, or wheresoever he is, sitting, standing or walking, always let him, with head bent and eyes fixed upon the ground, bethink himself of his sins and imagine that he is arraigned before the dread judgment of God. . . .

When all these steps have been mounted the monk will presently attain to that love of God which is perfect and casts out fear. By means of this love everything which he had observed before not without fear, he shall now begin to do by habit, without any trouble and, as it were, naturally. He acts now not through fear of hell, but for the love of Christ, out of a good habit and a delight in virtue. All this our Lord will vouchsafe to work by the Holy Spirit in his servant, now cleansed from vice and sin. (Benedict, *Rule*, Chapter 7)

19. Monks at Prayer

The prayer life for those Christians who chose to live in monastic communities was different in length and complexity from that of the ordinary Christian. Monks assembled at fixed hours of the day and night to join in reciting and chanting in unison what came to be called the "Divine Office" (what Benedict just referred to as the "Work of God"). Thus life in the Benedictine monastery chiefly comprised manual labor and the monastic liturgy par excellence, the recitation in common of Sacred Scripture, principally the Psalms, in sessions distributed across the day and night hours, so that in the course of a week the entire body of 150 psalms might be completed.

The Prophet says, "Seven times have I sung Your praises" (Ps. 118: 164). This sacred number of seven will be kept by us if we perform the duties of our service in the Hours of Matins [or daybreak], Prime [or full light], Terce [about 9 A.M.], Sext [about noon], None [about 3 P.M.], Vespers or Evensong and Compline. It was of these daytime Hours that the Prophet said, "Seven times a day I have sung Your praises," and of the nighttime vigils [begun about 2 A.M.] the same Prophet says, "At midnight I arose to confess to You" (Ps. 118:62). (Benedict, *Rule*, Chapter 16)

The Divine Office was celebrated in Western and Eastern monasteries with equal fervor. Here Symeon (949–1022 C.E.), surnamed "the New Theologian," a monastic reformer and mystic of the Eastern Church, describes the attitudes toward the Office appropriate to the monk.

Let it be noted that he who has already outwardly laid aside the earthly man with his attitude of mind, and by assuming the monastic habit has clothed himself with the heavenly man (1 Cor. 15:47–49), must rise at midnight before the Night Office and recite the prescribed (individual) prayer. After doing so he must rise with all to go to the service of praise, and with attention and vigilance go through the whole service. He must pay particular attention to the beginning of the hymnody, that is, the six psalms [Psalms 3, 38, and 63, then 88, 103, and 143], the psalm verses (usually chanted at this service) and the lections [that is, readings from the lives of the saints or the writings of the Fathers], with great concentration, without relaxation of body or putting one foot in front of another or leaning on walls or pillars, but holding the hands securely together, the feet equally on the ground, and the head immobile without nodding here and there. The mind must not wander nor the thoughts be occupied with curiosity or interest in the more careless brethren as they talk or whisper to each other. On the contrary the eye and the soul must be kept free from distraction and pay attention to nothing else but to the psalmody and the reading, and, as far as possible, to the meaning of the words of the Divine Scripture that are being sung or read. . . .

Once the morning Office of praise is finished do not, as soon as you have left the (monastery) church, start talking to one man or the other and so be distracted in idle talk. Rather pray in the solitude of your cell, and when you have recited the appointed prayers with tears and great recollection, take on some physical labor and at once go off to perform it. If it is some appointed task, go off to that task; if it is manual labor, go off to it; if it is study, go off to study. Refuse altogether to sit in your cell without some occupation, lest idleness teach you every kind of evil of which one may not even speak. Do not go about the monastery to inspect those who work or perform services, but observe that silence and detachment from all things in which true solitude consists. Take heed of yourself alone and of your manual work, whatever it is. (Symeon, *Discourses* 26: 2–3) [SYMEON NEOTHEOLOGUS 1980: 274–276]

Bonaventure (1221–1271 C.E.), a Franciscan monk, cardinal in the Roman Church and, like Symeon, a considerable mystical theologian, explores in the didactic fashion of the West the motives behind the monastic Divine Office.

The Holy Spirit has commanded the recitation of the Divine Office in the Church for five reasons. The first is to imitate the heavenly choirs. The saints and angels are ceaselessly engaged in singing His praises in the presence of God. "Blessed are they," says the Psalmist, "that dwell in Your house, O Lord; they shall praise You for ever and ever." Christ, according to His promise, "Behold, I am with you all days even to the consummation of the world," deigns to be truly with us here sacramentally as well as spiritually, and so it behooves us to the best of our ability to render Him honor and praise according to the example of the celestial spirits, so that even though we do not praise Him continuously, as those heavenly chanters do, we sing His praises at least from time to time despite our frailty.

The Divine Office has been established in the second place that we might render thanks to God at certain hours, mindful of His blessings and, praying for His grace, from time to time turn to Him, who was born of the Virgin Mary at night, dragged before the Sanhedrin at early morn, arose at daylight, was scourged at the third hour and a little latter (after the third hour) sent the Holy Spirit upon the Apostles, was crucified at the sixth hour, died upon the cross at the ninth, and being at supper in the afternoon gave us the Sacraments and was buried at Compline [that is, in the evening]. . . .

In the third place the Divine Office was established in order that through it we may be continuously incited to devotion and kindled with the love of God, to prevent our indolence and the great number of our occupations make our love grow lukewarm. In the Book of Leviticus the Lord says: "This is the perpetual fire which shall never go out on the altar . . . the priest shall feed it, putting wood on it every day in the morning." This fire is the fervor of devotion, which ought always to burn on the altar of our heart, which the devout priest ought to nourish constantly by putting on it the fuel of divine praises, that it may never be extinguished.

The fourth reason for which the Divine Office was instituted is that through it we may draw the faithful, who might thereby know how to set aside certain hours for prayer, to the practice of devotion, so that they may assemble in church at least when the offices of divine praise are being performed inside, and be less easily distracted when they see the clerics celebrating the Divine Office. . . . Most people would scarcely ever devote themselves to prayer if they were not called to church from worldly occupations at stated times to engage in divine service and listen to the word of God.

The fifth purpose of the Divine Office is to exhibit the beauty of the Christian religion. Jews, Gentiles and heretics from time to time assemble in their churches to celebrate their false rites. It is obviously far more proper and fitting for those who have the true and holy mysteries of the Sacraments to assemble often for the purpose of celebrating and venerating them and performing the solemn service of praise due to the Creator. (Bonaventure, *The Virtues of a Religious Superior* 6:5–9)

20. The Franciscan Spirit — *poverty*

In addition to celibacy and obedience, the other great wellspring of Christian ascet-icism flowing forth from the Egyptian deserts was that of poverty. It had its Gospel proof-texts, to be sure, and the Desert Fathers fervently cultivated the casting off of possessions. But theirs was an essentially private world of seclusion. Where the ideal of poverty was broadcast to society as a whole was in the life and work of Francis of Assisi (d. 1226 C.E.). He attempted, as many holy men before and after him, to convert that vision of spiritual perfection into a formal way of life, which in the Christian tradition meant the creation of a monastic order. This is how it was expressed in the version of the Franciscan Rule of the "Minor Brothers" submitted to and approved by Pope Honorius III in 1223 C.E.

In the name of the Lord thus begins the life of the Minor Brothers [or Friars Minor].

The Rule and Life of the Minor Brothers is this, namely to observe the Gospel of our Lord Jesus Christ, by living in obedience, without property and in chastity. Brother Francis promised obedience and reverence to the Lord Pope Honorius and to his canonically elected successors and to the Roman Church. And let the other brothers be bound to obey Brother Francis and his successors.

If any wish to embrace this life and come to our brothers, let them send them to their provincial ministers, to whom alone and not to others is accorded the power of receiving brothers. But let the ministers diligently examine them regarding the Catholic faith and the Sacraments of the Church. And if they believe all these things, and if they will confess them faithfully, and observe them firmly to the end, and if they have no wives, or, if they have and their wives have already entered a monastery, or have, with the authority of the diocesan bishop, given them permission to do so after having made a vow of continence, and if their wives be of a certain age that no suspicion may arise concerning them, let the ministers say to them the words of the Holy Spirit, that they should go and sell all their goods and strive to distribute them to the poor. If they should not be able to do this, their goodwill suffices. . . .

Afterwards let them give them clothes of probation, to wit, two tunics without a hood and a cord and breeches and a chaperon reaching to the cord. . . . The year of probation being finished, they shall be received to obedience, promising always to observe this life and this rule. . . . And let all the brothers be clothed in poor garments and they may patch them with pieces of sackcloth and other things, with the blessing of God. I exhort and admonish them not to despise and judge men whom they see clothed in fine and showy garments, using dainty meats and drink, but rather let each one judge and despise himself. . . .

I strictly enjoin on all the brothers that in no wise they receive coins or money, either themselves or through a third party. Nevertheless, for the necessities of the sick and for clothing the other brothers, let the ministers and guardians alone take watchful care through spiritual friends, according to places and times and cold climates, as they shall see expedient in the necessity, saving that, as I have said, they receive no coins or money. . . .

The brothers shall appropriate nothing to themselves, neither a house nor a place nor anything. And as pilgrims and strangers in this world, serving the Lord in poverty and humility, let them go confidently in quest of alms, nor ought they be ashamed, because the Lord made himself poor for us in this world. This, my dearest brothers, is the height of the most sublime poverty which has made you heirs and kings of the kingdom of heaven; poor in goods but exalted in virtue. Let that be your portion, for it leads to the land of the living; adhere to it without reservation, my best beloved brothers, for in the name of our Lord Jesus Christ, it never desires to possess anything under heaven. (*Franciscan Rule*)

21. This World and the Next:
The Islamic Preaching

Much in the manner of developed Christianity, the preaching of Islam drew a sharp distinction between this world and its values and that other world that is both the Hereafter and the abode of God.

Know that the life of this world is only a frolic and a mummery, an ornamentation, boasting and bragging among yourselves, and lust for multiplying wealth and children. It is like rain so pleasing to the cultivator for his vegetation which sprouts and swells, and then begins to wither, and you see it turn to yellow and reduced to chaff. There is severe punishment in the Hereafter, but also forgiveness from God and acceptance. As for the life of this world, it is no more than the merchandise of vanity. (Quran 57:20)

Al-Mustawrid ibn Shaddad told that he heard God's Messenger say, "I swear by God that this world in comparison to the world to come is just like one of you putting your finger in the sea. Let him consider what he brings out on it." (Baghawi, *Mishkat al-Masabih* 25.1.1)

Abu Hurayra reported God's Messenger as saying, "The world is the believer's prison and the infidel's Paradise." (Ibid.)

Abu Hurayra reported God's Messenger as saying, "The world is accursed and what it contains is accursed, except remembrance of God and what He likes, a learned man or a learner." (Ibid.)

Ibn Mas'ud told that God's Messenger slept on a reed mat and got up with the marks of it on his body, so Ibn Mas'ud said, "Messenger of God, I wish you would order us to spread something out for you and make something (on which you might rest)." He replied, "What do I have to do with the world? In relation to the world I am just like a rider who shades himself under a tree, and then goes off and leaves it." (Ibid. 25.1.2)

Ibn Umar told that God's Messenger caught hold of him and said, "Be in the world as though you were a stranger and a wayfarer, and reckon yourself to be among the inhabitants of the grave." (Ibid. 25.2.1)

There are echoes too of "Blessed are the poor . . . "

Usama ibn Zayd reported God's Messenger as saying, "I stood at the gate of Paradise, and the majority of those who entered it were poor, the rich being held back, except that those who were to go to Hell were ordered to be sent there. I stood at the gate of Hell, and the majority of those who entered it were women." This tradition is reported by Bukhari and Muslim. (Baghawi, *Mishkat al-Masabih* 25.2.1)

Anas told that the Prophet said: "O God, grant me life as a poor man, cause me to die as a poor man and resurrect me in the company of the poor." Aisha asked him why he said this, and he replied, "Because they will enter Paradise forty years before the rich. Do not turn away a poor man, Aisha, even if all you can give him is half a date. If you love the poor and bring them near you, Aisha, God will bring you near Him on the day of resurrection." (Ibid. 25.2.2)

Amr ibn al-Awf reported God's Messenger as saying, "I swear by God that it is not poverty I fear for you, but I fear that worldly goods may be given to you as lavishly as they were to your (pagan) ancestors, that you may vie with with one another in desiring them as they did, and that they may destroy you as they destroyed them." (Ibid. 25.1.1)

A belief in this Other World of God meant of course embracing its values. The classical collections of Prophetic traditions are filled with reported sayings of the Prophet on the virtues of prayer and fasting, not merely the canonically prescribed prayers and the equally obligatory fast of Ramadan, but the supererogatory performance of these spiritual exercises, though with cautious awareness that any practice attributed to the Prophet might be construed as a precedent for an additional obligation upon all Muslims.

Abu Hurayra and Abu Sa'id reported God's Messenger as saying, "People will not sit remembering God without angels surrounding them, mercy covering them, peace descending upon them, and God mentioning them among those who are with Him." (Baghawi, *Mishkat al-Masibih* 9.2.1)

Abu al-Darda reported God's Messenger as saying, "Would you like me to tell you the best and purest of your deeds in the estimation of your King, those which raise your degrees highest, those which are better for you than spending gold and silver, and better for you than that you should meet your enemy and cut off one another's head?" On receiving a reply in the affirmative, he said, "It is remembering God." (Ibid. 9.2.2)

Abdullah ibn Busr told of a desert Arab coming to the Prophet and asking who was the best among men, to which he replied, "Happy is he whose life is long and whose deeds are good." He asked God's Messenger what deed was most excellent, and he replied, "That you should leave the world with the mention of God fresh on your tongue." (Ibid.)

Abu Sa'id said God's Messenger was asked who would be the most excellent and most exalted in degree in God's estimation on the day of resurrection, and he replied, "The men and women who make frequent mention of God." He was asked if they would be superior even to the man who had fought in the path of God, and he replied, "Even though he plied his sword among infidels and polytheists till it was broken and smeared with blood, the one who made mention of God would have a more excellent degree than he." (Ibid. 9.2.3)

Abdullah ibn Shaqiq said than when he asked Aisha whether the Prophet used to fast the whole month of Ramadan, she replied, "I never knew him to fast a whole month except Ramadan, or to refrain from fasting some part of every month until he died." (Ibid. 7.7.1)

Aisha said that God's Messenger used to fast on Mondays and Thursdays. Abu Hurayra reported God's Messenger as saying, "Men's deeds are presented to God on Mondays and Thursdays, and I like mine to be presented when I am fasting." (Ibid. 7.7.2)

Abu Hurayra reported God's Messenger as saying, "There is an almsgiving that is applicable to everything, and the almsgiving of the body is fasting." (Ibid. 7.7.3)

22. The Catholic Tradition in Asceticism

True to its heritage as a "successor" religion to Judaism and Christianity, Islam entered early and easily into the "catholic" tradition of asceticism, as that was understood in the eighth century C.E. The authority cited here is Hasan al-Basri (d. 728), of the generation immediately following the Prophet and one of the founding fathers of the movement that was already being called "Sufism" in his day.

This world has neither worth nor weight with God; so slight is it, it weighs not with God so much as a pebble or a clod of earth. As I am told, God has created nothing more hateful to him than this world, and from the day He created it He has not looked upon it, so much He hates it. It was offered to our Prophet with all its keys and treasures . . . but he refused to accept it; and nothing prevented him from accepting it—for there is naught that can lessen him in God's sight—but that he knew God hated a thing and therefore he hated it. . . .

. . . As for Muhammad, he bound a stone upon his belly when he was hungry; and as for Moses, the skin of his belly showed as green as grass because of it all: he asked naught of God, the day he took refuge in the shade, save food to eat when he was hungry, and it is said of him in the

stories that God revealed to him, "Moses, when you see poverty approaching you, say, Welcome to the badge of the righteous! And when
you see wealth approaching, say, Behold! A sin whose punishment has
been put on aforetime."

*The next ascetic exemplar adduced by Hasan is Jesus, though there is no other record
of the saying attributed to him here.*

If you should so wish, you might name as a third the Lord of the
Word and the Spirit [that is, Jesus], for in his case there is a marvel. He
used to say, "My daily bread is hunger, my badge is fear, my raiment is
wool, my mount is my foot, my lantern at night is the moon, my fire by
day is the sun, and my fruit and fragrant herbs are such things as the earth
brings forth for the wild beast and cattle. All the night I have nothing and
yet there is none richer than I!"

And if you should so wish, you might name as a fourth instance
David, who was no less wonderful than these others: he ate barley bread
in his chamber and fed his family upon bran meal, but his people on fine
grain. And when it was night, he clad himself in sackcloth, and chained
his hand to his neck, and wept until dawn; eating coarse food and wearing
robes of hair.

All these men hated what God hates, and despised what God de-
spises; then the righteous thereafter followed in their path and kept close
to their tracks. (Abu Nu'aym, *The Ornaments of the Saints* 2:134–140)

[Cited by ARBERRY 1950: 34–35]

*The same broad Judeo-Christian horizons are apparent in the formation of the
Baghdad master Junayd (d. 910 C.E.) when he attempts to explain what Sufism is.*

Sufism is founded on eight qualities exemplified in eight apostles: the
generosity of Abraham, who sacrificed his son; Ishmael, who submitted
to the command of God and gave up his dear life; the patience of Job, who
patiently endured the affliction of worms and the jealousy of the Merciful; the symbolism of Zachariah [that is, the father of John the Baptist],
to whom God said: "Thou shall not speak to men for three days save
by signs" (Quran 3:36); and again to the same effect: "When he called
upon his Lord with a secret invocation" (Quran 19:2); the strangerhood
of John (the Baptist), who was a stranger in his own country and an alien
to his own kind among whom he lived; the pilgrimhood of Jesus, who
was so detached from worldly things that he kept only a cup and a
comb—the cup he threw away when he saw a man drinking in the palms
of his hand, and the comb likewise when he saw another man using his
fingers instead of a comb; the wearing of wool by Moses, whose garment

was woolen; and the poverty of Muhammad, to whom God Almighty sent the key of all treasures that are upon the face of the earth, saying, "Lay no trouble on yourself, but procure every luxury by means of these treasures," and he answered, "O Lord, I desire them not; keep me one day full fed and one day hungry." (Junayd, *Treatise*)

[Cited in HUJWIRI 1911: 39–40]

23. The Historical Origins of Sufism

Many of the early names to which the title of "Sufi" is attached in Muslim hagiography are little more than that, names alone. Hasan al-Basri is a firmly historical witness, however, and he stands close to the top of the page in every attempt, medieval and modern, to get back to the beginnings of the spiritual discipline that the Muslims call Sufism. And so he appears in the work of the Spanish philosopher-historian Ibn Khaldun (d. 1406 C.E.), who provides in his Prolegomenon to History *a schematic view of the origins of Sufism.*

The Science of Sufism. This science belongs to the sciences of religious law that originated in Islam. Sufism is based on the assumption that the method of those people (who later came to be called Sufis) had always been considered by the important early Muslims, the men around Muhammad and the men of the second generation, as well as those who came after them, as the path of true and right guidance. Their approach is based upon constant application to divine worship, complete devotion to God, aversion to the false splendor of the world, abstinence from pleasure, property and position to which the great mass aspires, and retirement from the world into solitude for divine worship. These things were general among the men around Muhammad and the early Muslims. (Ibn Khaldun, *Muqaddima* 6.10) [IBN KHALDUN 1967: 3:76]

The habit of a simple and unworldly life, if not actually the practice of what a later generation understood as asceticism, was traced back, then, to the earliest generation of Muslims, and even to the most eminent and powerful of them, as this account by the early Sufi author al-Kharraz (d. 890 C.E.) illustrates.

When Abu Bakr [Caliph, 632–634 C.E.] succeeded to the leadership, and the world in its entirety came to him in abasement, he did not lift up his head on that account, or make any pretensions; he wore a single garment, which he used to pin together, so that he was known as "the man of the two pins." Umar ibn al-Khattab [Caliph, 634–644 C.E.], who also ruled the world in its entirety, lived on bread and olive oil; his clothes were patched in a dozen places, some of the patches being of leather; yet there were opened to him the treasures of Khusraw and Caesar. As for Uthman [Caliph, 644–656 C.E.], he was like one of his slaves in appearance; of him it is related that he was seen coming out of one of the gardens with a faggot of firewood on his shoulders, and when questioned on the matter, he said, "I wanted to see whether my soul would refuse." Ali [Caliph, 656–661 C.E.] bought a waistband for four dirhams and a shirt for five dirhams; finding the sleeve of his garment too long, he went to a cobbler and taking his knife, he cut off the sleeve level with the tips of his fingers; yet this same man divided the world right and left. (Kharraz, *The Book of Truthfulness*) [Cited by ARBERRY 1950: 32]

It was at that point, at the death of Ali and the accession of the dynasty called the Umayyads, that there occurred a turning in the spiritual direction of Islam, according to what later became a commonly held view of the history of the community. Ibn Khaldun resumes.

Then worldly aspirations increased in the second century [that is, the eighth century C.E.] and after. People now inclined toward worldly affairs. At that time, the special name of "Sufis" was given to those who aspired to divine worship. . . . The most obvious etymology (of the term *Sufi*), if one uses one, is that which connects the word with *al-suf*, because Sufis as a rule were characterized by the fact that they wore woolen garments. They were opposed to people wearing gorgeous garments, and, therefore, they chose to wear wool.

Ibn Khaldun then passes to the transition within the still young Sufi movement from asceticism to mysticism, the latter here characterized by its possession of a "particular kind of perception."

The Sufis came to represent asceticism, retirement from the world and devotion to divine worship. Then, they developed a particular kind of perception which comes about through ecstatic experience. This comes about as follows. Man, as man, is distinguished from all the other animals by his ability to perceive. His perception is of two kinds. He can perceive sciences and matters of knowledge, and these may be certain, hypothetical, doubtful or imaginary. Also, he can perceive "states" persisting in himself, such as joy and grief, anxiety and relaxation, satisfaction, anger, patience, gratefulness and similar things. (Ibn Khaldun, *Muqaddima* 6.16) [IBN KHALDUN 1967: 3:76–78]

These "states" of self-awareness represent stages in the Sufi's training, as we shall see, and lead eventually to the mystical experience. All of this had been worked out in great detail by Ibn Khaldun's day. But the road to that point was a long one;

the Sufi had to make a place for himself in the Islamic experience, a process that was accompanied by opposition, rejection, suffering, and even on occasion death.

24. Conversions and Affirmations

By all accounts the earliest Muslims to bear the name "Sufi" were ascetics: Muslims whose rejection of "this world" bore all the signs of a religious conversion. Such was certainly the case for the early and much celebrated holy man Ibrahim ibn Adham, a prince of Balkh in eastern Iran who died sometime about 777 C.E.

My father was of Balkh, Ibrahim ibn Adham is reported to have said, and he was one of the kings of Khurasan. He was a man of wealth and taught me to love hunting. One day I was out riding with my dog, when a hare or a fox started. I spurred on my horse; then I heard a voice behind me saying, "It was not for this that you were created. It was not this you were charged to do." I stopped and looked right and left, but I saw no one; and I said, "God curse the devil!" Then I spurred on my horse again; and I heard a voice clearer than before, "O Ibrahim! It was not for this that you were created; it was not this you were charged to do." I stopped once more and looked right and left, but still I saw no one. And I repeated, "God curse the devil!" Then I spurred on my horse once again; and I heard a voice from the bow of my saddle, "O Ibrahim, it was not for this that you were created. It was not this that you were charged to do." I stopped and said, "I have been roused! I have been roused! A warning has come to me from the Lord of the Worlds. Truly, I will not disobey God from this day on, so long as the Lord shall preserve me." Then I returned to my people, and abandoned my horse. I came to one of my father's shepherds, and took his robe and cloak, and put my raiment upon him. Then I went toward Iraq, wandering from land to land. (Abu Nuᶜaym, *The Ornaments of the Saints* 7:368) [Cited by ARBERRY 1950: 36]

Or, in the manner of the holy in every religion, the saint is marked as such from birth. The following is told, with an interesting prologue, of Rabiᶜa, a famous holy woman of Basra in Iraq who died in 752 or 801 C.E.

If anyone asks, "Why have you included Rabiᶜa in the rank of men?" my answer is that the Prophet himself said, "God does not regard your outward forms." The root of the matter is not form, but intention, as the Prophet said, "Mankind will be raised up according to their intentions." Moreover, if it is proper to derive two-thirds of our religion from Aisha [referring to the great bulk of Prophetic traditions reported on the authority of the Prophet's wife Aisha], surely it is permissible to take religious instruction from a handmaiden of Aisha. When a woman becomes a "man" in the path of God, she is a man and one cannot any more call her a woman.

The night when Rabi'a came to earth, there was nothing whatsoever in her father's house; for her father lived in very poor circumstances. He did not possess even one drop of oil to anoint her navel; there was no lamp, and not a rag to swaddle her in. He already had three daughters, and Rabi'a was his fourth, which is why she was called Rabi'a, "the fourth."

"Go to our neighbor So and So and beg him for a drop of oil so I can light the lamp," his wife said to him. Now the man had entered into a covenant that he would never ask any mortal for anything. . . . The poor woman wept bitterly. In that anxious state the man placed his head on his knees and went to sleep. He dreamed that he saw the Prophet.

"Be not sorrowful," the Prophet bade him. "The girl child who has just come to earth is a queen among women, who shall be the intercessor for seventy thousand of my community." . . .

When Rabi'a had become a little older, and her mother and father were dead, a famine came upon Basra, and her sisters were scattered. Rabi'a ventured out and was seen by a wicked man who seized her and sold her for six dirhams. Her purchaser put her to hard labor.

One day as she was passing along the road a stranger approached her. She fled and, as she ran, she fell headlong and her hand was dislocated. "Lord God," she cried, bowing her face to the ground, "I am a stranger, orphaned of mother and father, a helpless prisoner fallen into captivity, my hand broken. Yet for all this I do not grieve; all I need is Your good pleasure, to know whether You are well pleased or not." "Do not grieve," she heard a voice say. "Tomorrow a station will be yours such that the cherubim in heaven will envy you."

So Rabi'a returned to her master's house. By day she continually fasted and by night she worshiped standing until day.

Her owner one night sees Rabi'a at her prayers, a lantern suspended without chain above her head, and whose light fills the house. He is moved and chastened and gives her her freedom.

She left the house and went into the desert. From the desert she proceeded to a hermitage where she served God for a while. Then she determined to perform the pilgrimage and set her face toward the desert (road from Basra to Mecca). She bound her bundle of possessions on a donkey. In the middle of the desert her donkey died. . . . "O God," she cried, lifting her head, "do kings so treat the powerless? You have invited me to Your House, then in the midst of the way, You have suffered my donkey to die, leaving me alone in the desert."

Hardly had she completed her prayer when her donkey stirred and rose up. Rabiʿa placed her load on its back and continued on her way. . . . She traveled on through the desert for some days, then she halted. "O God," she cried, "my heart is weary. Where am I going? I am a lump of clay and Your house is a stone! I need You here."

God spoke unmediated in her heart. "Rabiʿa, you are traveling in the lifeblood of eighteen thousand worlds. Have you not seen how Moses prayed for the vision of Me? And I cast a few motes of revelation upon the mountain, and the mountain shivered into forty pieces. Be content here in My name!" (Attar, *Recollections of the Saints* 1:73)

[ATTAR 1966: 40–43]

25. Ibn Khaldun Analyzes the Sufi Experience

The long process of experience and meditation upon that experience that constituted the beginnings of the Sufi path in Islam is largely concealed from our eyes. But, as occurred in Christianity, the "path" eventually became a broad and well-posted highway whose every turning had been charted by those who had gone before. That much is readily apparent in Ibn Khaldun's systematic and highly rationalized treatment.

Knowledge originates from evidence, grief and joy from the perception of what is painful or pleasurable, energy from rest, inertia from being tired. In the same way, the exertion and worship of the Sufi novice must lead to a "state" which is the result of his exertion. That "state" may be a kind of divine worship. Then it will be firmly rooted in the Sufi novice and become a "station" for him. Or, it may not be divine worship, but merely an attribute affecting the soul, such as joy or gladness, energy or inertia, or something else.

The "stations" form an ascending order. The Sufi novice continues to progress from station to station, until he reaches the (recognition of the) Oneness of God and the gnosis which is the desired goal of happiness. Muhammad says: "Whoever dies confessing that there is no god but the God, enters Paradise."

"Gnosis," a special intuitive understanding that differs radically from ordinary reflective knowledge, is the heart of the mystic's experience, as we shall observe in Chapter 4 below. It is the end of the quest. Ibn Khaldun returns to the novice standing at the very beginning.

Thus the novice must progress by such stages. The basis of them all is obedience and sincerity. Faith precedes and accompanies them all. Their result and fruit are states and attributes. They lead to others, and again to others, up to the station of the (recognition of the) Oneness of God and of gnosis. If the result [that is, the "state"] shows some shortcoming or defect, one can be sure that it came from some shortcoming that existed in the previous stage. The same applies to the ideas of the soul and inspirations of the heart.

The hallmark of Sufism is, according to Ibn Khaldun, the practice of self-scrutiny.

The novice therefore must scrutinize himself in all his actions and study their concealed import, because the results of necessity originate from actions, and shortcomings in the results thus originate from defects in the actions. The Sufi novice finds out about that through his mystical experience, and he scrutinizes himself as to its reasons. Very few people share the self-scrutiny of the Sufis, for negligence in this respect is almost universal. Pious people who do not get that far perform, at best, acts of obedience freed from the juridical study of how to be satisfactory and conforming. The Sufis, however, investigate the results of the acts of obedience with the help of mystical and ecstatic experience in order to learn whether they are free from deficiency or not. Thus it is evident that the Sufis' path in its entirety depends upon self-scrutiny with regard to what they do or do not do, and upon discussion of the various kinds of mystical and ecstatic experience that result from their exertions. This, then, crystallizes for the Sufi novice in a "station." From that station he can proceed to another, higher one. (Ibn Khaldun, *Muqaddima* 6.16)

[IBN KHALDUN 1967: 3:78–79]

26. A Quick Sketch of the Sufi Tradition

None of this analysis is original to Ibn Khaldun. By the time he was writing his Prolegomenon in 1377 there was already an extensive body of Sufi literature, much of it highly theoretical in nature. Indeed, Sufism constituted a well-defined discipline with its own somewhat ambivalent place in the hierarchy of Muslim religious disciplines, as Ibn Khaldun explains.

Thus the Sufis had their special discipline, which is not discussed by other representatives of the religious law. As a consequence, the science of the religious law came to consist of two kinds. One is the special field of jurists and muftis. It is concerned with the general laws governing the acts of divine worship, customary action and mutual dealings. The other is the special field of the "people" [that is, the Sufis]. It is concerned with pious exertion, self-scrutiny with regard to it, discussion of the different kinds of mystical and ecstatic experience occurring in the course of it, the mode of ascent from one mystical experience to another, and the interpretation of the technical terminology of mysticism in use among them.

When the sciences were written down systematically, and when the jurisprudents wrote works on jurisprudence and the principles of jurisprudence, on speculative theology, Quran interpretation and other subjects, the Sufis too wrote on their subject. Some Sufis wrote on the laws governing asceticism and self-scrutiny, how to act and not act in imitation of model (saints). That was done by Muhasibi [ca. 781–825 C.E.] in his *Consideration of the Truths of God*. Other Sufi authors wrote on the behavior of Sufis and their different kinds of mystical and ecstatic experiences in the "states." Al-Qushayri [986–1072 C.E.] in his *Letter* and Suhrawardi [1145–1234 C.E.] in his *Connoisseurs of Wisdom*, as well as others, did this. Al-Ghazali combined the two matters in his book called *The Revivification*. In it he dealt systematically with the laws governing asceticism and the imitation of models. Then he explained the behavior and customs of the Sufis and commented on their technical vocabulary. (Ibn Khaldun, *Muqaddima* 6.16) [IBN KHALDUN 1967: 3:79–80]

27. Two Sufi Autobiographies

All these authors regarded by Ibn Khaldun as critical in the formulation of the canons of Sufism are known to us, and one could easily compose a history of Sufism, particularly of its more moderate type, from their theoretical writings on the subject. Let us turn instead to personal statements by two very different men who experienced the Sufi life and left us their recollections: Abu Saʿid ibn Abi al-Khayr (967–1049 C.E.) and al-Ghazali (d. 1111 C.E.).

Whatever else it might eventually become, Sufism began, and to some extent always remained, an exercise in the same kind of self-restraint and even self-chastisement that was present in the early Christian tradition. The annals of Christianity, particularly as that faith was understood and practiced in Syria, are filled with tales of the most extraordinarily severe asceticism. Although Islamic piety rarely indulged in such extremes of self-abasement, physical and psychological severity were not entirely alien to it, as witnessed by this account of the early days of Abu Saʿid ibn Abi al-Khayr. The narrator at the outset is his father, who was curious about the doings of his son and one night followed him.

My son walked on till he reached the Old Cloister. He entered it and shut the gate behind him, while I went up on the roof. I saw him go into a chapel which was in the convent and close the door. Looking through the chapel window, I waited to see what would happen. There was a stick lying on the floor, and it had a rope fastened to it. He took up the stick and tied the end of the rope to his foot. Then, laying the stick across the top of a pit that was in a corner of the chapel, he slung himself head downwards, and began to recite the Quran. He remained in that posture until daybreak, when, having recited the whole Quran, he raised himself from the pit, replaced the stick where he found it, opened the door, came out from the chapel, and commenced to perform his ablution in the middle of the convent. I descended from the roof, hastened home and slept till he came in. (Abu Sa'id, *The Secrets of Oneness* 32:4)

[Cited by NICHOLSON 1921: 13–14]

Here Abu Sa'id himself explains his manner of life in those earliest days of his career as a Sufi, and incidentally provides an explanation of why he recited the Quran hanging upside down.

When I was a novice, I bound myself to do eighteen things: I fasted continually; I abstained from unlawful food; I practiced recollection of the name of God uninterruptedly; I kept awake at night; I never reclined on the ground; I never slept but in a sitting posture; I always sat facing the Ka'ba; I never leaned against anything; I never looked at a handsome youth or a woman whom it would have been unlawful for me to see unveiled; I did not beg; I was content and resigned to God's will; I always sat in the mosque and did not go into the market because the Prophet said that the market is the filthiest of places and the mosque the cleanest. In all my acts I was a follower of the Prophet. Every twenty-four hours I completed a recitation of the Quran.

In my seeing I was blind, in my hearing deaf, in my speaking dumb. For a whole year I conversed with no one. People called me a lunatic, and I allowed them to give me that name, relying on the Tradition that a man's faith is not made perfect until he is supposed to be mad. I performed everything I had read or heard of as having been done or commended by the Prophet. Having read that when he was wounded in the foot at the battle of Uhud, he stood on his toes in order to perform his devotions—for he could not set the sole of his foot on the ground—I resolved to imitate him, and standing on tiptoe I performed a prayer of forty genuflections. I modeled my actions, outward and inward, upon the Custom of the Prophet, so that habit at last became nature.

Whatever I heard or found in books concerning the acts of worship performed by the angels, I performed the same. I had heard and seen in

writing that some angels worship God on their heads. Therefore I placed
my head on the ground and bade the blessed mother of Abu Tahir tie my
toe with a cord and fasten the cord to a peg and then shut the door
behind her. Being left alone, I said "O Lord! I do not want myself; let me
escape from myself!" and I began a recitation of the entire Quran. When
I came to the verse, "God shall suffice you against them, for He hears and
knows all" (Quran 2:131), blood poured from my eyes and I was no
longer conscious of myself.

*At that point began Abu Saʿid's conversion from mere asceticism to the life of a
mystic saint. As he himself tells us, what had previously been simply his efforts were
now transformed into God's spiritual gifts, the "graces" and "blessings" with which
Sufi literature is filled.*

Then things changed. Ascetic experiences passed over me of a kind
that cannot be described in words, and God strengthened and aided me
therein, but I had fancied that all these acts were done by me. The grace
of God became manifest and showed me this was not so, and that these
acts were acts of divine favor and grace. I repented of my belief and
realized that it was mere self-conceit. Now if you say that you will not
tread this path because it is self-conceit, I reply that your refusal to tread
it is likewise self-conceit, and until you undergo all this, its self-conceit
will not be revealed to you. Self-conceit appears only when you fulfill the
Law, for self-conceit lies in religion and religion is of the Law. To refrain
from religious acts is unbelief, but to perform such acts self consciously
is dualism, because if "you" exists and "He" exists, then two exist, and
that is dualism. You must put your self away altogether.

I had a cell in which I sat, and sitting there I was enamored of passing
away from myself. A light flashed upon me, which utterly destroyed the
darkness of my being. God Almighty revealed to me that I was neither
that nor this: that this was His grace even as that was His gift.

*Abu Saʿid was well aware of the sudden adulation that accompanied Sufi "celeb-
rity" in medieval Islam, and the equally swift reversal to which all such celebrity is
subject.*

Then the people began to regard me with great approval. Disciples
gathered round me and converted to Sufism. My neighbors too showed
their respect for me by ceasing to drink wine. This proceeded so far that
a melon skin I had thrown away was bought for twenty pieces of gold.
One day when I was riding on horseback, my horse dropped dung. Eager
to gain a blessing, the people came and picked up the dung and smeared
their head and faces with it.

After a time it was revealed to me that I was not the real object of their veneration. A voice cried from the corner of the mosque, "Is not your Lord enough for you?" (Quran 41:53). A light gleamed in my breast and most veils were removed. The people who had honored me now rejected me, and even went before the judge to bear witness that I was an infidel. The inhabitants of every place that I entered declared that their crops would not grow on account of my wickedness. Once, while I was seated in a mosque, a woman went up on to the roof and bespattered me with filth; and still I heard a voice saying, "Is not your Lord enough for you?" The congregation desisted from their prayers, saying, "We will not pray together so long as this madman is in the mosque." . . .

This joyous transport was followed by a painful contraction of spirit. I opened the Quran and my eye fell on the verse, "We will prove you with evil and with good, to try you; and to Us shall you return" (Quran 21:36), as though God said to me, "All this which I put in your way is a trial. If it is good, it is a trial, and if it is evil, it is a trial. Do not stoop to good or to evil but swell in Me!" Once more my self vanished and His grace was all in all. (Abu Saʿid, *The Secrets of Oneness* 37:8)

[Cited by NICHOLSON 1921: 15–17]

What affected people's attitude toward Ibn Abi al-Khayr were changes in his external behavior. From a severe asceticism, he turned to what appeared to be a profligate life style, complete with luxurious feasts and splendid entertainments filled with song and dance (see Chapter 4 below). The turnabout caused another ambitious but somewhat naive Sufi to think that perhaps the famous Abu Saʿid had been overrated, a serious miscalculation. He approached the Master.

O Shaykh, (he said) I have come in order to challenge you to a forty days' fast. The poor man was ignorant of the Shaykh's novitiate and of his forty years of austerities: he fancied that the Shaykh had always lived in this same manner. He thought to himself, "I will chasten him with hunger and put him to shame in the eyes of the people, and I shall be the object of their regard." On hearing this challenge, the Shaykh said, "May it be blessed!" and spread his prayer rug. His adversary did the like, and they both sat down side by side.

While the ascetic, in accordance with the practice of those who keep a fast of forty days, was eating a certain amount of food, the Shaykh Abu Saʿid ate nothing; and though he never once broke his fast, every morning he was stronger and fatter and his complexion grew more and more ruddy. All the time, by his orders and under his eyes, his dervishes feasted luxuriously and indulged in spiritual concerts, and he himself danced with them. His state was not changed for the worse in any respect. The ascetic, on the other hand, was daily becoming feebler and thinner and paler, and the sight of the delicious viands which were served to the Sufis in his presence worked more and more upon him. At length he grew so weak that he could scarcely rise to perform the obligatory prayers. He repented of his presumption and confessed his ignorance.

When the forty days were finished the Shaykh Abu Sa'id said, "I have complied with your request: now you must do as I say." The ascetic acknowledged this and said, "It is for the Shaykh to command." Abu Sa'id said, "We have sat for forty days and eaten nothing and gone to the privy; now let us sit another forty and eat nothing but never go to the privy." His adversary had no choice but to accept the challenge, though he thought to himself that it was impossible for any human to do such a thing. (Abu Sa'id, *The Secrets of Oneness* 160:18) [Cited by NICHOLSON 1921: 71–72]

The man ended, of course, by becoming the disciple of Abu Sa'id ibn Abi al-Khayr.

Ghazali, whose distinguished intellectual career spanned philosophy, theology, and law, was a Sufi as well, and it was chiefly his moderate and sympathetic writing on the subject of Sufism that made the Islamic world a safer place for the sometimes extravagant likes of Ibn Abi al-Khayr. In addition to the extended treatment of Sufism in his Revivification of the Sciences of Religion, *Ghazali gives a personal but still highly schematic and intellectualized sketch of his own search for certitude in the autobiographical* Deliverer from Error. *After experimenting with the other disciplines, Ghazali tells us, he came at length to Sufism.*

When I had finished with those sciences, I next turned with set purpose to the method of Sufism. I knew the complete mystic "way" includes both intellectual belief and practical activity; the latter consists of getting rid of obstacles in the self and stripping off its base characteristics and vicious morals, so that the heart may attain to freedom from what is not God and to constant recollection of Him.

Ghazali, ever the intellectual, begins by reading the Sufi classics.

. . . I thus comprehended their fundamental teachings on the intellectual side, and progressed, as far as is possible by study and oral instruction, in the knowledge of Sufism. It became clear to me, however, that what is most distinctive of Sufism is something which cannot be apprehended by study, but only by tasting, by ecstasy and by moral change. . . . From the sciences I had labored at and the paths I had traversed in my investigation of the revelational and revealed sciences, there had come to me a sure faith in God Most High, in prophethood and the Last Day. These three credal principles were firmly rooted in my being, not through any carefully argued proofs, but by reason of various causes, coincidences and experiences which are not capable of being stated in detail.

It has already become clear to me that I had no hope of the bliss of the world to come save through a God-fearing life and the withdrawal of myself from vain desire. It was clear to me too that the key to all this was to sever the attachment of the heart to worldly things by leaving the mansion of deception and returning to that of eternity.

Next Ghazali, the distinguished professor on the faculty of Islamic law at the university of Baghdad, takes stock of his life.

I considered the circumstances of my life, and realized that I was caught in a veritable thicket of attachments. I also considered my activities, of which the best was my teaching and lecturing, and realized that in them I was dealing with sciences that were unimportant and contributed nothing to the attainment of eternal life. After that I examined my motive in my work of teaching, and realized that it was not a pure desire for the things of God, but that the impulse moving me was the desire for an influential position and public recognition. I saw for certain that I was on the brink of a crumbling bank of sand and in imminent danger of hell fire unless I set about to mend my ways. . . .

For nearly six months beginning in July 1095 I was continuously tossed about between the attractions of worldly desires and the impulses toward eternal life. In that month the matter ceased to be one of choice and became one of compulsion. God caused my tongue to dry up so that I was prevented from lecturing. One particular day I would make an effort to lecture to gratify the hearts of my following, but my tongue would not utter a single word nor could I accomplish anything at all.

Now in the full grip of spiritual impotence, Ghazali quits Baghdad, his family, and his post there and disappears into a ten-year seclusion, some of it spent in Jerusalem, some on pilgrimage to Mecca, and two years on spiritual retreat in Damascus.

In due course I entered Damascus and there I remained for nearly two years with no other occupation than the cultivation of retirement and solitude, together with religious and ascetic exercises, as I busied myself purifying my soul, improving my character and cleansing my heart for the constant recollection of God Most High, as I had learnt from my study of Sufism. I used to go into retreat for a period in the mosque of Damascus, going up the minaret of the mosque for the whole day and shutting myself in so as to be alone. . . .

I continued at this stage for the space of ten years, and during these periods of solitude there were revealed to me things innumerable and unfathomable. This much I shall say about that in order that others may be helped: I learnt with certainty that it is above all the Sufis who walk on the road of God; their life is the best life, their method the soundest method, their character the purest character; indeed, were the intellect of the intellectuals and the learning of the learned and the scholarship of the scholars, who are versed in the profundity of revealed truth, brought together in the attempt to improve the life and character of the Sufis, they would find no way of doing so; for to the Sufis all movement and all rest, whether external or internal, brings illumination from the lamp of pro- phetic revelation; and behind the light of prophetic revelation there is no other light on the face of the earth from which illumination may be received. (Ghazali, *Deliverer* 122–132) [GHAZALI 1953: 54–60]

28. "No Monasticism in Islam"

Christian monks in the Near East were to some extent characterized by their association with a woolen cloak—their version of the "religious habit" of Western Christendom—an association that at least suggests that "Sufism" owed more than a passing resemblance to Christian monastic practices on the Syrian steppe. Monks and monasticism are in fact mentioned in the Quran. In two of the citations it is not so much a question of the institution of monasticism as of praise for monks who "are not proud" (5:82) or the condemnation of those Christian monks "who devour the wealth of mankind wantonly" or "hoard up gold and silver and spend it not in the way of God" (9:34). If this were the end of it, one would assume that Muham- mad neither admired nor condemned Christian monasticism as such. But there is another, somewhat longer passage on the subject that is far more problematic. It occurs in the midst of the now familiar history of God's revelation.

We sent Noah and Abraham, and We gave prophethood to their progeny and the Book, and some of them were well-directed, but many of them were disobedient. Then in their train We sent Our apostles, and succeeding them Jesus, son of Mary, and gave him the Gospel, and put into the hearts of his followers and caused Our messengers," God de- clares, "to follow in their [that is, Noah and Abraham and their seed] footsteps; and We caused Jesus, son of Mary, to follow, and gave him the Gospel, and in the hearts of those who followed him We placed compas- sion and kindness. And monasticism, they created it, which had not been prescribed for them by Us except for seeking the pleasure of God; yet they did not observe it as it should have been rightly observed. (Quran 57:27)

"And monasticism. . . ." The meaning, and so the translation, of this bit of the verse is by no means certain. Is "monasticism" in parallel with "compassion and kindness," a virtuous practice begun by the Christians of their own volition, or is "monasticism" contrasted with what immediately precedes, a blameworthy human innovation? In Arabic the verse yields both meanings, and its inherent ambiguity is reflected in early Muslim comments upon it, as in this example from Muhasibi (d. 837 C.E.).

God blamed those among the Israelites [that is, the Christians] who, having instituted the monastic life to which He had not previously obliged them, did not observe it in an exact fashion. And He said, "this monastic life which they instituted; We ordained it not for them." . . .

There is disagreement on this verse. Mujahid interprets it as "We have not ordained it for them only to make them desire to conform themselves to the divine pleasure," that is to say, "We have prescribed it. . . . God placed in them, for their own good, the seeds of the monastic life, and then reprimanded them for abandoning it." But Abu Imama al-Bahili and others comment upon it as follows: "We have not prescribed, that is to say, it was not We who ordained this. They instituted it only to please God and even so God blamed them for abandoning it." This latter opinion is the more probable and one which embraces most of the scholars of the community. [MASSIGNON 1968: 149]

We cannot say which in fact is the more probable interpretation. Muhasibi is certainly correct in maintaining that the reading of the verse in a pejorative sense, namely that monasticism is a Christian innovation, unrequired, even undesired, by God, became the common interpretation of this verse among Muslims. It is no surprise, then, that there soon began to circulate a tradition on the subject attributed to Muhammad himself. "No monasticism in Islam," the Prophet is reported to have said.

29. Monks and Sufis

There was in fact no monasticism in Islam, not in the Christian sense of individuals or groups removing themselves from the world and society and living under perpetual vows of poverty, chastity, and obedience. But the spirituality of Muslims and Christians often took parallel paths, and both the similarities and differences appear in this advice given to an aspiring Sufi novice by one of the great masters, Ibn al-Arabi (1164–1240 C.E.) of Murcia.

Among the things you must possess, my brother, is (the grace) not to live at the expense of other people, to be a burden to no one, to accept no support from man either for yourself or anyone else, but to practice your own trade and be abstemious in the matter of your living expenses. (Exercise restraint) also in your words and glances on all occasions, whether you are moving about or are stationary. Be not extravagant in matters of housing or dress or food, for what is lawful (therein) is but little and leaves no room for lavishness. . . .

Among the things you must possess, my friend, is (the grace of doing with but) little food, for (abstinence) in this and cheerfulness in obedience drives away laziness. You must be careful to apportion out your time by day and by night. As for the hours when the religious law summons you to stand before God, they are the five prayer periods for the canonical prayers. But beyond them are the other times consecrated by the custom of the Prophet. So if you are a craftsman, labor diligently to make enough in one day to provide your needs for several days. If you are a business-man, do not hasten away from your place of prayer after the dawn prayer until the sun has risen, nor after the afternoon prayer until the sun has set. . . . Do not sleep until you are quite overcome by slumber. Do not eat save what is needful, nor dress save as is necessary to guard against heat and cold, with the intention of covering the genitals and removing a peremptory impediment to the worship of God. . . .

Among the things you must possess is (the grace of) having an ac-counting with yourself, a seasonable examination of your innermost thoughts, putting a shamefacedness before God as the raiment on your heart, for if you possess a true feeling of shame before God you will prevent your heart from harboring fancies which God would find blame-worthy, or from being moved by emotions with which God Most High would not be pleased. We ourselves used formerly to have a master who was accustomed to record his emotional states during the day in a book that he had, and when night came he would set the pages in front of him and have an accounting with himself for what was written therein. . . .

Take care to be continent. That is, avoid everything that would leave an impression on your soul. . . . If you live in that state of continence which is the foundation of religion and the path to God, your works will thrive and your undertakings be successful, your condition in life will prosper, supernatural blessings will hasten toward you, and you will be guided by divine care in all your affairs. We have no doubt about it. But whenever you turn aside from the path of continence and go straying in every valley (of desire), God departs from you and leaves you to yourself, so that Satan gets the mastery of you. (Ibn al-Arabi, *A Treatise on What the Novice Must Possess*) [JEFFERY 1962: 643–645, 653]

At times even the externals of the two types of spiritual endeavor, that of the monk and that of the Sufi, bore remarkable similarities, as one Muslim had occasion to observe. The era is the eleventh century, the Latin Crusader century in Palestine, and it is a community of Christian monks that first attracts the attention of the Muslim Usama.

I visited the tomb of John [the Baptist], the son of Zachariah—God's blessing on both of them—in the village of Sebaste in the province of Nablus [that is, the biblical Samaria]. After I said my prayers, I went into the square that was bounded on one side by the holy precinct (where the tomb was located). I found a half-closed gate, opened it and entered a church. Inside were about ten old men, their bare heads as white as combed cotton. They were facing eastward, and wore [embroidered?] on their breasts staffs ending in crossbars turned up like the rear of a saddle [that is, some form of a cross, as Usama likely knew very well]. They swore their oaths on this sign, and gave hospitality to those who needed it. The sight of their piety touched my heart, but at the same time it displeased and saddened me, for I had never seen such zeal and devotion among the Muslims.

I brooded on this experience for some time, until one day, as Muʿin al-Din and I were passing the Peacock House, he said to me, "I want to dismount here and visit the shaykhs." "Certainly," I said, and so we dismounted and went into a long building set at an angle to the road. At first I thought that there was no one there. Then I saw about a hundred prayer mats and on each one of them a Sufi, his face expressing a peaceful serenity, and his body humble devotion. This was a reassuring sight, and I gave thanks to Almighty God that there were among Muslims men of even more zealous devotion than those Christian priests. Before this I had never seen Sufis in their convent and so was ignorant of the way they lived. (Usama, *Book of the Staff* 528–529)

A century later, in 1183 C.E., the Muslim traveler Ibn Jubayr likewise had occasion to note communities of ascetics, now in Damascus, and he too was impressed and edified.

Ribats for Sufis, which are here called *khanaqas*, are numerous. They are adorned residences; water flows through all of them and they present the most delicious prospect imaginable. The members of this type of Sufi organization live like kings here since God has provided for them even beyond the necessities and so freed their minds from any concern for earning a living, and thus they can devote themselves entirely to His service. He has lodged them in halls which give them a foretaste of those of Paradise. So these fortunate men, the most favored of the Sufis, enjoy by God's favor the blessings of both this world and the next. They follow a praiseworthy vocation and their life in common is conducted in an admirable fashion.

Ibn Jubayr observed, and obviously approved of, something new and unusual about the Sufi life, their manner of prayer.

Their manner of worship is peculiar to them. Their custom of assembling for highly charged musical recitals is most pleasant. Sometimes, so carried away are some of these rapt ascetics when they are under the influence of this condition, that they can scarcely be thought of as belonging to this world at all. (Ibn Jubayr, *Travels* 284)

30. Sufi Communities

Ibn Jubayr had a name for the Sufis' common lodging, a ribat, *a familiar term to him, though in Damascus, he explains, the less familiar* khanaqa *is used. This latter, a Sufi cloister or convent, was the third, and in the end the most common, of a trio of institutions that served the needs and ends of ascetics and mystics in Islam. The oldest of the three was, as Ibn Jubayr intimates, the* ribat. *By tradition this was originally a fortified keep to protect the lands and coasts of Islam. In time, it evolved into a kind of cloistered hospice for Muslims who for reasons of need—widows were often housed in them—or by preference chose to separate themselves from the world. In the end the* ribat *became totally identified with Sufism, though it had neither the personal stamp of the shrine-tomb (zawiya) nor the official character and internal organization of what seems very akin to a Christian monastery—the text of Usama already suggests the comparison—the* khanaqa.

If the Sufi convent had some of the features of the Pachomian monastery, the shrine-tomb corresponded to an earlier development in Christian spirituality. As we have seen in the case of Antony and others, the earliest Christian holy men attracted others to themselves and provided both a model and an ideal for those admirers to follow. The shaykh of the Islamic tradition had much the same effect: his sanctity drew others to himself. At the same time, his quarters, perhaps enlarged to permit others to lodge there, became at once a very loosely organized "school" and shrine of sanctity. At the shaykh's death he was often buried in the same place, and so in the final stage of its evolution the zawiya *was both a shrine and a tomb, and not always on a modest scale. Ibn Battuta describes a shrine-tomb he visited near Wasit in Iraq in 1327 C.E.*

This gave me the opportunity of visiting the grave of the saint Abu al-Abbas Ahmad al-Rifaʿi [d. 1182 C.E.], which is set at a village called Umm Ubayda, one day's journey from Wasit. . . . It is a vast convent in which there are thousands of poor brethren. . . . When the afternoon prayers have been said, drums and kettle drums were beaten and the poor brethren began to dance. After this they prayed the sunset prayer and brought in the repast, consisting of rice bread, fish, milk and dates.

After the meal there begins the community "recollection," a widespread Sufi devotion already noted by Ibn Jubayr; it is performed in this instance under the direction of the master of the shrine-tomb together with his adepts. Shaykh Ahmad, as is noted, was a linear descendant of the saint buried there. Finally, the "Rifa'i" version of a "spiritual concert" was considered notorious even in its own day.

When all had eaten and prayed the first night prayer, they began to recite their "recollection," with the shaykh Ahmad sitting on the prayer carpet of his ancestor above mentioned, when they began the musical recital. They had prepared loads of firewood which they kindled into a flame, and went dancing into the midst of it; some of them rolled in the fire, and others ate it in their mouths, until finally they extinguished it entirely. This is their regular custom, and it is the peculiar characteristic of this corporation of Ahmadi brethren. Some of them will take a large snake and bite its head with their teeth until they bite it clean through. (Ibn Battuta, *Travels*) [IBN BATTUTA 1959–1962: 273–274]

The community resident within one of these convents or shrine-tombs might be formal or informal, loosely or tightly structured, made up of permanent members or with transient "sojourners." Where the life and the community was more formal was where it was associated with a "way," practices and blessings modeled on and derived from a saintly master. These are Islam's "religious orders," similar in some respects to the monastic confraternities of Christianity, though far more charismatic and with a greater orientation toward a master-novice relationship than their Christian, and particularly their Western Christian, counterparts. In the Sufi reception and training of postulants, for example, we can observe both the similarities to and the differences from Christian practice. Ibn Battuta describes the arrival at the gates of a Cairo convent of a postulant who has already had some training.

When a new arrival makes his appearance, he has to take up his stand at the gateway of the convent, girded about the middle, with a prayer rug slung over his back, his staff in his right hand and his ablution jug in his left. The gatekeeper informs the steward, who goes out and ascertains from what country he has come, what convents he has resided in during his journey [or earlier training], and who was his initiator. If he is satisfied with the truth of his replies, he brings him into the convent, arranges a suitable place for him to spread out his prayer mat and shows him the washroom. The postulant then restores himself to a state of ritual cleanliness, goes to his mat, ungirds himself and prays two prostrations. After this he clasps the hands of the shaykh [that is, the spiritual master] and of those who are present and takes his seat among them. (Ibn Battuta, *Travels* 1.20) [Cited by TRIMINGHAM 1971: 171]

The postulant has become a novice and is set upon the course of his spiritual training.

The Sufi masters observe the following rule. When a novice joins them with the purpose of renouncing the world, they subject him to a spiritual training for the space of three years. If he fulfills the requirements of this discipline, well and good; otherwise they declare that he cannot be admitted to the Path. The first year is devoted to the service of the people, the second year to service of God, and the third year to watching over his own heart.

At the end of his three-year training and probation, the novice is ready for investiture with the patched Sufi cloak, the "religious habit" of this way of life.

The adept, then, who has attained the perfection of saintship takes the right course when he invests the novice with the Sufi cloak after a period of three years during which he has educated him in the necessary discipline. In respect of the qualifications which it demands, the Sufi cloak is comparable to a winding sheet: the wearer must resign all his hopes of the pleasures of life, and purge his heart of all sensual delights, and devote his life entirely to the service of God. (Hujwiri, *The Unveiling*)
[HUJWIRI 1911: 54–55]

31. Convent Rules and Charters

Like their Christian counterparts, the earliest rules governing the life of Sufis living under a single convent roof were apparently quite simple. This set is attributed to Abu Sa'id ibn Abi al-Khayr (d. 1047 C.E.), a pioneer of the Sufi life in eastern Iran.

1. Let them keep their garments clean and themselves always pure.
2. Let them not sit in the mosque or in any holy place for the sake of gossiping.
3. In the first instance let them perform their prayers in common.
4. Let them pray much at night.
5. At dawn let them ask forgiveness of God and call upon Him.
6. In the morning let them read as much of the Quran as they can and let them not talk until the sun has risen.

7. Between the evening prayers and the bedtime prayers let them occupy themselves with repeating some litany.

8. Let them welcome the poor and the needy and all who join their company, and let them bear patiently the trouble of waiting upon them.

9. Let them not eat anything except when participating with another.

10. Let them not absent themselves without receiving permission from one another.

Furthermore, let them spend their hours of leisure in one of three things: either in the study of theology or in some devotional exercise or in bringing comfort to someone. Whoever loves his community and helps them as much as he can is a sharer in their merit and future recompense. (Abu Sa'id, *The Secret of Oneness*) [NICHOLSON 1921: 46]

The guidelines just cited are the teachings of an individual on the conduct of the spiritual life. More often in the Islam the monastic "rules" were the result of stipulations built into the founding charter of a convent by the founder-donor. The monasteries and convents of Islam were supported, like most other Muslim religious institutions, out of endowments. Generally, the details of both the finances and the internal organization of the institution were spelled out in the original endowment charter, as in this example preserved in inscriptional form from one of the convents of Jerusalem.

In the name of God, the Merciful, the Compassionate: the devoted servant of Almighty God, Ibn Abd Rabbihi ibn Abd al-Bari Sanjar al-Dawadari al-Salihi ordered the construction of this blessed convent called the House of the Saints. He made it a pious foundation for the sake of Almighty God and for the benefit of thirty members of the Sufi community and their disciples, both Arabs and Persians, of whom twenty are celibate and ten married. They are to live here and not depart, neither in summer nor in winter, neither spring nor fall, except in urgent cases and in order to extend hospitality to those Sufis and disciples who desire it for a period of ten days. He made its endowment (the income of) the village of Bir Nabala (of the territory of) the blessed Jerusalem and of the village of Hajla of (the territory of) Jericho; and also (the income of) a bakery and a mill and what is above these two enterprises in Jerusalem; of a soap factory, six shops and a paper factory in Nablus; of three gardens, three shops and four mills in Baysan. This is all endowment for the benefit of this convent and for instruction in the Shafi'ite rite; for a professor of Prophetic traditions and a reader to recite same; for ten persons who will memorize traditions and ten who will recite the Book of God in its entirety each day; also for a eulogist who will glorify the Prophet. All of this (latter) is to be done in the Aqsa mosque.

This (was done) on the first day of the year 695 [1295 C.E.], in the governorship of the devoted servant of God Sanjar al-Qaymari, may God grant him pardon. [VAN BERCHEM 1922: no. 70]

32. Convent Life in Islam

Sufi convent life evolved over a long period of time, from the most informal, almost anarchical arrangements, to institutions that rivaled Christendom's orderly monasteries. The first example here is from Muqaddasi, a professional traveler roaming the "Abode of Islam" sometime before 980 C.E., when Sufi congregations were still grasping for a sense of themselves.

When I entered Sus [a town in southwestern Iran] I went to the main mosque to seek out a shaykh whom I might question concerning certain points of Prophetic tradition. It happened that I was wearing a cloak of Cypriot wool and a Basran waist wrapper and so I was directed to a congregation of Sufis. As I approached they assumed that I too was a Sufi and welcomed me with open arms. They settled me among them and began questioning me. Then they sent a man with food. I felt uneasy about taking the food since I had had nothing to do with such (Sufi) congregations before this. They expressed surprise at my reluctance and my not joining in their rituals. But I felt drawn to associate myself with this congregation and find out about their method, and learn the true nature of Sufism. I said to myself, "This is your chance, here where nobody knows you."

I cast off all restraint in their regard. . . . At one time I joined in their antiphonal singing, on another occasion I shouted with them, and on another recited poems with them. I went with them to visit hospices and to engage in religious recitals, with the result that I won a remarkably high place in the affections of both the Sufis and the people there. I gained a great reputation; I was visited for my virtue and was sent presents of clothes and money, which I accepted but straightway handed over untouched to the Sufis, since I was well off. I spent every day in my considerable devotions, and they imagined that I did it out of piety. People began touching me and spreading reports of my fame, saying that they had never seen a more excellent ascetic. So it continued until, when the time came that I had penetrated into their secrets and learned all that I wished, I just ran away from them in the middle of the night and by the morning I was well away. (Muqaddasi, *The Best of Climes*, 415)

Three and a half centuries later, when Ibn Battuta describes the convents of Cairo ca. 1355 C.E., the institutional landscape looks very different.

Each convent in Cairo is affected to the use of a separate congregation of ascetics [here in Arabic, a *fakir*; the Persian equivalent is a dervish] most of whom are Persians, men of good education and adepts in the "way" of Sufism. Each has a shaykh and a warden, and the organization of their affairs is admirable. It is one of their customs in the matter of their food that the steward of the house comes in the morning to the dervishes, each of whom then specifies what food he desires. When they assemble for meals, each person is given his bread and soup in a separate dish, none sharing with another. They eat twice a day. They receive winter clothing and summer clothing and a monthly allowance varying from 20 to 30 dirhams each. Every Thursday evening they are given sugar cakes, soap to wash their clothes, the price of admission to the bathhouse and oil to feed their lamps. These men are celibate; the married men have separate convents. Among the stipulations required of them are attendance at the five daily prayers, spending the night in the khanaqa and assembly in mass in a chapel within the convent. (Ibn Battuta, *Travels*) [IBN BATTUTA 1959–1962: 44]

Or here, in even broader strokes, is Damascus of the same era.

The people of Damascus vie with one another in the building and endowment of mosques, religious houses, colleges and shrines. . . . Every man who comes to the end of his resources in any district of Damascus finds without exception some means of livelihood opened to him, either as a prayer leader in a mosque, or as a reciter in a law school or by occupation [of a cell] in a mosque, where his daily requirements are supplied to him, or by recitation of the Quran, or employment as a keeper at one of the blessed sanctuaries, or else he may be included in the company of Sufis who live in the convent, in receipt of a regular allowance for upkeep and clothing. Anyone who is a stranger there living on charity is always protected from [having to earn it at] the expense of his self-respect and dignity. Those who are manual workers or in domestic service find other means of livelihood, for example, as guardian of an orchard or intendant of a mill or in charge of children, going with them in the morning to their lessons and coming back with them in the evening, and anyone who wishes to pursue a course of studies or devote himself to the religious life receives every aid to the execution of his purpose. (Ibid.) [IBN BATTUTA 1959–1962: 149–150]

4. The Mystics' Ascent to God

Mysticism is sometimes taken as the esoteric understanding of God and His works given to a few chosen souls, or as the immediate apprehension of, and even identity with, God Himself. In either case, mysticism found a profound, if occasionally troubled, place in Judaism, Christianity, and Islam.

The sources of the trouble are not far to seek. For one thing, such a privileged understanding seemed to create "a church within a church," an elite group of believers who, if they did not often trouble those latter members of the flock, certainly troubled their shepherds. And among some of the adepts, their special understanding, their "gnosis," which they at least thought was more profound, and perhaps even more authentic, than that possessed by the ordinary believer, had the effect of reducing what might be called "ordinary revelation" to an inferior status and, as an occasional corollary, of freeing the adept from the "ordinary observance" prescribed by that other, public revelation. And finally, the mystic's intuitive leap into the neighborhood, or even the very bosom, of God seemed to violate one of the most profound and strongly held beliefs of the three monotheistic faiths, that in the utter transcendence, the absolute otherness, of God.

1. "O, Let Me Behold Your Presence"

The biblical worlds of God and man were unalterably separate. "The heavens are the Lord's heavens, but the earth He has given to the sons of man," as Psalm 115:16 put it. What, then, was the origin of this extraordinary idea that men could somehow approach God, could fathom His inscrutable secrets? The notion is not so wondrous, perhaps, as it might first appear. The seeds of it are already present at Sinai. It was during the sojourn of the Israelites in the wilderness of Sinai that the basic document of what later came to be called Judaism was given them. But there also occurs in the Sinai narrative an illuminating passage on the nature of God, His presence among His people, and the desire of at least some of the latter to draw closer to Him.

Now Moses would take the Tent and pitch it outside the camp, at some distance from the camp. It was called the Tent of Meeting, and whoever sought the Lord would go out to the Tent of Meeting that was outside the camp. Whenever Moses went out to the Tent, all the people would rise and stand, each at the entrance of his tent, and gaze after Moses until he had entered the Tent. And when Moses entered the Tent, the pillar of cloud would descend and stand at the entrance of the Tent, while He spoke to Moses. When all the people saw the pillar of cloud poised at the entrance of the Tent, all the people would rise and bow low, each at the entrance of his tent. The Lord would speak to Moses face to face, as one man speaks to another. And he would then return to the camp, but his attendant, Joshua son of Nun, a youth, would not stir out of the Tent.

Moses said to the Lord, "See, You say to me, 'Lead this people forward,' but You have not made known to me whom You will send with me. Further, You have said, 'I have singled you out by name, and you have indeed gained my favor.' Now, if I have truly gained Your favor, pray let me know Your ways, that I may know You and continue in Your favor. Consider, too, that this nation is Your people." And He said, "I will go in the lead and will lighten your burden." And he said to Him, "Unless You go in the lead, do not make us leave this place. For how shall it be known that Your people have gained Your favor unless You go with us, so that we may be distinguished, Your people and I, from every people on the face of the earth?" The Lord said to Moses, "I will also do this thing that you have asked; for you have truly gained My favor and I have singled you out by name."

Moses said, "O, let me behold Your Presence!" And He answered, "I will make all My goodness pass before you and I will proclaim before you the name Lord [that is, YHWH]."

Written, of course, in the Semitic fashion without vowels and generally vocalized as Yahweh. But there was a strict prohibition about pronunciation of the divine name, and one way of avoiding that was to substitute other vowels, thus "Yehoweh" or "Jehoveh." The text continues.

"... [A]nd the grace that I grant you and the compassion that I show. But," He said, "you cannot see My face, for man may not see Me and live." And the Lord said, "See, there is a place near Me. Station yourself on the rock and, as My Presence passes by, I will put a cleft in the rock and shield you with My hand until I have passed by. Then I will take My hand away and you will see My back; but My face must not be seen." (Exodus 33:7–23)

The Quran likewise recalls this incident.

When Moses arrived at the appointed time and his Lord spoke to him, he said: "O Lord, reveal Yourself to me that I may behold You." "You cannot behold Me," He said, "But look toward the mountain: if it remains firm in its place, then you may behold Me." But when his Lord appeared on the mountain in His effulgence, it crumbled to a heap of dust, and Moses fell unconscious. When he came to, he said: "All glory to You. I turn to You in repentance, and I am the first to believe." (Quran 7:143)

This protracted and intimate exposure to the presence of the Lord had its unmistakable physical effect, however.

Moses came down from Mount Sinai. And as Moses came down from the mountain bearing the two tablets of the Pact, Moses was not aware that the skin of his face was radiant, since he had spoken to Him. Aaron and all the Israelites saw that the skin of Moses' face was radiant; and they shrank from coming near him. But Moses called to them, and Aaron and all the chieftains in the assembly returned to him, and Moses spoke to them. Afterwards all the Israelites came near, and he instructed them concerning all the Lord had imparted to him on Mount Sinai. And when Moses had finished speaking with them, he put a veil over his face. (Exodus 34:29–35)

2. Visions of the Throne

The Israelites' "public" revelation was given not merely to Moses on Sinai but both before and after: from Adam and Enoch, Abraham and Jacob at one end of the biblical record to Daniel at the other, God had appeared or spoken to or otherwise communicated with, in a waking state or in dreams, many in Israel. Direct access to God was not, then, thought extraordinary among the Israelites, though some of its modalities and some of its effects certainly were, as in the case of Isaiah.

In the year King Uzziah died [742 B.C.E.], I beheld my Lord seated on a high and lofty throne, and the skirts of His robe filled the Temple. Seraphs stood in attendance on Him. Each had six wings: with two he covered his face, with two he covered his legs and with two he would fly.

> And one would call to the other,
> "Holy, holy, holy!
> The Lord of Hosts!
> His presence fills all the earth!"

The doorposts would shake at the sound of the one who called, and the House kept filling with smoke. I cried,

> "Woe to me; I am lost!
> For I am a man of unclean lips
> And I live among a people
> Of unclean lips;
> Yet my eyes have beheld
> The King Lord of Hosts."

Then one of the seraphs flew over to me with a live coal, which he had taken from the altar with a pair of tongs. He touched it to my lips and declared,

> "Now that this has touched your lips,
> Your guilt shall depart
> And your sin be purged away."

Then I heard the voice of my Lord saying: "Whom shall I send? Who will go for Us?" And I answered: "Here am I; send me." (Isaiah 6:1–8)

The following far more circumstantial, and obscure, account—the vision is highly personalized and idiosyncratic, and it is not always certain what the prophet was seeing or envisioning—is found in the opening chapter of the Book of Ezekiel. The prophet himself is speaking; the time is a few years into the Babylonian Exile.

In the thirtieth year, on the fifth day of the fourth month, when I was in the community of exiles by the Chebar Canal (in Babylonia), the heavens opened and I saw visions of God. On the fifth day of the month—it was the fifth year of the exile of King Jehoiachin [that is, 593 B.C.E.], the word of the Lord came to the priest Ezekiel son of Buzi the priest, by the Chebar Canal in the land of the Chaldeans. And the hand of the Lord came upon him there.

I looked, and lo, a stormy wind came sweeping out of the north—a huge cloud and flashing fire, surrounded by a radiance; and in the center of it, in the center of the fire, a gleam as of amber [or, "electrum"]. In the center of it were also the figures of four creatures. And this was their appearance:

They had the figures of human beings. However, each had four faces, and each of them had four wings. . . . The four of them had their faces and their wings on their four sides. Each one's wings touched those of the other. They did not turn as they moved; each could move in the direction of any of its faces.

Each of them had a human face (at the front); each of the four had the face of a lion on the right; each of the four had the face of an ox on the left; and each of the four had the face of an eagle (at the back). Such were their faces. . . . With them was something that looked like burning coals of fire. This fire, suggestive of torches, kept moving about among the creatures; the fire had a radiance, and lightning issued from the fire. Dashing to and fro (among) the creatures was something that looked like flares.

And here, as often, there is an ambiguity in the Hebrew between "wind" and what is called in English "spirit."

As I gazed on the creatures, I saw one wheel on the ground next to each of the four-faced creatures. As for the appearance and structure of the wheels, they gleamed like beryl. All four had the same form; the appearance and structure of each was as of two wheels cutting through each other. And when they moved, each could move in the direction of any of its four quarters; they did not veer when they moved. Their rims were tall and frightening, for the rims of all four were covered all over with eyes. And when the creatures moved forward, the wheels moved at their sides; and when the creatures were borne above the earth, the wheels were borne too. Wherever the spirit [or "the wind"] impelled them to go, they went—wherever it impelled them—and the wheels were borne alongside them; for the spirit of the creatures was in the wheels. . . .

Above the heads of the creatures was a form: an expanse, with an awe-inspiring gleam as of crystal, was spread out above their heads. . . . When they moved, I could hear the sound of their wings like the sound of mighty waters. . . . When they stood still, they would let their wings droop. From above the expanse over their heads came a sound. . . .

Above the expanse over their heads was the semblance of a throne, in appearance like a sapphire; and on top, upon this semblance of a throne, was the semblance of a human form. From what appeared as his loins up, I saw a gleam as of amber [or "electrum"]—what looked like a fire encased in a frame; and from what appeared as his loins down, I saw what looked like fire. There was a radiance all about him. Like the appearance of which shines in the clouds on a day of rain, such was the appearance of the surrounding radiance. That was the appearance of the semblance of the Presence of the Lord.

When I beheld it, I threw myself down on my face. And I heard the voice of someone speaking. And He said to me: "O mortal man, stand on your feet that I may speak to you." As He spoke, a spirit entered into me and set me on my feet; and I heard what was being spoken to me. (Ezekiel 1:1–2:3)

The Lord delivers to Ezekiel his commission, a warning to a rebellious Israel, and it is only then that Ezekiel begins to be transported. At the phrase "These are the words of the Lord God," the narrative continues.

Then a spirit [or wind] carried me away, and behind me I heard a great roaring sound: "Blessed is the Presence of the Lord, in His place," with the sound of the wings of the creatures beating against one another, and the sound of wheels beside them—a great roaring sound. A spirit seized me and carried me away. I went in bitterness, in the fury of my spirit, while the hand of the Lord was strong upon me. (Ezekiel 3:12–14)

3. Heavenly Journeys

The mere fact of God's revelations to Moses in person on Sinai, to various prophets like Isaiah and Ezekiel and Daniel in dreams or ecstatic states, and to any number of individuals through His angels makes it abundantly clear that God Most High was content to descend on occasion to that "earth He has given to the sons of man." Ezekiel's vision had shown him the highest heavens and the throne and very form of God, but he himself had remained on earth during the experience. More extraordinarily, the Bible records a number of cases where men were physically taken up alive into "the Lord's Heaven." Enoch, it appears from Genesis 5:24, did not die, as was said of all the other patriarchs in the biblical narrative, but was taken up by God.

All the days of Enoch came to 365 years. Enoch walked with God, then he was no more, for God took him. (Genesis 5:24)

Many centuries later, the Christian author of the "Letter to the Hebrews" can cite Enoch along with Abraham as a witness to the power of faith.

And what is faith? Faith gives substance to our hopes, and makes us certain of realities we do not see. It is for their faith that the men of old stand on record. . . . By faith Enoch was carried away to another life without passing through death; he was not to be found because God had taken him. For it is the testimony of the Scripture that before he was taken he had pleased God, and without faith it is impossible to please God. (Hebrews 11:1, 5–6)

The case of Elijah is considerably less mysterious, though no less miraculous. Elijah and his disciple Elisha are in Jericho.

The disciples of the prophets who were at Jericho came over to Elisha and said to him, "Do you know that the Lord will take your master away from you today?" He replied, "I know it too; be silent."

Elijah and Elisha approach the Jordan. Elijah strikes the waters with his cloak and they part so the two men can pass over on dry land.

As they were crossing, Elijah said to Elisha, "Tell me, what I can do for you before I am taken from you?" Elisha answered, "Let a double portion of your spirit pass on to me." "You have asked a difficult thing," he said. "If you see me as I am being taken from you, this will be granted to you; if not, it will not."

They kept on walking and talking; a fiery chariot with fiery horses suddenly appeared and separated one from the other; and Elijah went up to heaven in a whirlwind. Elisha saw it, and he cried out, "Oh, father, father! Israel's chariots and horsemen!" When he could no longer see him, he grasped his garments and rent them in two. (2 Kings 2:5–12)

The biblically certified presence of these two mortals alive in God's abode set in train a number of consequences. Enoch, as we shall see, became the central figure in a great many visionary accounts of the upper world, while the return of Elijah was associated in post-Exilic times with the End of Days. Here the Lord speaks through the mouth of His prophet Malachi.

Lo, I will send the prophet Elijah to you before the coming of that awesome, fearful day of the Lord. He shall reconcile fathers to sons and sons to fathers, so that, when I come, I do not strike the whole land with utter destruction. (Malachi 3:23)

The expectation of Elijah's return was still very much in the front of men's minds in Jesus' day.

When he came to the territory of Caesarea Philippi, Jesus asked his disciples: "Who do men say that the son of man is?" They answered: "Some say John the Baptist, others Elijah, others Jeremiah or one of the prophets." (Matthew 16:13)

Whatever others may have thought, Jesus himself publicly identified John the Baptist, recently imprisoned by Herod Antipas, with the returned Elijah.

I tell you this: never has there appeared on earth a mother's son greater than John the Baptist, and yet the least in the Kingdom of Heaven is greater than he. Ever since the coming of John the Baptist the Kingdom of Heaven has been subjected to violence and violent men are seizing it. For all the prophets and the Law foretold things to come until John appeared, and John is the destined Elijah, if you will but accept it. (Matthew 11:12–14)

And so he revealed to Peter, James, and John, immediately after they had beheld the transfigured Jesus in the company of Moses and Elijah.

On their way down the mountain, Jesus enjoined them not to tell anyone of the vision until the Son of Man had been raised from the dead. The disciples put a question to him: "Why then do our teachers say that Elijah must come first?" He replied, "Yes, Elijah will come and set everything right. But I tell you that Elijah has already come, and they failed to recognize him, and worked their will upon him; and in the same way the Son of Man is to suffer at their hands." Then the disciples understood that he meant John the Baptist. (Matthew 17:9–13)

The presence of Moses in the company of Jesus and Elijah on that hilltop in Galilee indicates that by Jesus' day he too had begun to be reckoned among those who had not suffered death but had been taken directly up into heaven. Moses did ascend Sinai to the presence of God in Exodus 24, but he descended as well, and the last chapter of Deuteronomy leaves no doubt that he later died.

Moses went up from the steppes of Moab to Mount Nebo, to the summit of Pisgah, opposite Jericho, and the Lord showed him the whole land. . . . "This is the land of which I swore to Abraham, Isaac and Jacob I will give to your offspring. I have let you see it with your own eyes, but you shall not cross there."

So Moses the servant of the Lord died there in the land of Moab, at the command of the Lord. He buried him in the valley in the land of Moab, near Beth Peor; and no one knows his burial place to this day. (Deuteronomy 34:1–6)

We cannot know why the final, apparently offhanded remark was added to the account, but it left open considerable space for the growth of a Moses ascension legend, and there certainly was such in full vigor in later times. This, for example, is how Josephus describes the final earthly moments of Moses.

And while he bade farewell to Eleazar and Joshua and was yet speaking with them, a cloud suddenly descended upon him and he disappeared into a ravine. But he has written of himself in the sacred book that he died, for fear that they might say by reason of his surpassing virtue he had gone back to the deity. (Josephus, *Antiquities* 4:48)

In all these cases it is more a matter of an assumption, a being taken up, rather than an ascension, a circumstantial voyage from earth to heaven. The earliest example of the latter occurs beyond the limits of Bible, in a third- or second-century B.C.E. work attributed to Enoch, the patriarch who had escaped death. The fourteenth chapter of the composite work that is now called the "First Book of Enoch" relates a fully articulated journey through the heavens.

Behold, clouds called me in the vision, and mist called me, and the path of the stars and flashes of lightning hastened me and drove me, and in the vision winds caused me to fly and hastened me and lifted me up into heaven. (1 Enoch 14:8)

And this is what he saw when he entered the heavens.

I proceeded until I came near to a wall which was built of hailstones, and a tongue of fire surrounded it, and it began to make me afraid. And I went into the tongue of fire and near to a large house which was built of hailstones, and the wall of that house was like a mosaic made of hailstones, and its floor was snow. Its roof was like the path of the stars and flashes of lightning, and among them fiery cherubim, and their heaven was like water. And there was a fire burning around its wall, and its door was ablaze.

And I went into that house, and it was hot as fire and cold as snow, and there was neither pleasure nor life in it. Fear covered me and a trembling took hold of me. And as I was shaking and trembling, I fell on my face. And I saw in the vision, and behold another house, which was larger than the former, and its doors were open before me, and it was built of a tongue of fire. And in everything it so excelled in glory and splendor and size that I am unable to describe to you its glory and its size.

If the model for this double-chambered house in heaven is likely the earthly Temple in Jerusalem, with its interior Holy of Holies, what follows is unmistakably drawn from Ezekiel's prophetic vision.

And I looked and I saw in it a high throne and its appearance was like ice and its surrounds like the shining sun and the sound of cherubim. And from beneath the high throne there flowed out rivers of burning fire so that it was impossible to look at it. And He who is great in glory sat upon it, and His raiment was brighter than the sun and whiter than any snow. And no angel could enter, and at the appearance of the face of Him who is honored and praised no creature of flesh could look. A sea of fire burnt round Him and a great fire stood before Him, and none of those round Him came near to Him. Ten thousand times ten thousand stood before Him, but He needed no holy counsel. And the Holy Ones who were near Him did not leave by night or day, and did not depart from Him.

And until then I had been prostrated on my face, as I trembled. And the Lord called me with His own mouth and said to me, "Come hither, Enoch, to My holy word." And He lifted me up and brought me near the door. And I looked, with my face down. (1 Enoch 14:9–25)

There are heavenly journeys attributed to others among the biblical patriarchs in the post-Exilic literature called "Pseudepigrapha" and not included in the Bible. One such work with one such journey is the so-called "Testament of Levi." It is later than 1 Enoch and adds another important motif to the genre, the voyage through the various heavens, with a description of the sights seen en route. It contains a somewhat confused description of the seven heavens, confused chiefly because the various versions of the "Testament of Levi" stand midway between belief in a three-tiered and a seven-tiered upper world. The doctrine of the seven heavens, founded on the domains of the seven planetary spheres of contemporary astronomy, was commonplace in Greco-Roman circles. The Jewish tradition supplied its own version of the function and contents of each, here set forth, not for the first time certainly, in rather crisp summary fashion in the Talmud.

Rabbi Judah said: There are two firmaments, for it is said: "Behold, to the Lord your God belongs heaven and the heaven of heavens" (Deuteronomy 10:14). Resh Lakish said: (There are) seven, namely, the Curtain, the Firmament, the Clouds, the Lofty Abode, the Dwelling, the Fixed Place and the Thick Darkness. (BT.Hagigah 12b)

4. The "Work of the Chariot"

Whatever the inherent interest of the accounts of cosmic and celestial voyages, it was Ezekiel's experience of the heavenly chariot that made the strongest impression on Jewish sensibilities. The Babylonian Talmud tells the following story.

Once Rabbi Yohanan ben Zakkai was riding on an ass when going on a journey, and Rabbi Eleazar ben Arak was driving the ass from behind. Rabbi Eleazar said to him: "Master, teach me a chapter from the 'Work of the Chariot.'" He answered: "Have I not taught you all thus: 'Nor the "Work of the Chariot" in the presence of one, unless he is a sage and understands of his own knowledge'?" (BT.Hagigah 14b)

Yohanan ben Zakkai, the sage who escaped Jerusalem just before its destruction by the Romans in 70 C.E., is here quoting his own words in order to discourage the request for instruction on the "Work of the Chariot." The full text of his ruling occurs in Mishna Hagigah and provides a little more context for the implied reprimand. The Mishna's caution about the "Work of Creation" begins with a warning against public discussion of the forbidden degrees of sexual relations and includes in its strictures the "Work of the Chariot."

The (subject of) forbidden relations may not be expounded in the presence of three persons, nor the Work of Creation in the presence of two, nor the (Work of) the Chariot in the presence of one, unless he is a sage and already has an independent understanding of the matter. (M.Hagigah 2:1)

We return to Yohanan ben Zakkai.

Rabbi Eleazar then said to him: "Master, then permit me to say [or perhaps "repeat"] to you something which you have taught me." He answered: "Say on!" Rabbi Yohanan ben Zakkai immediately dismounted from the ass, wrapped himself up (in his prayer shawl) and sat upon a stone beneath an olive tree. Rabbi Eleazar said to him: "Master, why did you dismount from the ass?" He answered: "Is it proper that while you are expounding the 'Work of the Chariot' and the Divine Presence is with us, and the ministering angels accompany us, I should be riding on the ass?"

Immediately Rabbi Eleazar ben Arak began his exposition of the "Work of the Chariot" and fire came down from heaven and encompassed all the trees in the field, and thereupon they all began to utter song. . . . An angel then said from the fire: "This is the very 'Work of the Chariot,' " whereupon Rabbi Yohanan ben Zakkai rose and kissed him on the head and said: "Blessed be the Lord God of Israel, who has given to Abraham our father a son who knows how to speculate upon, and to investigate, and to expound the 'Work of the Chariot.' " (BT.Hagigah 14b)

What is this "Work of the Chariot" that is subject to so many cautions and yet is so holy that Yohanan puts on his prayer shawl to hear it explained and that it summons down to earth the Shekina, the Divine Presence of God? The "Work of Creation," mentioned in the same cautions, was an esoteric exposition of what is sketched in Genesis, a kind of filling in the blanks of the biblical account out of a mélange of ideas, some of them palpably non-Jewish in origin, in circulation in late antiquity. The "Work of the Chariot" is a similar explanation of the first chapter of Ezekiel. The matter becomes clear as the Talmud begins to gloss Mishna Hagigah 2:1.

"Nor (the Work of) the Chariot in the presence of one": Rabbi Hiyya taught: But the headings of the chapters may be transmitted to that one person. Rabbi Zera said: The headings of chapters may be transmitted only to the Head of the Religious Court and to one whose heart is careful within him. Others say: *Only* if his heart is careful within him. Rabbi Ammi said: The mysteries of the Torah may be transmitted to "captains of companies, men of rank, counselor, magician and cunning enchanter" (Isa. 3:3).

Although there was some debate on how closely the circle was to be drawn, instruction on the "Work of the Chariot" was obviously to be restricted to individuals of maturity and sagacity. Whether the instruction was orally derived is unclear; it is conceivable, as some later commentators thought, that the "Work of the Chariot" was already an assembled and edited collection of teachings. The same Talmud passage continues.

Rabbi Joseph was studying the "Work of the Chariot"; the elders (of the Babylonian academy) of Pumbeditha were studying the "Work of Creation." The latter said to the former: Let the master teach us the "Work of the Chariot." He replied: Teach me the "Work of Creation." After they had taught him, they said to him: Let the master instruct us in the "Work of the Chariot." . . . We have already studied therein as far as "And He said to me: Son of Man . . ." (Ezek. 2:1). He replied: This is the very "Work of the Chariot."

The "Work of the Chariot" was, then, a certain understanding of the first chapter of the Book of Ezekiel.

An objection was raised: How far does the "Work of the Chariot" extend? Rabbi said: As far as the second "I saw" (in 1:27). Rabbi Isaac said: As far as "amber" (in 1:28). As far as "I saw" may be taught (publicly); thenceforward only the heads of the chapters may be transmitted. Some, however, say: As far as "I saw" the heads of chapters may be transmitted; thenceforward, if he is a sage capable of independent speculation, yes; if not, no.

This exchange seems to suggest that the heart of the esoteric understanding of the first chapter of Ezekiel turns on the word "amber" in 1:27 and 28. Two anecdotes are adduced to confirm this.

May one expound the mysteries of "the amber"? For behold, there was once a child who expounded the (mysteries of) "the amber" and a fire went forth and consumed him —The child is different, for he had not reached (the fitting) age. . . . The Rabbis taught: There was once a child who was reading at his teacher's house the Book of Ezekiel, and he apprehended what "the amber" was, whereupon a fire went forth from "the amber" and consumed him. So they sought to suppress the Book of Ezekiel, but Hananiah ben Hezekiah said to them: If he was a sage, all are sages! (BT.Hagigah 13a)

The two children were thus judged exceptional cases, and the Book of Ezekiel was left in the canon, its public reading and glossing permitted—the text of the Talmud proceeds to do exactly that—while the esoteric understanding of it was limited to those to whom it would do no harm.

Finally, there is a Christian testimony from the early third century. The author is Origen, the Alexandrian Christian who was well acquainted with the Hebrew Scriptures. The passage occurs in the prologue to his commentary on the biblical Song of Songs.

It is said that the custom of the Jews is that no one who has not reached full maturity is permitted to hold this book [that is, Song of Songs] in his hands. And not only this, but even though their rabbis and teachers are accustomed to teach all the Scriptures and their oral traditions to young boys, they postpone till last the following four texts: The opening of Genesis, where the creation of the world is described; the beginning of the prophecy of Ezekiel, where the teaching about the angels is expounded; the end (of the same book) which contains the description of the future Temple; and this present book, the Song of Songs. (Origen, *Commentary on the Song of Songs*, Prologue)

5. Jewish Gnosticism: The Temple-Palaces of God

The main line of Jewish mysticism, from late biblical times through the rabbinic and medieval eras, appears to be a type of what has come to be known by the convenient rubric of Gnosticism, that is, a special knowledge (gnosis) or, better, a special or esoteric understanding of exoteric texts, which is reserved for a chosen few and which, in the classical gnostic style, is closely associated with redemption.

The "Work of Creation" is esotericism purely and simply, secret meanings of public texts, in this case of the first chapter of Genesis. But that same kind of understanding of the first chapter of the Book of Ezekiel, the "Work of the Chariot," was linked, via a heavenly, Ezekiel-inspired journey, to the vicinity of the Throne of God. This is how it is described in summary—and how it came to be divulged—in a work known as "The Greater Treatise on the Temple-Palaces." The landscape is that of Ezekiel's vision.

Rabbi Ishmael said: When Rabbi Nehunyah ben ha-Qanah saw that wicked Rome had taken counsel to destroy the great ones of Israel, he at once revealed the secret of the world, the measure that appears to one who is worthy of gazing on the King, on His Throne, on His majesty and His beauty, on the Holy Creatures, on the mighty Cherubim, on the Offanim of the Shekina, on the swift lightning, on the terrible electrum, on Rigyon [that is, the river of fire] which surrounds His Throne, on the bridges, on the fiery flames that blaze up between one bridge and the next, on the dense smoke, on the bright wind that raises from the burning coals the pall of smoke which covers and conceals all the chambers of the Temple-Palace of Arabot, the (seventh) heaven, on the fiery clouds, on Surya, the Prince of the Divine Presence, the servant of TVTRKY'EL YHVH, the Majestic one. (*The Greater Treatise* 15:1) [ALEXANDER 1984: 120]

Although the word "chariot" does not occur in this passage, there are present many of the elements of what the rabbis were talking about when they referred to the "Work of the Chariot." The focus of the journey is manifold. There is the arrival in "Arabot," the seventh heaven and the site of the seven Hekalot, or "Temple-Palaces," which give their name to the literature. Each palace has its own guardian, and there is a considerable lore of gaining entry, chiefly by knowing the correct name of the guardian or seal. The names, many of them undecipherable or deliberately unintelligible at this remove, clearly owe a great deal to formula magic, as in this example.

When you come and stand at the gate of the sixth palace, show the three seals of the Gatekeepers of the sixth palace, two of them to Qizpiel the Prince, whose sword is unsheathed in his hand and from it lightning bolts shoot out, and it is drawn against anyone unworthy to gaze upon the King and on the Throne. . . . Show one seal to Dumiel. Is Dumiel really his name? Is not Abirghydrhm [or Abirghhydrpyr] his name? (*The Greater Treatise* 20:5) [ALEXANDER 1984: 123–124]

Here at any rate we understand. Dumiel, which straightforwardly means "the silence of God," is not only the guardian of this palace but also the ruler of the four elements. He has as well a magical title, Abirghhydrpyr, composed of a Hebrew transliteration of the elements' four Greek names: aer *(air),* ge *(earth),* hydor *(water), and* pyr *(fire).*

The Temple-Palaces writings have been called "a manual for mystics," and they do indeed contain what appear to be practical instructions for achieving the same difficult ascent as that undertaken by the famous four who, as we shall see, were thought to have entered Paradise. In the eleventh century Hai Gaon, the head of the Iraqi yeshiva, was asked to comment on a famous and difficult passage in the

Talmud that, whatever its original sense, was understood in his day to refer to a mystical ascent to Paradise. The Talmud passage begins: "Four men entered the Garden. . . ." Pardes, the Hebrew word borrowed from Persian via Greek and signifying "garden," is also used, as we have seen, in the sense of the same word in English, "Paradise," the abode of the blessed, or even of God. The text continues: "namely, Ben Azzai and Ben Zoma, and Somebody Else and Rabbi Akiba." The "Somebody Else" had a name, and it is used later in the passage: Elisha ben Abuya. He apostatized, however, and so even the mention of his name was avoided. The Talmud continues with Akiba's caution that they not confuse the marble walls of the heavenly palaces with the glitter of water.

Rabbi Akiba said to them: When you arrive at the stones of pure marble, do not say "Water! Water!" . . . Ben Azzai cast a look and died. . . . Ben Zoma looked and became demented. Somebody Else "mutilated the shoots" [that is, apostatized]. Rabbi Akiba departed unhurt. (BT.Hagigah 14b)

The outcome is not entirely clear. The implication is that Ben Azzai and Ben Zoma failed the ordeal and suffered accordingly, while both Rabbi Akiba and Elisha ben Abuya (his apostasy occurred after this incident) were successful and returned safely from the "Paradise." Already in this opaque passage the emphasis is on methodology, and it is precisely that aspect that Hai Gaon reflects upon in his comment on it.

You may be aware that many of the sages were of the opinion that an individual who possesses certain explicitly defined worthy characteristics, and who wants to look at the Chariot and to peer in the palaces of the celestial angels, has ways to achieve this. He must sit fasting for a specified number of days, place his head between his knees, and whisper to the earth many prescribed songs and hymns. He thus peers into the inner rooms and chambers as if he were seeing the seven palaces with his own eyes, and he observes as if he were going from palace to palace and seeing what is in all of them. The rabbis of the Mishna have taught two texts on this subject, called *The Greater Treatise on the Temple-Palaces* and *The Lesser Treatise on the Temple-Palaces*. (Hai Gaon)

[Cited by HALPERIN 1984: 543–544]

There are passages in the Temple-Palace texts that seem to confirm this prescription. In one of the best known a sage named Nehunyah ben ha-Qanah is described as experiencing a kind of mystic trance or transport, in which he witnesses "a marvelous majesty and strange dominion, a majesty of exaltation and a dominion of radiance, which is aroused before the Throne of Glory." He is "brought back" by members of his "brotherhood" to explain why not everyone is successful in what was begin-

ning to be called, somewhat inexplicably, "descent to the Chariot." The answer, as always, depends on showing the right seals to the right gatekeepers. But since these are rabbis, the account concludes on an appropriately legal note.

Dumiel [that is, the keeper of the gate leading out of the sixth of the Temple-Palaces] says to him: I testify and warn you of two things. He who descends does not descend to the Chariot unless he has these two qualities: (either he has read) the Torah, the Prophets and the Writings, and he studies Mishna, the statutes and the homiletic exegeses, and the legal decisions concerning what is forbidden and what is permitted, or else he has fulfilled every negative command that is written in the Torah, and keeps all the prohibitions of the statutes and judgments and teachings which were spoken to Moses on Sinai.

If a man says "I have one of these two qualities," immediately Dumiel summons Gabriel the scribe who writes for the man a document and hangs it on the shaft of the carriage of that man. It says: "Such and such is the learning of this person, and such and such are his deeds. He requests permission to enter before the Throne of Glory."

As soon as the gatekeepers of the seventh Temple-Palace see Dumiel, Gabriel and Qizpiel proceeding in front of the chariot of that man who is worthy to descend to the Chariot, they cover their faces and sit down—for they were standing erect. They loosen their strung bows and return their sharp swords to their sheaths. Nevertheless, it is necessary to show them a great seal and a fearful crown—T'DS VBR MNVGYH VK'SH YHVH the God of Israel. Then they enter before the Throne of Glory and bring out before him [that is, the "descender"] all kinds of melody and song, and, making music, they proceed before him till they lead him in and seat him with the Cherubim, the Offanim and the Holy Creatures and he sees wonders, powers, majesty, greatness, holiness, dread, humility and righteousness in that hour. (*The Greater Tractate* 21:4–22:2) [ALEXANDER 1984: 124–125]

We have no overwhelming conviction that either the authors of these texts or their readers held the achievement of such a heavenly ascent as a practical goal. The objective may well have been some more commonplace earthly good, a blessing perhaps, or even the acquisition of magical powers. So these passages associated with Rabbi Akiba seem to suggest.

Rabbi Akiba said: When I set forth this method of ascending and descending to the Chariot, they fixed for me a daily blessing in the heavenly court and in the earthly court. . . . A heavenly voice announced to me from beneath the Throne of Glory, "For my friend, who endures the

suffering of descending and ascending to the Chariot, I have fixed a blessing [to be recited] three times a day in the heavenly court and in the
earthly court. I will love and I will redeem any household where it is
repeated." (*Lesser Treatise on the Temple-Palaces* [SCHAEFER 1981: nos. 422–423]

*Akiba then describes what is required for this vicarious enjoyment of the fruits of the
heavenly ascent.*

Rabbi Akiba said: Anyone who wants to repeat this tradition and to
utter the name explicitly must sit fasting for forty days. He must put his
head between his knees until the fast gets control of him. He must whisper toward the earth and not toward heaven, so that earth may hear and
not heaven. If he is an adolescent, he may say it as long as he does not
have an emission. If he is married, he must be prepared [that is, conti-
nent] three days in advance, as it is written "Be prepared for the third
day" (Exodus 19:15).

The magical quality of what is being transmitted then becomes evident.

If he tells it to a friend, he must tell him one letter from among the
first ones and one letter from among the last ones. He should not make
the combination for him, lest he make a mistake and destroy's God's
world. If he wants to test him, he may test him once but not twice. He
must supervise him carefully, lest he make a mistake and destroy God's
world. He should make regular use of it month by month and year by
year, thirty days before Rosh Hashanah [to cover the forty-day period?]
from the first of Elul to Yom Kippur, to keep Satan from accusing him
and ruining his entire year. (*Lesser Treatise on the Temple-Palaces*)
[SCHAEFER 1981: no. 424]

6. The Divine Names

We have yet another mystical tradition that the whole Torah is comprised of names of the Holy One, blessed be He, and that the letters of
the words separate themselves into Divine Names when divided in a different manner, as you may imagine by way of example that the verse of
bereshit [that is, the first verse of Genesis] divides itself into these other
words: *berosh/yithbareh/Elohim*. This principle likewise applies to the entire
Torah, aside from the combinations and the numerical value of the Holy
Names. Our Rabbi Shlomo [that is, Rashi; d. 1105 C.E.] has already written in his commentaries on the Talmud concerning the manner in which
the Great Name of seventy-two letters is derived from the three verses

(Exod. 14:19–21): "And He went," "And He came," "And He stretched out." It is for this reason that the scroll of the Torah in which a mistake has been made in one letter being added or subtracted is disqualified, for this principle [namely, that the whole Torah is comprised of the Divine Names] obligates us to disqualify a scroll of the Torah in which one letter *vav* is missing from the word *otham*, or in which there are thirty-nine fully spelled [that is, spelled with *vav*] examples in the Torah, or if someone were to add a *vav* to any of the deficiently spelled ones. So it is in similar cases even though it matters not one way or the other for the sense. It is this principle that has caused scholars to count every fully and defectively spelled word in the Torah and Scripture and to compose books on the fully punctuated text, going back as far as Ezra the scribe and the prophet, so that we should be heedful of this, as the Sages derived it from the verse (Neh. 8:8): "And they read in the book of the Law of the Lord distinctly; and they gave the sense, and caused them to understand the reading."

It would appear that the Torah, "written with letters of black fire upon a background of white fire" (JT.Shekalim 13b) was in the form we have mentioned, namely that the writing was continuous, with break of words, which made it possible for it to be read by way of Divine Names and also by way of our normal reading which makes explicit the Torah and the commandment. It was given to Moses our teacher using the division of words which express the commandment, and orally it was transmitted to him in the rendition which consists of the Divine Names. Thus masters of the Kabbala write the letters of the Great Name I have mentioned all close to each other, and then these are divided into words consisting of three letters and many other divisions, as is the practice among the masters of the Kabbala. (Nachmanides, *Commentary on Genesis*) [NACHMANIDES 1971: 13–15]

7. Ascent by Intuition

The mystic was not the only one possessed of the conviction that it was possible to leap across revelation to an individual understanding of God. As we shall see in Chapter 5 below, the philosophers too shared that view. One such was Philo, who as a Jew as well as a philosopher had before him a double paradigm of an approach to God. Here he reflects upon biblical figures like Abraham, Jacob, and Moses who were particularly close to God.

These no doubt are truly admirable persons and superior to the other classes. They have, as I have said, advanced from down to up by a sort of heavenly ladder and by reason and reflection happily inferred the Creator from His works. But those, if such there be, who have had the power to apprehend Him through Himself without the cooperation of any reasoning process to lead them to the sight, must be recorded as holy and genuine worshipers and friends of God in truth. In their company is he who in the Hebrew is called Israel, but in our tongue the God-seer, who sees not His real nature—for that, as I said is impossible—but that He is. (Philo, *On Rewards and Punishments* 43)

Moses, of course, is the best-known example of someone who approached God and was rewarded with a vision of the deity, an event that Philo can treat in a bold allegorical fashion for the benefit of a wider audience of believers: the ascent of Sinai signifies a scaling of the heights of heaven itself.

Ex. 24 12a: What is the meaning of the words "Come up to Me to the mountain and be there"? This signifies that a holy soul is divinized not by ascending to the air or to the ether or to heaven higher than all but to a region above the heavens. And beyond the world there is no place but God. (Philo, *Questions on Exodus* 40)

In these instances Philo is meditating on Scripture, an unmistakably Jewish Scripture. But he could speak more generally, and more philosophically, as well. Earlier, the Greeks may have thought that it was possible to demonstrate the essence of the ultimate principle with the same ease and assurance as a theorem in geometry, but by the time that philosophical tradition reached Philo, its earlier intellectual optimism had necessarily to be trimmed to permit some place for intuitive knowledge, that sudden unreasoned and unreasoning seizure by understanding. Plato had already cleared a place for an intuitive leap in his own theology, and Philo, who stood in the midst of a still vital Platonic tradition in first-century B.C.E. Alexandria, describes just such an experience in his personal progress as a theologian.

The harvest of spontaneous good things is called "release," inasmuch as the mind is released from working on its own projects and is, we may say, emancipated from self-chosen tasks, by reason of the abundance of the rain and ceaseless shower of blessings. And these are of a most marvelous nature and passing fair. For the offspring of the soul's own travail are for the most part poor abortions, things untimely born; but those which God waters with the snow of heaven come to birth perfect, complete and peerless.

I feel no shame in recording my own experience, a thing I know from its having happened to me a thousand times. On some occasions, after making up my mind to follow the usual course of writing on philosophical doctrines, and knowing definitely the substance of what I was to set down, I have found my understanding incapable of giving birth to a single idea, and have given it up without accomplishing anything, reviling my understanding for its self-conceit and filled with amazement at the might of Him That Is, to Whom is due the opening and closing of soul-wombs. On other occasions, I have approached my work empty and suddenly became full, the ideas falling in a shower from above and being sown invisibly, so that under the influence of divine possession I have been filled with corybantic frenzy and been unconscious of anything, place, persons present, myself, words spoken, lines written. For I obtained language, ideas, an enjoyment of light, keenest vision, pellucid distinctness of objects, such as might be received through the eyes as a result of the clearest showing. (Philo, *The Migration of Abraham* 32–35)

[PHILO 1945: 72–73]

And again, less personally, but in an even more deeply Platonic vein, albeit taking his point of departure as usual from a biblical text:

"He who shall come out of you," Scripture says, "shall be your heir" (Gen. 15:4). Therefore, my soul, if you feel any yearning to inherit the good things of God, leave not only your land, that is, the body, your kins-folk, that is, the senses, your father's house, that is, speech, but be a fugi-tive from yourself also and issue forth from yourself. Like persons pos-sessed and corybants, be filled with inspired frenzy, even as the prophets are inspired. But it is the mind which is under the divine afflatus, and no longer in its own keeping, but is stirred to its depths and maddened by heavenward yearning, drawn by the Truly Existent and pulled upward thereto, with truth to lead the way and remove all obstacles before its feet, that its path may be smooth to tread, such is the mind which has this inheritance.

To that mind I say, "Fear not to tell us the story of your departure from the first three. For to those who have been taught to give ear to the things of the mind, you ever repeat the tale." "I migrated from the body," she answers, "when I ceased to regard the flesh; from sense, when I came to view all the objects of sense as having no true existence, when I denounced its standards as spurious and corrupt and steeped in false opinion, and its judgments equipped to ensnare and deceive and ravish truth away from its place in the heart of nature; from speech, when I sentenced it to long speechlessness, in spite of all its self-exaltation and self-pride. Great indeed was its audacity, that it should attempt the im-possible task to use shadows to point me to substances, words to point me to facts. And, amid all its blunders, it chattered and gushed about, unable to present with clear expression the distinctions in things. (Philo, *Who Is the Heir?* 69–73) [PHILO 1945: 73–74]

8. The Direct Apprehension of God

Thus Philo was schooled in a Greek philosophical tradition that, for all its relentless intellectualism, nonetheless conceded the possibility of a final direct approach to God, not by analogy or as the term of the final syllogism in the long process of discursive reasoning, but by a kind of sudden leap of the mind to God—the "flight of the alone to the Alone," as one of Philo's pagan successors in that same tradition put it. This is the gift enjoyed by the prophets; but according to Philo, it not restricted to them alone.

There is a mind more perfect and more purified, which has been initiated into the great mysteries, a mind that discovers the First Cause not from created things, as one may learn of the abiding object from its shadow, but transcends creation and obtains a clear impression of the Uncreated, so as from Him to apprehend both Himself and his shadow, that is, the Word (of God) and the world. This mind is Moses, who says, "Manifest Yourself to me that I may see You clearly" (Exod. 33:13). (Philo, *The Allegory of the Laws* 3.100–101) [PHILO 1981: 126–127]

This would not have been possible, for Moses or for anyone else, had not God previously "inspired" man in the very act of creation.

"Breathed into" (Gen. 2:7) is equivalent to "inspired" or "ensouled" the soulless; for heaven forbid that we should be infected with such far-out nonsense as to think that God employs for inbreathing organs such as mouth or nostrils; for God is without every quality, not only without human form. . . . And to what purpose, save that we may obtain a conception of Him? For how could the soul have conceived of God had He not infused it and taken hold of it as far as possible? For the human mind would never have made bold to soar so high as to apprehend the nature of God had not God Himself drawn it up to Himself, so far as it was possible for human mind to be drawn up, and imprinted it in accordance with the (divine) powers accessible to its reasoning. (Ibid. 1.36–38) [PHILO 1981: 127]

This "ensoulment" is given to all men. But there is something higher, the joint effect of human striving and God's graciousness. It is expressed by Philo in terms and images drawn directly from Plato.

After the self-taught, who enjoyed rich natural endowments, the third to reach perfection is the Man of Practice, who receives as his special reward the vision of God. For having applied himself to all aspects of human life and dealt with them in no offhand manner, and having evaded no toil or danger on the chance that he might be able to track down the truth, which is well worth pursuing, he found among mortal kind a profound darkness on land, water, air and ether. For the ether [that is, the fifth element and the substance of the heavenly bodies] and the entire heaven presented to him the appearance of night, since the whole sensible realm lacks determination, and the indeterminate is the brother of darkness and its kin. In his earlier period he kept the eye of his soul shut, but through unremitting struggles he laboriously began to open it and to part and throw off the obscuring mist. For an incorporeal beam purer than ether suddenly flashed over him and disclosed the intelligible world led by its charioteer. That charioteer, irradiated by a circle of undiluted light, was difficult to discern or divine, for the eye is enfeebled by the sparkling lights. Yet in spite of the abundant light that flooded it, it held its own in its extraordinary yearning to behold the vision. The Father and Savior, perceiving his genuine longing and desire, felt pity and, lending strength to the penetration of his sight, did not begrudge him a vision of Himself, to the extent that it was possible for created and mortal nature to contain it. Yet it was not a vision showing what He was, but only that He is. For the former, which is better than the good, more venerable than the monad, and purer than the unit, cannot be discerned by anyone else; but for Him alone is it allowed to comprehend Himself. . . .

This knowledge (that God exists) he has gained from no other source, not from things terrestrial or celestial, nor from the elements or compounds, mortal or immortal, but summoned by Him alone who is pleased to reveal His own proper existence to the suppliant. How this means of approach has come about is worth looking at through the use of a similitude. Do we see the sense-perceptible sun by anything other than the (light of the) sun or the stars by anything other than the (light of the) stars, and in general is not light seen by light? Similarly, God too has His own splendor and is discerned through Himself alone, without anything else assisting or being capable of assisting with a view to the perfect apprehension of His existence. They are but makers of inferences who strive to discern the Uncreated and the Creator of all from His creation, acting similarly to those who search out the nature of the One from the Two, whereas observation of the dyad should begin with the monad, which is its source. The pursuers of truth are they who form an image of God through God, light through light. (Philo, *On Rewards and Punishments* 36–46) [PHILO 1981: 127–129]

9. The Kabbalists' Torah and the Rabbis' Torah

In Philo, the mystic mounted up to God through man's purity and God's grace. Later Jewish works on "temple-palaces" show a much greater interest in esoteric techniques for the successful achievement of the journey to the throne of God. Many of those techniques appear magical—incantations, for example—but later Jewish mystics of the type interested in Kabbala, or The Tradition, were likewise concerned with techniques, though not always or necessarily magical ones.

One of the primary centers of Kabbala in the Muslim Near East was at Safed in Galilee, where many of the Jewish scholars exiled from Spain had migrated in the early years of the sixteenth century. One of the most illustrious there and in the entire history of Kabbala was Isaac Luria, dead at the age of thirty-eight in 1572 C.E.. His reflections on the acquisition of mystical knowledge are here passed on by one of his students.

My teacher's [that is, Isaac Luria's] comprehension of this knowledge proceeded along the following course. At first he studied the *Zohar*, and sometimes a whole week went by as he sought to grasp what he had studied. He studied one subject many times in order to understand in depth. He did this on many occasions. At times it was told to him that he still had not grasped that subject in its essence, and he continued to labor on the subject. Sometimes he was told the explanation of the subject according to Rabbi Simeon bar Yohai [that is, the second-century C.E. sage to whom the *Zohar* was attributed]. Sometimes he was told that this is how Rabbi Simeon bar Yohai understood the subject but that he [that is, Isaac Luria] still needed to go more deeply into it. Then did the prophet Elijah reveal himself to him, and then he understood everything, the great and the small, of all kinds of knowledge.

My teacher used to expound matters of the Law, according to their literal meaning, each of the six days of the week. But then he used to expound secret meanings in honor of the Sabbath.

(According to Isaac Luria,) the study of the Torah must have as its primary motive to attach the soul to its source through the Torah, in order to complete the supernal tree (of the Ten Primordial Numbers) and to complete and perfect the supernal man. This is the reason for the creation of man and the goal of his Torah study.

Commenting on Deuteronomy 22:3, "Thus you shall do with every lost object of your brother," Luria reveals another aspect of Kabbalism.

Know that a person may at times be perfected through "conjunction" [that is, a temporary joining to or indwelling in the body of another] or at times he may require reincarnation, which is much more painful. The penalty for anyone who finds a lost object and does not return it is that he cannot find justification through "conjunction" after his death but he must render it in some form of reincarnation. And this is the meaning of the concluding section of the verse cited above: "You may not hide yourself." This refers to "conjunction" alone, which involves being hidden in his neighbor's soul. Rather, he will require reincarnation, which is much more painful than "conjunction."

The eschatological punishment of reincarnation is also applied by Isaac Luria to the subject of mystical study.

If a person has not perfected himself by fulfilling all the 613 commandments in action, speech and thought, he will of necessity be subject to reincarnation (so that he may fulfill them). . . . And whoever has not studied Torah according to the four levels indicated by PRDS [= *pardes* = Paradise], (an acronym) which is a composite of the initial letters from four (Hebrew) words, *peshat* [that is, the literal], *remez* [the allegorical], *derash* [the homiletic], and *sod* [the mystical], will have his soul returned for reincarnation, so that he might fulfill each of them. (Jacob Zemah, *The Shulhan Arukh of the Divine Rabbi Isaac*) [BOKSER 1981: 145–146]

For all this patent esotericism, the rabbis' more intellectualistic tradition continued to run strongly through the writings of Luria and the most convinced Kabbalists. Moses of Cordova (1522–1570 C.E.), for example, was one of Luria's contemporaries and teachers at Safed. He too speaks of the need and the means of mystical study.

Undoubtedly, one of the duties laid down by the Torah is for a person to know God, in accordance with his powers of comprehension. Thus the text states, "I am the Lord your God" (Exod. 20:2), on which Maimonides offers the following comment in the beginning of his work (*Mishneh Torah*): The chief foundation and basis of all wisdom is to know that there is a First Cause, who brought all beings into existence. . . . And there is no doubt that our master intended to convey to us that included in this commandment is the understanding of the process by which existing things derived from Him, to the extent that this is within our human comprehension.

There can be no doubt concerning this, for how could one assume that the call to know as here used means only to believe in God's existence? The text would have stated that we have a positive commandment to *believe* that there is a God. But it is not written thus, it is written to *know*. This means specifically to attain knowledge, a comprehension of God in accordance with human intellectual capacity. And similarly did the Bible specify (Jer. 22:15): "Know the God of your fathers and serve Him." This is intended to teach us that to serve Him properly we must know Him, that is, know His Primordial Numbers and how He directs them and His unity with them. This is proper service, the unification of the Holy One, praised be He, and His Divine Presence. . . .

As to the appropriate time for commencing such study, I saw that the subject lends itself to a threefold division. First, there is the matter of preparing oneself to be fit to enter this holy domain. It is indeed true that it is not seemly that everyone who reaches out to robe himself in the holy garments in order to serve in the holy place shall come and so robe himself. One must first remove from oneself the coverings of crude pride which impede one from grasping the truth, and direct his heart toward heaven so that he shall not stumble. . . .

Second, it is important that a person train himself in the method of profound textual analysis so that he be accustomed and skillful in detaching from a text the illustrative elaborations, and this will enable him to reach the goal in this knowledge.

Thirdly, he shall dedicate himself to full acquisition of the laws of the Gemara [that is, the Talmudic discussions of the Mishna text], and the explanation of the commandments according to their simple meaning, as explained by Maimonides in the *Mishneh Torah*.

Fourth, he should also accustom himself to study Bible, whether much or little, so that he is perfected with sound knowledge, with Bible and Mishna, and he stumble not, and that he be not one of the group lost in error. . . .

After this, a person is to cleanse his mind of the follies and pleasures of the times, to the extent possible nowadays, and then will the gates of wisdom open to him. . . . Second, there is no doubt that a person will be unfit to pursue this knowledge unless, at the proper time, he marries and cleanses his thoughts. . . .

It is also necessary that a person reach at least his twentieth year, which brings him to the minimum of half the time fixed for the age of discernment [that is, forty, in M.Pirqe Aboth 5:24]. It is true that some held off until they reached their fortieth year, but we do not agree with this, for many followed our view and were successful. . . .

Third, as to the right time for engaging in this study, certainly it is easy to study any time in the day, but the time that is most conducive to study matters in depth is during the long nights, after midnight; or on the Sabbath, for the Sabbath itself lends predisposition to it; and on the holy days, especially Weeks [Shabuoth or Pentecost, that is, the holy day commemorating the giving of the Torah; see Chapter 1 above], for I have tried it many times and found this a time of wondrous propitiousness; and on the days of Tabernacles, in the "shelter" (*sukkah*) itself, for there it is most conducive. The times here mentioned were tested by me, and I speak from experience. (Moses of Cordova, *Deborah's Palmtree* 3:1–2)

[BOKSER 1981: 139–141]

10. Jesus' Transfiguration

Perhaps even as Philo was pondering the immediate contemplation of God, this event occurred, the Gospels tell us, in another, quite different Jewish milieu in Galilee.

Six days later Jesus took Peter, James and John, the brother of James, and led them up to a high mountain, where they were alone. And in their presence he was transfigured; his face shone like the sun and his clothes became as white as the light. And they saw Moses and Elijah appear, conversing with him. Then Peter spoke: "Lord," he said, "how good it is that we are here! If you wish it, I will make three shelters here, one for you, one for Moses and one for Elijah." While he was still speaking, a bright cloud overshadowed them, and a voice called from the cloud: "This is my Son, my Beloved, on whom my favor rests; listen to him." At the sound of the voice the disciples fell on their faces in terror. Jesus then came up to them, touched them, and said, "Stand up; do not be afraid." And when they raised their eyes they saw no one, but only Jesus. (Matthew 17:1–8)

In Matthew's Gospel this event occurs just after Peter's acknowledgment of Jesus' messiahship. The epiphany may have served to confirm and validate that acknowledgment, with at least the suggestion that Jesus too would be taken up to heaven alive, as those other figures in the scene, Moses and Elijah, were. If that was its original intent, what came to be called the Transfiguration in the Christian tradition eventually served a quite different end: what Peter, James, and John witnessed on Mount Tabor was the paradigm of the Christian mystic's face-to-face experience of God.

11. Prophecy, Ecstasy, and Heresy

But before the Tabor experience could be elevated into a prototype of the mystic experience there were problems to be faced and misunderstandings to be resolved. To begin with, the earliest Christian communities were far more charismatic and ecstatic than those that followed. Paul provides the context.

Put love first; but there are other gifts of the Spirit at which you should aim also, and above all prophecy. When the man is using the language of ecstasy he is talking with God, not with men, for no man understands him; he is no doubt inspired, but he speaks mysteries. On the other hand, when a man prophesies, he is talking to men, and his words have power to build; they stimulate and they encourage. The language of ecstasy is good for the speaker himself, but it is prophecy that builds up a Christian community. I should be pleased for you all to use the tongues of ecstasy, but better pleased for you to prophesy. The prophet is worth more than the man of ecstatic speech—unless indeed he can explain its meaning, and so help to build up the community. Suppose, my friends, that when I come to you I use ecstatic language; what good shall I do you, unless what I say contains something by way of revelation, or enlightenment, or prophecy, or instruction? (Paul, *To the Corinthians* 1.14:1–6)

Prophesy, then, and ecstatic visions and utterances were not uncommon phenomena in the Christian congregations of the first and second centuries. Indeed, they were reckoned a kind of revelation—but cautiously, and with controls, as also appears in that same letter of Paul to the Corinthians.

To sum up, my friends, when you meet for worship, each of you contributes a hymn, some instruction, a revelation, an ecstatic utterance, or the interpretation of such an utterance. All of these must aim at one thing, to build up the church. If it is a matter of ecstatic utterance, only two should speak, or at most three, at one time, and someone must interpret. If there is no interpreter, the speaker had better not address the meeting at all, but speak to himself and to God. Of the prophets, two or three may speak, while the rest exercise their judgment upon what is said. If someone else receives a revelation while still sitting in his place, let the first speaker stop. You can all prophesy, one at a time, so that the whole congregation may receive instruction and encouragement. It is for prophets to control prophetic inspiration, for the God who inspires them is a God not of disorder but of peace. (Paul, *To the Corinthians* 1.14:26–33)

Paul does not say who the interpreter was to be. With the increasing organization and institutionalization of Christian communities under a bishop, there is little doubt that eventually it was he who first controlled, and eventually suppressed, this freewheeling form of individual revelation. But not always and everywhere successfully.

There is said to be a certain village named Ardabau, in Mysia, on the borders of Phrygia. There they say that when Gratus was Proconsul in Asia, a recent convert named Montanus . . . first became inspired; and falling into a sort of frenzy and ecstasy raved and began to babble and utter strange sounds, prophesying in a manner contrary to the traditional and constant custom of the Church from the beginning. . . . And he stirred up in addition two women [Priscilla and Maximilla] and filled them with the false spirit so that they talked frantically, at unseasonable times, and in a strange manner, like the person already mentioned. . . . And the arrogant spirit taught them to revile the universal and catholic church under heaven, because the spirit of false prophecy received from it neither honor nor entrance into it; for the faithful in Asia met often and in many places throughout Asia to consider this matter and to examine the recent utterances, and they pronounced them profane and rejected the heresy, and thus these persons were expelled from the Church and shut out from the communion. (Eusebius, *Church History* 5.16)

These (next) are Phrygians by birth and they have been deceived, having been overcome by certain women called Priscilla and Maximilla, and they regard them as prophetesses, saying that in them the Paraclete Spirit dwelled. And they likewise glorify one Montanus before these women as a prophet. So with their endless books from these people they go astray, and they neither judge their statements by reason nor pay any attention to those who can judge them. But they rather behave without judgment in the faith they place in them, saying they have learned something more through them than through the Law and the Prophets and the Gospels. But they glorify these women above the Apostles and every gift, so that some of them presume to say that there was something more in them than in Christ. These confess God the Father of the universe and the creator of all things, like the Church, and all that the Gospel witnesses concerning Christ. But they invent new fasts and feasts and meals of dry food and meals of radishes, saying that thus they were taught by their women. (Hippolytus, *Refutation of All Heresies* 8.19)

12. From Asceticism to Mysticism

If one, perhaps aborted, source of Christian mysticism was the charismatic tradition present from the beginning in Christian communities, then another, and in the end a far more fruitful one, lay in the bosom of Christian asceticism. As we have already seen in Chapter 3 above, asceticism was for some early Christians an end in itself, a voluntary fulfillment of Jesus' invitation, "If you would be perfect . . . " But very early on it was understood, if not to have another end beyond itself, then to serve another joint purpose. Basil of Caesarea, the pioneer of Christian monasticism, points the direction.

There is only one way out of this, namely, total separation from the world. But withdrawal from the world does not mean physical removal from it. Rather, it is the withdrawal by the soul of any sympathy for the body. One becomes stateless and homeless. One gives up possessions, friends, ownership of property, livelihood, business connections, social life and scholarship. The heart is made ready to receive the imprint of sacred teaching, and this making ready involves the unlearning of knowledge deriving from evil habits. To write on wax, one must first erase the letters previously written there, and to bring sacred teaching to the soul one must begin by wiping out the preoccupations rooted in ordinary habits. (Basil, *Letter* 2)

The expectation that there were rewards beyond the practice of self-denial, rewards in this life and not in the hereafter, is already present in homilies attributed, falsely, to Macarius, one of the principal figures in Egyptian asceticism.

This is something that everyone ought to know, that we have eyes within, more penetrating than these eyes; and a hearing more acute than this hearing. As the eyes of sense behold and recognize the face of a friend or a loved one, so the eyes of the true and faithful soul, spiritually illumined with the light of God, behold and recognize the True Friend. (Macarius, *Homily* 28:5)

Christians behold as in a mirror the good things of eternity. . . . The sight of an earthly king is an object of desire to all men. Everyone in his capital longs to catch even a glimpse of his beauty, the magnificence of his apparel, the glory of his purple. . . . Thus carnal men desire to see the glory of the earthly king. But what of those upon whom has fallen the dew of the Spirit of life in the Godhead, smiting their hearts with a divine passion for Christ, their heavenly king? How much more are they bound fast to that beauty of that ineffable glory . . . of Christ the eternal King . . . and desire to obtain those unspeakable blessings which by the Spirit they see in a mirror? (Ibid. 5:4–5)

This expectation that monastic ritual might lead to visions, spiritual or otherwise, was by no means extraordinary, as witnessed by this encounter between Olympius, a monk of Skete in Egypt, and a pagan priest who paid him a visit. It is Olympius speaking in this anonymously recollected anecdote.

When he [that is, the pagan priest] had observed the life of the monks, he said to me: "With a life of this kind do you receive no visions from God?" "No," I said to him. Then the priest said to me: "As we minister our god conceals nothing from us but rather reveals to us his mysteries. And you, after you have endured so many labors and sleepless nights and days of silence and mortification, do you say 'We see nothing'? Why, then, if you see nothing, the thoughts of your heart must be evil that they separate you from your God." So I went and reported his words to the elders; and they were amazed and said: "So indeed it is. Unclean thoughts do indeed separate God from man." (*The Sayings of the Fathers* 1:583)

At times the experiences undergone by the early monks put us in the presence of genuine mystical transports and an intimate connection with God Himself (see the example of John Cassian below). Others simply received visions, glimpses of the spiritual world beyond this, as here in the deathbed recollections of the monk Anuph.

From the day when I [Anuph] first confessed my Redeemer under persecution, never has an untrue word passed my lips. Never have I allowed earthly desire to dim my spiritual longings. But God's grace has never failed me, and I have needed no earthly thing. Angels have given me all the sustenance I have craved. And God has hidden from me nothing that happens on earth. . . . Often He shows me the hosts of angels that stand before Him: often I behold the glorious company of the righteous, the martyrs and the monks, such as had no purpose but to honor and praise God in singleness of heart. And there too I behold Satan and his angels delivered to eternal torment, while the righteous for their part enjoy eternal bliss. (Rufinus, *Monastic History* 10)

13. Prayer and Contemplation

Spiritual "events" sometimes took the form of visions; more often the experience was associated with prayer. This is Cassian's description of the highest form of prayer, a "prayer without images," a "flame of fire" assisted by an illumination from on high.

It transcends all human thoughts and is distinguished, I will not say by no sound of the voice, but by no movement of the tongue, no utterance of words. It is a prayer which the mind, enlightened by the infusion of heavenly light, does not confine within stilted human speech but pours forth richly in an accumulation of thoughts, as from a plentiful fountain, and ineffably speaks to God, expressing in the shortest possible time such great things as the mind, when it returns to itself, could not easily speak or tell. (Cassian, *Collations* 9:25)

These more personal experiences, are amplified by Cassian sometime about 400 C.E. and echoed in the Homilies *attributed to Macarius and likewise dating from the fourth or fifth century.*

I was often caught up into such an ecstasy as to make me forget that I was clothed with the burden of a weak body. Suddenly my soul forgot all external notions and entirely cut itself off from all material objects so that neither my eyes nor my ears performed their proper functions. And my soul was so filled with devout meditations and spiritual contemplation that often in the evening I did not know whether I had taken any food, and on the next day I was very doubtful whether or not I had broken my fast on the day before. (Cassian, *Collations* 19:4)

(In this prayer) the soul leaves herself, as it were, and is transported into the heavenly regions. All earthly cares are buried in oblivion. The spirit is captivated by things divine, things infinite and incomprehensible, marvels which cannot be expressed in human words. At last it breaks out in longing: "O that my soul might leave the earth and soar away with my prayer!" (Macarius, *Homily* 8:1)

The Macarian Homilies give a graphic description of the act of contemplation. For others, contemplation might have been an intellectual act; here it is quite unmistakably visionary, albeit through the eyes of the soul.

This is something everyone ought to know, that there are eyes that are more inward than these eyes and hearing more inward than this hearing. As the eyes sensibly behold and recognize the face of a friend or loved one, so the eyes of the faithful and worthy soul, once spiritually enlightened by the light of God, behold and recognize the true friend, the sweetest and longed-for bridegroom, the Lord, while the soul is shone upon by the adorable Spirit; and thus beholding with the mind the desirable and only expressible beauty, it is smitten with a passionate love of God, and is directed into all the virtues of the Spirit, and thus possesses an unbounded, unfailing love for the Lord it longs for. (Macarius, *Homily* 28:5)

As time passed and experiences grew more profound, the essential difference between the prayer that is the obligation of every Christian and the mystic's characteristic activity of contemplation could be scored more clearly, as here by one of the Eastern masters of the the spiritual life, Isaac, monk and bishop of Nineveh in newly Muslim-occupied Iraq of the seventh century C.E.

Sometimes from prayer a certain contemplation is born which makes prayer disappear from the lips. And he to whom this contemplation happens becomes a corpse without a soul, in ecstasy. . . . The motions of the tongue and the heart during prayer are keys. What comes after them is the entering into the treasury. Here then all mouths and tongues are silent, and the heart, the treasurer of the thoughts, the mind, the governor of the senses, the daring spirit, that swift bird, and all their means and powers and the beseeching persuasions have to stand still there: for the master of the house has come.

Just as the whole force of the laws and the commandments which God has laid down for mankind have their term in purity of the heart, according to the words of the Fathers, so all kinds and habits of prayer with which mankind prays to God have their term in pure prayer. Lamentations and self-humiliations and beseechings and inner supplications and sweet tears and all other habits which prayer possesses have their boundary, and the domain within which they are set into motion is pure prayer.

As soon as the spirit has crossed the boundary of pure prayer and proceeded onward, there is neither prayer nor emotions nor tears nor authority nor freedom nor beseeching nor desire nor longing after any of those things which are hoped for in this world or in the world to be. Therefore there is no prayer beyond pure prayer . . . but beyond this limit it passes into ecstasy and is no longer prayer. From here onward the spirit desists from prayer; there is sight, but the spirit does not pray. (Isaac of Nineveh, *Mystical Treatises* 112–114)

Much the same type of distinction, though with more emphasis on the affects of contemplation, is drawn by the Spanish Carmelite nun Teresa of Avila (1515–1582 C.E.) in her Way of Perfection.

Do not mistakenly believe that one draws but little profit from vocal prayer when it is well made. I assure you that it is quite possible for our Lord to raise you to perfect contemplation while you are reciting the "Our Father" or some other vocal prayer. And thus His Majesty shows that He hears one who prays in such a manner. This Sovereign Master speaks to the soul in return, suspends its understanding, checks its thoughts and, as it were, forms the very words before they are pronounced. And thus one cannot utter a single word by oneself without the greatest effort. The soul then realizes that the Master teaches it without any sound of words. He suspends the activities of the faculties which, instead of gaining benefits, would only cause harm if they attempted to operate.

In this state the faculties are filled with delight, without knowing why it is they rejoice. The soul is inflamed with an increasing flow of love without perceiving how it loves. It knows that it enjoys the object of its love, but it does not understand the nature of this enjoyment. Nevertheless, it realizes that the understanding could not, of itself, yearn for so ineffable a good. It realizes too that the will embraces the good without the soul's knowing how the will does this. If the soul can understand anything at all, it is the fact that nothing could possibly merit this benefit. It is a gift of the Master of heaven and earth who in the end bestows this boon in a manner worthy of Him. This is contemplation. (Teresa of Avila, *The Way of Perfection*)

14. Origen: The Christian Platonist in Search of God

Early monastic mysticism appears highly personal, remote from any currents save those swirling in the mystic's own soul. But once those impulses moved from desert and wilderness to the wider world inhabited by Christianity in the fourth century, the Christian mystic had a double heritage upon which to draw: the biblical and the philosophical. For the third-century Christian, no less than for the first-century Jew Philo, Moses and Plato were the two principal guides along the mystical path, Moses as a paradigm, Plato as an instructor.

The Platonic tradition held firmly to the immortality of the highest faculty of the soul, that is to say, the human intellect. It also affirmed what has been called "the great chain of being," a linked and graduated unity from the First Cause at the head of creation to the lowest form of being at its base. This chain of being was the royal staircase by which creation proceeded gradually outward and downward from God by way of emanation; it was also the ladder by which men struggled, likewise gradually, back up to God by way of purification, understanding, and contemplation.

These were commonplaces of the tradition when the Philo was active in Alexandria and two centuries later when Origen (185–254 C.E.) was enrolled as the first known Christian in the philosophy faculty there. They provided Origen, as they had Philo, the theoretical bases for an approach to God.

That study is called "moral" which inculcates a seemly manner of life and lays down a foundation for virtuous habits. The study called "natural" is that in which the nature of each single thing is considered to the end that nothing may be done in life contrary to nature but rather that everything be assigned to those uses intended by the Creator in bringing it into being. The study called "inspective" is that by which we go beyond things seen and contemplate something of the heavenly and the divine, looking upon them with the mind alone, for they are beyond the range of bodily sight. (Origen, *Commentary on the Song of Songs*, Prologue)

*The nature of these studies becomes clearer when Origen links them with what were
to be the texts in a Christian version of an academic curriculum, namely, the three
biblical books ascribed to Solomon: Proverbs, Qohelet or Ecclesiastes, and the Song
of Songs.*

So as to distinguish each of these three branches of learning from the
other, that is, the moral, the natural and the inspective, and to differen-
tiate among them, Solomon issued them in three books, arranged in the
proper order. First, in Proverbs, he taught the moral science, casting the
rules for living into the form of brief and pithy maxims, as was appropriate. Second, he covered the science known as natural in Ecclesiastes.
There he discussed at length the things of nature, and by distinguishing
the useless and vain from the profitable and the essential, he counsels us
to forsake vanity and to cultivate useful and upright things. Similarly, the
inspective science he has explained in this little book now before us, that
is, the Song of Songs. In it he instills into the soul the love of things divine
and heavenly, using to this end the figures of the Bride and the Bridegroom, and he teaches us that communion with God must be attained by
the paths of charity and love.

If then a man has completed his course in the first subject, as it is
taught in Proverbs, by emending his behavior and keeping the commandments, and then, once he has seen how empty the world is and realized
how brittle are transitory things, he renounces the world and all that is
in it, he will proceed from that point to contemplate and desire the things
that are not seen and are eternal. But to attain these, we need God's
mercy, so that, once having beheld the beauty of the Word of God, we
may be kindled with a saving love for Him, and He Himself may deign to
love the soul whose longings for Himself He has discerned. (Ibid., Prologue)

*This state cannot be achieved, of course—and here the voices of the Platonist and
the Christian mingle in harmony—until after death, when the intellect is finally
freed of the carnal weight of the body and the earthbound soul.*

And so the rational being, growing at each successive stage, not indeed as it grew in this life, in the flesh or body and in the soul, but rather
increasing in mind and intellect, advances as a mind already perfect to a
perfect knowledge, now no longer hindered by its former carnal senses,
but developing in intellectual power, ever more closely approaches the
pure and it gazes "face to face," so to speak, on the causes of things.
(Origen, *On First Principles* 2.11.7)

15. Moses Enters the Darkness

What once seemed fitting and natural to Origen no longer seemed so to Christians a century later. The attraction of the emanationist theory of creation and the figure of the ladder had induced some to follow a certain Arius and place the person of Jesus a step or grade below the Father. The reaction against the Arians—and at the Council of Nicea in 325 C.E. this reaction was constituted Christian orthodoxy—was to insist once again, as Genesis itself seemed to insist, on an absolute creation of the universe from nothing: God—Father, Son, and Holy Spirit—stood on one side of what was now the great divide of being, all of creation on the other.

There would appear to be no hope of approaching God across that great abyss, none save that provided by the example of Moses on Sinai. Here the Christian Gregory of Nyssa (ca. 335–394 C.E.) follows Moses up Sinai. In the first, lighted stages of the ascent he walks step by step with Origen. Although Gregory speaks of Moses and Exodus, he is here commenting on what Origen taught the Christians should be the mystics' biblical vade mecum, the Song of Songs.

Moses' vision of God began with light; afterwards God spoke to him in a cloud. But when Moses rose higher and became more perfect, he saw God in the darkness. Now the doctrine we are taught here is as follows. Our initial withdrawal from wrong and erroneous ideas of God is a transition from darkness to light. Next comes a closer awareness of hidden things, and by this the soul is guided through sense phenomena to the world of the invisible. And this awareness is a kind of cloud, which overshadows all appearances, and slowly guides and accustoms the soul to look toward what is hidden. Next, the soul makes progress through all these stages and goes on higher, and as she leaves below all that human knowledge can attain, she enters within the secret chamber of the divine knowledge, and here she is cut off on all sides by the divine darkness. Now she leaves outside all that can be grasped by sense or by reason, and the only thing left for her contemplation is the invisible and the incomprehensible. And here God is, as the Scriptures tell us in connection with Moses: "But Moses went into the dark cloud wherein God was" (Exod. 20:21). (Gregory of Nyssa, *Commentary on the Song of Songs* 11)

Moses, then, is the type of the believer who crossed the abyss, who penetrated into that profound "otherness" that characterizes the divine and is hereafter represented in the Christian tradition by the figure of impenetrable darkness or a dense cloud. Gregory of Nyssa spoke of that darkness at length, and many of his thoughts on it are found in his Life of Moses. *Here he reflects on Moses' entry into the cloud on the summit of Sinai, as described in Exodus 24.*

What now is the meaning of Moses' entry into the darkness and the vision of God that he enjoyed in it? . . . The sacred text is here teaching us that . . . as the soul makes progress, and by a greater and more perfect concentration comes to appreciate what the knowledge of truth is, the more it approaches this vision, and so much the more does it see that the divine nature is invisible. It thus leaves all surface appearances, not only those that can be grasped by the senses but also those which the mind itself seems to see, and it keeps on going deeper until by the operation of the spirit it penetrates the invisible and the incomprehensible, and it is there that it sees God. The true vision and the true knowledge of what we seek consists precisely in not seeing, in an awareness that our knowledge transcends all knowledge and is everywhere cut off from us by the darkness of incomprehensibility. Thus that profound evangelist, John, who penetrated into this luminous darkness, tell us that "no man has seen God at any time," teaching us by this negation that no man—indeed, no created intellect—can attain a knowledge of God.

We can conceive of no limitation in an infinite nature, and that which is without limit cannot by its nature be understood. And so every desire for the Beautiful which draws us on in this ascent is intensified by the soul's very progress toward it. And this is the real meaning of seeing God: never to have this desire satisfied. By fixing our eyes on those things which help us to see, we must ever keep alive in us the desire to see more and more. And so no limit can be set on our progress toward God: first of all, because no limitation can be put upon the beautiful, and secondly, because the increase of our desire for the beautiful cannot be stopped by any sense of satisfaction. (Gregory of Nyssa, *Life of Moses* 2)

The figure is biblical, of course; and if the ethical and intellectual theory is still Platonic, the easy optimism of Plato, and of Origen, is gone. Aspiration has been converted into a series of paradoxes—the vision that consists in not seeing, a knowledge that transcends knowledge. These sentiments are the product of something new, a later and less confident Platonism perhaps, a Platonism at the same time more esoteric and more religious than that which Philo and even Origen knew, a Platonism tempered in its Christian form by the lessons learned from the Arian heresy condemned at Nicea. And it was profoundly to shape not so much the Christian experience of God as the understanding of the mode and meaning of that experience.

16. The Negative Theology of Dionysius the Areopagite

The classic exposition of later Platonic mysticism in Christian raiment is found in a series of works attributed to a certain Dionysius the Areopagite, one of Paul's converts mentioned in passing in Acts 17:34. In fact, he had nothing to do with the body of works circulating under his name; they were, as far as we can tell, an anonymous product of the early decades of the sixth Christian century. The essential themes of that system appear early in the tract entitled The Mystical Theology.

. . . As you look for a sight of the mysterious things, leave behind you everything perceived and understood, everything perceptible and understandable, all that is not and all that is, and, with your understanding laid aside, strive upward as much as you can toward union with Him who is beyond all being and knowledge. By an undivided and absolute abandonment of yourself and everything, shedding all and freed from all, you will be uplifted to the ray of the divine shadow which is above everything that is.

Equally characteristic is the emphasis on the esoteric nature of the mystic's knowledge. "Dionysius" is no more eager than his rabbinic contemporaries in the Talmud that this kind of speculation fall into the hands of the uninitiated.

See to it that none of this comes to the hearing of the uninformed, that is to say, to those caught up with the things of the world, who imagine that there is nothing beyond instances of individual being and who think by their own intellectual resources they can have a direct knowledge of Him who has made the shadow His hiding place. And if initiation into the divine is beyond such people, what is to be said of those others, still more uninformed, who describe the transcendent cause of all things in terms derived from the lowest order of being. . . . What has actually to be said about the cause of everything is this. We should posit and ascribe to it all the affirmations we make in regard to beings, and, more appropriately, we should negate all those affirmations, since it surpasses all being. Now we should not conclude that the negations are simply the opposites of the affirmations, but rather that the cause of all is considerably prior to this, beyond privations, beyond every denial, beyond every assertion.

This, at least, is what was taught by the Blessed Bartholomew. He says that the Word of God is vast and minuscule, that the Gospel is wide-ranging yet restricted. To me it seems that in this he is extraordinarily shrewd, for he has grasped that the good cause of all is both eloquent and taciturn, indeed wordless. It has neither word nor act of understanding, since it is on a plane above all this, and it is made manifest only to those who travel through foul and fair, who pass beyond the summit of every holy ascent, who leave behind them every divine light, every voice, every word from heaven, and who plunge into the darkness where, as Scripture proclaims, there dwells the One who is beyond all things.

The author now stands at the outer limit of paradox, and he is forced to resort more and more often to new and unusual compounds in hyper- ("super-" or "trans-") to express what he wants to but cannot say about God.

I pray we could come to this darkness so far above the light! If only we lacked sight and knowledge so as to see, so as to know, unseeing and unknowing, that which lies above all vision and knowledge. For this would be really to see and to know: to praise the Transcendent One in a transcending way, namely through the denial of all beings. We would be like sculptors who set out to carve a statue. They remove every obstacle to the pure view of the hidden image, and simply in this act of clearing aside they show up the beauty which is hidden.

Now it seem to me that we should praise the denials (concerning the First Cause) quite differently than we do the assertions. When we made assertions we began with the first things, moved down through the intermediate terms until we reached the last things. But now as we climb from the last things up to the most primary, we deny all things so that we may unhiddenly know that unknowing which is itself hidden from all those possessed of knowing amid all beings, so that we may see above being that darkness concealed from all the light among beings.

The figure of the sculptor abstracting, "clearing aside" to reveal the form inherent in the marble brings the author to a discussion of the "negative theology" that was to prove so useful in so many subsequent Christian explorations of mystical theology.

When we assert what is beyond every assertion, we must then proceed from what is most akin to it. . . . But when we deny that which is beyond every denial, we have to start by denying those qualities which differ most from the goal we hope to attain. . . . So this is what we say. The Cause of all is above all and is not inexistent, lifeless, speechless, mindless. It is not a material body, and hence has neither shape, nor form, quality, quantity, or weight. It is not in any place and can be neither seen nor touched. It is neither perceived, nor is it perceptible. . . . Again, as we climb higher we say this. It is not soul or mind, nor does it possess imagination, conviction, speech or understading. . . . It does not live nor is it life. It is not a substance nor is it eternity or time. . . . It falls within the predicate neither of non-being nor of being. . . . It is beyond assertion and denial. We make assertions and denials of what is next to it, but never of it, for it is both beyond every assertion, being the perfect and unique cause of all things, and, by virtue of its pre-eminently simple and absolute nature, free of every limitation, beyond every limitation; as it is also beyond every denial. (Dionysius the Areopagite, *Mystical Theology* 997b–1048b) [(PSEUDO)-DIONYSIUS 1987: 135–141]

17. God Experienced, East and West

The theology of "Dionysius the Areopagite" is, like most theological analyses, highly abstract, while the mystical experience is by its nature an intensely personal one. Here two Christians, one from Eastern Christendom, the other from the beginning of the European Middle Ages, attempt to describe it. The account of Symeon, the so-called "New Theologian" (949–1022 C.E.) who is closely linked with the Dionysian tradition in the Eastern Church, is here reported through one of his students.

As Symeon was praying one night, and his purified mind was thus united with the First Intelligence, he experienced a brilliant light coming from above, pure and great and casting its radiance over all, as bright indeed as the light of the day itself. He too was illumined by it, and it appeared to him as if the entire building, and his own cell within it, had all been annihilated in the merest instant. He was borne aloft into the air, forgetful of his own body, and in this condition—as he later told and wrote to his close associates, he experienced both happiness and scalding tears. He was lost in wonder at this extraordinary event, since he had never had such an experience before, was both filled with great happiness and overcome with hot tears. Amazed by the strangeness of this marvelous happening—for he had as yet no similar revelations—he cried out repeatedly, "Lord, have mercy on me." He was aware of this only after he returned to his normal state since at the time he was unaware that he was speaking or that his words were audible outside his cell. It was likewise during this state of illumination that the grace of (spiritual) sight was bestowed upon him, and a great a brilliant cloud, without form but suffused with the nameless presence of God, appeared to him. To the right of this cloud there appeared to him his (deceased) spiritual father, Symeon of Studium, standing erect and wearing his customary habit.

Symeon stared fixedly at the divine light and prayed without distraction, but since he had been in this ecstatic state for some time, he was unaware of whether he had left his own body or whether he was still within it, as he later told us. At length the great light began gradually to draw away and Symeon once more found himself conscious of his body and his cell. . . . Such is the effect of purity of heart and so great the operation of divine love in virtuous souls. (Nicetas Stethatus, *Life of Symeon the New Theologian*)

An equally circumstantial description is given to monastic brethren by Bernard of Clairvaux (1090–1153 C.E.), who had begun his career as a Cistercian in 1112 C.E.

Bear awhile with my foolishness. I would tell you, as indeed I promised, how it is with me in these matters. I confess, then, that the Word has come to me—I speak as a fool—and has come many times. Yet though He has often come in unto me, I never perceived the moment of His coming; I have perceived Him present, I remember he has been present; sometimes I have actually been able to have a premonition of His entry, but never to be aware of it when it happens, nor of His going out from me. For whence He came into my soul, and whither He went when He left it again, by what way He came in or went out, even now I confess I do not know. . . .

Certainly it was not by the eyes that He entered, for He has no color; nor by the ears, for He made no sound; nor by the nostrils, for He blends not with the air but with the soul; nor did He make the air fragrant—He *made* it. Nor again did He enter through the mouth, for He is not to be eaten or drunk; nor could He be discerned by touch, for He is impalpable. By what way then did He enter? Can it be that He did not enter at all because He did not come from outside? For He is not one of the things that is without. Yet again, He did not come from within me, for He is good and I know that "no good thing dwells within me."

I have gone up to the highest point in my powers, and behold, the Word was towering yet higher. My curiosity took me to my lowest depth to look for Him, nevertheless He was found still deeper. If I looked outside of me, I found He was beyond my farthest reach; if I looked within, He was more inward still. . . .

You ask, then, since His ways are thus beyond all searching out, how did I know the Word was present? Because He is living, and powerful to act and to do; and as soon as He came within He roused my sleeping soul. He stirred and softened and wounded my heart, for it was dry and stony and poor in health. He began, too, to pluck out and to destroy, to build up and to plant, to water the dry places, to lighten the dark corners, to throw open the closed doors, to enkindle the chilled regions, "to make the crooked straight and the rough places plain," so that "my soul blessed the Lord, and all that was within me praised His holy Name." So then the Word, the Bridegroom, though several times He has come unto me, had never made known His entry by any signs or tokens, either by voice or by sight or by step. In fine, it was by no movements of His that He became known to me, nor could I tell by any senses of mine that He had passed into my inmost parts; only by the movement of my heart, as I said at the outset, did I recognize His presence; and by the flight of all vices from me, and by the suppression of all carnal desires, I was aware of the power of His might; and from the discovery and conviction of my secret faults I came to wonder at the depth of His wisdom; and from the amendment, small though it was, of my life and conversation I learned of His goodwill and loving kindness; and through the renewing and refashioning of the spirit of my mind, that is, my inner man, I perceived in some measure His excellent beauty; and from gazing on all these things together, I was filled with awe at His abundant greatness. (Bernard of Clairvaux, *Sermons on the Song of Songs* 74:5–6)

18. Conjugal and Other Loves

Christian mystics of the Latin West took to heart Origen's advice to make the biblical Song of Songs—a rhapsody of conjugal, indeed of sexual, love—their guide to the spiritual life. Thus the mystics' quest for God is often expressed in terms of love of bridegroom and bride, as in Bernard of Clairvaux's meditation on the Song of Songs.

It is this conformity [that is, of the mystic with Jesus, the Word of God] that brings about the marriage of the soul with the Word, when the soul, which is already like Him in nature, shows itself like Him also in will, loving as itself is loved. Thus, if it loves so perfectly, it is wedded to Him. Is there anything more joyful than this conformity? Is there anything more to be desired than charity, charity which makes you, O soul, no longer content with human instruction, go forward on your own with full confidence to approach the Word, to cleave steadfastly to the Word, to address your questions to Him as a friend, to ask His counsel on every matter, as receptive in your intelligence as you are fearless in your desire? This is the marriage contract of a truly spiritual and holy union. No, contract is too weak a description; it is an embrace. . . .

The Bridegroom is not only loving, He is love. . . . God demands to be feared as Lord; to be honored as Father; as Bridegroom to be loved. Which of these is the highest, which the noblest? Love, we cannot doubt. Without love fear torments and honor has no grace. Fear remains servile because love does not set it free; and honor which does not flow from love is not real honor but mere flattery. Truly, honor and glory are due to God alone; but God will not accept either unless they are sweetened with the honey of love. Love is sufficient of itself, pleasant of and for itself. Love is a merit and love is its own reward. Love seeks neither cause nor outcome outside itself; the outcome is identical with the practice of it. I love because I love; I love that I may love. . . . Of all the movements of the soul, of all its feelings and affects, it is by love alone that the creator responds to its Creator, though in less than equal measure, and pays Him back something of what it has received. . . .

Love then is the great reality; but there are degrees of love, and highest of all is the love of the bride. Children love their fathers, but they are thinking of the inheritance they expect to get. . . . I am suspicious of that love which I see is animated by the hope of getting something. It is weak. . . . It is impure. . . . Pure love is not mercenary. Pure love does not draw its strength from hope, nor is it injured by distrust. This is the love the bride has; for all and everything she has is this: all her being, all her hope is love and love alone. The bride overflows with love, and the Bridegroom is content therein. He seeks nothing else from her; she has nothing else to give. It is this which makes Him the Bridegroom, her the bride. This is the love that belongs only to those who are joined in marriage, the love which none other but the bride, not even a son, can attain.

Rightly then does the bride renounce all other affections and give herself up wholly to love and to love alone, for she is able to make some return to love by loving him back again. For when she has poured her self forth in love, how little this is when compared with that fountain which flows in a never failing stream! Truly, they do not flow in equal volume, the lover and Love Himself, the soul and the Word, the bride and the Bridegroom, the Creator and the creature: it is as though we were to compare a thirsty man with the spring he drinks from. (Bernard, *Homilies on the Song of Songs* 83:3–6)

Elsewhere, in Bernard's analysis of the progressive types of love, there can be little doubt that in the fourth and highest stage he is speaking of the mystic's, and his own, personal experience.

Happy is the one who has deserved to gain the fourth stage, where a man does not love even himself except for the sake of God. Your justice, O Lord, is like the mountains of God. This love is a mountain, and a high mountain. . . . Who shall ascend into the mountain of the Lord? . . . When will the mind experience such an affection as this so that, inebriated with divine love, forgetful of self, and having become in its own eyes like a shattered vessel, the whole of it may continue on to God and, being joined to God, become one spirit with Him. . . .

Blessed and holy, I would say, is he to whom it has been granted to experience such a thing in this mortal life at rare intervals, or even once, and this suddenly and scarcely for the space of a single moment. In a certain manner to lose yourself as though you were not, and to be utterly unconscious of yourself and be emptied of yourself, and, as it were, brought to nothing, this, I say, belongs to heavenly intercourse and not human affection. And if indeed, a mortal is suddenly from time to time, as has been said, even for the space of a moment admitted to this, straightway the wicked world grows envious, the evil of the day throws everything into confusion, the body of death becomes a burden, the necessity of the flesh causes unrest, the fainting away of corruption offers no support; and what is more vehement than these, fraternal charity recalls one. Alas, he is forced to return to himself, to fall back upon his own, and in his wretchedness to cry out, "Unhappy man that I am, who shall deliver me from the body of this death?"

. . . O love, holy and chaste! O sweet and pleasing affection! O pure and undefiled intention of the will! The more surely undefiled and purer, as there is now mixed with it nothing of its own; so much the sweeter and more pleasing, as its every feeling is wholly divine. To be thus affected is to become one with God. Just as a little drop of water mixed with a lot of wine seems entirely to lose its own identity, while it takes on the taste and the color of the wine; just as iron, heated and glowing, looks very much like fire, having divested itself of its original and characteristic appearance; and just as air flooded with the light of the sun is transformed into the same splendor of light that it appears not so much lighted as to be light itself; so it will inevitably happen that in saints every human affection will in some ineffable manner melt away from self and will be entirely transfused in the will of God—be all in all, if in man there is left anything at all of man himself. The substance indeed will remain, but in another form, another glory, and another power. (Bernard of Clairvaux, *On the Love of Good* 10)

The love imagery drawn from the Song of Songs and elaborated by Bernard of Clairvaux occurs again and again in the writings of Christian mystics of the West. But occasionally the theme and image of love take other turns, as in this early-fifteenth-century meditation by Dame Julian of Norwich.

Jesus Christ that doeth good against evil is our Very Mother: we have our Being of Him—where the ground of Motherhood beginneth—with all sweet Keeping of Love that endlessly followeth. As verily as God is our Father, so verily God is our Mother; and that shewed He in all, and especially in those sweet words where He saith: I it am. That is to say, I it am, the Might and Goodness of the Fatherhood; I it am, the Wisdom of the Motherhood; I it am, the Light and the Grace that is all blessed Love; I it am, the Trinity. . . .

In these three is all our life: Nature, Mercy, Grace: whereof we have meekness and mildness; patience and pity; and hating of sin and of wickedness. And thus is Jesus our Very Mother in Nature by virtue of our first making. And He is our Very Mother in Grace, by taking on our nature made. All the fair working, and all the sweet natural office of dearworthy Motherhood is impropriated to the Second Person. . . . I understand three manners of beholding Motherhood in God: the first is grounded in our Nature's making; the second is tasking of our nature—and there beginneth the Motherhood of Grace; the third is the Motherhood of working—and therein is a forth-spreading by the same Grace, of length and breadth and height and of deepness without end. And all is one Love. (Julian of Norwich, *Revelations of Divine Love* 59)

The theme of the mystic's love of God appears early and urgently in Islam in the prayers of Rabiʿa (d. 801 C.E.), the Baghdad mystic who replied, when her hand was sought in marriage:

The contract of marriage is for those who lead a phenomenal existence. But in my case, there is no such existence, for I have ceased to exist and have passed out of self. I exist in God and I am altogether His. I live in the shadow of his command. The marriage contract must be asked of Him, not from me. (Attar, *Recollections of the Saints* 1:66)

[Cited by SMITH 1931: 186]

Rabiʿa was also the author of one the most famous poems in all Sufi literature, a brief meditation on the love of God.

I have loved you with two loves, a selfish love and a love that is worthy of You.

As for the love which is selfish, therein I occupy myself with You, to the exclusion of all others.

But in the love which is worthy of You, You raise the veil that I may
see You.

Yet is the praise not mine in this love or that,

But the praise is Yours in both that love and this.

(Rabiʿa) [Cited by SMITH 1931: 223]

The golden age of Sufism produced, this elegant little parable of mystic love from the pen of the Persian poet Attar, written in 1177 C.E.

A girl fell in a river—in a flash
Her lover dived in with a mighty splash,
And fought the current till he reached her side.
When they were safe again, the poor girl cried:
"By chance I tumbled in, but why should you
Come in after me and hazard your life too?"
He said: "I dived because the difference
of 'I' and 'you' to lovers makes no sense—
A long time passed when we were separate,
And now that we have reached this single state
When you are me and I am wholly you,
What use is it to talk of us as two?"
All talk of two implies plurality—
When two has gone there will be Unity.
(Attar, *The Conference of the Birds*) [ATTAR 1984: 194]

The tone of Attar's poetic parable is romantic but sober, and unmistakably hetero-sexual. It by no means exhausted the Sufis' emotional repertoire on the subject, however. The most famous of the Muslim poets of mystic love wrote much of his best work in the grip of an extraordinary passion for a fellow Sufi. Indeed, the love of Jalal al-Din Rumi (1207–1273 C.E.) for Shams al-Din Tabrizi was so all-consum-ing that in the end Rumi's son and disciples murdered the beloved Shams al-Din and told the master that he had simply disappeared. But not from Rumi's heart: the presence of Shams al-Din haunts the epic of love that is called the Mathnawi. *It opens with these lines.*

Hearken to this reed forlorn,
Breathing, ever since 'twas torn
From its rushy bed, a strain
Of impassioned love and pain.

The secret of my song, though near,
None can see and none can hear.
Oh, for a friend to know the sign
And mingle all his soul with mine!

'Tis the flame of Love that fired me,
'Tis the wine of Love inspired me.
Wouldst thou learn how lovers bleed,
Hearken, hearken to the Reed!
(Rumi, *Mathnawi*, Prologue) [Cited by ARBERRY 1950: 111]

And in these celebrated lines on human and divine love:

A certain man knocked at a friend's door: his friend asked:
> "Who is there?"
He answered: "I." "Begone," said his friend, "tis too soon!
> At my table there is no place for the raw.
How shall the raw be cooked but in the fire of absence? What else
> will deliver him from hypocrisy?"
He turned sadly away, and for a whole year the flames
> of separation consumed him;
Then he came back and again paced to and fro beside the house
> of his friend.
He knocked at the door with a hundred fears and reverence lest any
> disrespectful word might escape from his lips
"Who is there?" cried the friend. He answered: "Thou, O charmer
> of all hearts."
"Now," said the friend, "since thou art I, come in, there is no room
> for two I's in this house."
(Rumi, *Mathnawi*) [RUMI 1925–1940: 1:3056–3064]

19. The Spiritual Light

The path to God's presence traced by Gregory of Nyssa and "Dionysius," namely, the one that led into the realm of ineffable darkness that was the abode of the divine, continued to have its devotees in both the Eastern and the Western branch of Christendom. In the end, however, the Eastern Church came to prefer another way, that of God as Light. It is already clearly expressed in the fourth- or fifth-century Homilies attributed to the Egyptian desert master Macarius.

The soul which has been perfectly illuminated by the ineffable beauty of the glory of the light of the face of Christ, has achieved perfect participation in the Holy Spirit and has become worthy to be an abode and throne of God, that soul becomes wholly eye and wholly face and wholly Spirit, being so made by Christ who drives and guides and carries it about, and graces and adorns it with spiritual beauty. (Macarius, *Homilies* 1:2)

And if Moses on Sinai is the type of the mystic entering the cloud of unknowing, Jesus transfigured on that other mountain called Tabor in Galilee provides the most powerful image for the mysticism of light.

As the body of the Lord was glorified when he went up into the mountain, and was transfigured into the divine glory and into the infinite light, so are the bodies of the saints glorified and shine like lightning. The glory that was within Christ was spread out upon his body and shone forth there, and likewise the power of Christ in the saints shall on that day be poured outwardly upon their bodies. (Ibid. 15:38)

"That day" was for the author the day of the Last Judgment, but for later mystics the transfiguration could be achieved in this life in the mystic's transport. So it was in the tenth century for Symeon, the "New Theologian," whose Discourses gave the Byzantine Church a clear and highly personal understanding of what had by then come to be the single most powerful characterization of the mystic's encounter with God: to stand in the presence of God was to be bathed in and suffused with an ineffable immaterial light. Symeon, here referring to himself in the third person, informs the reader that he first had this experience while still living as a layman in Constantinople, though he was already well embarked upon a personal conversion.

During the day he managed a patrician's household and daily went to the palace, engaged in worldly affairs, so that no one was aware of his pursuits. Every evening tears welled from his eyes; more and more frequently he prostrated himself with his face to the ground, with his feet together, without moving from the spot where he stood. With all diligence he recited prayers to the Mother of God accompanied with groans and tears. . . . So as his prayer grew longer every evening he continued until midnight. Not a member of his body moved, his eye did not turn or look up, but he stood motionless as though he were a statue or an incorporeal spirit.

One day, as he stood and recited, "God have mercy upon me, a sinner," uttering it with his mind rather than his mouth, suddenly a flood of divine radiance appeared from above and filled all the room. As this happened he lost all awareness (of his surroundings) and forgot that he was in a house or that he was under a roof. He saw nothing but light all round him and did not know if he was standing on the ground. He was not afraid of falling; he was not concerned with the world, nor did anything pertaining to men and corporeal beings enter into his mind. Instead, he was wholly in the presence of immaterial light and seemed to himself to have turned into light. Oblivious of all the world, he was filled with tears and with ineffable joy and gladness. His mind then ascended to heaven and beheld yet another light, which was clearer than that which was close at hand. (Symeon, *Discourses* 22:3–4)

[SYMEON NEOTHEOLOGUS 1980: 245–246]

He describes, now in the first person, how it happened again not long after he had taken up the life of the monk.

I entered the place where I usually prayed and . . . I began to say "Holy God." At once I was so greatly moved to tears and loving desire of God that I would be unable to describe in words the joy and delight I then felt. I fell prostrate on the ground, and at once I saw, and behold, a great light was immaterially shining on me and seized hold of my mind and soul, so that I was struck with amazement at the unexpected marvel, and I was, as it were, in ecstasy. Moreover, I forgot the place where I stood, who I was, and where, and could only cry out, "Lord, have mercy," so that when I came to myself I discovered I was reciting this. . . . Who it was that was speaking, or who moved my tongue, I do not know—only God knows.

"Whether I was in the body or outside the body" (2 Cor. 12:2–3), I conversed with the light. The Light itself knows it; it scattered whatever mist there was in my soul and cast out every earthly care. It expelled from me all material denseness and bodily heaviness that made my members sluggish and numb. What an awesome marvel! It so invigorated and strengthened my limbs and muscles, which had been faint through great weariness, that it seemed to me as though I was stripping myself of the garment of corruption. Besides, there poured into my soul in unutterable fashion a great spiritual joy and perception and a sweetness surpassing all taste of visible objects, together with a freedom and forgetfulness of all thoughts pertaining to this life. In a marvelous way there was granted to me and revealed to me the manner of the departure from this present life. Thus all the perceptions of my mind and soul were wholly concentrated on the ineffable joy of the Light.

. . . When it [that is, the Light] appears, it fills one with joy, when it vanishes it wounds. It happens close to me and carries me up to heaven. It is a pearl (of great price) (Matt. 13:46). The light envelops me and appears to me like a star, and it is incomprehensible to all. It is radiant like the sun, and I perceive all creation encompassed by it. It shows me all that it contains, and enjoins me to respect my own limits. I am hemmed in by roof and walls, yet it opens the heavens to me. I lift up my eyes sensibly to contemplate the things that are on high, and I see all things as they were before.

The experience is over, but not the instruction.

I marvel at what has happened and I hear a voice speaking to me secretly from on high. "These things are but symbols and preliminaries, for you will not see that which is perfect as long as you are clothed in flesh. But return to yourself and see that you do nothing that deprives you of the things that are above. Should you fall, however, it is to recall you to humility! Do not cease to cultivate penitence, for when it is united with My love for mankind it blots out past and present failures." (Symeon, *Discourses* 16:3–5) [SYMEON NEOTHEOLOGUS 1980: 200–202]

Stepping back a bit from the immediacy of the event, Symeon explains that, for the believer who experiences it, this is nothing less than a kind of deification.

Let no one deceive you. God is light (1 John 1:5), and to those who have entered into union with him He imparts of His own brightness to the extent that they have been purified. When the lamp of the soul, that is, the mind, has been kindled, then it knows that a divine fire has taken hold of it and inflamed it. How great a marvel! Man is united to God spiritually and physically, since the soul is not separated from the mind, neither the body from the soul. By being united in essence man also [that is, like God] has three hypostases. He is a single god by adoption with body and soul and the divine Spirit, of whom he has become a partaker. . . . How He abides in us and how we in turn abide in Him, the Lord Himself taught us when He said, "You, Father, are in Me and I in You" (John 17:21) and "they are in Me and I in them" (John 17:23). (Symeon, *Discourses* 15:3) [SYMEON NEOTHEOLOGUS 1980: 195]

20. Jesus, the Eucharist, and the Transfiguration

Since the Son of God, in His incomparable love for man, not only united His divine hypostasis with our nature, by clothing Himself in a living body and a soul gifted with intelligence, but also united Himself . . . with the human hypostases themselves, in mingling Himself with each of the faithful by communion with His Holy Body, and since He becomes one single body with us (Eph. 3:6), and makes us a temple of the undivided Divinity, for in the very body of Christ dwells the fullness of the Godhead bodily (Col. 2:9), how should He not illuminate those who commune worthily with the divine ray of His Body, which is within us, lighting their souls, as He illumined the bodies of the disciples on Mount Tabor? For on the day of the Transfiguration, that Body, source of the light of grace, was not yet united with our bodies; it illuminated from the outside those who worthily approached it, and sent the illumination into the soul by the intermediary of the physical eyes; but now, since it is mingled with us and exists in us, it illuminates the soul from within. (Gregory Palamas, *The Triads* 1.3.38) [PALAMAS 1983: 19]

Thus, what was called by the Jews the Shekina, *the Divine Presence, became for Eastern Christians the Divine Light, which "illuminates the soul from within." It is, as Palamas (1296–1359), the most influential mystical theologian of the Eastern Church, attempts to explain, neither a sensible light nor yet only a symbol.*

The monks know that the essence of God transcends the fact of being inaccessible to the senses, since God is not only above all created things but is even beyond the Godhead. The excellence of Him who surpasses all things is not only beyond all affirmation but also beyond all negation, it exceeds all excellence that is attainable by the mind.

It is impossible to carry the Dionysian paradoxes much farther. Is God then totally unknowable? For an answer Palamas turns to the Divine Light, which he verifies from the experience of the saints:

This hypostatic light, seen spiritually by the saints, they know by experience to exist, as they tell us, and to exist not symbolically only, as do manifestations produced by fortuitous events, but it is an illumination immaterial and divine, a grace invisibly seen and ignorantly known. *What it is, they do not pretend to know.*

. . . This light is not the essence of God, for that is inaccessible and incommunicable; it is not an angel, for it bears the marks of the Master. Sometimes it makes a man go out from the body, it elevates him to an ineffable height. At other times it transforms the body, and communicates its own splendor to it when, miraculously, the light which deifies the body becomes accessible to the eyes of the body. Thus indeed did . . . Stephen (appear) when being stoned (Acts 6:15), and Moses, when he descended from the mountain (Exod. 34:29). Sometimes the light "speaks" clearly, as it were with ineffable words, to him who contemplates it. Such was the case with Paul (2 Cor. 12:4). According to Gregory the Theologian, "it descends from the elevated place where it dwells, so that He who in His own nature from eternity is neither visible nor containable by any being may in a certain measure be contained by a created nature. He who has received this light, by concentrating upon himself, constantly perceives in his mind that same reality which the children of the Jews called manna, the bread that came down from on high (Exod. 16:14 ff.)." (Gregory Palamas, *The Triads* 2.3.8–9) [PALAMAS 1983: 57–58]

21. The Lamp in the Niche

The scriptural accounts of Moses on Sinai and Jesus on Tabor served, when and where needed, as Jewish and Christian paradigms of the vision of God. The Muslim had no such straightforward narrative text in the Quran to certify Muhammad for the same purpose. The mystics of Islam turned instead for their inspiration to the famous "Light Verse."

> God is the Light of the heavens and the earth.
> The semblance of His Light is that of a niche
> in which is a lamp, the flame within the glass,
> the glass as it were a glittering star, lit with the oil
> of a blessed tree, the olive, neither of the East
> nor of the West, whose oil appears to light up
> even though fire touches it not—light upon light.
> God guides to His Light whom He will.
> So does God advance precepts [or "allegories"] for men,
> For God has knowledge of everything.
> (Quran 24:35)

The last sentence in the verse reads like an open invitation to allegorical exegesis, and so it was generally interpreted. One example is the work entitled The Pure in the Interpretation of the Quran, by the Shiʿite scholar al-Kashi (d. 1505 C.E.). His interpretation, which is overtly Shiʿite in intent, goes back, as he tells us, to another, much earlier eminence in that tradition, Ibn Babuya al-Qummi (d. 939). Qummi's authorities are no less than the fifth and sixth Shiʿite Imams, Muhammad al-Baqir (d. 731) and Jaʿfar al-Sadiq (d. 756).

In "The Oneness" (of al-Qummi) it is reported, on the authority of al-Sadiq: What is at question here is a simile that God has fashioned for us.

"God is the Light of the Heavens and the Earth": Just so, said al-Sadiq.

"His Light": al-Sadiq said: This refers to Muhammad.

"That of a niche": al-Sadiq said that what is meant here is Muhammad's breast.

"In which is a lamp": al-Sadiq said: In which is the light of knowledge, that is, of prophecy.

"The flame within the glass": al-Sadiq said: The knowledge of the Messenger of God went forth from the latter into the heart of Ali.

". . . neither of the East nor of the West": According to al-Sadiq these words refer to the Commander of the Believers, Ali ibn Abi Talib, who was neither a Jew nor a Christian.

"Whose oil appears to light up even though fire touches it not": al-Sadiq said: The knowledge would issue forth from the mouth of the knowing one of the family of Muhammad [that is, Ali] even if Muhammad had not spoken it.

"Light upon light": al-Sadiq said that this means from one Imam to the next.

Then Kashi turns to another Shiʿite commentator, al-Tabarsi (d. 1153 C.E.), for a somewhat more general interpretation of the same verse.

It is said . . . (by Tabarsi) from the Imam al-Baqir in a Tradition that the verse "God is the Light of the heavens and the earth" means: "I [that is, God] am the rightly guided director of the heavens and the earth. The knowledge that I have given, namely, My light through which the guidance results, 'is like a niche wherein is a lamp.' The niche is the heart of Muhammad, and the lamp is his light, wherein lies knowledge." Further, God's words "the flame in the glass" mean: "I [that is, God] want to lay hold of you and what is with you so that I might manifest the Executor [a standard Shiʿite designation for Ali] like the flame in the glass, 'as it were a glittering star.' Then will I give men news of the excellence of the Executor."

"Lit with the oil of a blessed tree": The root of that blessed tree is Abraham. This is referred to in God's words: "The mercy of God and His blessings be upon you, O people of the House. Surely he [that is, Abraham] is worthy of praise and glory" (Quran 11:76).

"That is neither of the East nor of the West" means: You are neither Jews, so that you would perform the prayer facing toward the west [that is, Jerusalem] nor Christians, so that you would face toward the east. Rather you follow the creed of Abraham, of whom God has said: "No, in truth Abraham was neither a Jew nor a Christian, but a *hanif* who had submitted to God. Certainly he was never one of the idolaters" (Quran 3:60). (Kashi, *The Pure, ad loc.*)

22. What Is the Mystic Way?

In Chapter 3 above we followed the jurist and theologian Ghazali (d. 1111 C.E.) on his voyage of discovery of Sufism as he described it in his Deliverer from Error. At the end of his quest, in attempting to define what he has found, he begins with a comparison with the ablution that purifies a Muslim for prayer.

In general, then, how is the mystic way described? The purifying which is the first condition of it is the purification of the heart completely from what is other than God Most High; the key to it, which corresponds to the opening act of adoration in prayer, is the sinking of the heart completely in the recollection of God; and the end of it is complete annihilation in God. At least this is its end relative to those first steps which almost come within the sphere of choice and personal responsibility; but in reality in the actual "way" it is the first step, what comes before it being, as it were, the antechamber for those who are journeying toward it.

With this first stage of the "way" there begin the revelations and visions. The mystics in their waking state now behold angels and the spirits of the prophets; they hear these speaking to them and are instructed by them. Later, as a higher stage is reached, instead of beholding forms and figures, they come to stages in the "way" which it is hard to describe in language; if a man attempts to express these, his words inevitably contain what is clearly erroneous.

In general what the mystics manage to attain is nearness to God; some, however, would conceive of this as "infusion," some as "union," and some as "identity" (with God). All that is erroneous. He who has attained the mystic state need do no more than say that "Of the things I do not remember, what was, was; think it good; do not ask an account of it." . . .

In general, the man to whom He has granted no immediate experience at all apprehends no more of what prophetic revelation really is than the name alone. The miraculous graces given to the saints are in truth the beginnings of the prophecy, and that was the first "state" of the Messenger of God, peace be upon him, when he went out to Mount Hira, and was given up entirely to his Lord, and worshiped Him so that the bedouin said, "He loves his Lord passionately."

Now this is a mystical "state" which is realized in immediate experience by those who walk in the way leading to it. Those to whom it is not granted to have the immediate experience can become assured of it by trial [that is, observation of Sufis] and by hearsay, if they have sufficiently numerous opportunities of associating with mystics to understand that [that is, the mystical experience] with certainty by means of what accompanies the states. Whoever sits in their company derives from them this faith; and no one who sits in their company is pained. (Ghazali, *Deliverer* 132–135) [GHAZALI 1953: 60–62]

Ibn Khaldun too attempts to explain the Sufi experience, though now not through the sensibilities of one who had himself traveled the path but from the perspective of the cultural historian.

Mystical exertion, retirement, and the recollection exercise are as a rule followed by the removal of the veil of sensual perception. The Sufi beholds divine worlds which a person subject to the senses cannot. The spirit belongs to those worlds. The reason for the removal of the veil is the following. When the spirit turns from external sense perception to inner perception, the senses weaken and the spirit grows strong. It gains predominance and a new growth. The recollection exercise helps to bring that about. It is like food to make the spirit grow. The spirit continues to grow. It had been knowledge; now it becomes vision. The veil of sensual perception is removed, and the soul realizes its essential existence. This is identical with perception. The spirit now is ready for the holy gifts, for the sciences of divine presence, and for the outpouring of the Deity. Its essence realizes its own true character and draws close to the highest sphere, the sphere of the angels.

The removal of the veil often happens to people who exert themselves in mystical exercise. They perceive the realities of existence as no one else does. They also perceive many future happenings in advance. With the help of their minds and psychic powers they are active among the lower existents, which thus become obedient to their will. The great Sufis do not think much of the removal of the veil and of activity among the lower existents. They give no information about the reality of anything they have not been ordered to discuss. They consider it a tribulation when things of that sort occur to them, and try to escape them whenever they afflict them.

By the "great Sufis" Ibn Khaldun means the earliest generation of Muslims, beginning with the men of Muhammad's own generation. Although they received abundant visitations of the divine grace, they paid little attention to such manifestations. The self-conscious pursuit of such experiences set in only at a later date, among more recent mystics.

Recent mystics have turned their attention to the removal of the veil and the discussion of perceptions beyond sensual perception. Their ways of mystical exercise in this respect differ. They have taught different methods of mortifying the sensual perception and nourishing the reasoning spirit with recollection exercises, so that the soul might fully grow and attain its own essential perception. When this happens they believe that the whole of existence is encompassed by the perceptions of the soul, that the essences of existence are revealed to them, and that they perceive the reality of all the essences from the divine throne to light rain. This was said by al-Ghazali in the *Revivification*, after he had mentioned the forms of spiritual exercises. . . .

The recent Sufis who have occupied themselves with this kind of removal of the veil talk about the real character of the higher and lower existents and about the real character of the kingdom, the spirit, the throne, the seat, and similar things. Those who did not share their approach were not able to understand their mystical and ecstatic experiences in this respect. The muftis partly approve of these Sufis and partly accept them. Arguments and proofs are of no use in deciding whether the Sufi approach should be rejected or accepted, since it belongs to intuitive experience. (Ibn Khaldun, *Muqaddima* 6.16) [IBN KHALDUN 1967: 3:81–83]

23. Junayd on Oneness of and with God

It is not always easy to understand where Ibn Khaldun is drawing his systematic line between the "earlier" and "later Sufis," but the Baghdad master Junayd (d. 910 C.E.) certainly falls in the very heart of the earlier category. He stands midway between the Sufi pioneer Muhasibi (d. 837) and his erstwhile disciple, the far more extreme Hallaj, executed at Baghdad in 922 C.E. Like Muhasibi and most of the other "sober" Sufis, Junayd was a skilled director of souls, as this brief analysis indicates.

There are three types of people: the man who seeks and searches, the man who reaches the door and stays there, and the man who enters and remains.

As for the man who seeks God, he goes toward Him guided by a knowledge of the religious precepts and duties (of Islam), concentrating on the performance of all external observances toward God. Regarding the man who reaches the doorway and stays there, he finds his way there by means of his internal purity, from which he derives his strength. He acts toward God with internal concentration. Finally, as for the man who enters into God's presence with his whole heart and remains before Him, he excludes the vision of anything other than God, noting God's every sign to him, and is ready for whatever his Lord may command. This readiness is characteristic of the man who recognizes the Oneness of God. (Junayd, *Treatises*) [JUNAYD 1962: 176]

This last perception of the "Oneness of God," an expression that in Arabic also does service as "Oneness with God," was for Junayd and his ninth-century Baghdad contemporaries both the touchstone and the climax of the mystical experience. It was not an easy notion either to grasp or to describe. Although Junayd defined the "Oneness of/with God" in typically aphoristic fashion as "the separation of the Eternal from the contingent"—a phrase not uncommonly offered by his successors as a definition of Sufism, or rather of mysticism purely and simply—he also addressed the central concept of Oneness in a somewhat fuller fashion.

Know that the first condition of the worship of God—may He be exalted and magnified—is the knowledge of God, and the basis of the knowledge of God is the recognition of His being One, and that His Oneness precludes the possibility of describing God in terms of responses to the questions "How?" or "Where?" or "When?" . . .

God's Oneness connotes belief in Him. From belief follows confirmation which in turn leads to knowledge of Him. Knowledge of Him implies obedience to His commands, obedience carries with it the ascent toward Him, which leads ultimately to reaching Him.

This apparent success in the mystical quest leads only to a further paradox, however.

When God is attained His manifestation can be expounded, but from His manifestation there also follows bewilderment which is so overwhelming that it inhibits the possibility of the exposition of God, and as a result of losing this manifestation of God the elected worshiper is unable to describe God. And there, when the worshiper is unable to describe God, he finds the true nature of his existing for God. And from this comes the vision of God, together with the loss of his individuality. And with the loss of his individuality he achieves absolute purity . . . he has lost his personal attributes: . . . he is wholly present in God . . . wholly lost to self.

But then there is an inevitable return to a more normal condition, though not without permanent alterations in spiritual temperament.

He is existent in both himself and in God after having been existent in God and non-existent in himself. This is because he has left the drunkenness of God's overwhelming presence and come to the clarity of sobriety. Contemplation is once again restored to him, so that he can put everything in its right place and assess it correctly. Once more he assumes his individual attributes, after the "obliteration" his personal qualities persist in him and in his actions in this world, when he has reached the height of spiritual perfection granted by God, he becomes a pattern for his fellow men. (Junayd, *Treatises*) [JUNAYD 1962: 171–172]

Know that this sense of the Oneness of God exists in people in four different ways. The first is the sense of Oneness possessed by ordinary people. Then there is the sense shared by those well versed in formal religious knowledge. The other two types are experienced by the elect who have esoteric knowledge. (Ibid.) [JUNAYD 1962: 176]

God's Oneness is in fact the cornerstone of Islam—every Muslim's profession of faith begins with the statement that "There is no god but the God"—and Junayd bases his analysis on its simple assertion.

As for the sense of Oneness possessed by ordinary people, it consists in the assertion of God's Oneness, in the disappearance of any notion of gods, opposites, equals or likenesses to God, but with the persistence of hopes and fears in forces other than God. This level of Oneness has a certain degree of efficacy since the simple assertion of God's Oneness does in fact persist.

As for the conception of Oneness shared by those who are well versed in religious knowledge, it consists not only in the assertion of God's Oneness, in the disappearance of any conception of gods, opposites, equals or likenesses to God, but also in the performance of the positive commands (of religion) and the avoidance of that which is forbidden, so far as external action is concerned, all of this being the result of their hopes, fears and desires. This level of Oneness likewise possesses a degree of efficacy since there is a public demonstration of the Oneness of God.

As for the first type of esoteric Oneness, it consists in the assertion of the Oneness of God, the disappearance of the conception of things referred to, combined with the performance of God's command externally and internally, and the removal of hopes and fears in forces other than God, all of this is the result of ideas that conform with the adept's awareness of God's presence with him, with God's call to him and his answer to God.

A second type of esoteric Oneness consists in existing without individuality before God with no intermediary between, becoming a figure over which His decrees pass in accordance with His omnipotence, a soul sunk in the flooding sea of His Oneness, all sense lost of himself, God's call to him and his response to God. It is a stage wherein the devotee has achieved a true realization of the Oneness of God in true nearness to Him. He is lost to both sense and action because God fulfills in him what He has willed of him. . . . His existence now is like it was before he had existence. This, then, is the highest stage of the true realization of the Oneness of God in which the worshiper who sustains this Oneness loses his own individuality. (Junayd, *Treatises*) [JUNAYD 1962: 176–178]

24. Self-Obliteration

Obliteration, the loss of one's personal or individual characteristics before God, is also the key to attaining that same state: It is both the method and the goal of the mystic's pursuit, as Ghazali explains in his great work of spiritual renewal, The Revivification of the Sciences of Religion.

Whoever looks upon the world only because it is God's work, and knows it because it is God's work, and loves it because it is God's work, does not look except to God and knows nothing except God, and loves naught except God—he is the true One-maker who does not see anything but God, indeed, he does not regard even himself for his own sake but because he is God's servant, and of such a person it is said that he is annihilated in Oneness and he is annihilated from himself. (Ghazali, *Revivification* 4:276)

According to Junayd, the first step on the path to self-annihilation consists in training the will.

The obliteration of attributes, characteristics and natural inclinations in your motives when you carry out your religious duties, making great efforts and doing the opposite of what you may desire, and compelling yourself to do the things which you do not wish to do.

Nor must asceticism be neglected.

The obliteration of your pursuit of pleasure and even the sensation of pleasure in obedience to God's commands; so that you are exclusively His, without intermediary means of contact.

Finally, the mystic achieves true obliteration, a complete loss of self-awareness, and with it, a higher level of existence.

The obliteration of the consciousness of having attained the vision of God at the final stage of ecstasy when God's victory over you is complete. At this stage you are obliterated and have eternal life with God, and you exist only in the existence of God because you have been obliterated. Your physical being continues but your individuality has departed. (Junayd, *Treatises*) [JUNAYD 1962: 81]

25. Oneness with God Is Not Identity with God

Sufi theoreticians on the one hand cut their definitions of annihilation of self and Oneness with God exceedingly fine; ecstatics on the other, the "drunken Sufis" who did not share Junayd's measured sobriety, followed whither their fevered experience and expressions led them. The result was, not unpredictably, a conservative reaction, or at least a degree of caution, and in the first instance on the part of certain Sufi masters themselves. One such was al-Sarraj (d. 988 C.E.), whose great systematic treatise on Sufism ends with a kind of syllabus of errors directed at Sufi theory and practice.

Some mystics of Baghdad have erred in their doctrine that, when they pass away from their qualities, they enter into the qualities of God. This involves "infusion" or leads to the Christian belief concerning Jesus. The doctrine in question has been attributed to some of the earlier (Muslim) mystics, but its true understanding is this: when a man goes forth from his own qualities and enters into the qualities of God, he goes forth from his own will, which is a gift to him from God, and enters into the Will of God, knowing that his will has been given to him by God, and that by virtue of this gift he can stop regarding himself and become entirely devoted to God. This is one of the stages of those who seek after Oneness. Those who have erred in this teaching are the ones who have failed to note that the qualities of God are not the same as God. To make God identical with His qualities is to be guilty of infidelity, because God does not descend into the heart but what does descend into the heart is faith in God and belief in His Oneness and reverence for the thought of him. (Sarraj, *The Splendor of Sufism* 432) [Cited in JUNAYD 1962: 84]

Some have abstained from food and drink because they fancy that, when a man's body is weakened, it is possible that he may lose his humanity and be invested with the attributes of divinity. The ignorant persons who hold this doctrine cannot distinguish between humanity and the innate qualities of humanity. Humanity does not depart from a man any more than blackness departs from that which is black or whiteness from that which is white, but the innate qualities of humanity are changed and transmuted by the all-powerful radiance that is shed upon them from the Divine Realities. The attributes of humanity are not the essence of humanity. Those who speak of the doctrine of obliteration mean the cessation of our regarding our own actions and works of devotion through continuously regarding God as the doer of those acts on behalf of His servants. (Ibid. 426) [Cited in JUNAYD 1962: 84–85]

26. "All That Matters for the Ecstatic Is That His Only One Bring Him to His Oneness"

We have already seen Ghazali's reflections on his spiritual career. But these are thoughts recollected and reshaped in tranquillity. Indeed, some Sufi lives may have been tranquil, but certainly not that of Islam's most notorious seeker after God, the Baghdad saint and mystic, Husayn ibn Mansur, surnamed al-Hallaj, "the carder," who was put to death, a martyr of esoteric Sufism, in 922 C.E. A brief memorial of his father's much troubled, peripatetic life was set down by Hallaj's son Hamd.

My father, Husayn ibn Mansur, was born in Bayda (in Iran), in a place called al-Tur. He was brought up in Tustar, and for a period of two years he became the disciple of Sahl ibn Abdullah Tustari, after which he went to Baghdad. He walked around sometimes dressed in hairshirts, other times in two coats of dyed material, other times in a woolen robe with a turban, or in a greatcoat with sleeves, like a soldier.

He left Tustar first for Basra (in Iraq) and was eighteen years old at the time. Next he left dressed in two coats to see Amr al-Makki and Junayd and he lived near Amr for eighteen months. After that he married (in Basra) my mother Umm al-Husayn, daughter of Abu Ya'qub Aqta; but Amr al-Makki was unhappy about this marriage and a great quarrel flared up between Abu Ya'qub and Amr over this subject. My father went at that time alone to Junayd and told him how unbearable the crisis ... was making the situation in Baghdad. Junayd advised him to keep calm and to show them respect, which he did patiently for some time.

Next he left for Mecca and remained there a year on a pious visit. Afterwards he returned to Baghdad with a group of Sufi ascetics. He went to Junayd to pose a question, which the latter did not, however, answer, judging it to be motivated by the desire for a personal mission.

The break with Junayd, at this point or later, was more substantial, as we shall see. The account of Hallaj's son continues.

My father, hurt by this, returned, together with my mother, to Tustar, where he remained for nearly two years. And there he received such a warm personal welcome that all his (Sufi) contemporaries hated him, particularly Amr ibn Makki, who persisted in sending letters about him to eminent persons in Khuzistan in which he accused him of very grave errors. To such a degree and so effectively that my father put aside the religious garb of the Sufis, rejected it, and put on a sleeved coat, frequenting the company of worldly society.

He left Tustar after that and we saw no more of him for five years. During this time he traveled through Khurasan and Mawaranahr (in eastern Iran); from there he went (southward) into Sijistan and Kirman, and afterwards returned to (his home region of) Fars. He began to speak in public, to hold meetings, to preach God to the people. In Fars people knew him as "the ascetic" and he wrote several works for them. Then he went from Fars back to Ahwaz, and called for her who brought me into the world to come to him. He spoke in public and everyone, great and small, approved of him. He spoke to his listeners of their consciences, of what was in their hearts, which he unveiled for them. They called him "the carder of consciences," and the name "the carder" (al-hallaj), for short, stayed with him.

Next he left for Basra; he stayed there only a little while, leaving me in Ahwaz with his disciples. He went a second time to Mecca, dressed this time in a coat of rags and patches and an Indian cloak. Many people accompanied him on this journey, during which Abu Ya'qub Nahrajuri, out of hatred, spread the charge against him (of being a magician) with which people are familiar.

Hallaj returns to Basra and then installs himself, with his family and a number of disciples, in Baghdad. But he does not rest there for long. He is soon off once again, this time to the "land of idolatry," India and Turkestan. And, his son adds, "the gossip about him increased after this journey."

He departed again after that and made a third pilgrimage, including a two-year spiritual retreat in Mecca. He returned this time very changed from what he had been before. He purchased property in Baghdad and built a house. He began to preach in public a doctrine only half of which which I understood. In the end (the lawyer) Muhammad Dawud rose against him, together with a whole group of *ulama*; and they took their accusations against his views to (the Caliph) al-Mu'tadid. . . . Some people said: he is a sorcerer. Others: he is a madman. Still others: he performs miracles and his prayer is granted (by God). And tongues wrangled over his case up to the moment when the government arrested and imprisoned him.

At that time (the Grand Chamberlain) Nasr Qushuri went to the Caliph, who authorized him to build my father a separate cell in prison. Then a little house was constructed for him adjoining the prison; the outside door to the building was walled up, the building itself was surrounded by a wall, and a door was made opening into the interior of the prison. For about a year he received visits from people there. Then that was forbidden him, and he went for five months without anyone being able to see him. . . . At that time I was spending my night with my maternal family outside, and staying during the day near my father. Then they imprisoned me with him for a period of two months. At that time I was eighteen years old.

And when the night came in which my father was to be taken, at dawn, from his cell (for execution), he stood up for the prayer, of which he performed one of two prostrations. Then, with this prayer completed, he continued repeating over and over again the word "illusion . . . illusion," until the night was almost over. Then for a long time he was silent, when suddenly he cried out "truth . . . truth." He stood up again, put on his head cloak and wrapped himself in his coat, extended his hands, turned toward the prayer-direction and went into ecstatic prayer. . . .

When the morning came, they led him from the prison, and I saw him walking proudly in his chains. . . . They led him then (to the esplanade) where they cut off his hands and feet, after having flogged him with 500 lashes of the whip. Then he was hoisted up onto the cross, and I heard him on the gibbet talking ecstatically with God: "O my God, here I am in the dwelling place of my desires, where I contemplate Your marvels. O my God, since You witness friendship even to whoever does You wrong, how is it You do not witness it to this one to whom wrong is done because of You?" . . .

At the time of the evening prayer, the authorization by the Caliph to decapitate Hallaj came. But it was declared: "It is too late; we shall put it off until tomorrow." When morning came, they took him down from the gibbet and dragged him forth to behead him. I heard him cry out then, saying in a very high voice: "All that matters for the ecstatic is that his Only One bring him to his Oneness." Then he recited this verse: "Those who do not believe in the Final Hour call for its coming; but those who believe in it await it with loving shyness, knowing that this will be (the coming of) God" (Quran 42:17). These were his last words.

His head was cut off, then his trunk was rolled up in a straw mat, doused with fuel and burned. Later his ashes were carried to Lighthouse Point (on the Tigris) to disperse them to the wind. [MASSIGNON 1982: 10–18]

27. "I Am the Truth"

Hallaj's son's account of his father's life and death makes no mention of his trial, which, as we have seen in Chapter 2, had to do with the examination of Hallaj's views on the pilgrimage. This apparent attack on Islamic ritual may indeed have merited Hallaj the death sentence in 922, but it was by no means his only, or perhaps even his most scandalous, view of Islamic religious teaching. What attracted even more attention in later generations was another remark let drop, in what appears to be utter simplicity, to Junayd.

It is related that Hallaj met Junayd one day, and said to him, "I am the Truth." "No," Junayd answered him, "it is by means of the Truth that you are! What gibbet will you stain with your blood!" [MASSIGNON 1982: 127]

That appears to be the full extent of the incident and the exchange. But there is little doubt as to how Hallaj intended Junayd to understand the expression "I am the

Truth"—or, as it has been translated, "My 'I' is God"—or how Junayd understood it. "The Truth" is a title of God, and Hallaj was arrogating it to himself, and not, it is noted, in a state of ecstatic "intoxication" but in its aftermath, the believer's normal state of "sobriety," a distinction that meant little to Hallaj but was of crucial importance to Junayd. Our source is the Persian Sufi Hujwiri (fl. 1057 C.E.).

I have read . . . that when Husayn ibn Mansur, in a sort of trance, broke with Amr al-Makki and came over to Junayd, the latter said: "Why did you come?"

"To live in community with you as a master."

"I do not live in community with madmen; community life requires balance, otherwise what happened to you with Sahl Tustari and Amr occurs."

"O master, sobriety and intoxication are only the two human aspects of the mystic, who remains separated from his Lord as long as these two aspects are not both annihilated."

"O Ibn Mansur, you are wrong in your definition of those states, sobriety and intoxication; the first means the state of norm⌐¹ equilibrium of the faithful before God; it is not a qualification of the   ul that he may get it through his own effort as a creature; likewise the second, which signifies extremes of desire and love. O Ibn Mansur, I see in your language an indiscreet curiosity and some expressions that are useless."
(Hujwiri, The Unveiling 235) [Cited by MASSIGNON 1982: 125–126]

28. Ecstatic Utterances

What Junayd tactfully characterized as "some expressions that are useless" many other Muslims called "ecstatic utterances," cries like Hallaj's "I am the Truth" or Bistami's "Glory be to Me," uttered in a moment of mystical transport—valid for the mystic, no doubt, but the cause of some disturbance, and even scandal, to the ordinary Muslim. Both Ghazali and Ibn Khaldun tried to put the best face upon what was admittedly a difficult subject.

Those gnostics, when they return from their ascent into the heaven of Reality, confess with one voice that they saw no existent there save the One Real Being. Some of them arrived at this scientifically, others experimentally and subjectively. For these last the plurality of things entirely fell away; they were drowned in the absolute Oneness, and their intelligences were lost in Its abyss. . . . They became like persons struck dumb, and they had no power within them except to recall God, not even the power to recall themselves. So there remained with them nothing save

God. They became drunk with a drunkenness wherein the sense of their own intelligence disappeared, so that one cried out "I am the Truth," and another "Glory be to Me! How great is My Glory!" and still another "Within this robe is nothing but God!" . . . But the words of lovers passionate in their intoxication and ecstasy must be hidden away and not spoken of. (Ghazali, *Niche for Lights*)

There are the suspect expressions which the Sufis call "ecstatic utterances" and which provoke the censure of orthodox Muslims. As to them, it should be known that the attitude that would be fair to the Sufis is that they are people who are removed from sense perception. Inspiration grips them. Eventually, they say things about their inspiration that they do not intend to say. A person who is removed from sense perception cannot be spoken to. More, he who is forced to act is excused. Sufis who are known for their excellence and exemplary character are considered to act in good faith in this and similar respects. It is difficult to express ecstatic experiences, because there are no conventional ways of expressing them. This was the experience of Abu Yazid al-Bistami and others like him. However, Sufis whose excellence is not known and famous deserve censure for utterances of this kind, since the (data) that might cause us to interpret their statements (so as to remove any suspicion attached to them) are not clear to us. Furthermore, any Sufis who are not removed from sense perception and are not in the grip of a (mystical) state when they make such utterances, also deserve censure. Therefore the jurists and the great Sufis decided that al-Hallaj was to be killed, because he spoke (ecstatically) while not removed from sense perception but in control of his state. And God knows better. (Ibn Khaldun, *Muqaddima* 6.16) [IBN KHALDUN 1967: 3:102]

29. The Face in the Mirror

Ghazali's moderating influence won for Sufism a respected, if always somewhat suspect, place in the Sunni household, and Nasafi's libertines were banished to the realm of the heterodox. But as the Sufi movement continued to develop, instances of what Juyawni would doubtless have considered "indiscreet curiosity" and "useless expressions" continued to occur in Sufi circles. Even the fate of Hallaj did nothing to dampen the adventuresome thought of some Sufi masters. His example, however, when accompanied by continuing vigil on the part the Sunni authorities, may have counseled some mystics to resort to the somewhat safer ground of allegory or inference.

One of the more prolonged and celebrated of the Sufi allegories is a long poem in Persian, The Conference of the Birds, *written by Farid al-Din Attar in 1177 C.E. Its premise is that the birds of the world collect to go in search of an ideal king. In the end they discover him, but not before they tell and have told to them a great number of stories illustrative of the Sufi life, whose path they are themselves in fact allegorically tracing. Attar's allegorical birds finally reach their goal, the abode of a mythical king called Simorgh, whose Persian name derives etymologically from* si = "thirty" *and* morgh = "birds."

> A world of birds set out, and there remained
> But thirty when the promised goal was gained,
> Thirty exhausted, wretched, broken things,
> With hopeless hearts and tattered, trailing wings.

The king's herald counsels them to turn back.

> The herald said: "The blaze of Majesty
> Reduces souls to unreality,
> And if your souls are burnt, then all the pain
> That you have suffered will have been in vain."
> They answered: "How can a moth flee fire
> When fire contains its ultimate desire?
> And if we do not join Him, yet we'll burn,
> And it is for this that our spirits yearn—
> It is not union for which we hope;
> We know that goal remains beyond our scope." . . .
>
> Though grief engulfed the ragged group, love made
> The birds impetuous and unafraid;
> The herald's self-possession was unmoved,
> But their resilience was not reproved—
> Now gently he unlocked the guarded door;
> A hundred doors drew back, and there before
> The birds' incredulous, bewildered sight
> Shone the unveiled, the inmost Light of Light.
> He led them to a noble throne, a place
> Of intimacy, dignity and grace,
> Then gave them all a written page and said
> That when its contents had been duly read
> The meaning that their journey had concealed,
> And of the stage they'd reached, would be revealed. . . .
>
> The thirty birds read through the fateful page
> And there discovered, stage by detailed stage,

Their lives, their actions, set out one by one—
All their souls had ever been or done. . . .

The chastened spirits of these birds became
Like crumbled powder, and they shrank with shame.
Then, as by shame their spirits were refined
Of all the world's weight, they began to find
A new life flow toward them from that bright
Celestial and ever-living Light—
Their souls rose free of all they'd been before;
The past and all its actions were no more.
Their life came from that close and insistent sun
And in its vivid rays they shone as one.
There in the Simorgh's radiant face they saw
Themselves, the Simorgh of the world—with awe
They gazed, and dared at last to comprehend
They were the Simorgh and the journey's end.
They see the Simorgh—at themselves they stare,
And see a second Simorgh standing there;
They look at both and see the two are one,
That this is that, that this, the goal is won.
They ask (but inwardly; they make no sound)
The meanings of these mysteries that confound
Their puzzled ignorance—how is it true
That "we" are not distinguished here from "You"?
And silently their shining Lord replies:
"I am a mirror set before your eyes,
And all who come before my splendor see
Themselves, their own unique reality."
(Attar, *The Conference of the Birds*) [ATTAR 1984: 214–219]

The image of the face in the mirror was not original with Attar. It had appeared in one of its most striking forms in the work of the dominant figure in all of Islamic mysticism, the Spaniard Muhyi al-Din ibn al-Arabi (1165–1240 C.E.). It is introduced at the very beginning of his Bezels of Wisdom, *in the expression of one of his fundamental themes: the ultimate and primordial unity of Reality or Being, polarized into the God and the Cosmos only after and because of the Reality's desire to experience itself in another.*

The Reality wanted to see the essences of His Most Beautiful Names, or, to put it another way, to see His own Essence in an all-inclusive object encompassing the whole (divine) Command, which, qualified by existence, would reveal to Him His own mystery. For the seeing of a thing, itself by itself, is not the same as its seeing itself in another, as it were in a mirror; for it appears to itself in a form that is invested by the location of the vision by that which would only appear to it given the existence of the location and its [that is, the location's] self-disclosure to it.

The reality gave existence to the whole Cosmos (at first) as an undifferentiated thing without anything of the spirit in it, so that it was like an unpolished mirror. It is in the nature of the divine determination that He does not set out a location except to receive a divine spirit, which is also called "the breathing into him" (Quran 21:91). The latter is nothing other than the coming into operation of the undifferentiated form's (innate) disposition to receive the inexhaustible overflowing of Self-Revelation, which has always been and will ever be. . . .

Thus the (divine) Command required (by its very nature) the reflective characteristic of the mirror of the Cosmos, and Adam was the very principle of reflection for that mirror and the spirit of that form. (Ibn al-Arabi, *Bezels of Wisdom*, "Adam") [IBN AL-ARABI 1980: 50–51]

Here the image is turned around, and it is God who is the mirror.

If you are a believer, you will know that God will manifest Himself on the Day of Resurrection, initially in a recognizable form, then in a form unacceptable (to ordinary belief), He alone being the Self-manifesting One in every form, although it is obvious that one form is not the same as another.

It is as if the single Essence were a mirror, so that when the observer sees in it the form of his belief about God, he recognizes and confirms it, but if he should see it in the doctrinal formulation of someone of another creed, he will reject it, as if he were seeing in the mirror His form and then that of another. The mirror is single, while the forms (it reveals) are various in the eye of the observer.

None of the forms are in the mirror wholly, although a mirror has an effect on the forms in one way and not in another. For instance, it may make the form look smaller, larger, taller or broader. Thus it has an effect on their proportions, which is attributable to it, although such changes occur only due to the different proportions of the mirrors themselves. Look, then, into just one mirror, without considering mirrors in general, for it is the same as your beholding (Him) as being one Essence, albeit that He is beyond all need of the worlds. Insofar as He is Divine Names, on the other hand, He is like (many) mirrors. In which Divine Name have

you beheld yourself, or who is the one who beholds? It is only the reality
of the Name that is manifest in the beholder. Thus it is, if you will but
understand. (Ibn al-Arabi, *The Bezels of Wisdom*, "Elias")

[IBN AL-ARABI 1980: 232-233]

*Ibn al-Arabi returns to the relationship of the Reality and the Cosmos, now in terms
of light and shadow.*

Know that what is "other than the Reality," which is called the
Cosmos, is, in relation to the Reality, as a shadow is to what casts the
shadow, for it is the shadow of God, this being the same as the relationship between Being and the Cosmos, since the shadow is, without doubt,
something sensible. What is provided there is something on which the
shadow may appear, since if that whereon it appears should cease to be,
the shadow would be an intelligible and not something sensible, and
would exist potentially in the very thing that casts the shadow.

The thing on which this divine shadow, called the Cosmos, appears
is the (eternally latent) essences of contingent beings. The shadow is
spread out over them, and the (identity of the) shadow is known to the
extent that the Being of the (original) Essence is extended upon it. It is
by His Name, the Light, that it is perceived. This shadow extends over the
essences of contingent being in the form of the unknown Unseen. Have
you not observed that shadows tend to be black, which indicates their
imperceptibility (as regards content) by reason of the remote relationship
between them and their origins? If the source of the shadow is white, the
shadow itself is still so [that is, black].

*This is how the universe exists. Ibn al-Arabi then begins to move from its existence
to our way of knowing both this world of ours called the Cosmos and its source.*

No more is known of the Cosmos than is known from a shadow, and
no more is known of the Reality than one knows of the origin of a
shadow. Insofar as He has a shadow, He is known, but insofar as the form
of the one casting the shadow is not perceived in the shadow, the Reality
is not known. For this reason we say that the Reality is known to us in
one sense and unknown in another.

We are, then, seriously misled about the "real existence" of the sensible universe.

If what we say is true, the Cosmos is but a fantasy without any real
existence, which is another meaning of the Imagination. That is to say,
you imagine that it [that is, the universe] is something separate and self-
sufficient, outside the Reality, while the truth is that it is not so. Have you
not observed (in the case of the shadow) that it is connected to the one

who casts it, and would not its becoming unconnected be absurd, since nothing can be disconnected from itself?

It is, Ibn al-Arabi immediately continues, in the mirror we should look.

Therefore know truly your own self [that is, your own essence], who you are, what is your identity and what your relationship with the Reality. Consider well in what way you are real and in what was (part of) the Cosmos, as being separate, other, and so on.

Thus God is seen in many different modes: in one way—"green"—by the ordinary believer relying on the givens of Scripture, in another—"colorless"—by the theologian with his refined deductive portrait. And they are both correct, and, of course, both wildly wrong.

The Reality is, in relation to a particular shadow, small or large, pure or purer, as light in relationship to the glass that separates it from the beholder to whom the light has the color of the glass, while the light itself has no particular color. This is the relationship between your reality and your Lord; for, if you were to say that the light is green because of the green glass, you would be right as viewing the situation through your senses, and if you were to say it is not green, indeed it is colorless, by deduction, you would also be right as viewing the situation through sound intellectual reasoning. That which is seen may be said to be a light projected from a shadow, which is the glass, or a luminous shadow, according to its purity. Thus, he of us who has realized in himself the Reality manifests the form of the Reality to a greater extent than he who has not. . . .

God created shadows lying prostrate to right and left only as clues for yourself in knowing yourself and Him, that you might know who you are, your relationship with Him, and His with you, and so you might understand how or according to which divine truth all that is other than God is described as being completely dependent on Him, as being (also) mutually independent. Also that you might know how and by what truth God is described as utterly independent of men and all worlds, and how the Cosmos is described as both mutually independent with respect to its parts and mutually dependent. (Ibn al-Arabi, *The Bezels of Wisdom,* "Joseph") [IBN AL-ARABI 1980: 123–126]

30. Al-Jili and the Perfect Man

Sufism from Ibn al-Arabi onward developed a repertory of esoteric learning that was as vast and at times as impenetrable as the Kabbala. This was theosophy pure and

simple, an arcane and transcendental way of looking at this world in terms of a
higher reality, a blend of knowing and doing, of gnosis and theurgy, with strong
derivative roots in the late Platonic tradition of the fifth and sixth century C.E. One
of the central themes of this world view was the theory of the "Perfect Man," a
figure who simultaneously embraces the Holy Spirit, the Word, Adam, Muhammad,
and the fully enlightened mystic himself. Ibn al-Arabi was one of the pioneers in the
development of this motif, but it found its classic expression in the treatise called The
Perfect Man *by Abd al-Karim al-Jili (d. ca. 1410 C.E.).*

God created the angel called Spirit from His own light, and from him
He created the world and made him His organ of vision in the world. One
of his names is the Word of God. He is the noblest and most exalted of
all existent beings. The Spirit exercises a Divine guardianship, created in
him by God, over the whole universe. He manifests himself in his perfection in the Ideal Muhammad: therefore the Prophet is the most excellent
of all mankind. While God manifests Himself in His attributes to all other
created beings, He manifests Himself in His essence to this angel [that is,
the Spirit] alone. Accordingly, the Spirit is the Pole of the present world
and the world to come. He does not make himself known to any creature
of God but to the Perfect Man. When the saint knows him [that is, the
Perfect Man] and truly understands the things which the Spirit teaches
him, then he too becomes a pole around which the entire universe re-
volves. But Poleship belongs fundamentally to the Spirit, and if others
hold it, they are only his delegates. (Jili, *The Perfect Man* 2:12)

[Cited by NICHOLSON 1921: 110–111]

The Perfect Man is the Pole on which the spheres of existence re-
volve from first to last, and since things came into being he is one forever
and ever. He has various guises and appears in diverse bodily tabernacles:
in respect of some of these his name is given to him, while in respect to
others it is not given to him. His original name is Muhammad, his name
of honor is Abu al-Qasim [that is, "father of Qasim," the latter the name
of Muhammad's first son], his description is Abdullah [that is, "servant of
God"], and his title is Shams al-Din [that is, "the sun of religion"]. In
every age he bears a name suitable to his guide in that age. I once met him
[that is, the Perfect Man, Muhammad] in the form of my Shaykh, Sharaf
al-Din Isma'il al-Jabarti, but I did not know that he [that is, the Shaykh]
was the Prophet, though I knew the Prophet was the Shaykh. . . . The real
meaning of this matter is that the Prophet has the power of assuming
every form. When the adept sees him in the form of Muhammad which
he wore during his life, he names him by that name, but when he sees him

in another form but knows him to be Muhammad, he names him by the name of the form in which he appears. The name Muhammad is not applied except to the Real Muhammad. . . . If you perceive mystically that the Reality of Muhammad is displayed in any human form, you must bestow upon the Reality of Muhammad the name of that form and regard its owner with no less reverence than you would show our Lord Muhammad, and after having seen him therein you may not behave toward it in the same manner as before.

This appearance of the Real Muhammad in the form of another could be miscon-strued as the condemned doctrine of the transmigration of souls, and so al-Jili hastens to dissociate the two.

Do not imagine that my words contain any tincture of the doctrine of metempsychosis. God forbid! I mean that the Prophet is able to assume whatever form he wishes, and the Tradition declares that in every age he assumes the form of the most perfect men (of that age) in order to exalt their dignity and correct their deviation: they are his Caliphs externally and he is their reality inwardly.

In the Perfect Man himself are identified all the individualizations of existence. With his spirituality he stands with the higher individualizations, in his corporeality with the lower. His heart is identified with the Throne of God, his mind with the Pen, his soul with the Well-Guarded Tablet, his nature with the elements, his capability of receiving form with matter. . . . He stands with the angels with his good thoughts, with the demons and the devils with the doubts that best him, with the beasts in his animality. . . .

You must know that the Perfect Man is a copy of God, according to the saying of the Prophet, "God created Adam in the image of the Merciful," and in another Tradition, "God created Adam in His own image." . . . Further, you must know that the Essential names and the Divine attributes belong to the Perfect Man by fundamental and sovereign right in virtue of a necessity inherent in his essence, for it is he whose "reality" is signified by these expressions and whose spirituality is indicated by these symbols: they have no other subject in existence (to which they might be attached) except the Perfect Man.

Once again the figure of the mirror is adduced, and in a manner familiar from Ibn al-Arabi: man, and in particular the Perfect Man, is the mirror in which God sees and recognizes and admires Himself, as does man.

As a mirror in which a person sees the form of himself, and cannot see it without the mirror, such is the relation of God to the Perfect Man, who cannot possibly see his own form but in the mirror of the name "God." And he is also a mirror to God, for God laid upon Himself the necessity that His names and attributes should not be seen save in the Perfect Man. (Jili, *The Perfect Man* 2:58) [Cited by NICHOLSON 1921: 105–107]

31. Ibn Khaldun: An Evaluation of the Sufi Tradition

Ibn Khaldun had all these developments before him, from the earliest Muslim ascetics, through the "ecstatic utterances" of Bistami and Hallaj, to the daring "existential monism" of Ibn al-Arabi and the theosophical speculation of his successors, when he composed his thoughts on Sufism for the Prolegomenon to History. *He was well aware of the strong current of disapproval, or at least of reservation, that many in the Islamic legal establishment had expressed on the subject of Sufis and Sufism. For his part, however, Ibn Khaldun attempts to isolate the dubious areas in Sufi speculation, in the first instance by laying out the topics with which Sufis generally concerned themselves.*

Many jurists and muftis have undertaken to refute these . . . recent Sufis. They summarily disapproved of everything they came across in the Sufi "path." The truth is that discussion with the Sufis requires making a distinction. The Sufis discuss four topics. (1) Firstly, they discuss pious exertions, the resulting mystical and ecstatic experiences, and self-scrutiny concerning one's actions. They discuss these things in order to obtain mystical experience, which then becomes a station from which one progresses to the next higher one. . . . (2) Secondly, they discuss the removal of the veil and the perceivable supernatural realities, such as the divine attributes, the throne, the seat, the angels, revelation, prophecy, the spirit, and the realities of everything in existence, be it supernatural or visible; furthermore, they discuss the order of created things, how they issue from the Creator Who brings them into being. . . . (3) The third topic is concerned with activities in the various worlds and among the various created things connected with the different kinds of divine grace. (4) The fourth topic is concerned with expressions which are suspect if understood in their plain meaning. Such expressions have been uttered by most Sufi leaders. In Sufi technical terminology they are called "ecstatic utterances." Their plain meaning is difficult to understand. They may be something that is disapproved of, or something that can be approved, or something that requires interpretation.

Now that the territory has been charted, Ibn Khaldun can proceed to his critique. First, on the matter that by all accounts constituted the main stream of Sufism and

that had won, at least since the time of Ghazali, a recognized place among accept-
able Islamic practices and experiences.

As for their discussion of pious exertions and stations, of the mystical and ecstatic experiences that result, and of self-scrutiny with regard
to shortcomings in the things that cause these experiences, this is something that nobody ought to reject. These mystical experiences are sound
ones. Their realization is the very essence of happiness.

Ibn Khaldun then reverses the second and third points he had established above,
treating first the Sufis' perceptions about the operation of divine grace, which he is
inclined to accept, and their description, after the "removal of the veil," of that
other, higher world where God and His angels and the other higher realities have
their being, about which he is much less certain.

As for their discussion of the acts of divine grace experienced by the
Sufis, the information they give about supernatural things, and their activity among created things, these are sound and cannot be disapproved
of, even though some religious scholars tend to disapprove . . . since they
might be confused with prophetic miracles.

There is no problem here. The scholastic apparatus of theology had its distinctions
well in order.

Competent orthodox scholars have made a distinction between
(miracles and acts of divine grace) by referring to "the challenge (in
advance)" that is, the claim made (by the prophet in advance) that the
miracle would occur in agreement with the prophetic revelation. It is not
possible, they said, that a miracle could happen in agreement with the
claim of a liar. Logic requires that a miracle indicate truthfulness. By
definition a miracle is something that can be verified. If it were performed
by a liar it could not be verified and thus would have changed its character, which is absurd. In addition, the world of existence attests the occurrence of many such acts of divine grace. Disapproval of them would be
a kind of negative approach. Many such acts of divine grace were experienced by the men around Muhammad and the great early Muslims. This
is a well-known and famous fact.

The Sufis' charting of the higher realities, on the other hand, might appear to
constitute a kind of private, intuitive, and so unverifiable revelation. In this case Ibn
Khaldun recommends a kind of circumspect neglect.

Most of the Sufi discussion about the removal of the veil of the
reception of the realities of the higher things, and of the order in which
the created things issue, falls, in a way, under the category of ambiguous

statements. It is based upon the intuitive experience of the Sufis, and those who lack such intuitive experience cannot have the mystical experience that the Sufis receive from it. No language can express what the Sufis want to say in this connection, because languages have been invented only for the expression of commonly accepted concepts, most of which apply to sensible reality. Therefore, we must not bother with the Sufi discussion of those matters. We ought merely to leave it alone, just as we leave alone the ambiguous statements in the Quran and the Prophetic custom. Those to whom God grants some understanding of these mystical utterances in a way that agrees with the plain meaning of the religious law do, indeed, enjoy happiness. (Ibn Khaldun, *Muqaddima* 6.16) [IBN KHALDUN 1967: 3:99–101]

32. Sufis and Shiʿites

Ibn Khaldun then turns his attention to trends that began to develop in Sufism after its heroic period. In his reading of Sufi history it was the Shiʿites who led Islamic mysticism astray.

The ancient Sufis did not go into anything concerning the Mahdi [that is, the expected Muslim messiah]. All they discussed was their mystic activity and exertion and the resulting ecstatic experiences and states. It was the Imamite and extremist Shiʿa who discussed the preferred status of Ali, the matter of his Imamate, the claim made on his behalf to have received the Imamate through the last will of the Prophet, and the rejection of the two Shaykhs [that is, Abu Bakr and Umar]. . . . Among the later Sufis, the removal of the veil and matters beyond the veil of sense perception came to be discussed. A great many Sufis came to speak of incarnation and oneness. This gave them something in common with the Imamites and the extremist Shiʿa who believed in the divinity of the Imams and the incarnation of the deity in them. The Sufis also came to believe in the "Pole" and in "saints." This belief looked like an imitation of the opinions of the extremist Shiʿa concerning the Imam and the Alid "chiefs."

Ibn Khaldun will return to the Shiʿa-Sufi theory of "Poles" and "saints." He continues:

The Sufis thus became saturated with Shiʿa theories. Shiʿa theories entered so deeply into their religious ideas that they based their practice of using a cloak on the fact that Ali clothed al-Hasan al-Basri in such a cloak and caused him to agree solemnly that he would adhere to the mystic path. This tradition (begun by Ali) was continued, according to the Sufis, through al-Junayd, one of the Sufi shaykhs.

However, it is not known for a certainty whether Ali did any such thing. The mystic path was not reserved to Ali, but all men around Muhammad were models of the various paths of religion. The fact that the Sufis restrict precedence in mysticism to Ali smells strongly of pro-Shiʿa sentiments. This and other aforementioned Sufi ideas show that the Sufis have adopted pro-Shiʿa sentiments and have become enmeshed in them. (Ibn Khaldun, *Muqaddima* 3.51) [IBN KHALDUN 1967: 2:186–187]

And so, on Ibn Khaldun's view as a Sunni historian, the chief tenets of the "recent Sufis" that show the influence of Shiʿism are, first, their discussions of the God-head's becoming incarnate in certain chosen souls and, second, their insistence on the Divine Oneness to the extent that it became in effect pantheism.

Tradition scholars and jurists who discuss the articles of faith often mention that God is separate from His creatures. The speculative theologians say that He is neither separate nor connected. The philosophers say that He is neither in the world nor outside it. The recent Sufis say that He is one with the creatures in the sense that He is incarnate in them or in the sense that He is identical with them and there exists nothing but Himself either in the whole or in any part of it. . . .

A number of recent Sufis who consider intuitive perceptions to be scientific and logical hold the opinion that the Creator is one with His creatures in His identity, His existence and His attributes. They often assume that this was the position of philosophers before Aristotle, such as Plato and Socrates. . . . The Oneness assumed by the Sufis is identical with the incarnation the Christians claim for the Messiah. It is even stranger, in that it is the incarnation of something primeval in something created and the Oneness of the former with the latter.

The Oneness assumed by the Sufis is also identical with the stated opinion of the Imamite Shiʿa concerning their Imams. In their discussions, the Shiʿa consider the ways in which the oneness of the Deity with the Imams is achieved. (1) The essence of the primeval Deity is hidden in all created things, both sensible and intelligible, and is one with them in both kinds of perception. All of them are manifestations of it, and it has control over them—that is, it controls their existence in the sense that, without it, they would not exist. Such is the opinion of the people who believe in incarnation.

(2) There is the approach of those who believe in absolute Oneness. It seems as if in the exposition of those who believe in incarnation, they

have sensed the existence of an (implicit) differentiation contradicting the concept of Oneness. Therefore, they disavowed the (existence of any differentiation) between the primeval Deity and the creatures in essence, existence, and attributes. In order to explain the difference in manifestations perceived by the senses and the intellect, they used the specious argument that those things were human perceptions that are imaginary. By imaginary . . . they mean that all those things do not exist in reality and exist only in human perception. Only the primeval Deity has real existence and nothing else, either inwardly or outwardly. (Ibn Khaldun, *Muqaddima* 6.16) [IBN KHALDUN 1967: 3:83–86]

Ibn Khaldun has no doubts about whence these notions derived, or about their essential falsehood.

The recent Sufis who speak about the removal of the veil and supersensory perception have delved deeply into these subjects. Many of them have turned to the theory of incarnation and oneness, as we have indicated. They have filled many pages with it. That was done, for instance, by al-Harawi [ca. 1010–1089 C.E.] in the *Book of Stations* and by others. They were followed by Ibn al-Arabi [1165–1240 C.E.] and Ibn Sab'in [1226–1271 C.E.] and their pupils, and then by Ibn Afif [ca. 1260–1289 C.E.], Ibn al-Farid [d. 1235 C.E.] and Najm al-Din al-Isra'ili [1206–1278 C.E.] in the poems they composed.

The early Sufis had had contact with the Neo-Isma'ili Shi'ite extremists who also believed in incarnation and in the divinity of the Imams, a theory not known to the early Isma'ilis. Each group came to be imbued with the dogmatics of the other. Their theories and beliefs merged and were assimilated. In Sufi discussion there appeared the theory of the "Pole," meaning the chief gnostic. The Sufis assumed that no one can reach his station in gnosis until God takes him to Himself and gives his station to another gnostic. . . .

The theory of successive "Poles" is not, however, confirmed by logical arguments or evidence from the religious law. It is a sort of rhetorical figure of speech. It is identical with the theory of the extremist Shi'a about the succession of the Imams through inheritance. Clearly, mysticism has plagiarized this idea from the extremist Shi'a and come to believe in it.

The Sufis furthermore speak about the order of existence of the "saints" who come after the "pole," exactly as the Shi'a speak of their "representatives." They go so far (in the identification of their own concepts with those of the Shi'a) that when they construed a chain of transmitters for the wearing of the Sufi cloak as a basic requirement of the mystic way and practice, they made it go back to Ali. This points in the same direction. Among the men around Muhammad, Ali was not distinguished by any particular practice or way of dressing or by any special condition. Abu Bakr and Umar were the most ascetic and pious people after the Messenger of God. Yet, none of these men was distinguished by the possession of any particular religious practice peculiar to him. In fact, all the men around Muhammad were models of religion, austerity, asceticism, and pious exertion. This is attested by their way of life and history. Indeed, with the help of these stories, the Shiʿa try to suggest that Ali is distinguished from the other men around Muhammad by being in possession of certain virtues, in conformity with well-known Shiʿa beliefs. (Ibn Khaldun, *Muqaddima* 6.16) [IBN KHALDUN 1967: 3:92–93]

5. Thinking about God

1. The Birth of Philosophy

If God's revelation through Scripture was an unveiling of Himself to man, there were other ways of coming to a knowledge of God, ways that had been equally deliberately provided by the Creator, as Philo, the Hellenized Jew of Alexandria, explains in his meditation on the Torah. The theme is not new: Philo's Greek and Roman mentors all had their eyes cast heavenward, seeking traces of God. But for a Jew to attempt to elicit such a rationalized portrait from Scripture was a novel enterprise, one with enormous consequences: Yahweh, who had been for the Jews pre-eminently the purposeful God of history, their history, was about to begin His equally purposeful career as the God of philosophy, and so the common property of all men, with or without the benefit of revelation.

Its Maker arrayed the heaven on the fourth day with a most divine adornment of perfect beauty, namely the light-giving heavenly bodies; and knowing that of all things light is best, He made it the indispensable means of sight, the best of the senses; for what the intellect is in the soul, this the eye is in the body; for each of them sees, the one the things of the mind, the other the things of sense; and they have need, the mind of knowledge, that it may become cognizant of incorporeal objects, the eye of light, for the apprehending of bodily forms. Light has proved itself the source of many other boons to mankind, but pre-eminently of philosophy, the greatest boon of all. For man's faculty of vision, led upward by light, discerned the nature of the heavenly bodies and their harmonious movement. He saw the well-ordered circuits of the fixed stars and planets, how the former moved in unchanging orbit and all alike, while the latter sped round in two revolutions out of harmony with each other. He marked the rhythmic dances of all these, how they were marshaled by the laws of perfect music, and the sight produced in his soul an ineffable delight and pleasure. Banqueting on sights displayed to it one after another, his soul was insatiate in beholding. And then, as usually happens, it went on to busy itself with questioning, asking what is the essence of these visible objects? Are they in nature unoriginated or had they a beginning of existence? What is the method of their movement? And what are the principles by which each is governed? It is out of the investigation of these problems that that philosophy grew, than which no more perfect good has come into the life of mankind. (Philo, *The Creation of the World* 53–54) [PHILO 1945: 53–54]

2. Saadya on Reason and Revelation

Opening the door to philosophy—that is, to all the demonstrative sciences of the Greeks, "than which no more perfect good has come into the life of mankind," as Philo put it in such an apparently unself-conscious manner—seemed upon reflection to close the door to other avenues of truth, or at least to raise questions about their usefulness or necessity, as we shall see shortly. Christianity would have its own debate about this scientific certitude offered by the Greek sciences, but its claims were essentially messianic and not prophetic. And so the burden of the resolution of the conundrum of reason and revelation fell most heavily on the Jews and the Muslims.

The response of both groups begins from a simple proposition: truth is one, whether discovered by philosophy or revealed by a special act of God. In his Book of Doctrines and Beliefs, *Saadya (d. 942 C.E.), the chief luminary of the Jewish community in Muslim Baghdad, begins by describing the "bases of truth and the vouchers of certainty, which are the sources of all knowledge and the mainspring of all cognition." Three of them could have come from any textbook on Greek philosophy: empirical observation, intellectual intuition, and logical demonstration. But there is a fourth, and it is there that the Jew and the scripturalist begins to speak.*

As for ourselves, the community of monotheists, we hold these three sources of knowledge to be genuine. To them, however, we add a fourth source, which we have derived by means of the (other) three, and which has thus become for us a further principle. That is, the validity of authentic tradition, by reason of the fact that it is based upon the knowledge of the senses as well as that of reason. . . . At this point, however, we remark that this type of knowledge, I mean that which is furnished by authentic tradition and the books of prophetic revelation, corroborates for us the validity of the first three sources of knowledge. (Saadya, *Book of Doctrines and Beliefs*, Introduction) [SAADYA 1948: 18]

This is a relatively modest role assigned to revelation, that of confirming the other sources of true and certain knowledge. But Saadya has not finished with the topic. When he returns to it, he deftly moves the cart out before the horse.

Now someone might, of course, ask: "But how can we take it upon ourselves to indulge in speculation about objects of knowledge and their investigation to the point where these would be established as convictions according to the laws of geometry and become firmly fixed in the mind, when there are people who disapprove of such an occupation, being of the opinion that speculation leads to unbelief and is conducive to heresy?" Our reply is that such an opinion is held only by the uneducated among them. Thus you see the masses of this country [that is, Baghdad] labor under the impression that whoever goes to India becomes rich. . . . It is also related that some of the ignorant people in Arabia are under the impression that whoever does not have a she-camel slaughtered on his grave, is brought to the Last Judgment on foot. And many other such ridiculous stories are circulated.

Should one say, however, "But did not the greatest of the sages of Israel forbid this sort of occupation, and especially speculation on the beginning of time and place, saying, 'Whosoever speculates on the following four matters would have been better off had he not been born; namely, "What is below and what is above, what was before and what will be behind" (M.Hagigah 2:1)?' " Our answer is this, and we ask the Merciful One to stand by us, that it is inconceivable that the sages should have prohibited us from (rational inquiry). For did not our Creator Himself command us to do this very thing apropos of authentic tradition, as is evident from the declaration (of the prophet): "Know you not? Hear you not? Has it not been told to you from the beginning? Have you not understood the foundations of the earth?" (Isa. 40:21). . . .

What, however, the sages forbade was only to lay the books of the prophets aside and to accept any private notion that might occur to an individual about the beginning of place and time. For whoever speculates in this wise may either hit the mark or miss it. Until he hits it, however, he would be without religious faith, and even when he has hit upon the teaching of religion and has it firmly in hand, he is not secure against being deprived of it again by some uncertainty that might arise in his mind and corrupt his belief. We are agreed, then, on charging one who behaves in this fashion with sin, even though he be a professional thinker. As for ourselves, the congregation of the Children of Israel, we engage in research and speculation in a way other than this. It is this method of ours which I wish to describe and clarify with the help of the Merciful One.

Know then, and may God direct you aright, you who studies this book, that we inquire into and speculate about the matters of our religion with two objectives in mind: (1) in order to have verified in fact what we have learned from the prophets of God theoretically; and (2) in order to refute him who argues against us in anything pertaining to our religion. For our Lord, may He be blessed and exalted, instructed us in everything which we require by way of religion, through the medium of His prophets, after having established for us the truth of prophecy by signs and miracles. Thus He enjoined us to accept these matters as binding and observe them. He has furthermore informed us, however, that if we would engage in speculation and diligent research, inquiry would produce for us in each instance the complete truth, tallying with His announcements to us by the speech of His prophets. Besides that He has given us the assurance that the godless will never be in a position to offer a proof against our religion, nor the skeptics (to produce) an argument against our creed. (Ibid., Introduction) [SAADYA 1948: 27–28]

3. On the Usefulness of Revelation

If, then, speculative knowledge can produce "the complete truth, tallying with His announcements to us by the speech of His prophets," what need was there of revelation in the first place? This is the classic question for the scripturalist, Jewish, Christian, or Muslim, and Saadya faces it directly and responds.

Inasmuch as all matters of religious belief, as imparted to us by our Lord, can be attained by means of research and correct speculation, what was the reason that prompted (divine) wisdom to to transmit them to us by way of prophecy and support them by means of visible proofs and miracles rather than by intellectual demonstrations? We say: the All-Wise knew that the conclusions reached by means of the art of speculation can be attained only in the course of a certain measure of time. If, therefore, He had referred us for our acquaintance with His religion to that art (of speculative knowledge) alone, we should have remained without religious guidance for some time, until the process of reasoning was completed so that we could make use of its conclusions. But many of us might never complete the process because of some flaw in his reasoning. Again, he might not succeed in making use of its conclusions because he was overcome by worry or overwhelmed by uncertainties that confuse and befuddle him. That is why God, may He be exalted and magnified, afforded us a quick relief from all these burdens by sending us His messengers through whom He transmitted messages to us, and by letting us see with our own eyes the signs and proofs supporting them, about which no doubt could prevail and which we could not possibly reject. . . . Thus it became immediately incumbent upon us to accept the religion, together with all that was embraced in it, because its authenticity has been proven by the testimony of the senses. Its acceptance is also incumbent upon anybody to whom it has been transmitted because of the attestation of authentic tradition. . . . Furthermore women and children and people who have no aptitude for speculation can thus have a perfect and accessible faith, for the knowledge of the senses is common to all human beings. (Saadya *Book of Doctrines and Beliefs*, Introduction) [SAADYA 1948: 31–32]

4. On the Necessity of Revelation

In the tractate on Command and Prohibition, *Saadya divided the Law into "revelational" and "rational" precepts, and it is in connection with these latter that he makes his strongest and most direct case, not merely for the usefulness of revelation but for its necessity.*

. . . I have heard that there are people who say that men have no need for divine messengers and prophets because their reason is enough of a guide for them to distinguish between good and evil. I, therefore, went back to the touchstone of truth and I noted that if the matter were really as they said it was, the Creator would have known it best and He would not have sent any messengers to mankind, since He does nothing that has no purpose. Then I pondered the matter deeply and I found that there was considerable need for the dispatch of messengers to God's creatures, not only that they might be informed by them about revealed laws, but also on account of the rational precepts. For these latter too are carried out practically only when there are messengers to instruct men concerning them.

Thus, for example, reason calls for gratitude toward God for His kindness, but does not define how this gratitude is to be expressed or at what time or in what form it is to be shown. There was, then, need for messengers who defined it and designated it as "prayer" and assigned to it certain set times and gave it a particular formulation and prescribed a specific posture and direction. . . .

Another instance is the measure of punishment for crimes. Reason considers it proper that whoever commits a crime should expiate for it, but it does not define what form this expiation ought to take: whether a reprimand alone is sufficient, or should include the defamation of the evildoer, or include, in addition, flogging. In the event that the punishment take the form of flogging, again, the question is how much, and the

same applies to the defamation and the reprimand. Or whether nothing short of the death of the criminal would suffice. And again it might be asked whether the punishment should be the same for whoever commits a certain crime or whether it should vary from person to person. So the prophets came and fixed for each crime its own penalty, and grouped some of them with others under certain conditions, and imposed monetary fines for some. For these considerations, then, that we have enumerated and other such reasons, it is necessary for us to have recourse to the mission of God's messengers. (Saadya, *Book of Doctrines and Beliefs* 3.3)
[SAADYA 1948: 146]

5. Moses the Philosopher

If human reason requires revelation as its necessary complement for the attainment of the end of man, the way of reason and the way of revelation were in some respects parallel paths to that end, the one being traveled by the philosopher, the other by the prophet. Did it follow, then, that the philosopher, the pagan wise man, was the peer of the prophet? Was Plato the equal of Moses? The germ of one response appears in Philo's attempt to make the prophetic experience an ecstatic one. On this view prophecy occurred only when the soul dispossessed its normal intellectual faculty and permitted the divine afflatus to take over and give light and even voice to the prophet. An "unlettered" prophet, a spiritual "natural" uninstructed in worldly wisdom, might serve very well for this purpose, and this was in fact the Muslim point of view with regard to Muhammad. But it was not Philo's with respect to Moses. For the Jewish thinker, prophecy was not another, alternative way to the truth but a phenomenon superadded to the philosopher's apprehension of truth.

I intend to record the life of Moses, whom some consider the lawgiver of the Jews, others as the interpreter of the Holy Laws, a man who is in every respect the greatest and most perfect, and whom it is my wish to make known to those who deserve not to be uninformed of him. For while the fame of the laws he left behind has traveled throughout the inhabited world and reached the ends of the earth, the man himself as he was in reality is known to few. This was due to the unwillingness of Greek men of letters to consider him worthy of mention, probably through envy and also the disagreement of his laws in many instances with those ordained by the legislators of many states. (Philo, *Life of Moses* 1.1–2)
[PHILO 1981: 267]

Later in the same treatise, part of an ongoing commentary on the Jewish Scriptures, Philo takes up Moses' education in Egypt. Jesus was God-taught, as his youthful instruction of the rabbis on the Law illustrates (Luke 2:46–47), and so too was the "unlettered" Muhammad. But Moses had other teachers. Even though his education "seemed to be a case of recollection rather than of learning," Philo's description of those teachers and what they taught him effectively integrates Moses into the intellectual tradition of the ancient world, particularly that of Egypt, which in Philo's day was regarded as the birthplace and font of wisdom.

Teachers arrived forthwith from various places, some unbidden from the bordering areas and the Egyptian provinces, others summoned from Greece under promise of great bounty. But he [Moses] soon outstripped their capacities, for his happy natural gifts anticipated their instruction, so that it seemed to be a case of recollection rather than of learning, and he himself even further devised conundrums for them. For great natures open up new spheres of knowledge . . . and the naturally endowed soul goes forward in advance to meet its instruction and derives more profit from itself than from its teachers, and having grasped some first principles of knowledge rushes forward, as the saying goes, like the horse to the pasture. Arithmetic, geometry, the theory of rhythm, harmony, meter, and the entire field of music as exhibited by the use of instruments or in the accounts of more specialized manuals and expositions, were transmitted to him by learned Egyptians. They further instructed him in the philosophy conveyed through symbols, which they display in the so-called "holy characters" [that is, the hieroglyphs] and through the approbation accorded animals, to which they [the Egyptians] even pay divine honors. Greeks taught him the rest of the universal curriculum, and savants from the bordering lands taught him Assyrian letters and the Chaldean science of the heavenly bodies. The latter he also acquired from the Egyptians, who especially pursue astronomy. And when he had learned with precision from either nation both that on which they agree and that on which they disagree, avoiding politics and strife, he sought the truth, since his mind was incapable of accepting anything false, as is the wont of sectarians, who maintain the doctrines proposed, whatever they happen to be, without examining whether they are trustworthy, thus acting exactly like hired lawyers who have no concern for justice. (Ibid. 1.21–24) [PHILO 1981: 267–268]

6. The Prophet Is Also a Philosopher

Moses was, then, the most learned man of his time and, on the chronological evidence, the predecessor of vaunted Greek masters like Plato. It was Plato who was the borrower, as the sequel to the argument shows, and the point was taken up with avidity by the Christian Fathers, Augustine among others.

Certain partakers with us in the grace of Christ wonder when they hear and read that Plato had conceptions concerning God in which they recognize considerable agreement with the truth of our religion. Some have concluded from this that when Plato went to Egypt he had heard the prophet Jeremiah or, while traveling in the same country, had read the prophetic Scriptures, which opinion I myself have expressed in certain of my writings.

Augustine has, however, reinvestigated the chronological question and concluded that Plato was in Egypt too late to have encountered Jeremiah and too early to have been able to read the Septuagint translation of the Scriptures commissioned by King Ptolemy.

. . . [U]nless, indeed, we say that, as Plato was most earnest in the pursuit of knowledge, he also studied those writings [that is, the Bible] through an interpreter, as he did those of the Egyptians . . . or learned as much as he possibly could concerning their contents by means of conversation. What warrants this supposition are the opening verses of Genesis, "In the beginning God made heaven and earth. And the earth was invisible and without order; and darkness was over the abyss: and the Spirit of God moved over the waters." For in the *Timaeus*, when writing on the formation of the world, Plato says that God first united heaven and fire; from which it is evident that he assigns fire a place in heaven. This opinion bears a certain resemblance to the statement, "In the beginning God made heaven and earth." Plato next speaks of those two intermediary elements, water and air, by which the other two extremes, namely, earth and fire, were mutually united; from which circumstances he is thought to have so understood the words, "The Spirit of God moved over the waters." For, not paying sufficient attention to the designations given by those Scriptures to the Spirit of God, he may have thought that the four (physical) elements are spoken of in that place, because the air is also called "spirit."

Then, as for Plato's saying that the philosopher is a lover of God, nothing shines forth more conspicuously in those Sacred Writings. But the most striking thing in this connection, and that which most of all inclines me almost to assent to the proposition that Plato was not ignorant of those Writings, is the answer which was given to the question elicited from the holy Moses when the words of God were conveyed to him by the angel; for, when he asked what was the name of that God who was commanding him to go and deliver the Hebrew people out of Egypt, this answer was given: "I am who am; and you shall say to the Children of Israel, He who is sent me to you" (Exod. 3:14); as though compared with Him who truly is, because He is unchangeable, these things which have been created mutable are not—a truth which Plato zealously held and most diligently commended. And I know not whether this sentiment is anywhere to be found in the books of those who are before Plato, unless in that Book where it is said, "I am who am; you shall say to the Children of Israel, He who is sent me to you." (Augustine, *City of God* 8.11)

[AUGUSTINE 1948: 2:112–113]

Many centuries later Maimonides pursues the argument much in the same vein.

Know that the true prophets indubitably grasp speculative matters, though by means of his speculation alone man is unable to grasp the causes from which what a prophet has come to know necessarily follows. . . . For the very overflow that affects the imaginative faculty, with the result of rendering it perfect so that its activity brings about its giving information about what will happen and its apprehending those future events as if they were things perceived by the senses and had reached the imaginative faculty through the senses, this is the same overflow that renders perfect the activity of the rational faculty so that its activity brings about its knowing things that are real in their existence, and it achieves this apprehension as if it had apprehended it by starting from speculative premises. . . . The overflow of the Active Intellect goes in its true reality only to it [the human rational faculty], causing it to pass from potentiality to actuality. It is from the rational faculty that the overflow comes to the imaginative faculty. How then can the imaginative faculty be perfected in so great a measure as to apprehend what does not come to it from the senses without the rational faculty being affected in a similar way so as to apprehend without having apprehended by way of premises, inference and reflection? (Maimonides, *Guide of the Perplexed* 2.39)

[MAIMONIDES 1963: 377]

7. Philo on the Limits of Speculative Theology

Philo stands at the beginning of a long debate on reason and revelation among the Peoples of the Book, but he too had before him an already long tradition of attempts to reason about God. It had begun among the Greeks with an attempt to arrive at the principle of all things, a quest that pondered various material possibilities. Once the basic distinction between matter and spirit had been established, however, the investigation took a new course. It accepted that its object was God, the same supernatural presence or force or power commemorated under various human guises

by the Greeks' own mythology. Thereafter theology, the "science of God," at-
tempted to apply its refined tools of conceptual analysis and demonstrative proof—
methods that had been spectacularly vindicated in the science of mathematics—to
understanding, in as rigorous a way as possible, the essence, attributes, and opera-
tions of God.

As we have already seen in Chapter 4 above, Philo was willing to concede the
possibility of an intuitive knowledge of God to the man endowed with both a rigorous
training in philosophy and the gift of God's grace. But he was careful to insist that
this was a knowledge of God's existence only; knowledge of His essence was restricted
to God Himself. For Philo, the substance of God was not only unknown but unknow-
able, which was likely a new position in the Greek philosophical tradition from which
he had come, though after him it became a commonplace in Jewish, Christian, and
Muslim theology.

Do not suppose that the Existent, which truly exists, is apprehended
by any man; for we have in us no organ by which we may form any image
of It, neither sense organ, for it is not sense-perceptible, nor mind. So
Moses, the student of invisible nature—for the divine oracles [that is,
Scripture] say that he entered the darkness (Exod. 20:21), a figure intimating the invisible and incorporeal existence—searched everywhere
and into everything and sought to see with distinct clarity the object of
his great yearning and the only good. But finding nothing, not even an
idea that resembled what he hoped for, in despair and learning from
others, he flies for refuge to the object of his search itself and makes the
following supplication: "Reveal Yourself to me that I may see You
clearly" (Exod. 33:13). And yet he does not attain his purpose, since the
knowledge of things both material and immaterial that come after the
Existent is considered a most ample gift for the best race among mortals.
For we read: "You will see what is behind Me, but My face will not be
seen by you" (Exod. 33:23), meaning that all that comes after the Existent, both material and immaterial, is accessible to apprehension, even if
it is not all already apprehended, but He alone by His very nature cannot
be seen. And why is it astonishing if the Existent is inapprehensible to
men when even the mind in each of us is unknown to us? For who has
seen the true nature of the soul, whose obscurity has bred innumerable
disputes among the sophists who propose opinions contrary to each other
or even completely opposed in kind?

The very name of God is, then, unknown.

It follows that not even a proper name can be given to the Truly
Existent. Observe that when the prophet earnestly inquires what he must

answer those who ask about His name, He says, "I am He that is" (Exod. 3:14), which is equivalent to "My nature is to be, not to be spoken." But that mankind should not be in complete want of a designation for the Supremely Good, He allows them to use analogically, as though it were His proper name, the title of Lord God of the three natures, teaching, perfection and practice, whose recorded symbols are Abraham, Isaac and Jacob. For this, He continues (Exod. 3:15), is "My name through the ages," inasmuch as it belongs to our time period, not to the precosmic, "and My memorial," not a name set beyond memory and thought, and again, "for generations," not for beings ungenerated. For those who have entered the realm of mortal creation require the analogical use of the divine name, so that they may approach, if not the facticity, then at least the name of the Supremely Good, and be ruled according to it.

This is also shown by an oracle revealed as from the mouth of the Ruler of the universe that no proper name of Him has been disclosed to anyone. "I appeared," He says, "to Abraham, Isaac and Jacob, being their God, and My name of 'Lord' I did not reveal to them" (Exod. 6:3). For if the order of the words is changed back to the normal grammatical sequence, the meaning would be as follows: "My proper name I did not reveal to them," but only the one for analogical use, for the reasons already mentioned. So ineffable indeed is the Existent that not even the ministering powers tell us a proper name. Thus after the wrestling match that (Jacob) the Man of Practice fought in his quest for virtue, he says to the unseen master, "Declare to me your name," and He said, "Why do you ask this My name?" (Gen. 32:29), and He does not disclose His personal and proper name. "Suffice it for you," He says, "to profit from My blessing, but as for names, those symbols of created things, seek them not among imperishable natures." Do not then be thoroughly perplexed if you find the highest of all things to be ineffable, when His Word too, cannot be expressed by us through His own name. And indeed, if He is ineffable, He is also inconceivable and incomprehensible. (Philo, *On the Changing of Names* 7–15) [PHILO 1981: 141–143]

8. Paul on the Wisdom of the World and the Wisdom of God

Paul, like Philo, was a Diaspora Jew living in a world suffused with Greek philosophical ideas and ideals. Both men could use those ideas as seemed appropriate, but Paul had public reason to condemn them to the new Christians.

This doctrine of the cross is sheer folly to those on their way to ruin, but to those of us who are on our way to salvation, it is the power of God. Scripture says, "I will destroy the wisdom of the wise, and bring to nothing the cleverness of the clever." Where is your wise man now, your man of learning, or your subtle debater—limited, all of them, to this passing age? God has made the wisdom of this world look foolish. As God in His wisdom ordained, the world failed to find Him by its wisdom, and He chose to save those who have faith by the folly of the Gospel. Jews call for miracles, Greeks look for wisdom; but we proclaim Christ—yes, Christ nailed to the cross. And though this is a stumbling block for the Jews and folly to the Greeks, yet to those who have heard his call, Jews and Greeks alike, he is the power of God and the wisdom of God. . . .

As for me, brothers, when I came to you, I declared the attested truth of God, without display of fine words or wisdom. I resolved that while I was with you I would think of nothing but Jesus Christ—Christ nailed to the cross. I came before you weak, nervous and shaking with fear. The word I spoke, the Gospel I proclaimed, did not sway you with subtle arguments; it carried conviction by spiritual power, so that your faith might not be built upon human wisdom but upon the power of God. (Paul, *To the Corinthians* 1.1:18–2:5)

9. Christ and Socrates

In the generation after Paul the wisdom of Hellenism did not appear quite so threatening, particularly to intellectuals like Justin who were raised in that tradition. Christ was immeasurably greater than Socrates; but truth is one, and even the pagan Greeks had some share in it.

Our teachings appear to be greater than all human teaching, because Christ, who appeared for our sakes, became the whole rational being, body and reason and soul. For whatever either lawgivers or philosophers uttered well they elaborated by finding and contemplating some part of the Logos. But since they did not know the whole of the Logos, which is Christ, they often contradicted themselves. And those who by human birth were older than Christ, when they attempted to consider and prove things by reason, were brought before the tribunals of the impious and busybodies. And Socrates, who was more zealous in this direction than all of them, was accused of the very same crimes as ourselves. For they said he was introducing new divinities, and did not consider those to be gods whom the state recognized. But Socrates cast out from the state

Homer and the rest of the poets, and taught men to reject the wicked demons and those who did the things which the poets related; and he exhorted them to become acquainted with the God who was unknown to them, by means of the investigation of reason, saying that "it is not easy to find the Father and Maker of all, nor, having found him, to declare Him to all."

But these things our Christ did through his own power. For no one trusted in Socrates to the point of dying for this teaching, but in Christ, who was partially known to Socrates—for he was and is the Logos who is in every man, and who foretold the things that were to come to pass both through the prophets and in his own person when he was made of like passions and taught these things—not only philosophers and scholars believed, but also artisans and people entirely uneducated, despising alike glory and fear and death, since he is the power of the ineffable Father, and not the mere instrument of human reason. . . .

I prayed and strove with all my might to be found a Christian, not because the teachings of Plato are contrary to those of Christ, but because they are not in all respects like them, as is the case with the doctrines of the others, Stoics, poets and prose authors. For each discoursed rightly, seeing that which was kin to Christianity through sharing in the seminal divine reason; but they who have uttered contrary opinions seem not to have had the invisible knowledge and the irrefutable wisdom. Whatever has been uttered aright by any man in any place belongs to us Christians; for next to God we worship and love the Logos which is from the unbegotten and ineffable God, since on our account He has been made man so that, being partaker of our sufferings, He may also bring us healing. For all the authors were able to see that truth darkly, through the implanted seed of *logos* dwelling in them. For the seed and imitation of a thing, given according to a man's capacity, is one thing; far different is the thing itself, the sharing of which and its representation is given according to His grace. (Justin, *Apology* 2.10, 13)

10. The Fathers Debate the Role of Greek Philosophy

With a greater familiarity with this "wisdom of the world," as Paul called it, a new generation of Christians pondered somewhat more carefully the attractions and the dangers of the demonstrative, discursive, and at times utterly convincing science of the Greeks. To some it seemed almost like a form of revelation.

Philosophy was necessary for the Greeks for righteousness, until the coming of the Lord. And it now helps toward true religion as a kind of preparatory training for those who come to faith by the way of demonstration. For "your foot shall not stumble" if you assign all good to Providence, whether it belongs to the Greeks or to us. For God is the source of all good things; of some in a primary sense, like the Old and New Testaments; of others by way of consequence, like philosophy. But it may be that philosophy was given to the Greeks immediately and primarily, until the Lord should call the Greeks. For philosophy served as a pedagogue to bring the Greek mind to Christ, as the Law brought the Hebrews. Thus philosophy was a preparation, paving the way toward perfection in Christ. (Clement of Alexandria, *Stromateis* 1:5)

If that was the view from highly Hellenized Alexandria at the beginning of the third century, the matter appeared somewhat differently in the nearly contemporary Latin-speaking Western Church.

These are the teachings of men and of demons born of the spirit of this world's wisdom, for itching ears; and the Lord called this foolishness, choose the foolish things of this world to the confusion of philosophy. It is this philosophy which is the subject matter of this world's wisdom, that rash interpreter of the divine nature and order. In fact, heresies are themselves prompted by philosophy. It is the source of the "Aeons" and I know not what infinite "forms" and the "trinity of man" in the system of Valentinus. He was a Platonist. It is the source of Marcion's "better God," "better" because of his tranquillity. Marcion came from the Stoics. Again, when it is said that the soul perishes, that opinion is taken from the Epicureans. The denial of the restoration of the flesh is taken over from universal teaching of the philosophers; the equation of matter with God from Zeno, and when any assertion is made about a God of fire, then Heraclitus comes in. Heretics and philosophers handle the same subject matter; both treat of the same subjects: Whence came evil? And why? Whence came man? And how? And the question lately posed by Valentinus: Whence came God? His answer: From *enthymesis* and *ektroma*! Wretched Aristotle who taught them dialectic, that art of building up and demolishing, so protean in statement, so far-fetched in conjecture, so unyielding in controversy, so productive of disputes; self-stultifying since it is ever handling questions but never settling anything. . . . What is there in common between Athens and Jerusalem? Between the Academy and the Church? Between heretics and Christians? Away with all projects for a "Stoic" or a "Platonic" or a "dialectical" Christianity! After Christ Jesus we desire no subtle theories, no acute inquiries after the Gospel. (Tertullian, *On the Prescription of Heretics* 7)

By the fifth Christian century, however, an accommodation had been made, even in Latin circles, though with continuing echoes of Paul's warnings.

Although a Christian man instructed in ecclesiastical literature may perhaps be ignorant of the very name of the Platonists, and may not even know that there have existed two schools of philosophers speaking the Greek tongue, to wit, the Ionian and Italic, he is nevertheless not so deaf with respect to human affairs as not to know that philosophers profess the study, and even the possession, of wisdom. He is on his guard, however, with respect to those who philosophize according to the elements of this world and not according to God, by whom the world itself was made; for he is warned by the precept of the Apostle (Paul) and faithfully hears what has been said, "Beware that no one deceive you through philosophy and vain deceit, according to the elements of the world" (Col. 2:8). Then, that he may not suppose that all philosophers are such as do this, he hears the same Apostle say concerning certain of them, "Because that which is known of God is manifest among them, for God has manifested it to them. For His invisible things from the creation of the world are clearly seen, being understood by the things which are made, also by His eternal power and Godhead" (Rom. 1:19–20). And, when speaking of the Athenians, after having spoken a mighty thing concerning God, which few are able to understand, "In Him we live and move and have our being" (Acts 17:28), he goes on to say, "as certain also of your own people have said."

Paul knows well too to be on his guard even against these philosophers (who understand the truth) in their errors. For where it has been said by him that God has manifested to them His invisible things by those things which are made that they might be seen by the understanding, there it has also been said that they did not rightly worship God Himself because they paid divine honors, which are due to Him alone, to other things also to which they ought not to have paid them, "because, knowing God, they glorified Him not as God: neither were they thankful, but became vain in their imaginings and their foolish hearts were darkened. Professing themselves to be wise, they became fools and changed the glory of the incorruptible God into the likeness of the image of corruptible man, and of birds, and of four-footed beasts, and of creeping things" (Rom. 1:21–23), where the Apostle would have us understand him as meaning the Romans, the Greeks and the Egyptians, who gloried in the name of wisdom; but concerning this, we will dispute with them afterwards.

With respect, however, to that wherein the philosophers agree with
us, we prefer them to all others, namely, concerning the one God, the
author of this universe, who is not only above everybody, being incorporeal, but also above all souls, being incorruptible: our principal, our light,
our good. And though the Christian man, being ignorant of their writings,
does not use in disputation words which he has not learned—not calling
that part of philosophy natural, which is the Latin term, or physical,
which is the Greek one, which treats of the investigation of nature; or
that part rational or logical which deals with questions of how truth may
be discovered; or that part moral or ethical which concerns morals and
shows how the good is to be sought and evil to be shunned—he is not
for all that ignorant that it is from the one true and supremely good God
that we have that nature in which we are made in the image of God, and
that doctrine by which we know Him and ourselves, and that grace
through which, by cleaving to Him, we are blessed. This, then, is the
reason why we prefer these to all others, because while other philosophers have worn out their minds and powers in seeking the causes of
things, and endeavoring to discover the right mode of learning and of
living, these, by knowing God, have found where resides the cause by
which the universe has been constituted, and the light by which truth
is to be discovered, and the fountain at which felicity is to be drunk.
All philosophers, then, who have had these thoughts concerning God,
whether Platonists or not, agree with us. But we have chosen to argue our
case with the Platonists, because their writings are better known. For the
Greeks, whose tongue holds the highest place among the languages of the
Gentiles, are loud in their praise of their writings; and the Latins, likewise
taken by their excellence or their renown, have studied them more heartily than other writings, and by translating them into our tongue, have
given them greater celebrity and notoriety. (Augustine, *City of God* 8.10)
[AUGUSTINE 1948: 2:111–112]

11. Despoiling the Egyptians

*As is clear in the case of Clement, and even earlier of Philo, philosophy and science
inspired no terror in many of the religious intellectuals of the eastern, Greek-
speaking provinces of the Roman Empire. They themselves had been to Greek schools
before their conversion, had learned the methods, literary and philosophical, in use*

there, and had begun to apply them, and teach others to apply them, to their newly found Christian faith. One of them, Origen, a graduate of the philosophy faculty of the university of Alexandria, composed ca. 225 C.E. the first systematic treatment of the principles of the Christian faith. Here we see this pioneer Christian theologian and his work through the eyes of one of his students, Gregory, called "the Wonder-worker," whom Origen not only converted to the Christian faith but whose view of the world he had altered forever.

He [Origen] taught us to consider not only the obvious and evident arguments, but sometimes even erroneous and sophistical ones, to probe and sound each to see whether it gave any echo of hollowness. Thus he provided us with a reasonable training for the critical part of our soul. . . . He also raised within us a humility of the soul, as we were amazed by the great and marvelous and manifold and all-wise workmanship of the universe. . . . By physics he established a reasonable, in place of an unreasonable, wonder in our souls. This divine and lofty science is taught by the study of nature, a subject most delectable to all. What need to mention the sacred studies, geometry dear to all and irrefragable, and astronomy, whose path is on high? . . . He made heaven accessible to us by "the ladder reaching up to heaven" of either study.

He was the first and only one to direct me to Greek philosophy, persuading me by his own manner of life to listen and adhere to the study of ethics. He thought it right that we should philosophize, and collate with all our powers every one of the writings of the ancients, whether philosophers or poets, excepting and rejecting nothing, save only those of the atheists. (Gregory Thaumaturgus, *To Origen*)

Origen responded to Gregory's encomium and, in the course of his reply, contrived what was to become Christianity's most familiar scriptural justification for helping itself to the riches of Greek philosophy and science, namely, the example of the Israelites' "despoiling of the Egyptians" described in Exodus 11:2–35.

Greetings in God, sir, my most excellent and revered son Gregory, from Origen: . . . Your abilities are such as to make you an accomplished Roman lawyer, or a Greek philosopher in one of the most prestigious of the schools. But my desire has been for you to focus all the force of your abilities on Christianity as your end, and to this effect I implore you to take from Greek philosophy whatever matters are capable of being generalized into serving as studies preparatory to Christianity, and likewise from geometry and astronomy such things as might be useful for the exposition of Holy Scripture, so that what the sons of the philosophers said about geometry and music and grammar and rhetoric and astronomy, namely, that they are the handmaidens of philosophy, we may also say of philosophy in relation to Christianity.

It is possibly just something of this sort that is hinted at in Exodus, which was written from the mouth of God, where it is said that the Children of Israel were to ask from their neighbors and their fellow residents silver and gold vessels as well as clothes, so that having thus despoiled the Egyptians, they might have material for the construction of the (prescribed) things . . . in the Holy of Holies, the ark with its cover, and the cherubim, and the seat of mercy, and the golden vessel in which was stored the manna, the bread of angels.

But, my son, make your first and foremost concern the reading of the Holy Scriptures. For we need great attention in reading the Scriptures, that we may not speak or think too rashly about them. . . . Do not be satisfied with merely knocking and seeking; what is most important is our prayer to understand divine matters. (Ibid.)

12. Faith and Knowledge

Early in the encounter with the wisdom of the Hellenes, the new breed of Christian theologians had to address the issue of adherence to the truth through faith and its understanding through knowledge. Here one of the first of them, Clement of Alexandria, speaks to the point.

Knowledge [*gnosis*] is, so to speak, the perfecting of man as man, which is accomplished through acquaintance with divine things; in character, life and word it is harmonious and consistent with itself and with faith. For by it faith is made perfect, since it is through it alone that the man of faith becomes perfect. Faith is an internal good, and without searching for God confesses His existence and glorifies Him as existent. Hence, by starting with this faith, and being developed by it through the grace of God, the knowledge of Him is likewise to be acquired to as great an extant as possible. . . .

But it is not doubt about God but rather belief that is the foundation of knowledge. Christ is both the foundation and the superstructure, through whom both the beginning and the end come to be. And the beginning and the end, by which I mean faith and love, are not taught. Knowledge [*gnosis*], which is conveyed as a deposit through communication by the grace of God, is entrusted to those who show themselves worthy of it. . . .

Faith is, then, a kind of compendious knowledge of the essentials, while knowledge is the sure and firm demonstration of what is received by faith, built upon faith by the Lord's teaching and carrying us onward to unshaken conviction and certainty. And, as it seems to me, the first saving change is that from paganism to faith; and the second, that from faith to knowledge. And this latter passing on to love thereafter brings about a mutual friendship between that which knows and that which is known. And he who has arrived at this state has already perhaps attained equality with the angels. He continues to advance, at any rate, after he has reached the final ascent in the flesh, and passes on through the Holy Sevenness into the Father's house, to that which is indeed the Lord's abode. (Clement, *Stromateis* 7.10)

13. "Knowing Not What He Is, But Knowing What He Is Not"

Clement understands the passage from faith to knowledge not as a simple progress to a more profound understanding of what one had previously simply accepted but as a true ascent, out of and beyond the flesh, into the realms of an almost mystical theology.

The sacrifice acceptable to God is unchanging alienation from the body and its passions. This is the really true piety. And is not philosophy, therefore, rightly called by Socrates the meditation on death? For he who neither applies his eyes in the exercise of thought nor draws upon his other senses but rather applies himself to objects purely with mind practices the true philosophy. . . .

. . . In the great mysteries concerning the universe nothing remains to be learned; we have only to contemplate and comprehend with the mind nature and things. We shall understand more about purification by confession and more about contemplation by analysis, advancing through analysis to the first notion, beginning with the properties underlying it; abstracting from the body its physical properties, taking away the dimension of depth, then of breadth, then of length. The point that remains is the unit, possessing only position. If we abstract position, what remains is the conception of unity.

If, then, we abstract all that belongs to bodies and things called incorporeal, we cast ourselves in the greatness of Christ, and thence advancing into immensity by holiness, we may reach somehow to the conception of the Almighty, knowing not what He is, but knowing what He is not. And form and motion, or standing, or a throne or place, or right hand or left, are not at all to be conceived as belonging to the Father of the universe, although it is so written. . . . The First Cause is not in space but above time and space and name and conception. (Clement, *Stromateis* 5.11)

14. The Father and the Son: Some Preliminary Proposals

It was one thing, perhaps, to lay down as Origen did the philosophical bases upon which the Christian faith might rest; it was quite another to take Christian teachings themselves, couched, as they inevitably were, in the language of Scripture, and attempt to explain them in philosophical terms. One attractive area of investigation was the nature of the relationship of Jesus to his "Father who is in heaven," or, somewhat more elusively, how Jesus could be eternal and one with the Father and at the same time man. Hippolytus, in his Refutation of All Heresies, *presents two sharply contrasting second-century views of the matter, which bear within them the seeds of a great many later theological postures. In the first, which Hippolytus identifies as coming from heretical Jewish-Christian circles, the Ebionites, the human Jesus is made to appear as a kind of "adopted" son of the Father.*

Jesus [it was alleged] was a man, born of a virgin, according to the counsel of the Father, and after he had lived in a way common to all men and had become pre-eminently religious, he afterwards at his baptism in the Jordan received Christ, who came from above and descended upon him. Therefore miraculous powers did not operate in him prior to the manifestation of that Spirit which descended and proclaimed him as the Christ. But some others (who share this view) are disposed to think that this man never was God, even at the descent of the Spirit, whereas others of them maintain that he was made God after the resurrection from the dead. (Hippolytus, *Refutation of All Heresies* 7.35)

Almost exactly the opposite view of the Father and the Son was proposed by one Noetus of Smyrna, "a reckless babbler and trickster," as Hippolytus calls him.

There is one Father and Son of the universe, and that He who had made all things was, when He wished, invisible to those who existed, and when He wished, He became visible; that He is invisible when He is not seen and visible when He is seen; that the Father is unbegotten when He is not generated but begotten when He was born of a virgin; that He is not subject to suffering and is immortal when He does not suffer and die, but when His passion came upon Him, Noetus admits that the Father suffers and dies. The Noetians think that the Father is called the Son according to events at different times. (Hippolytus, *Refutation of All the Heresies* 10.27)

15. An Early Theological Discussion in Christian Circles

These views of Jesus and the Father are already identified as heretical in the source that transmits them to us. To pass from a condemnation of what is false to a statement of what actually constituted an orthodox view of the matter was a more complex task, however, and one that required considerable discussion. We are given some insight into one such dialectical inquiry that took place at the ecumenical council of Nicea in 325 C.E. As we have already seen, the bishops put forth a draft statement of the Christian faith as follows.

We believe in one God, the Father All-sovereign, maker of heaven and earth, and all things visible and invisible.

And in one Lord Jesus Christ, the Son of God, Begotten of the Father, the Only-begotten, that is, from the substance of the Father; God from God, Light from Light, True God of True God, begotten not made, consubstantial with the Father, through whom all things were made, those in heaven and those on earth;

Who for us men and for our salvation came down and was made flesh, suffered and rose again on the third day, ascended into heaven, and is coming to judge the living and the dead.

And in the Holy Spirit.

And those who say "there was time when he was not," and "before his generation he was not," and "he came to be from nothing," or those who pretend that the Son of God is "of other hypostasis or substance," or "created" or "alterable," the catholic and apostolic church anathematizes.

Eusebius, the Church historian and bishop of Caesarea who was present at the synod, and who had earlier proposed his own formula, reports on what followed.

At their suggesting this formula, we did not let it pass without inquiry in what sense they were using the expressions "of the substance of the Father" and "consubstantial with the Father." Accordingly, questions and explanations took place and the discussion tested the meaning of these phrases. And they professed that the phrase "of the substance" meant the Son's being indeed from the Father, yet without being as it were a part of Him. And with this understanding we thought good to assent to the meaning of the pious teaching suggesting that God was from the Father, though not a part of His substance. On this account we too assented to this meaning, without declining even the term "consubstantial," since peace was the aim we set before us and in fear of deviating from the correct meaning.

In the same way, we also accepted "begotten, not made," since they [the proposers] said that "made" was an appellation to the other creatures which came to be through the Son, to whom the Son bore no likeness. Wherefore the Son was not a work resembling the things which through him came to be, but was an essence too high for any level of work, and which the Divine Oracles [that is, the Scriptures] teach to have been generated from the Father, the mode of generation being ineffable and inexplicable to every originated nature.

And so too on examination there are grounds for saying that the Son is "consubstantial" with the Father; not in the way of bodies, or like mortal beings, for he is not by division of essence or by severance, no, nor by any affect or alteration or changing of the Father's substance and power, since from all such the unoriginate nature of the Father is alien; but because "consubstantial with the Father" suggests that the Son of God bears no resemblance to the originated creatures, but that to his Father alone who begot him is he in every way assimilated, and that he is not of any other hypostasis and substance but from the Father. To this term too, understood in such a way, it appeared well to assent, since we were aware that even among the ancients some learned and illustrious bishops and writers have used the term "consubstantial" in their theological teaching concerning the Father and the Son.

So much then for the (statement of) Faith which was published, to which we all assented, not without inquiry, but according to specified meanings mentioned before the most religious Emperor himself and justified by the aforementioned considerations. And as for the anathemas published by them at the end of the Faith, we thought them without offense because they forbade the use of expressions not found in Scripture, from which almost all the confusion and disorder in the Church have come. Since, then, no divinely inspired Scripture has used the phrase "out of nothing" and "once he was not" and the rest which follow, there appeared no ground for using or teaching them; to which also we assented as a good decision since it had not been our (own) custom hitherto to use these terms.

Moreover, to anathematize "before his generation he was not" did not seem preposterous in that it is confessed by all, that the Son of God existed before the generation according to the flesh. Nay, our most religious Emperor proved in a speech made on that occasion that he [the Son] was in being even according to his divine generation which is before all ages, since even before he was generated in actuality, he was potentially with the Father ingenerately, the Father being always the Father, as King always, as Savior always, being all things potentially, and always being in the same respects and in the same way.

This we have been forced to transmit to you, beloved brethren, to make clear to you the deliberations that surrounded our inquiry and assent, and how reasonably we resisted even to the last minute, so long as we were offended at statements which differed from our own, but received without contention what no longer pained as soon as, on candid examination of the sense of the words, they appeared to us to coincide with what we ourselves have professed in the (statement) of Faith which we previously declared. (Eusebius in Sozomen, *Church History* 1.8)

16. The Divine Trinity

Trinitarian—or better, triadic—thinking about the primary principle or principles of being was not a Christian innovation. Dyads and triads were philosophical commonplaces among the later Platonist philosophers, and Philo's triune, "Lord God of three natures, teaching, perfection and practice, whose recorded symbols are Abraham, Isaac and Jacob," is a notion that can be found, as a whole or in its distinct parts, scattered through many passages in his writings, here, for example, in his work called Abraham.

Spoken words are symbols of that which is apprehended by the intellect alone. When, therefore, at high noon, the soul is fully illuminated and, entirely filled with intelligible light, it is rendered shadowless by the rays of light diffused all around it, it perceives a triple vision of a single object, one representing it as it really is, the other two like shadows reflected from it. This occurs also for those living in the sensible light; whether standing or moving, objects often cast two shadows simultaneously. No one, however, should suppose that the shadow can properly be referred to God. It is only an analogical use of words in order to afford a clearer view of the fact being set forth, for the truth is not so. Rather, as anyone who stands closest to the truth would say, in the central position is the Father of the Universe, who in Holy Scriptures is properly called the Existent One, and on either side are the senior powers that are nearest to Him, the Creative and the Regent. The Creative is designated God, since through it He established and ordered the universe; the Regent is called Lord, for it is right that the Creator should rule and hold sway over what He has brought into being.

The central Being, then, attended by each of His powers, presents to the mind that has vision the appearance, now of one, now of three: of one when perfectly purified and transcending not only the multitude of numbers but even the dyad, neighbor to the unit, it hastens to the form that is unmixed and uncombined, and is in itself in need of nothing whatever; of three, when as yet uninitiated into the greater mysteries, it still celebrates the lesser ones, and is unable to apprehend the Existent by Itself alone and apart from anything else, but only through Its actions, either creative or ruling. This is, as they say, a "second best voyage"; yet it shares in a view that is no less dear to God. But the former mode has not merely a share, it is itself the God-beloved view, or rather it is truth, more venerable than any point of view, more precious than any act of thinking. (Philo, *Abraham* 119–125) [PHILO 1981: 222–223]

Although in other places Philo identifies what is here called "the Creative" with the Word of God, or even His Son, the difference between his notion and the Christian Trinity is readily apparent. For Philo, the "triune God" is a matter of human perception, a useful analogical way of grasping the nature of God through secondary affects of creating and ruling rather than immediately through His essence. For the Christian, the Trinity is a mode of being, and its three constituents of Father, Son, and Holy Spirit are fully articulated existential persons, as Augustine explains.

All those Catholic expounders of the divine Scriptures, both Old and New, whom I have been able to read, who have written before me concerning the Trinity, Who is God, have purposed to teach, according to the Scriptures, this doctrine, that the Father, and the Son, and the Holy Spirit intimate a divine unity of one and the same substance in an indivisible equality; and that therefore they are not three Gods but one God: although the Father has begotten the Son, and so He who is the Father is not the Son; and the Son is begotten by the Father, and so He who is the Son is not the Father; and the Holy Spirit is neither the Father nor the Son, but only the Spirit of the Father and the Son, Himself co-equal with the Father and the Son, and pertaining to the unity of the Trinity; . . . the Father and the Son and the Holy Spirit, as they are indivisible, so work indivisibly. This is also my faith, since it is the Catholic faith.

Some persons, however, find a difficulty in this faith; when they hear that the Father is God and the Son God and the Holy Spirit God, and yet that the Trinity is not three Gods but one God; and they ask how they are to understand this, especially when it is said that the Trinity works indivisibly in everything that God works, and yet that a certain voice of the Father spoke, which is not the voice of the Son; and that none except the Son was born in the flesh, and suffered, and rose again, and ascended into heaven; and that none but the Holy Spirit came (upon Jesus at his baptism) in the form of a dove. (Augustine, *On the Trinity* 1.4–5)

[AUGUSTINE 1948: 2:672–673]

17. A Scriptural Demonstration of the Trinity

Parts of Augustine's proof for a triune God are derived from Scripture, many of them from the New Testament, with its frequent references to "Father" and "Son." But a number too are drawn from the Bible, the Christians' Old Testament, where there appear to be distinct and multiple manifestations of God on occasion.

In that which is written in Genesis, to wit, that God spoke with man whom He had formed out of the dust, if we set apart the figurative meaning and treat it so as to place faith in the letter of the narrative, it should appear that God spoke with man in the appearance of a man. This is not indeed expressly laid down in the Book, but the general tenor of its reading sounds in this sense, especially in that which is written, that Adam heard the voice of the Lord God, walking in the garden in the cool of the evening. . . . Adam too says that he hid himself from the face of God. Who then was He? Whether the Father, or the Son or the Holy Spirit? Whether altogether indiscriminately did God the Trinity speak to man in the form of man? The context itself of Scripture nowhere, it would seem, indicates a change from person to person, but He seems still to speak to the first man who (earlier) said, "Let there be light" and "Let there be firmament," and so on through each of those days, (the One) whom we usually take to be God the Father, making by a word whatever He willed to make. For He made all things by His word, which Word we know, by the right rule of faith, to be His only Son. . . . Why are we not to go on to understand that it was He also [that is, the Father] who appeared to Abraham and to Moses, and to whomever He would, through the changeable and visible creature subjected to himself, while He Himself remains in Himself and in His own substance, in which He is unchangeable and invisible? But possibly it might be that the Scripture passed over in a hidden way from person to person, and while it related that the Father said, "Let there be light," and the rest which it mentioned Him to have done by the Word, went on to indicate the Son as speaking to the first man; not unfolding this openly, but intimating it to be understood by those who could understand it.

Augustine passes to the Christians' most cogent and frequently cited biblical proof-text, Abraham's encounter with the three men in Genesis 18:1ff.

Under the oak at Mamre he [Abraham] saw three men, whom he invited and hospitably received and ministered to them as they feasted. Yet Scripture at the beginning of that narrative does not say that three men appeared to him but "The Lord appeared to him." And then, setting forth in due order after what manner the Lord appeared to him, it has added the account of the three men, whom Abraham invites to his hospitality in the plural number, and afterwards speaks to them in the singular number as one; and as one He promises Abraham a son by Sarah, namely, the one whom the Scripture calls "Lord" in the beginning of the same narrative. "The Lord," it says, "appeared to Abraham." He invites them then, and washes their feet, and leads them forth at their departure, as though they were men; but he speaks as with the Lord God, whether when a son is promised to him or when the destruction is shown to him that was impending over Sodom.

There is a subtext to Augustine's argument throughout this section of On the Trinity: *whether or not Jesus, the pre-existent Son of God in the Christians' Trinity, had appeared in human form before his birth. And that is the first issue addressed in his reflections on the scene of Abraham at Mamre.*

That place in Scripture demands neither a slight nor a passing consideration. For if one man had appeared (to Abraham), what else would those at once cry out, who say that the Son was visible also in His own substance before He was born of the Virgin, but that it was He? . . . And yet I would go on to demand in what manner "He was found in fashion as a man" before He had taken our flesh, seeing that His feet were washed and He fed upon earthly food? How could that be, when He was still "in the form of God and thought it not robbery to be equal to God" (Phil. 2:6–7)? For, tell me, had He already "emptied Himself, taking upon Him the form of a servant, and made in the likeness of man and found in fashion as a man" (ibid.) when we know when it was that He did this through His birth of the Virgin? How, then, before He had done this, did He appear as one man to Abraham? Or was not that form a reality?

I could put these questions if it had been one man that appeared to Abraham, and if that one were believed to be the Son of God. But since three men appeared, and no one of them is said to be greater than the rest either in form or age or power, why should we not here understand, as visibly intimated by the visible creature, the equality of the Trinity and one and the same substance in three persons? For, lest anyone should think that one among the three is in this way intimated to have been the greater, and that this one is understood to have been the Lord, while the other two were His angels, because, whereas three appeared, Abraham there speaks to one as the Lord: Holy Scripture has not forgotten to anticipate, by a contradiction, such future thoughts and opinions, when a little while after it says (Gen. 18:33) that two angels came to Lot, among whom that just man also . . . speaks to one as to the Lord. For so Scripture goes on to say, "And the Lord went His way, as soon as He left communing with Abraham; and Abraham returned to his place." (Augustine, *On the Trinity* 2.10–11) [AUGUSTINE 1948: 2:711–714]

18. A Jewish Rebuttal

The Jews' first polemical concern with the Christians was, of course, with Jesus' messianic claims simply as such and then perhaps, as Christian theology progressively unfolded, with the anomaly represented by the Christians' assertion that Jesus was also the eternal Son of God. There was not much incentive for the Jews to continue the debate in the overwhelmingly Christian Roman Empire after Constantine. But six centuries later Jews and Christians once again stood as political equals, now as protected minorities under Islam, and the dialogue was resumed, particularly when the changed circumstances and the Muslim example brought Jewish thinkers once again to explore the possibilities of a scriptural theology in the manner of Philo. The pioneer in that enterprise was Saadya (d. 942 C.E.), head of the Jewish schools in Iraq, and its chief testament is his Book of Doctrines and Beliefs, *where he confronts the Christians directly on the matter of the Trinity.*

Let me say that in this matter (of God's attributes) the Christians erred when they assumed a distinction in God's personality which led them to make of him a trinity and to deviate from the orthodox belief. I shall, therefore, take occasion here to make note of what refutation of their doctrine is offered by reason, invoking the aid of the truly One and His Uniqueness.

Now I do not have in mind when I present this refutation the uneducated among them who profess only a crass materialistic trinity. For

I would not have my book occupy itself with answering people like that, since what that answer must be is quite clear and the task simple. It is rather my intention to reply to their elite, who maintain that they adopted their belief in the trinity as a result of rational speculation and subtle understanding, and it was thus that they arrived at these three attributes and adhered to them. Declaring that only a thing that is living and omniscient is capable of creating, they recognized God's vitality and omniscience as two things distinct from His essence, with the result that these became for them a trinity. (Saadya, *Doctrines and Beliefs* 2.5)
[SAADYA 1945: 103]

Part of Saadya's rebuttal of the doctrine of the Trinity is dialectical, as were the Christians' own arguments on the matter; but part too is addressed to the Christians' use of Scripture. He was not concerned with what use the Christians made of their own writings; the question of biblical interpretation, on the other hand, is one he must and does contend.

If, again, they derive their proof from Scripture, as for example, some one of them might assert, I see that Scripture says that God is possessed of a spirit and a word, as is borne out by the statement, "The spirit of the Lord spoke to me and His word was upon my tongue" (2 Sam. 23:2), our answer is that this "spirit" and "word" are things specially created by God, constituting the detailed speech revealed by God to His prophet. We know, in fact, that the Scripture calls the name of God "soul," as Scripture says, "Who has not taken My soul in vain" (Ps. 24:4) instead of "My name." Now inasmuch as in the case of creatures "soul" and "spirit" have one connotation, and the Creator also has a "soul" by which is meant His name, the "spirit" which is attributed to Him means "revelation" and "prophecy." This misinterpretation of these terms on the part of these individuals is, then, due to their unfamiliarity with the Hebrew language.

Similarly, I find that some of these (trinitarians) cite as proof (of their doctrine) the fact that the Scriptures declare that the spirit of God engages in Creation. They say (for example): "The spirit of God has made me, and the breath of the Almighty gives me life" (Job 33:4). Also they assert that the word of God engages in Creation. That is the import of their statement, "By the word of the Lord were the heavens made, and by the breath of His mouth" (Ps. 33:6). I note, however, that this too is due to unfamiliarity with the language of Scripture. For the Scriptures mean to say by these assertions only that the Creator created all things by means of His word, His command, His will or His wish, that He created them with intent, not wantonly, unintentionally or from necessity. This is borne out by the scriptural remark: "But He is at one with Himself, and who can turn Him? And what His soul desires, even that He does" (Job 23:13). (Ibid. 2.5) [SAADYA 1948: 105–106]

And on the celebrated incident at Mamre:

Others, conjecturing about the implication of the passage, "And the Lord appeared to him by the terebinths of Mamre," declare that the thing that appeared to Abraham and was designated by this name was a trinity, because Scripture later explicitly states: "And behold, three men stood before him." Let me explain, then, that these are more ignorant than all of those who have been mentioned earlier, because they did not wait until they reached the end of the passage. For had they patience until they heard the verse, "And the men turned from there and went toward Sodom; but Abraham yet stood before the Lord" (Gen. 18:22), they would have realized that the men had departed while the light of God remained stationary with Abraham, who was in its presence. The thought, therefore, that God was identical with these men is completely refuted.

The truth of the matter is that the light of God appeared to Abraham first in order that he might infer therefrom that his visitors were good and saintly men. That is why Abraham said to them: "My Lord, if I have now found favor in your sight" (Gen. 18:3). What was actually meant was angels of the Lord or messengers of the Lord, by way of ellipsis, which is of frequent occurrence in the language of the Children of Israel, as well as in other languages. (Ibid. 2.6) [SAADYA 1948: 107–108]

19. And a Muslim Rebuttal

The theologian Ghazali interpreted the prologue of the Gospel of John in a manner consistent with Muslim beliefs. These opening verses of John were a capital text for the Christians' assertion of the divinity of Jesus; and so after his new exegesis of the text, Ghazali turns to some more general reflections on the Christian view of the Trinity.

In interpreting the doctrine of the hypostases, the Christians have followed a procedure which has obliged them to proclaim the existence, conceptually and objectively, of three Gods, distinct in their essence and natures, or else deny the Essence of God, glorious is His Name. For they use the term "Father" for the Essence as defined by fatherhood, "Son" for the Essence as defined by sonship, and "Holy Spirit" for the Essence

as defined by the aspect of "proceeding." And after all that they still speak
of One God!

If they are cornered in this matter and realize that the Essence of the
Father as particularized by the attribute of fatherhood cannot admit the
attribute of sonship—and the same argument applies to the Son and
the Holy Spirit—and that it is not one of those relative essences, so as
to be considered a father to one person and a son to another, they then
state that the Essence is one, but that it is perfectly possible to describe
it by all of those attributes; except that when we describe it by one
attribute, we apply the negation of whatever is different from it. That is
the pitch of their ignorance and stupidity: they proclaim the pre-eternity
of these Essences and their attributes. So the Essences are inseparably
attached to the attributes and the attributes are inseparably attaching to
the Essences: whenever the thing attached exists, the thing attaching to
it exists as well; and whenever the thing attaching to it is removed, the
thing attached to is removed also. So if we suppose that the attribute
attaching to the Essence is negated, we must also suppose the Essence
itself is negated. This is the meaning behind that solemn reference in the
Holy Book:

> They are unbelievers
> Who say, "God is the Third of Three." (Quran 5:73)

(Ghazali, *The Elegant Refutation*) [ARBERRY 1964: 306–307]

20. The Philosopher and the Rabbi

The premise of Judah Halevi's The Khazar King, *which was written as an apologia
for traditional Judaism sometime between 1130 and 1140 C.E., was that the ruler
of the Crimean people called the Khazars was visited by God in a dream and told
that his actions were not pleasing to God. In an effort to practice the true religion,
he summoned to his presence a philosopher, a Muslim and a Christian theologian,
and a rabbi to explain their positions to him. The first three make only a token
appearance in the work, but at the outset the philosopher sets forth his creed, with
particular emphasis on the points that separated him from the adherents of the
scriptural religions.*

There is no favor or dislike in the nature of God because He is above
desire and intention, since a desire intimates a want in the person who
feels it, and not until it is satisfied does he become, so to speak, complete;
if it remains unfulfilled, he lacks completion. In the same way God is, in
the opinion of the philosophers, above the knowledge of individuals,

because the latter change with the times, while there is no change in God's knowledge. He, then, does not know you, much less your thoughts or actions, nor does He listen to your prayers or see your movements. If philosophers say that He created you, they only use a metaphor, because He is the Cause of causes in the creation of all creatures, but not because this (specific act) was His intention from the beginning. He never created man. For the world is without beginning, and there never arose a man except through one who came into existence before him, in whom are united forms, gifts, characteristics inherited from father, mother and other relations, besides the influences of climate, countries, food and water, spheres, stars and constellations. Everything is reduced to a Prime Cause, not to a Will proceeding from this, but an Emanation from which emanated a second, a third, and a fourth cause. (Judah Halevi, *The Khazar King*) [HALEVI 1905: 36]

The rabbi responds:

There is an excuse for the philosophers. Being Greeks, science and religion did not come to them as inheritances. They belong to the descendants of Japheth, who inhabited the north, while that knowledge coming from Adam, and supported by the divine influence, is only to be found among the progeny of Shem, who represented the successors of Noah and constituted, so to speak, his essence. This knowledge has always been connected with this essence, and will always remain so. The Greeks only received it when they became powerful, from Persia. The Persians had it from the Chaldeans [or Babylonians]. It was only then that the famous Greek philosophers arose, but as soon as Rome assumed political leadership, they produced no philosopher worthy of the name.

The Khazar King: Does this mean that Aristotle's philosophy is not deserving of credence?

The Rabbi: Certainly. He exerted his mind, because he had no tradition from any reliable source at his disposal. He meditated on the beginning and end of the world, but found as much difficulty in the theory of a beginning as in that of the eternity of the world. Finally, these abstract speculations which made for the eternity of the world prevailed, and he found no reason to inquire into the chronology or derivation of those who had lived before him. Had he lived among a people with well-authenticated and generally acknowledged traditions, he would have applied his deductions and arguments to establish a theory of creation, however difficult, instead of the eternity of the world, which is even more difficult to accept.

The Khazar King: Is there any decisive proof?

The Rabbi: Where could we find one for such a question? Heaven forbid that there should be anything in the Bible to contradict that which is manifest or proved! On the other hand, it tells of miracles and changes of ordinary things, newly arising, or changing one into the other. This proves that the Creator of the world is able to accomplish what He wills, and whenever He wills. The question of eternity and creation is obscure, while the (rational) arguments on either side are evenly balanced. But the theory of creation derives greater weight from the prophetic tradition of Adam, Noah and Moses, which is more deserving of credence than mere speculation. If, after all, a believer in the Law finds himself compelled to admit an eternal matter and the existence of many worlds prior to this one, this would not impair his belief that this world was created at a certain epoch, and that Adam and Noah were the first human beings. (Judah Halevi, *The Khazar King*) [HALEVI 1905: 53–54]

21. Theology among the Jews, Christians, and Muslims

Halevi attempted to put philosophy and theology into some kind of historical perspective for the Khazar king. The Spaniard Maimonides (d. 1204 C.E.) attempted much the same, though in a far more analytical fashion, for the Jewish readers of his Guide of the Perplexed. *He begins by discussing the condition of theology in Judaism.*

As for that small bit of dialectical theology concerning the question of the Oneness of God and what depends from this notion, which you will discover in the writings of some of the Gaons [that is, the heads of the Jewish academies] and in those of the Karaites, that the subject matter of this argument was taken over by them from the dialectical theologians of Islam, and they are brief indeed when compared to what the Muslims have also had to say on this subject.

Furthermore, it happened that the first Muslims to follow this path belonged to a certain sect, namely the Muʿtazilites, from whom our (Jewish) coreligionists borrowed and whose way they followed. After a time another sect arose in Islam, namely the Ashʿarites, who had other opinions, noneʿof which will be discovered among our coreligionists. The reason is not because they preferred the first opinion to the second, but simply because they happened to have taken over and adopted the first opinion and assumed that it was something that had been proven by demonstration.

Maimonides now moves back to the era before Islam and lays out his understanding of the origins of dialectical theology among the Christians, both the Hellenized Christians and the Syriac-speaking ones of the interior Near East.

You should realize that all the statements that the Muslims—both the Muʿtazilites and the Ashʿarites—have made on these subjects [that is, on the Oneness of God and its consequences] are all of them opinions founded on premises that were derived from the books of the (Christian) Greeks and the Syrians who had wished to disagree with the opinions of the (pagan) philosophers and to disprove their statements. Why this occurred was because when the Christian community came to include those communities (of Greeks and Syrians)—the Christian doctrine being what it is—and since the opinions of the (pagan) philosophers were widespread in those communities—philosophy had first risen there, and there were kings who protected religion—the learned of the time from among the Greeks and the Syrians saw that those (Christian) doctrines were strongly and obviously opposed to philosophical opinion. Thus there arose among them this science of dialectical theology.

They [that is, the early Christian theologians] began to establish premises that would be useful for (establishing) their beliefs and for countering those opinions that might undermine the foundations of their Law. Thus when the community of Islam later arrived on the scene and the books of the (pagan) philosophers were translated for them, those (same Christian) polemics that had been composed against the books of the (Greek) philosophers were likewise translated for the Muslims. Thus the Muslims discovered the dialectical theology of John Philoponus (ca. 525 C.E.) and Yahya ibn Adi (d. 974 C.E.) and others with regard to those notions, made it their own, and thought they had achieved something great. . . .

Afterwards dialectical theology became broader in scope and these people [that is, the Muslim theologians] went down other peculiar roads that had never been taken by the dialectical theologians from among the (Christian) Greeks and others, for these (roads) were near to those of the philosophers. There subsequently appeared among the Muslims statements of the Law that were particular to them and that they necessarily had need to defend. Furthermore, differences occurred among them with regard to these questions, so that every one of their sects attempted to establish premises that would be useful for the defense of its opinion.

There is no doubt that there are things that are shared by all three of us (religious communities), I mean the Jews, the Christians and the

Muslims: namely, the assertion of the creation of the world in time, the validity of which entails the validity of miracles, and other things. As for the other matters into which these two latter communities chose to plunge—for instance the notion of the Trinity into which the Christians plunged and the dialectical theology into which certain sects of the Muslims plunged—so that they found it necessary to establish premises and to establish, by means of these premises . . . the notions that are peculiar to each of the two communities, these are things that we (Jews) do not in any way require. (Maimonides, *Guide of the Perplexed* 1:71)

22. Ibn Khaldun on the Origins of Theology in Islam

Somewhat later than Maimonides, Ibn Khaldun gives his own rapid survey of what he calls the "traditioned sciences." In the Prolegomenon to History *he takes up the question of theology, first offering his rather general definition of its nature and function.*

The duties of the Muslim may concern either the body or the heart. The duties of the heart are concerned with faith and the distinction between what is to be believed and what is not to be believed. This concerns the articles of faith which deal with the essence and the attributes of God, the events of the Resurrection, Paradise, punishment and predestination, and entails discussion and defense of these subjects with the help of intellectual arguments. (Ibn Khaldun, *Muqaddima* 6.9)
[IBN KHALDUN 1967: 2:438]

Islam in fact knew two theologies. The first was the Greeks' science about God, often called metaphysics after the Aristotelian work that was the Muslims' chief source of instruction in it. The second was what was called in Arabic by Jews, Muslims, and Christians kalam *and has been translated here throughout as "dialectical theology." Unlike the Greeks' metaphysics, which began with the premises of pure reason, the method of dialectical theology in Islam more closely resembled that of the Christians' "sacred theology," which, as Maimonides pointed out, took the givens of revelation as its starting point and then attempted to demonstrate dialectically the conclusions that flowed from them. These two aspects of Islamic dialectical theology are clearly underlined in Ibn Khaldun's description of it, which includes both the Quranic menu of its subject matter and a generic characterization of its method, to wit, "intellectual arguments."*

Ibn Khaldun returns to the earliest days of Islam and undertakes to provide a sketch of the conditions that brought this discipline into being, though with a notable, and understandable, reluctance to trace it to Christian origins, as Maimo-

nides had. Ibn Khaldun begins by summing up what might be called the "articles of faith," the propositions that every Muslim must believe in order to be saved. He then continues.

These main articles of faith are proven by the logical evidence that exists for them. Evidence for them from the Quran and the Prophetic traditions also is ample. The scholars showed the way to them and the religious leaders verified them. However, later on, there occurred differences of opinion concerning the details of these articles of faith. Most of the difference concerned the "ambiguous verses" of the Quran. This led to hostility and disputation. Logical argumentation was used in addition to the traditional material. In this way, the science of dialectical theology originated.

We shall now explain this summary statement in detail. In many verses of the Quran the worshiped Master is described as being absolutely devoid (of human attributes), and this in absolute terms requiring no interpretation. All these verses are negative (in their statements). They are clear on the subject. It is necessary to believe them, and statements of the Lawgiver (Muhammad) and the men around him and the men of the second generation have explained them in accordance with their plain meaning.

Then there are a few verses in the Quran suggesting anthropomorphism, with reference to either the essence or the attributes of God. The early Muslims gave preference to the evidence for God's freedom from human attributes because it was simple and clear. They knew that anthropomorphism is absurd, but they decided that those (anthropomorphic) verses were the word of God and therefore believed them, without trying to investigate or interpret their meaning. . . . But there were a few innovators in their time who occupied themselves with those "ambiguous verses" and delved into anthropomorphism. One group operated with the plain [that is, literal] meaning of the relevant verses. They assumed anthropomorphism for God's essence, in that they believed that He had hands, feet and a face. Thus they adopted a clear-cut anthropomorphism and were in opposition to the verses stating God is devoid of human attributes. . . . The people who gave consideration to the anthropomorphic verses then tried to escape from the anthropomorphic abomination by stating that God has "a body unlike (ordinary human) bodies." . . . Another group turned to anthropomorphism with regard to the attributes of God. They assumed direction, sitting, descending, voice, letter (sound) and similar things on the part of God. Their stated opinions imply

anthropomorphism, and like the former group they took refuge in statements like "a voice unlike voices," "a direction unlike directions," "descending unlike descending." . . .

Later on the sciences and the crafts increased. People were eager to
write systematic works and to do research in all fields. The speculative
theologians wrote on God's freedom from human attributes. At that
juncture the Mu'tazila innovation came into being. The Mu'tazila extended the subject (of God's freedom from human physical attributes) to
the negative verses and decided to deny God's possession of the ideational
attributes of knowledge, power . . . and life, in addition to denying their
consequences. . . . The Mu'tazila further decided to deny God's possession of volition. This forced them to deny predestination, because predestination requires the existence of a volition prior to the created things.
They also decided to deny God's hearing and vision, because both hearing
and vision are corporeal accidents. . . . They further decided to deny God
speech for reasons similar to those they used in connection with hearing
and vision. . . . Thus the Mu'tazila decided that the Quran was created.
This was an innovation; the early Muslims had clearly expressed the
contrary view. The damage done by this innovation was great. Certain
leading Mu'tazilites indoctrinated certain Caliphs with it, and the people
were forced to adopt it. The Muslim religious leaders opposed them.
Because of their opposition, it was permissible to flog and kill many of
them. This caused orthodox people to rise in defense of the articles of
faith with logical evidence and to push back the innovations.

The leader of the speculative theologians, Abu al-Hasan al-Ash'ari
[d. 935 C.E.] took care of that. He mediated between the different approaches. He disavowed anthropomorphism and recognized the (existence of the) ideational attributes. He restricted God's freedom from
human attributes to the extent to which it had been recognized by early
Muslims, and which had been recognized by the proofs stating the general
applicability (of the principle) to special cases. He recognized the four
ideational attributes [that is, of knowledge, power, volition, and life], as
well as hearing, vision and speech, as an essential function of God, and
this with the help of both logical and traditional methods. He refuted the
innovators in all these respects. He discussed with them their stated
opinions with regard to (God's concern for) human welfare and what is
best for man, and their definition of good and evil, which they had invented on the basis of their innovation. He perfected the dogmas concerning the rising of the dead, the circumstances of the Resurrection,
Paradise and Hell, and reward and punishment. Ash'ari added a discus-

sion of the Imamate because the Imamite Shi‘ites at that time suggested the novel idea that the Imamate was one of the articles of faith and that it was the duty of the Prophet as well as of the Muslim nation to fix (the succession to) the Imamate and to free the person who would become the Imam from any responsibility in this respect. However, the Imamate is at best a matter of public interest and social organization; it is not an article of faith. But it was added to the problems of this discipline. The whole was called "the science of dialectical theology." (Ibn Khaldun, *Muqaddima* 6.14) [IBN KHALDUN 1967: 3:45–50]

23. The Intrusion of Philosophy into Dialectical Theology

Even as this rationalist tradition was developing in Islamic circles, during the century and a half spanning the Mu‘tazilite beginnings about 800 C.E. and the death of Ash‘ari in 935, a great many Greek philosophical works were translated into Arabic, as Maimonides had pointed out in his summary. This project proceeded under the patronage of the very Caliph Ma’mun (813–833 C.E.) who had given an ear to the Mu‘tazilites. The effects were not long in being felt on the nascent discipline of dialectical theology, not directly from the translations but from the adaptation of the analytical method into their own work by certain Muslim thinkers, as Ibn Khaldun continues.

Thus Ash‘ari's approach was perfected and became one of the best speculative disciplines and religious sciences. However, the forms of its arguments are, at times, not technical [that is, not scientifically rigorous] because the scholars (of Ash‘ari's time) were simple and the science of logic which probes arguments and examines syllogisms had not yet made its appearance in Islam. Even if some of it had existed, the theologians would not have used it because it was so closely related to the philosophical sciences, which are altogether different from the beliefs of the religious law and were, therefore, avoided by them. . . . After that the science of logic spread in Islam; people studied it. And they made a distinction between it and the philosophical sciences in that logic was merely a norm and yardstick for arguments and served to probe the arguments of the philosophical sciences as well as those of other disciplines.

Then, (once they had accepted the legitimacy of logic) scholars studied the premises the earlier theologians had established. They refuted most of them with the help of arguments leading them to a different opinion. Many of these (earlier) arguments were derived from philosophical discussions of physics and metaphysics, and when the scholars now

probed them with the yardstick of logic, it showed that the earlier arguments (like those used by Ash'ari) were applicable only to those other
(philosophical) disciplines and not to dialectical theology. But they did
not believe that if the arguments were wrong, the conclusion was also
wrong. . . . This approach differed in its technical terminology from the
earlier one; it was called "the school of recent scholars" [or, "the modern
school"], and their approach often included a refutation of the philosophers as well, where the opinions of the latter differed from the articles
of faith. They considered the philosophers the enemies of the articles of
faith because in most respects there is a relationship between the opinions
of the innovators and the opinions of the philosophers.

The first scholar to write in accordance with the (new) theological
approach was al-Ghazali [d. 1111 C.E.]. He was followed by the imam Ibn
al-Khatib [Fakhr al-Din al-Razi; d. 1209]. A large number of scholars
followed in their steps and adhered to their tradition. (Ibn Khaldun,
Muqaddima 6.14) [IBN KHALDUN 1967: 3:50–52]

*Ibn Khaldun follows the evolution of dialectical theology down closer to his own
time.*

If one considers how this discipline (of dialectical theology) originated and how scholarly discussion was incorporated in it step by step,
and how, during this process, scholars always assumed the correctness of
the articles of faith and paraded proofs and arguments in their defense,
one will realize that the character of this discipline is as we have established it, and that the discipline cannot go beyond those limits. However,
the two approaches have been mixed up by recent scholars: the problems
of theology have been confused with those of philosophy. This has gone
so far that one discipline is no longer distinguishable from the other. The
student cannot learn theology from the books of the recent scholars, and
the same situation confronts the student of philosophy. Such mixing was
done by Baydawi [d. 1286 C.E.] . . . and by later, non-Arab scholars in all
their works. . . .

The approach of the early Muslims can be reconciled with the beliefs
of the science of dialectical theology only if one follows the old approach
of the theologians (and not the mixed approach of more recent scholars).
The basic work here is the *Right Guidance* of al-Juwayni [d. 1083 C.E.], as
well as works that follow its example. Those who want to inject a refutation of the philosophers into their dogmatic beliefs must use the books of
Ghazali and Fakhr al-Din Razi. These latter do show some divergencies
from the old technique, but do not make such a confusion of problems

and subjects as is found in the approach of the recent scholars who have come after them.

Ibn Khaldun then sums up with his own reflections on speculative or dialectical theology. The year, it will be recalled, is 1377 C.E.

In general, it must be known that this science, the science of dialectical theology, is not something that is necessary to the contemporary student. Heretics and innovators have been destroyed. The orthodox religious leaders have given us protection against heretics and innovators in their systematic works and treatments. Logical arguments were needed only when they defended and supported (their views with them). Now, all that remains of those arguments is a certain amount of discussion, from most of whose ambiguities and inferences the Creator can be considered to be free. (Ibn Khaldun, *Muquaddima* 6.14)

[IBN KHALDUN 1967: 3:53–54]

24. The Limited Role of Dialectical Theology

It was not, then, an entirely successful enterprise in Islam, this dialectical theology. The fundamentalists regarded its use of intellectual arguments as unnecessarily rationalistic, while more philosophically sophisticated Muslims criticized its lack of scientific rigor. Ghazali—for Ibn Khaldun the first of the "modernists" in theology—was a scholar who understood the methods of discursive reasoning used by Greek and Muslim philosophers, and he recognized both the usefulness and the limits of dialectical theology. Like Ibn Khaldun, he emphasized its essentially defensive function.

God sent to His servants by the mouth of His Messenger, in the Quran and the Prophetic traditions, a creed which is the truth and whose contents are the basis of man's welfare in both religious and secular affairs. But Satan too sent, in the suggestions of heretics, things contrary to orthodoxy; men tended to accept his suggestions and almost corrupted the true creed for its adherents. So God brought into being the class of (dialectical) theologians, and moved them to support traditional orthodoxy with the weapon of systematic theology by laying bare the confused doctrines invented by the heretics at variance with traditional orthodoxy. This is the origin of (dialectical) theology and theologians.

In due course a group of theologians performed the task to which God invited them; they successfully preserved orthodoxy, defended the creed received from the prophetic source and rectified heretical innovations. Nevertheless in so doing they they based their arguments on premises which they took from their opponents and which they were compelled to admit by naive belief or the consensus of the community or bare acceptance of the Quran and the Prophetic traditions. For the most part their efforts were devoted to making explicit the contradictions of their opponents and criticizing them in respect of the logical consequences of what they admitted.

This method might serve with Muslims who were willing to start at the same shared premises, but it would hardly do with those other philosophers and theologians trained in the Hellenic mode and committed to beginning with the first principles of reason.

This method was of little use in the case of one who admitted nothing at all save logically necessary truths. . . . It is true that, when theology appeared as a recognized discipline and much effort had been expended on it over a considerable period of time, the theologians, becoming very earnest in their endeavors to defend orthodoxy by the study of what things really are, embarked on the study of substances and accidents with their natures and properties. But since that was not the (principal) aim of their science, they did not deal with the question thoroughly in their thinking and consequently did not arrive at results sufficient to dispel universally the darkness of confusion due to the different views of men. I do not exclude the possibility that for others than myself these results have been sufficient; indeed, I do not doubt that this has been so for quite a number. But these results were mingled with naive beliefs in certain matters which are not included among first principles. (Ghazali, *Deliverer from Error* 81–83) [GHAZALI 1953: 27–29]

25. Theology Is to Piety as Scansion Is to Poetry

As Maimonides pointed out, medieval Jewish theology from Saadya onward went through many of the same stages of excitement and doubt as its Islamic counterpart. There is little surprise in this, since the enterprise was being pursued by Muslims and Jews with a similar, sometimes an identical, culture, often writing in the same language in the very same cities. And, of course, both Muslims and Jews were attempting to protect revelation from a rationalism that at times threatened to overwhelm it. Thus Judah Halevi shared many of his contemporary Ghazali's reservations about dialectical theology and incorporated them in his dialogue with the Khazar king. Tell me, the king asks, about the "masters of dialectical theology." His Jewish interlocutor responds.

This theology has no value, save as an exercise in dialectics. . . . A simple, wise man, such as a prophet, can impart to others little by way of formal instruction, nor can he solve a problem by dialectical methods, while the master of dialectical theology possesses such an aura of learning that those who hear him consider him as superior to the simple pious man whose learning consists of beliefs which no one can induce him to abandon. Yet the supreme achievement of the master of dialectical theology, in all that he learns and teaches, would be that there should come into his own soul and the souls of his students those very same beliefs which are present by nature in the soul of the simple man.

It happens that the science of dialectical theology destroys many true beliefs in a man's heart by leading him into doubts and conflicting opinions. The masters of dialectical theology are like experts on poetic meters who investigate scansion. Such experts make a great fuss and use a lot of formidable terms to describe a skill which comes easily to someone naturally gifted in poetry, who senses the meter and so never breaks in any way the rules of scansion. . . . The same may be said about those who possess a natural aptitude for living according to the divine law and for drawing near to God: through the words of the pious sparks are kindled in their souls, which become rays of illumination in their hearts. A man not endowed with such a natural gift has necessarily to resort to dialectical theology, which may not bring him any benefit, and indeed may conceivably cause him positive harm. (Judah Halevi, *The Khazar King* 5.16) [HALEVI 1905: 56–57]

26. The Fundamentalist Position: "Without Howing" versus Dialectical Theology

One of the areas in which the early Muslim proponents of dialectical theology used their newly discovered skills was in explaining the various attributes attached to God in the Quran: "merciful," "compassionate," "powerful," "seeing," "knowing," "hearing," and so on. Some raise an immediate problem: How indeed can God see without eyes, or shall we credit Him with eyes as well? The problem is anthropomorphism, a problem that, upon closer inspection, all the attributes raise in one form or another. The early dialectical theologians attempted to address the problem in the same time-honored fashion invoked by Jewish and Christian theologians, the prudent use of allegorical exegesis.

The allegorizing of the divine attributes is an issue that never quite disappeared in Islam, and it was one of the grounds of choice for Muslim conservatives— the overwhelming number of them lawyers—to confront the theologians. Among the lawyers, it was the followers of Ahmad Ibn Hanbal (d. 855 C.E.) who took the most conservative positions of all. A Hanbalite spokesman in late-twelfth-century Damas-

cus was Ibn Qudama (d. 1223 C.E.), whose works include one pointedly entitled The Prohibition of the Study of the Works of the Dialectical Theologians. Here he concludes.

We have already pointed out by the preceding, the evil of the science of dialectical theology that originates in its very source, the censure of it by our religious leaders, the unanimous agreement of the learned men that its advocates are partisans of heretical innovations and error, that they are not regarded as belonging to the ranks of learned men, and that whoever occupies himself with it becomes a heretic and will not prosper. (Ibn Qudama, Prohibition 90)

The issue is a familiar one, and it serves to clarify what precisely constitutes heresy in Islam.

Allegorical interpretation is an innovation in religion. Now an innovation is any doctrine in religion which the Companions [that is, the generation of Muhammad's "contemporaries," the latter term construed broadly] had died mentioning. Innovation in religion is the heresy against which our Prophet has cautioned us, and which he informed us was the most evil of things. He has said (in a tradition): "The most evil things are the innovated ones." He has also said (likewise in a tradition): "Keep to my course of conduct and the course of conduct of the (first four) rightly guided Caliphs after me; hold fast to it." "Beware of innovations; for every innovation is a heretical innovation, and every heretical innovation is an error." Now, the allegorical interpreter has deserted the course of conduct of the Apostle of God and that of the rightly guided Caliphs; he is an inventor of heretical innovations, and has gone astray by virtue of the aforementioned tradition. (Ibn Qudama, Prohibition 56)

How, then, is one to deal with all the apparent anthropomorphisms used to characterize God in the Quran and the Prophetic traditions? Simply by accepting them, Ibn Qudama asserts. He offers a clear exposition of the conservative position in theology, the doctrine known in shorthand fashion as "Without Howing." The authority is no less than the eponym of the school himself.

An (earlier) Hanbalite has said: I asked Abu Abdullah Ahmad ibn Muhammad ibn Hanbal about those traditions which say that God will be seen, and that He plants His foot and other statements similar to these. Whereupon Abu Abdullah answered: We believe in them, and accept them as true, without rejecting any part of them, whenever their chains of transmitters are sound; nor do we deny the statements of the Apostle, for we know that what he has brought to us is true.

God should not be described in excess of His own description of Himself, boundless and immeasurable: "There is nothing like Him! He is the Hearing, the Seeing" (Quran 42:11). Therefore we say precisely what He has said, and describe Him as He has described Himself, without going beyond His description, or depriving Him any of His attributes merely for fear of some possible slander which might be leveled against us. We believe in these traditions, we acknowledge them, and we allow them to stand exactly as they have come down to us, without being able to understand the how of them, or fully understand their intended sense, except in accordance with His own description of Himself; and He is, according to His own description, the Hearing, the Seeing, boundless, immeasurable. His attributes proceed from Him and are His own. We do not go beyond the Quran or the traditions of the Prophet and his Companions; nor do we know the how of these, save by the acknowledgment of the Apostle and the confirmation of the Quran. (Ibn Qudama, *Prohibition* 19)

27. Ash'ari on the Charge of Heretical Innovation

Ibn Qudama's view that dialectical theology constituted a reprehensible innovation in Islam was hardly novel. The charge had been leveled against theologians almost from the beginning. Indeed, Ash'ari himself (d. 935 C.E.), one of the fathers of the discipline, had taken up arms against this allegation in a tract called On Thinking Well of Engaging in the Science of Theology. *The Prophet, it was said by the opponents of theology, knew nothing about such new-fangled notions, a "motion and rest, body and accident, accidental modes and states." Wrong, says Ash'ari.*

The Apostle of God did know these questions about which they have asked, and he was not ignorant of any detail involved in them. However, they did not occur in his time in such specific form that he should have, or should not have, discussed them—even though their basic principles were present in the Quran and the tradition of the Prophet. But whenever a question arose which was related to religion from the standpoint of the Law, men discussed it, and inquired into it, and disputed about it, and debated and argued. . . . Such questions, too numerous to mention, arose in their days, and in the case of each one there had come no explicit determination from the Prophet. For if he had given explicit instructions concerning all that, they would not have differed over those questions, and the differences would not have lasted till now.

The mere fact of these differences of opinion shows that men investigated, and will continue to investigate, matters of importance on which neither the Quran nor the tradition gives guidance. Moreover, Ash°ari continues, the analogical method so typical of theology was the same one used in these investigations.

But even though there was no explicit instruction of the Apostle of God regarding each one of these questions, they referred and likened each to something which had been determined explicitly in the Book of God, and the Tradition, and their own independent judgment. Such questions, then, which involved judgments on unprecedented secondary causes, they referred to those determinations of the Law which are derivative, and which are to be sought only along the line of revelation and the Prophetic tradition. But when new and specific questions pertaining to basic dogmas arise, every intelligent Muslim ought to refer judgment on them to the sum of principles accepted on the grounds of reason, sense experience, intuition, etc. . . .

Judgment on legal questions which belong to the category of what is passed down by tradition is to be based on reference to legal principles which likewise belong to the category of the traditioned, and judgment on questions involving the data of reason and the senses should be a matter of referring every such instance to (something within) its own category, without confounding the rational with the traditioned or the traditioned with the rational. So if dialectical theology on the creation of the Quran and on the atom . . . had originated in those precise terms in the Prophet's time, he would have discussed and explained it, just as he explained and discussed all the specific questions which did originate in his time. (Ash°ari, *The Science of Dialectical Theology* 21–22)

[ASH°ARI 1953: 130–131]

28. The Fatal Flaw of Sacred Theology

Judah Halevi thought dialectical theology dangerous; Ibn Qudama regarded it as an unjustified and heretical innovation. But for the philosophically more astute Maimonides, who "knew the difference between demonstration, dialectic, and sophistry," this theology based on revelation had a fatal flaw: in truth it could not demonstrate anything.

All the first dialectical theologians from among the Greeks who had adopted Christianity and from among the Muslims did not conform to the appearance of that which exists, but considered how existence ought to be in order that it should furnish a proof for the correctness of a particular opinion, or at least should not refute it. And when such a fantasy held good, they assumed that what exists corresponds to that form and started to argue in order to establish the truth of the assertions from which are taken the premises that show the correctness of the doctrine, or at least do not refute it.

This was the way of the men of intellect who first used this method, put it down in books, and claimed that speculation alone impelled them to do so, and that they did not seek thereby to protect a doctrine or a preconceived opinion. Men of later periods who study these books know nothing about all this and consequently find in these ancient books a vigorous argument and a powerful endeavor to establish the truth of a certain thing or to refute a certain thing. . . . (They also believe) that their predecessors did what they did only in order to confuse the opinions of the philosophers and to make them doubt that which they regarded as a demonstration. Those who say this are not aware, and do not know, that the matters are not as they thought, but that their predecessors toiled to establish what they desired to establish and to refute what they desired to refute because of the harm that would come if this were not done— even if it were after a hundred propositions—to the opinion whose recognition as correct was desired by them. These ancient dialectical theologians did away with the disease starting with its root. . . .

When I studied the books of these dialectical theologians, as far as I had the opportunity—and I have likewise studied the books of the philosophers, as far as my capacity went—I found that the method of all the dialectical theologians was one and the same in kind, though subdivisions differed from one another. For the foundation of everything is that no consideration is due to how that which exists is, for it is merely a custom [or, the way it happens to be], and from the point of view of the intellect, it could well be different. Furthermore, in many places they follow the imagination [that is, the faculty wherein likely or probable truths reside] and call it intellect [that is, the faculty of necessary truths].

To illustrate his case, Maimonides chooses what was the absolute base issue between the philosophers on the one hand and the dialectical theologians and, indeed, all the partisans of revelation on the other. Genesis said, and the latter maintained, that the universe had been created in time; reason demonstrates, the philosophers had argued from the beginning, that the universe is eternal. Maimonides continues.

Thus when they [that is, the dialectical theologians] propound the premises that we will let you hear, they found by their demonstrations the (affirmative) judgment that the world is created in time. And when it is thus established that the world is created in time, it is likewise undoubtedly established that it has a Maker who has created it in time.

Then they infer that this Maker is One; whereupon, basing themselves on His being One, they affirm that He is not a body. This is the way of every dialectical theologian from among the Muslims in anything concerning this subject. Thus also do those belonging to our community who imitate them and follow their ways. . . .

Now when I considered this method of thought, my soul felt a very strong aversion to it, and had every right to do so. For every argument deemed to be a demonstration of the temporal creation of the world is accompanied by doubts and is not a decisive demonstration except to those who do not know the difference between demonstration, dialectic and sophistry. As for those who know these arts, it is clear and evident to them that there are doubts with regard to all these proofs and that premises that have not been demonstrated have been used in them. . . .

If you are one of those who are persuaded by what the dialectical theologians say, and if you believe that the demonstration with regard to the creation of the world in time is correct, bravo for you. If, however, it is not demonstrated in your opinion, and if you take over from the prophets, through obeying their authority, the doctrine that it was created in time, there is no harm in that. . . .

There may be no harm in allowing oneself to be convinced by the dialectical theologians, or even in simply taking one's beliefs straight out of Genesis, but that is not what Maimonides had in mind. His was a far more adventuresome project, one that Ibn Qudama would surely have objected to and one that many of Maimonides' own Jewish successors did in fact have grave doubts about. Maimonides explains.

The correct way, according to me, which is the method of demonstration about which there can be no doubt, is to establish the existence and the oneness of the deity and the negation of corporeality through the methods of the philosophers, which methods are founded upon the doctrine of the eternity of the world—not because I believe in the eternity of the world or because I concede this point to the philosopher, but because it is through this method that the demonstration becomes valid and perfect certainty is obtained with regard to those three things: I mean the existence of the deity, His oneness and His not being a body; all this without regard to reaching a judgment as to the world's being eternal or created in time. When these three great and sublime problems have been validated for us through a correct demonstration, we shall thereafter return to the question of the creation of the world in time and we shall enounce with regard to it all the argument that is possible. (Maimonides, *Guide of the Perplexed* 1: Chapter 71) [MAIMONIDES 1963: 178–183]

29. Rationalist Theology

Maimonides was assuredly not the only one aware of the dark little secret of the dialectical theology of the medieval Muslims and their Jewish imitators: that it was mostly dialectic, with very little theology. There were also those who, as Ghazali described them, "admitted nothing at all save logically necessary truths," to wit, the partisans of metaphysics or rationalistic theology on the Greek model. In his autobiographical Deliverer from Error *Ghazali offers a capsule history of this kind of theology from its point of origin among the Hellenes.*

The study of philosophy began, Ghazali explains, with the "Materialists," who simply denied a Creator and posited an eternal cycle of everlasting generation, "animals from seed and seed from animals." The second group, the "Naturalists," were constrained by the order and excellence of nature to admit the existence of a Creator God, but they denied any spiritual existence and so the immortality of the soul and an afterlife. Finally, there are the "more modern" philosophers, called "Theists," who include Socrates, Plato, and Aristotle, the latter of whom "systematized logic for them and organized the sciences, securing a higher degree of accuracy and bringing them to maturity."

The Theists in general attacked the two previous groups, the Materialists and the Naturalists and exposed their defects so effectively that others were relieved of the task. . . . Aristotle, moreover, attacked his predecessors among the Theistic philosophers, especially Plato and Socrates, and went so far in his criticisms that he separated himself from them. Yet he too retained a residue of their unbelief and heresy from which he did not manage to free himself. We must therefore reckon as unbelievers both those philosophers themselves and their followers among the Islamic philosophers, such as Ibn Sina [or Avicenna], al-Farabi and others; in transmitting the philosophy of Aristotle, however, none of the Islamic philosophers has accomplished anything comparable to the two men named. (Ghazali, *Deliverer from Error* 87–88) [GHAZALI 1953: 31–32]

The principal area of unbelief lay, according to Ghazali, in the science called theology or metaphysics.

Here occur most of the errors of the philosophers. They are unable to satisfy the conditions of proof they lay down in logic and consequently differ much from one another here. The views of Aristotle, as expounded by Farabi and Avicenna, are close to those of the Islamic writers. All their errors are comprised under twenty heads, on three of which they must be reckoned infidels and on seventeen heretical innovators. . . . The three points on which they differ from all Muslims are as follows:

(1) [On the physical reality of Paradise and Hell], they say that for bodies there is no Resurrection: it is bare spirits which are rewarded or punished; and the rewards and punishments are spiritual, not bodily. They certainly speak true in affirming the spiritual ones, since these do exist as well; but they speak falsely in denying the bodily ones and in their pronouncements disbelieve the revelation.

(2) [On divine providence], they say that God knows universals, but not particulars. This too is plain unbelief. The truth is that "there does not escape Him the weight of an atom in the heavens or in the earth" (Quran 34:3).

And what Maimonides too had earmarked has a basic disagreement.

(3) [On the eternity of the world], they say that the world is ever-lasting, without beginning. But no Muslim has adopted any such view on this question. (Ghazali, *Deliverer from Error* 96–97) [GHAZALI 1953: 35–36]

30. Farabi on God's Providence

We note the issue between theology and Islam on the subject of the afterlife in Chapter 6 below. Here we see one of Islam's premier philosophers, al-Farabi, attempting to pick his careful way through the thorny and dangerous subject of divine providence.

Different beliefs are held by many people about the care of the Lord for His creation. Some maintain that He cares for His creation as a king cares for his subjects and their welfare, without conducting personally the affairs of any of them, and without connection between Him and partner or wife, but by appointing for the task one who will undertake it and discharge it, and do in regard to it what right and justice demand.

Farabi makes no comment on that view, so it may be his own, though we cannot be certain. The second is distinctly not his opinion, however.

Others think that the Creator is not sufficient unless He undertakes the personal management of each one of His creatures in each one of their actions, and directs them aright, and leaves none of his creatures to (the care of) others. It would follow that He is responsible for many actions which are defective, blameworthy, ugly actions, errors and abominable words and deeds, and when any of His creatures aims at attacking one of His clients—a reversal of truth by way of argument—He is his helper and responsible for leading him and guiding him. . . . And if they deny that He directs and helps such for some things, they must deny the whole doctrine. Such principles give rise to wrong ideas and give rise to vicious and abominable ways. (Farabi, *Aphorisms of the Statesman* 82) [FARABI 1961: 69]

31. Ghazali on Theology and Muslim Belief

Ghazali remained unconvinced by explanations such as Farabi's.

Among the most extreme and extravagant of men are a group of scholastic theologians who dismiss the Muslim common people as unbelievers and claim that whoever does not know scholastic theology in the form they recognize and does not know the prescriptions of the Holy Law according to the proofs which they have adduced is an unbeliever.

These people have constricted the vast mercy of God to His servants and made paradise the preserve of a small clique of theologians. They have disregarded what is handed down by the Prophetic traditions, for it is clear that in the time of the Prophet, may God bless and save him, and in the time of the Companions of the Prophet, may God be pleased with them, the Islam of whole groups of rude Arabs was recognized, though they were busy worshiping idols. They did not concern themselves with the science of analogical proof and would have understood nothing of it if they had.

Whoever claims that theology, abstract proofs and systematic classification are the foundations of belief is an innovator. Rather is belief a light which God bestows on the hearts of His creatures as a gift and a bounty from Him, sometimes through an explainable conviction from within, sometimes because of a dream in sleep, sometimes by seeing the state of bliss of a pious man and the transmission of his light through association and conversation with him, sometimes through one's own state of bliss. (Ghazali, *The Decisive Criterion* 202) [LEWIS 1974: 2:20–21]

32. The Truth of Philosophy

And yet Ghazali was by no means a fundamentalist in the mold of Ibn Qudama. He understood both the attractions and the dangers of philosophy and science, but he was unwilling to permit the dangers to be used as a reason for dismissing the truth and the certitude that philosophy brought. Mathematics provides an almost classic instance.

None of its results are connected with religious matters, either to deny or affirm them. They are matters of demonstration which it is impossible to deny once they have been understood and apprehended. Nevertheless there are two drawbacks which arise from mathematics. The first is that every student of mathematics admires its precision and the clarity of its demonstrations. This leads him to believe in the philosophers (and scientists generally) and to think that all their sciences resemble this one in clarity and cogency. Further, he has already heard the accounts on everyone's lips of their unbelief, their denial of God's attributes and their contempt for revealed truth; he becomes an unbeliever merely by accepting them as authorities, and says to himself, "If (revealed) religion were true, it would not have escaped the notice of these men since they are so precise in this science."

That is one extreme: seduction by mathematics. The other is no more attractive.

The second drawback arises from the man who is loyal to Islam but ignorant. He thinks that religion must be defended by rejecting every science connected with the philosophers, and so rejects all their sciences and accuses them of ignorance therein. He even rejects their theory of the eclipse of the sun and the moon, considering that what they say is contrary to religion. . . . A grievous crime indeed against religion has been committed by the man who imagines that Islam is defended by the denial of the mathematical sciences, seeing that there is nothing in revealed truth opposed to these sciences by way of either negation or affirmation, and nothing in these sciences opposed to the truths of revelation. (Ghazali, *Deliverer from Error* 90–91) [GHAZALI 1953: 33–34]

33. Rationalist Ethics and Revealed Morality

Ghazali had no brief for or interest in mathematics; it simply provided him, by the clarity and cogency of its demonstrations, a casebook model for the truth of science, even the foreign and often heretical science of the Greeks and the Muslim followers. Ethics, on the other hand, with its judgments about conduct and morality, is a rival and competitor of revealed religion, and so a more interesting and complicated case. There are, for example, the instances where the teachings of philosophical ethics, a well-defined branch of the Hellenic philosophical tradition, are identical with those of the Muslim moral theologians working with the data of revelation, as Ghazali saw himself doing. Two explanations are possible: that the former borrowed from the latter—an argument already familiar from Philo—or that the truth of God is essentially one and so there should be little wonder that different groups can reach it by different means. "Ethics," Ghazali begins, "consists in defining the characteristics and moral constitution of the soul and enumerating the various types of soul and the method of moderating and controlling them." He continues.

This they [that is, the philosophers] borrow from the teaching of the mystics, those men of piety whose chief occupation is to meditate upon God, to oppose the passions, and to walk in the way leading to God by withdrawing from worldly pleasure. In their spiritual warfare they have learned about the virtues and vices of the soul and the defects in its actions, and what they have learned they have clearly expressed. The philosophers have taken over this teaching and mingled it with their own disquisitions, furtively using this embellishment to sell their rubbishy wares more readily. . . .

From this practice of the philosophers of incorporating in their books conceptions drawn from the prophets and the mystics, there arise two evil tendencies, one in their partisans and one in their opponents.

The evil tendency in the case of the opponent is serious. A crowd of men of slight intellect imagines that, since these ethical conceptions occur in the books of the philosophers mixed with their own rubbish, all reference to them must be avoided, and indeed any person mentioning them must be considered a liar. They imagine this because they heard of the conceptions in the first place only from the philosophers, and their weak intellects have concluded that, since their author is a falsifier, they must be false.

We have heard the argument before from Ghazali, in the case of those who wished to throw out all of mathematics, baby, bathwater, and eclipses of the sun and moon. Here, however, the instance is different.

This is like a man who hears a Christian assert, "There is no god but the God, and Jesus is the Messenger of God." The man rejects this, saying, "This is a Christian conception," and does not pause to ask himself whether the Christian is an infidel only in respect of his denial of the prophethood of Muhammad, peace be upon him. If he is an infidel only in respect of his denial of the prophethood of Muhammad, then he need not be contradicted in other assertions, true in themselves and not connected with his unbelief, even though these are also true in his eyes (like the Christian statement cited above).

Ghazali then passes on to far more personal terrain than a defense of the Christians' right to be correct on certain religious matters.

To some of the statements made in our published works on the principles of the religious sciences an objection has been raised by a group of men whose understanding has not fully grasped the sciences and whose insight has not penetrated to the fundamentals of the systems. They think that these statements are taken from the works of the ancient philosophers, whereas the fact is that some of them are the product of reflections which occurred to me independently—it is not improbable that one foot should fall on another footprint—while others come from the revealed Scriptures, and in the case of the majority the sense, though perhaps not the actual words is found in the works of the mystics.

After this not entirely spirited defense of his own originality, Ghazali comes to the difficult heart of the matter, the spoliatio Aegyptorum, *or, to use Ghazali's own figure, honey in a cupping glass.*

Suppose, however, that the statements [that is, certain moral teachings] are found only in the philosophers' books. If they are reasonable in themselves and supported by proof, and if they do not contradict the Book and the Custom of the Prophet, then it is not necessary to abstain from using them. If we open this door, if we adopt the attitude of abstaining from every truth that the mind of a heretic has apprehended before us, we should be obliged to abstain from much that is true. We should be obliged to leave aside a great number of verses of the Quran and the traditions of the Messenger and the accounts of the early Muslims, and all the sayings of the philosophers and the mystics. . . . The lowest degree of education is to distinguish oneself from the ignorant ordinary man. The educated man does not loathe honey even if he finds it in the surgeon's cupping glass; he realizes that the cupping glass does not essentially alter the honey. The natural aversion from it in such a case rests on popular ignorance, arising from the fact that the cupping glass is made only for impure blood. Men imagine that the blood is impure because it is in the cupping glass, and are not aware that the impurity is due to a property of the blood itself. (Ghazali, *Deliverer from Error* 99–105) [GHAZALI 1953: 38–42]

34. Ibn Rushd: The Law Commands the Study of Philosophy

There were few in Islam who were willing to dispute Ghazali on this point; indeed, as is clear from Ibn Qudama's position, many Muslims found Ghazali's stance far too liberal when it came to the use of reason in thinking about God. The one voice raised against Ghazali in the name of philosophy was that of the Spanish scholar Ibn Rushd (d. 1198 C.E.), demonstrably the greatest student of the Hellenic philosophical tradition ever produced in Islam. Ghazali's Incoherence of the Philosophers *was countered point by point in Ibn Rushd's* Incoherence of the Incoherence. *Here, however, we hear the man the West knew as Averroes speaking to the issue*

*of philosophy in Islam in more general, and very Muslim, terms. We are now at the
opposite pole from Ibn Qudama: not only is intellectual investigation not heresy; it
is commanded by the Islamic law.*

Praise be to God with all due praise, and a prayer for Muhammad,
His chosen servant and Messenger. The purpose of this treatise is to
examine, from the standpoint of the study of the (Islamic) Law, whether
the study of philosophy and logic is allowed by the Law, or prohibited,
or commanded, either by way of recommendation or as obligatory.

We say: If the activity of philosophy is no more than the study of
existing beings and the reflection on them as indications of the Artisan [or
Creator], that is, inasmuch as they are products of art, for beings also
indicate the Artisan through our knowledge of the art in them, and the
more perfect this knowledge is, the more perfect the knowledge of the
Artisan becomes, and if the Law has encouraged and urged reflection on
beings, then it is clear that what this name (of philosophy) signifies is
either obligatory or recommended by the Law.

That the Law summons us to reflection on beings, and the pursuit
of knowledge about them by the intellect is clear from the several verses
of the Book of God, blessed be He and exalted, such as the saying of the
Exalted, "Reflect, you have vision" (Quran 59:2); this is textual authority
for the obligation to use intellectual reasoning, or a combination of intellectual and legal reasoning. Another example is His saying, "Have you not
studied the kingdom of the heavens and the earth, and whatever things
God has created?" (Quran 8:185); this is a text urging the study of the
totality of beings. Again, God the Exalted has taught that one of those
whom He singularly honored by this knowledge was Abraham, peace be
upon him, for the Exalted said, "So we made Abraham see the kingdom
of the heavens and the earth, that he might be . . . " etc. (Quran 2:5–6).
The Exalted also said, "Do they not observe the camels, how they have
been created, and the sky, how it has been raised up?" (Quran 2:6–7); and
He said, "and they gave thought to the creation of the heavens and the
earth" (Quran 2:7), and so in countless other verses.

Since it has now been established that the Law has rendered obligatory the study of beings by the intellect, and reflection on them, and since
reflection is nothing more than inference and drawing out of the unknown from the known, and since this is reasoning or at any rate done
by reasoning, therefore we are under an obligation to carry on our study
of beings by intellectual reasoning. It is further evident that this manner
of study, to which the Law summons and urges, is the most perfect kind

of study using the most perfect kind of reasoning; and this is the kind called "demonstration."

The Law, then, has urged us to have demonstrative knowledge of God the Exalted and all the beings of His creation. But it is preferable and even necessary for anyone who wants to understand God the Exalted and the other beings demonstratively to have first understood the kinds of demonstration and their conditions (of validity), and in what respects demonstrative reasoning differs from dialectical, rhetorical and fallacious reasoning. But this is not possible unless he has previously learned what reasoning as such is, and how many kinds it has, and which of them are valid and which invalid. This in turn is not possible unless he has previously learned the parts of reasoning, of which it is composed, that is, the premises and their kinds. Therefore he who believes in the Law and obeys its commands to study beings, ought prior to his study to gain a knowledge of these things, which have the same place in theoretical studies as instruments have in practical activities. (Ibn Rushd, *The Decisive Treatise* 1—2) [AVERROES 1961: 44—46]

One objection can be easily dispensed with.

It cannot be objected: "This kind of study of intellectual reasoning is a heretical innovation since it did not exist among the first believers." For the study of legal reasoning and its kinds is also something which has been discovered since the (time of) the first believers, yet it is not considered a heretical innovation. So the objector should believe the same about the study of intellectual reasoning. For this there is a reason, which is not the place to answer here. But most (masters) of this religion (that is, Islam) support intellectual reasoning, except a small group of gross literalists, who can be refuted by (sacred) texts. (Ibid. 3) [AVERROES 1961: 46]

Ibn Rushd is not naive; he is well aware of the dangers to the faith, real or alleged, that are associated with the study of Greek philosophy.

From (all) this it is evident that the study of the books of the ancients is obligatory by (Islamic) Law, since their aim and purpose in their books is just the purpose to which the Law has urged us, and that whoever forbids the study of them to anyone who is fit to study them, that is, anyone who unites the two qualities of natural intelligence and religious integrity and moral virtue is blocking people from the door by which the Law summons them to knowledge of God, the door of theoretical study which leads to the truest knowledge of Him; and such an act is the extreme of ignorance and estrangement from God the Exalted.

And if someone errs or stumbles in the study of these books owing to a deficiency in his natural capacity, or bad organization of his study of them, or being dominated by his passions, or not finding a teacher to guide him to an understanding of their contents, or a combination of all or more than one of these causes, it does not follow that one should forbid them to anyone who is qualified to study them. For this manner of harm which arises owing to them is attached to them by accident, not by essence; and when a thing is beneficial by its nature and essence, it ought not to be shunned because of something harmful contained in it by accident. This was the thought of the Prophet, peace be upon him, on the occasion when he ordered a man to give his brother honey to drink for his diarrhea, and the diarrhea increased after he had given him the honey; when the man complained to him about it, he said, "God spoke the truth; it was your brother's stomach that lied." We can even say that a man who prevents a qualified person from studying books of philosophy, because some of the most vicious people may be thought to have gone astray through their study of them, is like a man who prevents a thirsty person from drinking cool, fresh water until he dies from thirst because some people have choked to death on it. For death from water by choking is an accidental matter, but death by thirst is essential and elementary. (Ibid. 5–6) [AVERROES 1961: 48–49]

35. The Ban on the Greeks

As we have already seen, the ninth-century discovery, via translation, of the works of Greek philosophers like Plato and Aristotle encouraged the growth of a rationalist movement in Islam. We have also noted the reaction that soon appeared in traditionalist circles, particularly among the Hanbalites. The balance between faith and reason was indeed a perilous one, and when a thinker like Ibn Sina or Maimonides was seen to have conceded too much to the claims of reason, disclaiming voices were soon raised. Ibn Sina provoked the reaction of Ghazali, and Maimonides too, for his part, provoked a great many protests, especially among Western Jews.

Maimonides was a particularly complicated case, since he stood behind, as Ibn Sina did not, a large body of impeccably orthodox writing on the subject of the Mosaic Law. But the tone and the argument of the Guide of the Perplexed *delivered a quite different message to many. Notable among the defenders of the traditional approach to Judaism was Solomon ben Adret, a prestigious rabbi of Barcelona, here writing in response to a query sometime about a generation after the death of Maimonides in 1204 C.E.*

You have made inquiry about my attitude toward that traditional story according to which the world will come to an end after a certain time; you say that you have discovered statements in the writings of Rabbi Moses Maimonides which contradict this (traditional belief).

You should know that in these and all similar matters, when we attempt to investigate them through pure science, the latter view must inevitably prevail; thus we are indeed forced to conclude that the world will never cease to exist, since science is based upon perceptions and observations of nature, and we can observe that all the planets as well as the earth are in perpetual motion without alteration. But the belief in an end to the world is not founded on any sense perception but on the evidence of the sages, with the result that this belief cannot be undermined.

What has been founded on tradition or prophetic inspiration cannot be undermined by any science in the world, since science ranks (in certitude) far below prophetic inspiration. This is a principle agreed upon by the adherents of all positive religions, and in particular by the adherents of our own true faith. We believe in the entire tradition, as we believe in the supernatural miracles which were done for the patriarchs, for example, as we believe in the passing through the Red Sea and the Jordan, in the sun's standing still, etc. To be sure, all this is denied by the philosophers, and for them neither Moses nor any of the prophets avails anything.

The philosophers pure and simple are one thing, but what of those Jews who were attempting to reconcile tradition and philosophy?

If Jewish scholars were to accept the point of view maintained by science in general, they would be constrained to interpret many passages of Scripture in a forced way in order to bring them into agreement with science, and to explain many things allegorically because philosophy cares not at all for prophets or commandments. If we wish, then, as true Jewish scholars, to remain in agreement with tradition, we must explain the words of the Bible without concern as to whether or not they agree with the conclusions of science. It is possible, for example, to interpret all the passages in the Bible which refer to resurrection allegorically, particularly the narrative of the dry bones (Ezek. 37). But though there is in this way no necessity to apply any particular verse of Scripture to an actual general resurrection, tradition nevertheless obliges us to do so, and this is enough to oblige us to interpret the respective verses in a corresponding way, since divine wisdom is of far greater value to us than human wisdom, and as we must give unconditional preference to a tradition preserved by our forefathers, which is deeply rooted and founded in the prophets, rather than to the results of our limited human knowledge. (Solomon ben Adret, *Letter to an Anonymous Inquirer*)

For some, these public pronouncements of private sentiments were not enough. Ben Adret was urged to act more officially in this situation when "the sanctuary is being consumed by rotten books," as one partisan put it. He did. Solomon wrote to various communities advising them to forbid the study of philosophy to men under thirty. The advice provoked in 1304 C.E. the following retort from Jacob ben Machir, a mathematician of Montpellier.

. . . If such (scientific) studies do damage to faith, why then do you permit them at all and require only that a line should be drawn between youth and maturity? Is a man of advanced years, then, entitled to expose his faith in religious truths which he learned in his youth to the temptations of philosophical scepticism later on? I am perfectly aware that your true but secret intention is to deny the validity of science altogether, because you have often spoken in a derogatory manner about it and its pioneers, and have even declared that Maimonides' positions on cosmology are without foundation. . . .

I concede that there are some unacceptable notions expressed in the writings of the philosophers, but this hardly justifies your refusal to allow us to acquaint ourselves with the good ideas they contain. Our scientific efforts demonstrate to the nations [that is, the Gentiles] that we have an open mind and an appreciation for everything that is beautiful and good. We might even take them as an example in this regard, since they honor the scholars of other denominations who translate their writings into the languages spoken by those denominations even though they may be in profound disagreement with the latter's ideas. The convictions of a people are in no way weakened by such an attitude, and their faith is nowhere and never undermined, and certainly not ours, for the truth of which we possess the best possible proofs. Besides, there is no one among us who wants to dissolve all biblical stories into allegories; I myself know very well the frontier which philosophy must not cross in its criticism of the Bible, and the most ardent fanatic has no grounds for criticizing me for going too far in this respect. I neither overestimate nor underestimate the value of philosophy, and I am thankful to anybody who can give me a satisfactory explanation of one of those wondrous Talmudic legends.

Solomon ben Adret responded almost immediately.

. . . I regret the injury to your dignity, which you yourself endanger by lowering yourself to practices unworthy of the height to which your peers rightly elevated you by reason of your learning, and by joining the children who can scarcely cry "Daddy" or "Mommy" but who nonetheless throw themselves into the arms of secular science and make a hobby of astrological reveries and overhasty syllogisms. It is true that such studies may be of profit to men of experience whose hair has grown gray while they studied Torah, and that they offer to reasonable people a somewhat deeper insight into the essence of religion, than which no better evidence can be found than Maimonides himself. Besides, mathematics and medicine do not at all belong to the sciences interdicted by me. Even so, a complete peace between philosophy and revealed religion is inconceivable. (Solomon ben Adret, *To Jacob ben Machir*)

In Barcelona in July 1305 C.E. Solomon ben Adret published the final version of his interdiction. A formal ban or excommunication was pronounced upon all those Jews under the age of twenty-five who studied the books of the Greeks on natural science—medicine excepted—or the first philosophy or metaphysics, whether in the original or in translation. It is difficult to measure the effects of the ban in either the short or the long term. Ben Adret died in 1310 and his edict does not seem to have long survived him.

36. The Mystic's Gnosis and the Theologian's Science

The philosopher and the theologian both claimed, then, a privileged access to a knowledge of God, claims resting essentially on the primacy and autonomy of reason. But there was another such claim in Islam, as there had been in the two Abrahamic faiths that preceded it: the mystic too claimed the benefit of a privileged knowledge of God, primary, authentic and immediate, visionary, intuitive—a genuine gnosis.

Ghazali, who was in the unique position of being both a theologian and a mystic, has left us a comparative evaluation of the mystic's inspired gnosis and the theologian's discursively developed understanding in his Revivification of the Sciences of Religion. *Both ways of knowing do indeed open a way to God, but there are fundamental and crucial differences between them, as he pedagogically explains in a chapter subtitled: "Wherein there is set forth the difference between inspiration and study, between the way of the Sufis in discovering the truth and the way of those given over to speculative knowledge."*

Be aware that the types of knowledge which are not necessarily possessed by everyone come into the heart in different ways and the mode by which they arrive varies. At times they appear unexpectedly in the heart as if they had been thrown in from the heart knows not what source. At other times they are acquired by the method of intellectual elaboration and study. The knowledge which arises neither by way of acquisition nor by the operation of a deductive chain is called inspiration;

that which comes about from intellectual elaboration is called examination or reflection.

The knowledge which presents itself in the heart of a sudden and without striving, study or work on the part of the subject is of two types: the first is of the kind that a man is unaware how it came to him or whence; the second carries with it an understanding of the means whereby it came, that is, the vision of the angel who cast it into the heart. The first type is called inspiration and breathes in the depths of the heart; the second is called revelation and properly belongs to the prophets. As for the first, it is characteristic of the saints and the pure of heart, while the previously mentioned type of knowledge, the kind acquired by means of intellectual elaboration, that is proper to the learned.

After this somewhat scholastic introduction, Ghazali turns to more Quranic—and more mystic—images and language.

What can be truly said of the subject (of such inspired knowledge) is that his heart is ready to receive the irradiation of the Truth of Truths which is in all things. Nothing in effect can interpose itself between the heart and things . . . a kind of veil which puts itself between the mirror of the heart and the Well-Guarded Tablet upon which is inscribed all that God has decreed until the Day of Resurrection. The truths of knowledge radiate from the mirror of the tablet onto the mirror of the heart, as an image produced on a mirror will imprint itself on another placed in front of it.

The veil which is between the two mirrors is sometimes drawn aside by the hand, sometimes by the breaths of air that move it. Thus there blow at times the breaths of grace; the veils are then lifted from before the eyes of the heart and certain of the things inscribed on the Well-Guarded Tablet are reflected in him. That occurs from time to time in sleep and by this means one knows what will happen in the future. As for the complete removal of the veil, that will occur at the point of death when there will be removed that which conceals. But it also happens that the veil is drawn aside during the waking state to the extent of being lifted by a hidden grace of God Most High, and then something of the marvels of knowledge gleams in hearts from behind the veil of the Mystery. At times it is like a quick lightening flash; at other times a whole series of them, but limited, and it is extremely rare that this condition is much prolonged.

Just as it is only the mode of its acquisition that distinguishes the mystic's grace-inspired knowledge from the scholar's—whether he is one of the philosophers or one of the ulama class—the same distinction prevails between inspiration—God's gift to the saint—and revelation, God's gift to the prophet.

Inspired knowledge differs from acquired knowledge by neither its nature nor its locus nor its cause but only with respect to the removal of the veil: that is not within the power of man. And revelation in turn does not differ from inspiration with respect to any of these but only by the vision of the angel who brings the knowledge, which comes into our hearts only through the agency of angels. God Most High alludes to it in His words, "It is not given to man that God should speak to him, except by a revelation, or from behind a veil, or by sending an apostle in order that this latter, by God's permission, reveals to man what God wishes" (Quran 42:50–51).

With these preliminaries out of the way, the mystics' most influential and respected spokesman in Islam comes to the parting of the paths and follows the one that leads to his real subject, the Sufi way to God.

With this introduction, know that Sufis prefer the knowledge that comes by inspiration, to the exclusion of that acquired by study. Again, they desire neither to study such learning nor to learn anything of what authors have written on the subject: to inspect neither their teachings nor their arguments. They maintain on the contrary that the "way" consists in preferring spiritual combat, in getting rid of one's faults, in breaking one's ties and approaching God Most High through a single-minded spiritual effort. And every time those conditions are fulfilled, God for His part turns toward the heart of His servant and guarantees him an illumination by the lights of understanding.

Since God Most High has reserved to Himself the power of governing the heart, when the Mercy of God is extended upon this latter, light shines there, his breast expands, the secret of the Kingdom is revealed to him, the veil which blinded him disappears from before his face by the grace of the Mercy and the Truths shine out before him. The only thing in the power of the believer is that he prepare by the purification that strips him clean and that he arouse in himself a care for such things, as well as a sincere will, a consuming thirst and an attentive observation in the constant expectation of what God most High will reveal to him of His Mercy.

As for the prophets and the saints, this object was never revealed to them and the light was never expanded in their breasts either by dint of study or intellectual labors or by things written in books, but they arrived at it by renouncing the world to lead an ascetic life, by freeing themselves of their attachments, by emptying their hearts of their earthly occupations and by approaching God Most High by a single-minded spiritual effort. And he who is God's, God is his.

The Sufis say that the way that leads to such an end consists first of all in cutting off all one's attachments to the world, to cease preoccupying oneself with family, wealth, children, one's homeland, as well as with learning, with authority, with honor; and more, to bring the heart to a state where the existence or non-existence of everything is a matter of indifference. Then the Sufi retires into his own company, into a cell, obliging himself to fulfill the obligatory religious precepts and obligations. He remains thus, his heart empty, concentrating on a single objective. He does not dissipate his thoughts either by reading the Quran or meditating on one of its commentaries, or on the books of Prophetic traditions or any other. He attempts to achieve just the opposite, that nothing should enter his spirit save God Most High.

When he is seated in solitude, he does not cease to say "God, God" continuously and with a recollected heart. And he carries on until he comes to a state where he abandons the movement of his tongue and imagines the word [that is, the name of God] rolling off his tongue. Then he arrives at the point of obliterating any trace of the word from his tongue and he finds his heart continuously applied to (the exercise of) recollection. And he perseveres in it with determination until he reaches the point where he effaces the image of this word from his heart, the letters and the form of the word, and only the sense of the word remains in his heart, present within him, as if joined to him and never leaving him.

It is within his power to arrive at this point and to make this stage endure while resisting temptations. He cannot, however, draw upon himself the Mercy of God Most High. Rather, by his efforts he makes himself ready to receive the breaths of the divine Mercy and there remains nothing else for him to do but to await what God will reveal to him of His Mercy, as He revealed it, by this same way, to the prophets and the saints.

Then, if the will (of the Sufi) has been sincere, his spiritual effort a pure one, and his perseverance perfect; if he has not been carried in the opposite direction by his passions or preoccupied by an unrest arising from his attachments to the world, then the rays of the Truth will shine in his heart. At the outset this will be like a sudden lightening that does not last, then returns, but slowly. If it does return, sometimes it remains and sometimes it is only passing. If it remains, sometimes its presence is extended and sometimes not. And at times illuminations like the first appear, one following the other; at other times they are reduced to a single experience. The saints' "resting" in that state are without number, just as their natures and characters are innumerable.

In sum: this way leads solely, insofar as it concerns you, to a complete purity, purification and clarity, and then to being ready, expectant.

Finally, Ghazali returns to the opening theme, the difference between the inspired knowledge of the Sufi and the discursive knowledge of the theologian.

As for those who practice speculation and discursive examination, they do not deny the existence of this way (of the Sufi), or its possibility, or that it can arrive at such an end on rare occasions: it is, after all, the state often achieved by the prophets and the saints. But they have looked upon it as an arduous way, slow to yield its fruits, requiring a complex of conditions rarely achieved. They have maintained that at this point it is almost impossible to break one's attachments to the world and that to arrive at a "state" and remain there is more difficult still. . . . As a consequence of this kind of spiritual struggle (they say), the temperament is spoiled, the reason disordered and the body made ill. If the soul has not been exercised (by the practices of piety) and formed by the realities of the sciences to begin with, the heart is monopolized by corrupt imaginings in which the soul takes its rest over an extended period of time, to the point that one's life is past and over without success having been achieved. How many Sufis who have followed this route have remained for twenty years in the grip of some imaginary fantasy, while someone who had previously been solidly grounded in learning would have immediately recognized the dubious quality of this product of the imagination. To devote oneself to following a course of study is the surest way of proceeding and accomplishing the end.

(The dialectical theologians) say that this attitude of the Sufis is like that of a man who neglects the study of the religious law by maintaining that the Prophet, may the peace and blessing of God be upon him, did not study but became expert in this discipline by revelation and inspiration, without studying texts or writing commentaries on them, and so will I, perhaps, by the practice of asceticism and sheer perseverance. Whoever thinks that way, they maintain, does ill to himself and is squandering his life. Indeed, he is like a man who leaves off trying to earn a living and cultivating the soil in the hope of chancing upon some buried treasure or other, something that is possible but highly improbable. (Ghazali, *Revivification* 3:16–17)

37. Ibn al-Arabi on the Irrelevance of Ibn Rushd

Jewish respect for Maimonides may have prevented a more radical reaction to the rationalist tradition that he so brilliantly and profoundly represented. In Islam, too, the scholastics' reverence for Ghazali and Ghazali's moderating influence may have prevented a full-scale reaction to the rationalist strain. But there are responses other than reaction, and the more radical mystical thinkers in Islam—more radical than al-Ghazali at any rate—illustrate another view of rationalism. For example, Ibn al-Arabi (1165–1240 C.E.), from his own supremely confident position—the text of his book The Bezels of Wisdom, *he informs the reader at the outset, was handed to him by no other than Muhammad himself in Damascus in the month of Muharram, 1230 C.E.—simply dismisses the rationalizing and rationalist ways of trying to understand God as at worst ignorant and at best irrelevant. In his* Meccan Revelations *Ibn al-Arabi tells this highly revealing anecdote about a meeting in Cordova between himself, the still very young patron saint of Islamic theosophy, and Ibn Rushd, the "second Aristotle" of Islam.*

I spent a good day in Cordova at the house of Abu al-Walid ibn Rushd. He had expressed a desire to meet with me in person, since he had heard of certain revelations I had received while in retreat, and had shown considerable astonishment concerning them. In consequence, my father, who was one of his close friends, took me with him on the pretext of business, in order to give Ibn Rushd the opportunity of making my acquaintance. I was at the time a beardless youth.

As I entered the house the philosopher rose to greet me with all the signs of friendliness and affection, and embraced me. Then he said to me, "Yes!" and showed pleasure on seeing that I had understood him. I, on the other hand, when I became aware of the motive of his pleasure, replied, "No!" At this Ibn Rushd drew back from me, his color changed and he seemed to doubt what he had thought of me. He then put to me the following question: "What solution have you found as a result of mystical illumination and divine inspiration?" I replied "Yes and No. Between the Yea and the Nay the spirits take their flight beyond matter, and the necks detach themselves from their bodies." At this Ibn Rushd became pale, and I saw him tremble as he muttered the formula, "There is no power save from God." This was because he had understood my allusion. (Ibn al-Arabi, *Meccan Revelations* 1:153) [IBN AL-ARABI 1980: 2]

We are somewhat less certain than Ibn Rushd about the meaning of the allusion, but there is no mistaking Ibn al-Arabi's views on what and how we know about God—or better, the Reality. He begins with an attack on the very foundation of the rationalist enterprise, the principal of causality.

An indication of the weakness of intellectual speculation is the notion that a cause cannot be (also) the effect of that to which it is a cause. Such is the judgment of the intellect, while in the science of divine Self-revelation it is known that a cause may be the effect of that for which it is a cause. . . . The most that the intellectual will admit to on this matter, when he sees that it contradicts speculative evidence, is that the essence, after it is established that it is one among many causes, in some form or other, of a (given) effect, cannot be an effect to its effect, so that that effect should become its cause, while the first still remains a cause, but that if its determination becomes changed by its transformation in forms, then it may thus become an effect to its own effect, which might then become its cause. This then is as far as he will go, when he perceives that the matter does not agree with his rational speculation.

There have been none more intelligent than the Apostles, God's blessing be on them, and what they brought us derives from the divine Majesty. They indeed confirmed what the intellect confirms, but added more that the intellect is not capable of grasping, things the intellect declares to be absurd, except in the case of one who has had an immediate experience of divine manifestation; afterwards, left to himself, he is confused as to what he has seen. If he is a servant of the Lord, he refers his intelligence to Him (to respond to his perplexities), but if he is a servant of reason, he reduces God to reason's yardstick. This happens only so long as he is in this worldly state, being veiled from his otherworldly state in this world. (Ibn al-Arabi, *The Bezels of Wisdom*, "Elias") [IBN AL-ARABI 1980: 234]

The "servant of the Lord" and the "servant of reason" are thus neatly distinguished. Other similar distinctions, all to the same point, appear often in his work.

For the believers and men of spiritual vision it is the creation that is surmised and the Reality that is seen and perceived, while in the case of those not in these two categories, it is the Reality Who is surmised and the creation that is seen and perceived by the senses. . . .

Men are divided into two groups. The first travel a way they know and whose destination they know, which is their "Straight Path" (of Quran 11:56). The second group travel a way they do not know and of whose destination they are unaware, which is equally the Straight Path. The gnostic calls on God with spiritual perception, while he who is not a gnostic calls on Him in ignorance and bound by a tradition.

Such a knowledge is a special one stemming from "the lowest of the low" (Quran 95:5), since the feet are the lowest part of the person, what is lower than that being the way beneath them. He who knows that the

Reality is the way knows the truth, for it is none other than He that you progress and travel, since there is naught to be known save Him, since He is Being Itself and therefore also the traveler himself. Further, there is no Knower save Him; so who are you? Therefore, know your true reality and your way, for the truth has been made known to you on the tongue of the Interpreter [that is, Muhammad], if you will only understand. He is a true word that none understands, save that his understanding be true; the Reality has many relations and many aspects. . . .

. . . You may say of Being what you will; either that it is the creation or that it is the Reality, or that it is at once both the creation and the Reality. It might also be said that there is neither creation nor the Reality, as one might admit to perplexity in the matter, since by assigning degrees the difficulties appear. But for the limitation (that arises in defining the Reality), the Apostles would not have taught that the Reality transforms Himself in cosmic forms nor would they have described Him (at the same time) as abstracting Himself from all forms. . . .

Because of this (inevitable limitation by definition), He is both denied and known, called incomparable and compared. He who sees the Reality from His standpoint, in Him and by Him, is a gnostic. He who sees the Reality from His standpoint, in Him, but with himself as the seer, is not a gnostic. He who does not see the Reality in this way, but expects to see Him by himself, he is ignorant.

In general most men have perforce an individual concept of their Lord, which they ascribe to Him and in which they seek Him. So long as the Reality is presented to them according to it, they recognize Him and affirm Him, whereas if it is presented in any other form, they deny Him, flee from Him and treat Him improperly, while at the same time imagining that they are acting toward Him fittingly. One who believes (in the ordinary way) believes only in a deity he has created in himself, since a deity in "beliefs" is a (mental) construction. They see (in this deity) only themselves and their own constructions within themselves. (Ibn al-Arabi, *The Bezels of Wisdom*, "Hud") [IBN AL-ARABI 1980: 132–133]

6. The Last Things

All religions agree on the fact that souls experience states of happiness and misery after death, but they disagree in the manner of symbolizing these states and explaining their existence to men. (Ibn Rushd, *Unveiling of the Programs of Proof* 122) [AVERROES 1961: 76]

So Ibn Rushd, a Muslim philosopher of Spain in the waning years of the twelfth century. It is the beginning of a chapter on the "Future Life." His mood in writing it was more defensive, perhaps, than philosophical, as we shall see, but he knew whereof he spoke. Again, referring to the future life, Ibn Rushd remarks:

This is a problem which is not found in the older philosophers, although resurrection has been mentioned in different religions for at least a thousand years, and the philosophers whose theories have come to us are of more recent date. The first to mention bodily resurrection were the prophets of Israel after Moses, as is evident from the Psalms and many books attributed to the Israelites. Bodily resurrection is also affirmed in the New Testament and attributed by tradition to Jesus. (Ibn Rushd, *Incoherence of the Incoherence* 580) [AVERROES 1954: 359]

And, the Muslim Ibn Rushd had no need of adding, resurrection sounds like a trumpet throughout the Quran.

1. The Darkness Below

The Israelites unmistakably had some notions of a type of survival beyond the grave, although, despite Ibn Rushd's flat assertion, the concept does not seem to have been integrated into God's or their own thinking about the Covenant or the Law. Indeed, there is no sure biblical reference to a resurrection or an authentic form of life after death until the Book of Daniel, the last work included in the Bible. Enoch and Elijah were immortal only in the sense that they did not die. The fear of eternal punishment or the promise of an eternal reward are never offered in the Torah as motives for fidelity to the Covenant.

According to the biblical evidence, the dead were thought to survive, after a fashion, and they may have been the subject of some kind of tomb cult in Israel. This passage in Deuteronomy addressed to the Lord seems to imply that untithed food offered to the dead is right and appropriate.

I have neither transgressed nor neglected any of Your commandments. I have not eaten any of the tithe while in mourning; I have not cleared out any of it while I was unclean, and I have not deposited any of it with the dead. (Deuteronomy 26:13–14)

The abode of these not-quite dead—the "strengthless dead," as they are later called—where the Bible does give it a name, is Sheol. Descriptions of it and its location are vague. Sheol is generally a dark, underground place—its other names are "the grave" or "the abyss"—and its principal inhabitants seem to be those who died violently or did not receive appropriate burial, as here in Isaiah and Ezekiel.

> Once you thought in your heart,
> "I will climb to the sky,
> Higher than the stars of God
> I will set my throne.
> I will sit on the mount of assembly,
> On the summit of Zaphon:
> I will mount the back of a cloud—
> I will match the Most High."
> Instead, you are brought down to Sheol,
> To the bottom of the Pit . . .
> All the kings of nations
> Were laid, every one,
> Each in his tomb.
> While you were left unburied,
> Like loathesome carrion,
> Like a trampled corpse
> In the clothing of the slain gashed by the sword
> Who sink to the very stones of the Pit.
> (Isaiah 14:13–19)

Thus said the Lord God: On the day he [that is, the Pharaoh] went down to Sheol, I closed the deep over it and covered it; I held back its streams and great waters were checked. . . . When I cast him down to Sheol with those who descend into the Pit. . . . You too shall be brought down . . . to the lowest parts of the netherworld; you shall lie among the uncircumcised and those slain by the sword. Such shall be the fate of Pharaoh and all his hordes—declares the Lord. (Ezekiel 31:15–18)

O mortal, (the Lord said) wail (the dirge)—along with the women of the mighty nations—over the masses of Egypt, accompanying their descent to the lowest part of the netherworld, among those who have gone down into the Pit. Whom do you surpass in beauty? Down with you, and be laid to rest with the uncircumcised! . . .

From the depths of Sheol the mightiest of warriors speak to him [that is, the Pharaoh] and his allies; the uncircumcised, the slain by the sword, have gone down and lie there. (Ezekiel 32:18–21)

Israelite malefactors too are plunged into Sheol.

Scarcely had Moses finished speaking all these words when the ground under them burst asunder, and the earth opened its mouth and swallowed them up with their households, all Korah's people and all their possessions. They went down alive into Sheol with all that belonged to them; the earth closed over them and they vanished from the midst of the congregation. (Numbers 16:31–33)

But there is another, more neutral view of Sheol as a "quiet grave" shared by high and low alike.

Why did I not die at birth, expire when I came forth from the womb? . . . For now I would be lying in repose, asleep and at rest, with the world's kings and counselors who rebuild ruins for themselves, or with nobles who possess gold and fill their houses with silver. Or why was I not like a buried stillbirth, like babies who never saw the light? There the wicked cease from troubling; there rest those who strength is spent. Prisoners are wholly at ease; they do not hear the taskmaster's voice. Small and great alike are there, and the slave is free of his master. (Job 3:11–19)

2. The Resurrection

Then, in the Book of Daniel, written sometime about 165 B.C.E., when Israel was in the grip of what appeared might be a fatal pogrom at the hands of Antiochus Epiphanes, this apparently new perspective appears in Daniel's vision.

At that time, the great prince, Michael, who stands beside the sons of your people, will appear. It will be a time of trouble, the like of which has never been since the nation came into being. At that time the people will be rescued, all who are found inscribed in the book. Many of those who sleep in the dust of the earth will awake, some to eternal life, others to reproaches, to everlasting abhorrence. And the knowledgeable will be radiant like the bright expanse of sky, and those who lead the many to righteousness will be like the stars forever and ever. (Daniel 12:1–4)

Thus the first unmistakable reference to a future life is connected, as it will often be in subsequent references, with righting life's wrongs—the collective wrongs to Israel, as here, or the injustices suffered by an individual. In the Jewish tradition at least, a belief in immortality was born of a desire for theodicy.

But there is something else in the text as well. Unless the word "like" is here signaling only a metaphor, there is a connection of the just with heaven and the stars. We are perhaps at the Jewish beginning—it was fairly commonplace among the pagans—of the notion that the good "go to heaven."

3. Sadducees, Pharisees, Rabbis, and Others on the Afterlife

The point of view put forward in Daniel 12, though it was taken up and elaborated by many in the period between the two Testaments, did not entirely drive out the old Israelite denial of a life after death, not at least until 70 C.E. and the triumph of the Pharisees. Chief among the Jews who denied an afterlife were the Sadducees, the conservative and aristocratic party who constituted the ruling group in the Sanhedrin for most of the period. Opposing them on the issue of immortality were the Pharisees. Josephus first offers this general characterization of the two parties.

The Pharisees had passed on to the people certain regulations handed down by former generations and not recorded in the Laws of Moses [that is the Torah, the Pentateuch], for which reason they are rejected by the Sadducees, who hold that only those regulations should be considered valid which were written down (in Scripture), and those that were (only) handed down by former generations need not be observed. (Josephus, *Antiquities* 13:297)

As a consequence of that fundamental difference in deriving the Law there followed these opposed views of the afterlife.

The Pharisees . . . believe that souls have the power to survive death and that there are rewards and punishments under the earth for those who have led lives of virtue or vice: eternal imprisonment is the lot of evil souls, while the good souls receive an easy passage to a new life. . . . The Sadducees hold that the soul perishes along with the body. (Josephus, *Antiquities* 18:14–16)

Paul plays upon that same fundamental difference of opinion when he is taken in custody before the council of the Sanhedrin for a hearing.

Paul was well aware that one section of them [that is, of the San-hedrin] were Sadducees and the other Pharisees, so he called out in the Council, "My brothers, I am a Pharisee, a Pharisee born and bred; and the true issue in this trial is our hope of the resurrection of the dead." At these words the Pharisees and the Sadducees fell out among themselves, and the assembly was divided—the Sadducees deny that there is any resurrection, or angel or spirit, but the Pharisees accept them. So a great uproar broke out; and some of the doctors of the Law belonging to the Pharisaic party openly took sides and declared, "We can find no fault with this man; perhaps an angel or spirit has spoken to him." The dissension was mounting, and the (Roman) commandant was afraid that Paul would be torn to pieces, so he ordered the troops to go down and bring him into the barracks. (Acts 23:6–10)

Paul was in fact a Pharisee, or at least educated as one, as he tells us elsewhere, and so it is not remarkable that he should follow the Pharisaic position on the question of life after death. But what of his master, Jesus? In Mark 12 Jesus is approached by some Sadducees, who, as the Gospel remarks, "say that there is no resurrection" (Mark 12:18). They pose him a legal conundrum: a woman has married seven different husbands in series, all of whom predecease her. To which of them will she be married at the resurrection, "when they all come back to life"? The intent was probably to demolish belief in the afterlife by a legal reduction to the absurd, but Jesus takes the question seriously and gives a serious answer.

Jesus said to them, "You are mistaken, and surely this is the reason: you do not know either the Scriptures or the power of God. When they rise from the dead, men and women do not marry; they are like angels in heaven. But about the resurrection of the dead, have you never read in the Book of Moses, in the story of the burning bush, how God spoke to him and said, "I am the God of Abraham, the God of Isaac and the God of Jacob" (Exod. 3:6). God is not the God of the dead but the God of the living.

Thus Jesus' answer too is in perfect agreement with the teaching of the Pharisees, and his attempt to establish it out of the Torah is precisely the polemical tack taken by the later rabbis when they debated the resurrection question in the tractate "Sanhedrin" in the Talmud. "Debate" is not perhaps the word. The Sadducees were no longer a force in Jewish life after 70 C.E., and so the Pharisaic view that there was an afterlife, a place of punishment and reward, had become in fact Jewish "orthodoxy." Witness, for example, the second of the Eighteen Blessings introduced into standard synagogue worship in this era (see Chapter 1 above).

You, O Lord, are mighty forever, You quicken the dead, are mighty to save. You sustain the living with loving kindness, quicken the dead with great mercy, support the falling, heal the sick, loose the captive, and keep Your faith with those who sleep in the dust. Who is like You, Lord of mighty deeds, and who resembles You, O King, who kills and quickens and causes salvation to spring forth.

Yes, faithful You are to quicken the dead. Blessed are You, O Lord, who quickens the dead. (Shemoneh Esreh 2)

The starting point of the Talmudic discussion was, in any event, this Mishnaic text.

All Israel have a portion in the world to come, for it is written, "Your people are all righteous; they shall inherit the land forever, the branch of My planting, the work of My hands, that I may be glorified" (Isa. 60:22). But the following have no portion therein: he who maintains that resurrection is not a biblical doctrine, the Torah was not divinely revealed and an Apiqoros [that is, an "Epicurean"]. (M.Sanhedrin 10:1)

He who holds that "resurrection is not a biblical doctrine" is obviously the Sadducee or a connected group. "Epicurean" here and elsewhere in the Talmud seems to extend farther than the Greek philosophical school of that name, and at times it seems to be used generically as "heretic." But there was a connection between the philosophy and the Talmud's "Apiqoros," and nowhere more clearly than here, since a central tenet of Greco-Roman Epicureanism was its denial of the afterlife.

So the discussion proceeds in BT.Sanhedrin 90b–92b. Texts are brought forth; and although there is no clear-cut statement to that end, there is an attempt to show that the resurrection can at least be deduced from or was intimated in the Bible. Many of the adduced texts depend on allegorical interpretations or the presence in a cited text of an indefinite future tense that is then construed to refer to the afterlife. There is a passing, almost casual reference to Daniel 12 but, interestingly, no use of Exodus 3:6, the text cited by Jesus.

If we cannot hear Jesus' rabbinic voice in BT.Sanhedrin 90b–92b, we can certainly hear Paul's. First, Rabbi Meir (d. ca. 175 C.E.) responds to a query not from the queen of Egypt but from the name that stood in the text at that point before it got garbled, the chief of the Samaritans.

Queen Cleopatra [that is, the Samaritan patriarch] asked Rabbi Meir: "I know that the dead will revive, for it is written, 'And they [that is, the righteous] shall blossom forth out of the city like the grass of the earth' (Ps. 72:16). But when they arise, shall they be nude or in their clothes?" He replied: "You may deduce an answer a fortiori from a grain of wheat: if a grain of wheat, which is buried naked, sprouts in so many robes, how much more so the righteous, who are buried in their raiment?"

And Paul, in response to a very similar question:

You may ask, how are the dead raised? In what kind of a body? How foolish! The seed you sow does not come to life unless it has first died, and what you sow is not the body that shall be, but a naked grain; and God clothes it with the body of His choice, each seed with its own particular body. All flesh is not the same flesh: there is flesh of men, flesh of beasts, of birds, and of fishes—all different. . . . So it is with the resurrection of the dead. What is sown in the earth as a perishable thing is raised imperishable. Sown in humiliation, it is raised in glory; sown in weakness, it is raised in power; sown as an animal body, it is raised as a spiritual body. (Paul, *To the Corinthians* 1.15:35–44)

4. Gehinnom

Together with a growing conviction from the second century B.C.E. onward that there was an afterlife went the elaboration of its function and features, largely through the agency of the "heavenly journey" discussed in Chapter 4 above. There was, to begin with, the older Sheol; but although the Septuagint and the Christian Latin version of the Bible both translate "Sheol" by "Hades" and "Infernus," respectively, it does not appear that Sheol was the Hell of those somewhat later traditions. It was not created for punishment, and if there was torment in Sheol, it was the torment of privation, aloneness, ineffectiveness.

A place of explicit damnation does eventually appear in the Jewish tradition, as a separate phenomenon from Sheol. There was a valley immediately to the south of Jerusalem known as "the valley of the Children of Hinnom," in Hebrew, Ge ben Hinnom or Ge Hinnom. Under the the later monarchy, during the reigns of Ahaz and Menasseh, the place called "the Valley of Hinnom" was used as the site of ritual sacrifice, where Jews offered their children as burnt sacrifice to the god Moloch. Then, with the restoration of the Law under Josiah, official action was taken concerning the shrine called Topheth in the Gehinnom.

He [Josiah] desecrated Topheth in the valley of the Ben Hinnom, so that no one might make his son or daughter pass through the fire in honor of [or: as an offering to] Moloch.

The people of Judah have done what displeases Me—declares the Lord. They have set up their abominations in the House which is called by My name, and they have defiled it. And they have built the shrines of

Topheth in the Valley of Ben Hinnom to burn their sons and daughters in fire—which I never commanded, which never came to My mind.

Assuredly, a time is coming—declares the Lord—when men shall no longer speak of Topheth or the Valley of Ben Hinnom, but of the Valley of Slaughter; and they shall bury in Topheth until no room is left. The carcasses of this people shall be food for the birds of the sky and the beasts of the earth, with none to frighten them off. (Jeremiah 7:30–33)

Possibly Isaiah is thinking of this same place of filth, pollution, and smoldering fires in a passage where the Lord predicts His final victory over His enemies. A later generation of Jews certainly understood it to mean Gehinnom, as we shall see.

All flesh . . . shall go out and gaze on the corpses of the men who rebelled against Me; their worms shall not die, nor their fire be quenched; they shall be a horror to all flesh. (Isaiah 66:23–24)

And this passage too from Zechariah was read by later rabbis as referring to a judgment after death, though there is no sign in the text itself that it refers to such an eschatological event.

Throughout the land—the Lord declares—two-thirds shall perish, shall die, and one-third of it shall survive. That third I will put into the fire, and I will smelt them as one smelts silver and test them as one tests gold. (Zechariah 13:8–9)

5. A Moral Hell

When we turn to "The Wisdom of Solomon," a work composed by an Alexandrian Jew of the first century B.C.E., we can see the new notions at work on the moral plane. The case is put forward by "the wicked" that life is short and there is nothing afterwards, so come, let us enjoy.

A passing shadow, such is our life, and there is no postponement of our end, man's fate is sealed and none returns. Come then and let us enjoy the good things while we can, and make full use of creation, with all the eagerness of youth. Let us have costly wines and perfumes to our heart's content and let no flower of spring escape us. (Wisdom of Solomon 2:5–8)

So they argued, and very wrong they were; blinded by their own malevolence, they did not understand God's hidden plan; they never expected that holiness of life would have its recompense; they thought that innocence had no reward. But God created man for immortality, and made him the image of His own immortal Self; it was the devil's spite that brought death into the world, and the experience of it is reserved for those who take his side.

But the souls of the just are in God's hand, and torment shall not touch them. In the eyes of foolish men they seemed to be dead; their departure was reckoned as defeat, and their going from us disaster. But they are at peace, for though in the sight of men they may be punished, they have a sure hope of immortality; and after a little chastisement they will receive great blessings, because God has tested them and found them worthy to be His. Like gold in a crucible he put them to the proof and found them acceptable like an offering burnt whole upon the altar. (Wisdom of Solomon 2:21–3:6)

The hope of the godless man is like down flying on the wind, like spindrift swept before a storm, and smoke which the wind whirls away, or like the memory of a guest who stayed for one day and passed on. But the just live forever: their reward is in the Lord's keeping and the Most High has them in His care. Therefore royal splendor shall be theirs, and a fair diadem from the Lord Himself. (Wisdom of Solomon 5:14–16)

In 2 Maccabees, likewise written in Egypt ca. 124 B.C.E., King Antiochus is depicted as bent on executing seven brothers for their fidelity to the Law. They respond:

Fiend though you are, you are setting us free from this present life, and since we die for His laws, the King of the universe will raise us up to a life everlastingly made new. (2 Maccabees 7:9)

Or again:

Better to be killed by men and cherish God's promise to raise us again. There will be no resurrection to life for you. (2 Maccabees 7:14)

The passage in 2 Maccabees that most interested later Christians in the Latin West seemed like a scriptural verification—the Books of Maccabees were included in the Christian canon of Scripture—of their belief in Purgatory as a place of temporary punishment where the pains of the dead sinner could be alleviated by the prayers of the living.

Regrouping his forces, he [that is, Judah Maccabeus] led them to the town of Adullam. The seventh day was coming on so they purified themselves, as custom dictated, and kept the Sabbath there. Next day they went, as had now become necessary, to collect the bodies of the fallen (in battle) in order to bury them with their relatives in the ancestral graves. But on every one of the dead, they found, under the tunic, amulets sacred to the idols of Jamnia, objects which the Law forbids to Jews. It was evident to all that here was the reason why these men had fallen. Therefore they praised the work of the Lord, the Just Judge who reveals what is hidden; and turning to prayer, they asked that this sin might be entirely blotted out.

The noble Judah called on the people to keep themselves free from sin, for they had seen with their own eyes what had happened to the fallen because of their sin. He levied a contribution from each man and sent the total of two thousand silver drachmas to Jerusalem for a sin offering. (2 Maccabees 12:38–44)

A sin offering is normal; what is unusual here is that it is for the dead. It is perhaps the novelty of it that elicits the immediately following remark, or defense, from the author of 2 Maccabees.

... [A] fit and proper act in which he took due account of the resurrection. For if he had not been expecting the fallen to rise again, it would have been foolish and superfluous to pray for the dead. But since he had in view the wonderful reward reserved for those who die a godly death, his purpose was a holy and pious one. And this is why he offered an atoning sacrifice to free the dead from their sin. (2 Maccabees 12:45)

6. The New Testament Vision of the Beyond

A later generation of Christians combed the Bible as carefully as the rabbis did for texts in support of their vision of the afterlife as a place of punishment and reward. And like the rabbis they found them. But save for the one example of Daniel, the exegesis seems forced in the extreme. Yet if the Israelites had no such view of the afterlife, many post-Exilic Jews certainly did, including Jesus and Paul. The later Christians were correct in supposing that they had inherited their notions of the afterlife from the Jews, but the legacy came from those generations of Jews who composed the Apocrypha, the Mishna, and the Talmud and who believed firmly in an eternal Hell and an eternal Paradise and described them in a series of vivid apocalypses.

The Synoptic Gospels all have their apocalyptic chapters, as we have seen. Taken as a whole, their view of the afterlife was a traditional one, as that word was understood in conservative Jewish circles after the Exile: there was a life after death characterized by God's judgment, His punishments, and His rewards in places set aside for that purpose. This, for example, is Enoch's version of the end from the second century B.C.E.

And in those days the earth will return what has been entrusted to it, and Sheol will return what has been entrusted to it, that which it has received, and destruction will return what it owes. And he [that is, the

Chosen One] will choose the righteous and holy from among them, for the day has come near that they must be saved. And in those days the Chosen One will sit on his [or "My"] throne, and all the secrets of wisdom will flow from the counsel of his mouth, for the Lord of the Spirits has appointed him and glorified him. And in those days the mountains will leap like rams, and the hills will skip like lambs satisfied with milk, and all will become angels in heaven. Their faces will shine with joy, for in those days the Chosen One will have risen; and the earth will rejoice, and the righteous will dwell upon it, and the chosen will go and walk upon it. (1 Enoch 61)

Such visions of future glory doubtless colored the Christians' expectation of the coming Kingdom, but the Gospels show the darker side of the End Time as well. Its themes are already present in the teaching of John the Baptist.

The people were on the tiptoe of expectation, all wondering about John, whether he was perhaps the Messiah, but he spoke out and said to them all: I baptize you with water; but there is one to come who is mightier than I. I am not fit to unfasten his shoes. He will baptize you with the Holy Spirit and with fire. His threshing fork is ready in his hand, to winnow his threshing floor and gather the wheat into his granary; but he will burn the chaff on a fire that will never go out. (Luke 3:15–17)

On Jesus' own teaching there can be no doubt. These remarks are from the Sermon on the Mount. The place of eternal punishment is now firmly "Gehenna," the Bible's Gehinnom.

Anyone who nurses anger against his brother must be brought to judgment. If he abuses his brother he will have to answer for it to the court; if he sneers at him he will have to answer for it in the fires of Gehenna. (Matthew 5:22)

If your right eye is your undoing, tear it out and fling it away; it is better for you to lose one part of your body than for the whole of it to be thrown into Gehenna. (Matthew 5:29)

To which there is added, in Mark's version of the saying, the characterization already cited from Isaiah 66:24.

. . . Gehenna, where the devouring worm never dies and the fire is not quenched. (Mark 9:48)

Not everyone who calls me "Lord, Lord" will enter the kingdom of Heaven but only those who do the will of my heavenly Father. (Mark 7:21)

And on curing the servant of the Gentile centurion:

Many, I tell you, will come from east and west to feast with Abraham, Isaac and Jacob in the kingdom of heaven. But those who were born to the kingdom will be driven out into the dark, the place of wailing and grinding of teeth. (Matthew 8:11–12)

The same theme and images show up in the parables, in the story of a man's enemy sowing weeds among his wheat, for example. Both crops are allowed to grow together until harvest time, when they are harvested separately, first the weeds for burning and then the wheat for storage in barns.

His disciples came to him [that is, Jesus] and said, "Explain to us the parable of the weeds in the field." And this was his answer: "The sower of the good seed is the Son of Man. The field is the world; the good seed stands for the children of the Kingdom, the weeds for the children of the evil one. The enemy who sowed the weeds is the devil. The harvest is the end of time. The reapers are angels. As the weeds, then, are gathered up and burnt, so at the end of time the Son of Man will send out his angels, who will gather out of his kingdom whatever makes men stumble and all whose deeds are evil, and these will be thrown into the blazing furnace, the place of wailing and grinding of teeth. And then the righteous will shine as brightly as the sun in the kingdom of their Father. If you have ears, then hear." (Matthew 13:36–43)

When the Son of Man comes in his glory and all the angels with him, he will sit in state upon his throne, with all the nations gathered before him. He will separate men into two groups, as a shepherd separates the sheep from the goats, and he will place the sheep on his right hand and the goats on his left. Then the king will say to those on his right hand, "You have my Father's blessing; come, enter and possess the kingdom that has been ready for you since the world was made." . . . Then he will say to those on his left hand, "The curse is upon you; go from my sight to the eternal fire that is ready for the devil and his angels." . . . And they will go away to eternal punishment and the righteous will enter eternal life. (Matthew 25:31–46)

Like the place of torment, Gehenna, the place of eternal life has also been localized. Jesus refers to it in his final moments of life. As he hangs on the cross, the criminal crucified next to him turns to Jesus.

And he said, "Jesus, remember me when you come to your throne." He answered, "I tell you this. Today you shall be with me in Paradise." (Luke 23:43)

It was, as we shall see, a promise fulfilled.

7. The Charting of Hades

The Gospels do not offer many details of Paradise and Gehenna, but Jewish apoca-
lypses from 1 Enoch in the second century B.C.E. to 4 Ezra in the late first century
C.E. provide elaborate "eyewitness" reports, particularly of the now elaborate geog-
raphy of the underworld of the damned.

 Enoch was the enigmatic biblical presence described simply in Genesis 5:24:
"Having walked with God, Enoch was seen no more, because God took him away."
Where God took him is not explained in the Bible. But in the period after the Exile,
and for long afterwards, Enoch became the subject of an elaborate visionary litera-
ture among the Jews, part of which professed to describe, in his name, the regions
of the afterlife. The shadowy biblical Sheol has now been fleshed out with many of
the features, geographical and cosmological, of the Greek underworld.

And they took me to a place where those who were there were like
burning fire, and when they wished, they made themselves look like men.
And then they led me to a place of storm and a mountain the tip of whose
summit reached to heaven. And I saw lighted places and thunder in the
outermost ends, in its depths a bow of fire and arrows and their quivers,
and a sword of fire, and all the flashes of lightning. And they took me to
the water of life, as it is called, and to the fire of the west which receives
every setting of the sun. And I came to a river of fire whose fire flows like
water and pours into the great sea which is toward the west. And I saw
all the great rivers, and I reached the great darkness and went where all
flesh walks. And I saw the mountains of the darkness of winter and the
place where all the water of the deep pours out. And I saw the mouths
of all the rivers of the earth and the mouth of the deep.

This is, then, the subbasement of the universe. It is also the place of future punish-
ment. In Enoch's account, as in almost all its successors, it will be populated by
exemplary sinners, here the immortal "sons of the gods" who had defiled themselves
by intercourse with the "daughters of men" in Genesis 6:4, as is explained to Enoch
by the archangel Uriel.

And Uriel said to me: "The spirits of the angels who were promis-
cuous with women will stand here; and they, assuming many forms, made
men unclean and will lead men astray so that they sacrifice to demons as
gods—that is, until the great judgment day on which they will be judged
so that an end will be made of them. And their wives, having led astray
the angels of heaven, will become sirens. And I, Enoch, alone saw the
sight, the ends of everything, and no man has seen what I have seen." (1
Enoch 17–19)

As happened later in Christian and Muslim circles, though Gehenna had its un-doubted interest for visionaries and storytellers, it fell to the rabbinic lawyers to extract the appropriate judicial conclusions from the mass of scriptural and tradi-tional material that lay before them. Here the question is twofold: who is in Gehenna and what is the duration of their punishments?

Rabbi Shammai teaches this: that there will be three groups at the judgment: one of the truly holy, another of the truly wicked, and a third in between. It is immediately written and sealed that the truly holy shall live until the end of time, and it is likewise written that the truly wicked shall remain in Gehenna, as it is written (Dan. 12:2). As for the third group, they shall go down to Gehenna for a time and then come up again, as it is written (Zech. 13:9 and 1 Sam. 2:6). But the Hillelites say: He who is abundant in mercy inclines toward mercy, and it is of them that David speaks (Ps. 116:1) to God, who hears him and responds in these terms: . . . Sinners, Jew and Gentile alike having sinned in their body, shall be punished in Gehenna for twelve months and then reduced to nothingness. (BT.Rosh Hashanah 16b–17a)

Or as the Tosefta to Sanhedrin refines it, making it very clear that Gehenna is not a Purgatory but rather the antechamber to annihilation:

. . . [T]heir souls are reduced to nothing and their bodies burned and Gehenna vomits them up; they become ash and the wind disperses them to be trodden underfoot by the holy. (Tosefta Sanhedrin 13:3)

8. A Rabbinic Discussion of Gehenna

By the time the Babylonian Talmud was assembled in the sixth or early seventh century C.E., the notion of a Hell for grave sinners was a familiar one in Jewish circles, learned and unlearned. Here in Talmud "Erubin" the subject of Gehenna comes up, entirely naturally, in the course of a discussion of other matters. The par-ticipants deal with both the scriptural topoi and the legal issues with practiced ease.

Rabbi Joshua ben Levi has said: What (is the meaning of) what is written (in Ps. 65:2): "Passing through the valley of Baca they make it a place of springs; yes, the early rain clothes it with blessings"?

Joshua ben Levi's exegesis, which follows, is not so arbitrary as perhaps it appears in translation. Each interpretation is based on the root of the Hebrew word under examination.

"Passing" is an allusion to men who transgress the will of the Holy One, blessed be He; "valley" (is an allusion to these men) for whom Gehenna is made deep; "of Baca" (signifies) that they weep and shed tears; "they make it a place of springs," like the constant flow of the altar drains; "the early rains clothe it with blessings," that is, they acknowledge the justice of their punishment and declare before Him, "Lord of the universe, You have judged well. You have condemned well and provided Gehenna for the wicked and Paradise for the righteous."

It would seem, then, on the basis of Rabbi Joshua ben Levi's exegesis of the verse in Psalms that even the wicked acknowledge the justice of God's judgment. We are not entirely surprised, however, to discover that there is another point of view, here expressed through Simeon ben Lakish, relying on his own understanding of the famous passage in Isaiah 66:24. The apparent conflict of opinions is soon resolved in favor of Joshua ben Levi.

[It might be objected that] this is not (so). For did not Rabbi Simeon ben Lakish state: The wicked do not repent even at the gate of Gehenna, for it is said, "And they shall go forth and look upon the carcasses of men who rebel against me . . . " (Isa. 66:24), where it is not said "who have rebelled" but "who rebel" (implying) that they go on rebelling forever? There is no contradiction since the former [that is, Ben Levi] refers to transgressors in Israel and the latter [Ben Lakish] to transgressors among idol worshipers. Logical argument also leads to this conclusion, since otherwise a contradiction would arise between two statements of Resh Lakish. For Resh Lakish (also) stated: The fire of Gehenna has no power over the transgressors in Israel, as may be inferred *a minori ad majus* from the golden altar: if (the gilt veneer) on the golden altar, which was only the thickness of a dinar, lasted for many years and the fire had no power over it, how much more would that be the case with the transgressors in Israel who are as full of good deeds as a pomegranate (with seed), as is said in Scripture, "Your temples are like a pomegranate" (Song of Songs 6:7), and Rabbi Simeon ben Lakish remarked: Do not read "Your temples" but "Your empty ones" (signifying) that even the worthless among you are as full of good deeds as a pomegranate.

If one is to follow Resh Lakish in this matter and maintain that Israelites do not suffer in Gehenna, are we forced to go back and reinterpret "passing through the valley of Baca"? No, the text continues.

. . . [T]hat (refers to the fact) that they [that is, the wicked Israelites] are at the time under sentence to suffer in Gehenna, but our father Abraham comes, brings them up and receives them, except such an Israelite as had immoral intercourse with the daughter of an idolater, since his foreskin is drawn forward and he cannot be discovered (by Abraham). Rabbi Kahana demurred. Now that you have laid down that "who rebels" implies that they go on rebelling, would you also maintain that where it is written in Scripture "who brings out" or "who brings up," that (the meaning is) "who always brings up" or "who always brings out"? So you must admit that (the meaning is) "who brought up" or "who brought out" and so too here "who rebelled."

The thread of the discussion returns to the authority with whom it began, Rabbi Jeremiah ben Eleazar, but it remains firmly on the last subject, Gehenna.

Rabbi Jeremiah further stated: Gehenna has three gates: one in the wilderness, one in the sea and one in Jerusalem. In the wilderness since it is written in Scripture, "Since they [Korah and his sons], and all that belongs to them, went down alive into the pit" (Num. 16:33). In the sea, since it is written in Scripture, "Out of the belly of the underworld I cried, and You heard my voice" (Jon. 2:3). In Jerusalem, since it is written in Scripture, "Says the Lord, whose fire is in Sion and His furnace in Jerusalem" (Isa. 31:9), and the school of Rabbi Ishmael taught that "whose fire is in Sion" refers to Gehenna and "His furnace in Jerusalem" refers to the gate of Gehenna.

Are there no more (gates) than that? Has not Rabbi Meryon in fact stated in the name of Rabbi Joshua ben Levi . . . : There are two palm trees in the Valley of Ben Hinnom and between them smoke rises, and it is (in connection with) this spot that we have learned "The stone palms of the iron mountain are fit (for the lulab), and this is the gate of Gehenna"? Is it possible that this is the same as "the one in Jerusalem"?

Rabbi Joshua ben Levi stated: Gehenna has seven names, and they are Sheol, Destruction, the Pit, Tumultuous Pit, Miry Clay, Shadow of Death and the Underworld. . . . Are there no more (names) than this? Is there not in fact the name of Gehenna? (This means) a valley that is as deep as the valley of Hinnom and into which all go down for gratuitous acts. . . .

(As for) Paradise, Resh Lakish said: If it is in the Land of Israel, its gate is Beth Shean; if it is in Arabia, its gate is Beth Gerem; and if it is Between the Rivers [that is, Syria-Mesopotamia], its gate is Damascus. (BT.Erubin 19a)

Sheol survives in Jewish thought as a dark and underground place, the world of graves and tombs, the abode of the dead. But it is Gehinnom, or Gehenna as it is called when it appears in the Greek of the Gospels, that is the place of punishment. It is somewhere far below, under the abyss or the ocean, but its original geographical site stays firm: the vent hole of Hell remains in the Ge ben Hinnom south of Jerusalem.

9. The Heavenly Garden

As we have seen, the "good thief" in Luke's Gospel is told that he will be with Jesus in Paradise. "Paradise," the Greek term borrowed from the Persian word for "royal park" or "plantation," was there and thereafter doing service as a translation for the Hebrew "Gan Eden," the Garden of Eden: Jesus' kingdom, and the abode of the blessed in the afterlife, is identical with the biblical Eden.

Throughout the Bible the name Eden is used only of Genesis' terrestrial paradise of Adam. Eventually, however, in post-Exilic times, the Garden of Eden became the name for the abode of the just after death. This was a new development. At first a place had been reserved, almost as a kind of celestial storage, for Enoch and Elijah, the two mortals taken up alive to heaven. By the first century B.C.E., when the later parts of the first Book of Enoch came to be written, there were others as well: "the elect who dwell in the garden of life" (1 Enoch 61:12). It is Enoch who speaks.

And he was lifted on the chariots of the spirit, and his name vanished from among men. And from that day I was not counted among them, and he placed me between two winds, between the north and the west, where the angels took the cords to measure for me the place of the chosen and the righteous. And there I saw the first fathers and the righteous who from the beginning of the world dwelt in that place. (1 Enoch 70: 2–4)

At about the same time, the Garden was being relocated from some not very certain site on earth into the remote heavens. The point was probably to move His saints closer to God after death. Indeed, some refer to Paradise as the abode of both God and the just, while others place the righteous and their Paradise in the third heaven, or even the seventh heaven, the highest of the firmaments and just below the abode of God. The following is Enoch's version of Paradise: it is located in the third heaven, and its physical features are now considerably more detailed than Genesis' rather spare account of the earthly Garden of Eden.

And these men [that is, Enoch's angel guides] led me from there to the third heaven and set me in the midst of Paradise. And that place is more beautiful than anything there is to see—all trees in full bloom, all fruit ripe, every kind of food always in abundance, every breeze fragrant. And there are four rivers flowing by in silent course: the whole garden is good, producing what is good to eat.

And the tree of life is in that place, where the Lord rests, when He goes into Paradise. And that tree is indescribable for the quality of its fragrance. . . . And every tree is laden with good fruit: there is no tree that is without fruit; and the whole place is blessed.

Paradise appears swept and garnished, but as yet uninhabited. Enoch's guides explain.

And I said, how very blessed is this place. The men answered me, This place, Enoch, is prepared for the righteous, who will endure hardships in this life, and mortify themselves, and turn their eyes away from unrighteousness, and execute true justice, to give bread to the hungry, and to cover the naked with a garment, and to lift up anyone who has fallen, and to help those who have been wronged, who live their lives in God's presence and serve Him alone. For them is this place prepared as their eternal inheritance. (2 Enoch 5:1–10)

This vision remained, in its essence, the standard Jewish conception of the positive side of the afterlife throughout the rabbinic period: there was a heavenly garden called Paradise whose still palpably physical pleasures were reserved for the righteous after the Judgment. Although who precisely might be included among its residents was debated, neither the reality nor the location of Paradise was cast into doubt by the masters of the Talmud.

10. Signs of the Times

Far more consequential than changes in Jewish ideas about the habitat of the dead and what befell them there was a radically new view of the destiny of God's creation. In the literature produced after the Exile there appears the entirely novel idea that this world will come to an end; and that end, far from being the outcome of a theorem, was sensed as imminent. It was assuredly a physical event. More important, it was God's providentially ordered moral happening: the End Time, though accompanied by unimaginable hardships and trials, would represent the Lord's vindication of His people. And it would be achieved by an agent from on high: a Messiah.

These themes begin in the prophets, but they find their most urgent and vivid presentations in the anonymous or pseudepigrapical works that were in wide circulation in Jewish circles from the second century B.C.E. onward. Since this End Time was felt, in varying degrees in different circles, to be rapidly approaching, one of the most popular themes in the new literature of eschatological visions and warnings was a description of the signs that would precede the End. There would be, the prophets and others warned, a time of troubles before the resolution. Joel, for example, describes in graphic terms both that "great and terrible day" and the ingathering of "the remnant" that will follow.

> After that,
> I will pour out My Spirit on all flesh;
> Your sons and your daughters shall prophesy,
> Your old men shall dream dreams,
> And your young men shall see visions;

I will even pour out My Spirit
Upon male and female slave in those days.
I will set portents in the sky and on the earth,
Blood and fire and pillars of smoke;
The sun shall be turned to darkness
And the moon into blood.

But everyone who invokes the name of the Lord shall escape, for
there shall be a remnant on Mount Sion and in Jerusalem, as the Lord
promised. Anyone who invokes the Lord will be among the survivors.

For lo! in those days and in that time,
When I restore the fortunes of Judah and Jerusalem,
I will gather all the nations,
And bring them down to the Valley of Jehoshaphat.
There I will contend with them
Over My very own people, Israel,
Which they scattered among the nations.
For they divided My land among themselves
And cast lots over My people;
And they bartered a boy for a whore,
And sold a girl for wine, which they drank.
(Joel 3:1–4:3)

11. "No Man Knows the Hour": The Second Coming of the Christ

For the Christians, with their ambiguity on whether the Kingdom had come or was still to be expected, the coming of the Messiah had to be converted into a twofold event: the historical incarnation of Jesus and a second, eschatological return to complete the messianic work. Indeed, Jesus himself foretold it: all three Synoptics have versions of Jesus' discourse about the Last Day, when the Son of Man will return for a second time. He will be preceded by the almost unimaginable catastrophes that Joel had already predicted for the "Day of the Lord." There will be impostors and false prophets, but then at last the true Messiah will come to gather his chosen ones to himself. This is Jesus' apocalyptic vision as Mark recounts it in his Gospel.

As he was leaving the Temple, one of his disciples exclaimed, "Look master, what huge stones! What fine buildings!" Jesus said to him, "You see these great buildings? Not one stone will be left upon another. All will be thrown down."

When he was sitting on the Mount of Olives facing the Temple, he was questioned privately by Peter, James, John and Andrew. "Tell us," they said, "when this will happen. What will be the sign when the fulfillment of this is at hand?"

Jesus began: "Take care that no one misleads you. Many will come claiming my name and saying, 'I am he'; and many will be misled by them. When you hear news of battle near at hand and the news of battles far away, do not be alarmed. Such things are bound to happen; but the end is still to come. For nation will make war upon nation, kingdom upon kingdom; there will be earthquakes in many places; there will be famines. With these things the birth pangs of the new age begin. . . . Those days will bring distress such as never has been until now since the beginning of the world which God created—and will never be again. If the Lord had not cut short that time of troubles, no living thing could survive. However, for the sake of his own, whom He has chosen, He has cut short the time.

"Then if anyone says to you, 'Look, here is the Messiah,' or, 'Look, there he is,' do not believe it. Impostors will come claiming to be messiahs, or prophets, and they will produce signs and wonders to mislead God's chosen, if such a thing were possible. But you, be on your guard; I have forewarned you of it all.

"But in those days, after that distress, the sun will be darkened; the moon will not give her light; the stars will come falling from the sky, the celestial powers will be shaken. Then will you see the Son of Man coming in the clouds with great power and glory, and he will send out his angels and gather his chosen from the four winds, from the farthest bounds of earth to the farthest bounds of heaven. . . .

"But about that day or that hour no one knows, not even the angels in heaven, not even the Son; only the Father." (Mark 13:1–32)

The Christian congregation that Paul committed to his care still had a vivid expectation of the "Day of the Lord." Paul's own interest in the Last Things was not particularly strong, as we shall see, but he did his best to reassure his flock at Thessalonica, who seemed particularly preoccupied with the Second Coming. Paul seeks to restrain their anxieties by referring them to Jesus' own pointing to the signs, as we have just seen in Mark.

And now, brothers, about the coming of our Lord Jesus Christ and his gathering us to himself: I beg you, do not suddenly lose your heads or alarm yourselves, whether at some oracular utterance, or pronouncement, or some letter purporting to come from us, alleging that the Day of the Lord is already here. Let no one deceive you in any way whatever. That day cannot come before the final rebellion against God, when wickedness will be revealed in human form, the man doomed to perdition. He is the enemy. . . . You cannot but remember that I told you this when I was still with you; you must now be aware of the restraining hand which ensures he shall be revealed only at the proper time. For already the secret power of wickedness is at work, secret only for the present until the Restrainer disappears from the scene. And then he will be revealed, that wicked man whom the Lord Jesus will destroy with the breath of his mouth and annihilate with the radiance of his coming. But the coming of that wicked man is the work of Satan. It will be attended by all the powerful signs and miracles of the Lie, and all the deception that sinfulness can impose on those doomed to destruction. Destroyed they shall be, because they did not open their minds to love of the truth, so as to find salvation. Therefore God puts them under a delusion, which works upon them to believe the lie, so that they may all be brought to judgment, all who do not believe the truth but make sinfulness their deliberate choice. (Paul, *To the Thessalonians* 2.2:1–12)

There were other questions as well. What of those believers who died before that Final Coming, for example?

This we tell you as the Lord's word: we who are left alive until the Lord comes shall not forestall those who have died; because at the word of God's command, at the sound of the archangel's voice and God's trumpet call, the Lord himself will descend from heaven; first the Christian dead will rise, then we who are left alive shall join them, caught up in clouds to meet the Lord in the air. Thus we shall always be with the Lord. Console one another, then, with these words.

About dates and times, my friends, we need not write to you, for you know perfectly well that the Day of the Lord comes like a thief in the night. . . . Sleepers sleep at night, and drunkards are drunk at night, but we, who belong to the daylight, must keep sober, armed with faith and love for coat of mail, and hope of salvation for helmet. For God has not destined us to the terrors of judgment, but to the full attainment of salvation through our Lord Jesus Christ. He died for us so that we, awake or asleep, might live in company with him. Therefore hearten one another, fortify one another, as indeed you do. (Paul, *To the Thessalonians* 1.4:15–5:13)

1 2. A Christian Apocalypse

The brief apocalypses in the three Synoptic Gospels were later fleshed out in highly imaginative detail by the final work included in the New Testament canon, the Revelation of John, from the pen of someone generally thought to be identical with the "beloved disciple" of Jesus and the author of the fourth Gospel, though the date of composition of the Revelation was probably close to the end of the first century. Here too the terrors of the Day of the Lord are spelled out, but there is the glory and the resurrection as well. The narrative begins with Jesus' return at the final act of the End Time.

I saw heaven open wide, and there was before me a white horse; and its rider's name was Faithful and True, for he was just in judgment and just in war. His eyes flamed fire and on his head were many diadems. Written upon him was a name known to none but himself, and he was robed in a garment drenched in blood. He was called the Word of God, and the armies of heaven followed him on white horses, clothed in fine linen, clean and shining. . . . And on his robe and on his thigh was written the name "King of Kings and Lord of Lords."

Then I saw an angel standing in the sun, and he cried aloud to all the birds flying in mid-heaven: "Come and gather for God's great supper, to eat the flesh of kings and commanders and fighting men, of horses and their riders, the flesh of all men, slave and free, great and small!" Then I saw the beast [that is, Rome and its divinized emperor] and the kings of the earth and their armies mustered to do battle with the Rider and his army. The beast was taken prisoner, and so was the false prophet who had worked miracles in its presence and deluded those that had received the mark of the beast and worshiped its image. The two of them were thrown alive into the lake of fire with its sulphurous flames. The rest were killed by the sword which went out of the Rider's mouth; and all the birds gorged themselves on their flesh.

Then I saw an angel coming down from heaven with the key of the abyss and a great chain in his hands. He seized the dragon, that serpent of old, the Devil or Satan, and chained him up for a thousand years; he threw him into the abyss, shutting and sealing it over him, so that he might seduce the nations no more until the thousand years were over. After that he must be let loose for a short while.

Then I saw thrones, and upon them sat those to whom judgment was committed. I could see the souls of those who had been beheaded for the sake of Christ's word and their testimony to Jesus, those who had not worshiped the beast and its image or received its mark on their forehead or hand. These came to life again and reigned with Christ for a thousand years, though the rest of the dead did not come to life until the thousand years were over. This is the first resurrection. Happy indeed, and one of God's own people, is the man who shares in this first resurrection! Upon such the second death has no claim; but they shall be priests of God and of Christ, and shall reign with him for the thousand years.

At the end of the thousand years Satan will return, according to this vision, and muster his forces for the final battle. The battle is ended by God himself in a great rain of fire from heaven; Satan is consigned to hell forever together with the Antichrist. It is then that the Final Judgment begins.

Then I saw a great white throne, and the One who sat upon it; from His presence earth and heaven vanished away, and no place was left for them. I could see the dead, great and small, standing before the throne; and the books were opened, the roll of the living. From what was written in these books the dead were judged upon the record of their deeds. . . . Then Death and Hades were flung into the lake of fire. This lake of fire is the second death, and into it were flung any whose names were not to be found in the roll of the living.

Then I saw a new heaven and a new earth, for the first heaven and the first earth had vanished, and there was no longer any sea. I saw the Holy City, the New Jerusalem, coming down out of heaven from God, made ready like a bride adorned for her husband. I heard a loud voice proclaiming from the throne, "Now at last God has His dwelling among men! He will dwell among them and they shall be His people, and God Himself will be with them. He will wipe every tear from their eyes; there shall be an end to death, and to mourning and crying and pain; for the old order has passed away."

Then He who sat on the throne said, "Behold, I am making all things new!" And He said to me, "Write this down for these words are trustworthy and true. Indeed, they are already fulfilled. 'I am Alpha and Omega, the beginning and the end. A draught from the water springs of life will be My free gift to the thirsty. All this is the victor's heritage; and I will be his God and he will be My son. But as for the cowardly, the faithless, and the vile, murderers, fornicators, sorcerers, idolaters and liars of every kind, their lot will be the second death, in the lake that burns with sulphurous flames.' " (Revelation 19:11–21:9)

13. The Second Coming: The Muslim Tradition

Muslims believed that Jesus did not die on the cross, as the Christians alleged, but had been taken up alive by God to heaven. He would, then, have to return to earth and suffer the death that is the common fate of all mankind. But his return had for the Muslims as much eschatological significance as it did for the Christians, and it was closely connected with the events of the End Time, as appears in this summary statement of Muslim messianism by Ibn Khaldun (d. 1406 C.E.).

It has been well known by all Muslims in every epoch, that at the end of time a man from the family of the Prophet will without fail make his appearance, one who will strengthen the religion and make justice triumph. The Muslims will follow him, and he will gain domination over the Muslim realm. He will be called the Mahdi [that is, the "Guided One"]. Following him, the Antichrist will appear, together with all the subsequent signs of the Hour (of the Last Judgment), as established in the sound tradition. After the Mahdi, Jesus will descend and kill the Antichrist. Or, Jesus will descend with the Mahdi, and help him kill the Antichrist, and have him as the leader in his prayers. (Ibn Khaldun, *Muqaddima* 3.51) [IBN KHALDUN 1967: 2:156]

The matter did not rest there, of course. The Muslim tradition had filled in many of the details regarding Jesus' return.

Abu Salih Shu ͨayb ibn Muhammad al-Bayhaqi has informed us with a chain of authorities back to Abu Hurayra how this latter related that the Messenger of God, upon whom be God's blessing and peace, said: "The Prophets are brethren, though of different mothers, and their religion is one and the same. I am the nearest of mankind to Jesus son of Mary, on both of whom be peace, because there has been no Prophet between him and me. It will come to pass that the son of Mary will descend among you as a just ruler. He will descend to my community and be my deputy [or Caliph] over them, so when you see him, give him recognition. He will be a man symmetrical in stature, of reddish-white (complexion), lank-haired, as though his hair were dripping perfume though it had not been moistened. He will come down in a greenish-yellow garment, will break crosses and kill swine, will put an end to the poll tax [that is, the tax paid by non-Muslims under Islam], will raise the welcoming cry from al-Rawha when he comes for the Greater and the Lesser Pilgrimage, undertaking them both with zeal. He will make war on behalf of Islam, until in his time he destroys all religions save that of Islam, and there will thenceforward be but one single prostration of obeisance, namely that to God,

Lord of the Worlds. Also in his time God will destroy the Antichrist, the lying al-Dajjal. Then there will be such security on earth that lions will pasture freely with camels, tigers with cattle, wolves with sheep, children will play with serpents and no one will do harm to anyone. Then he will die, and the Muslims will pray over him and bury him at Medina beside the grave of Umar. Read, if you will, the words 'There are none of the People of the Book but will believe in him before his death, and on the Day of Resurrection he will be a witness against them' (Quran 4:159)."
(Tha'alibi, *Stories of the Prophets*) [JEFFERY 1962: 596–597]

Additional specifics are given in a series of traditions cited by Ibn Khaldun.

The final descent of Jesus will be at the time of the afternoon prayer, when three-fourths of the Muslim day has passed. . . . It has been stated in the tradition that Jesus will descend at the white minaret east of Damascus. He will descend between two yellowish-colored ones, that is, two light-saffron-yellow-colored garments. He will place his hands upon the wings of two angels. His hair is as long as though he had just been released from a dungeon. When he lowers his head, it rains, and when he lifts it up, jewels resembling pearls pour down from him. He has many moles on his face. Another tradition has: "Square built and reddish white." Still another has: "He will marry in the *gharb*," *gharb* meaning a bucket as used by the Bedouins. Thus the meaning is that he will take a woman from among the Bedouins as his wife. She will bear his children. The tradition also mentions that Jesus will die after forty years. It is also said that Jesus will die in Medina and be buried at the side of Umar ibn al-Khattab. And it is said that Abu Bakr and Umar [that is, the first two Caliphs of the Muslim community] will rise from the dead between two Prophets (Muhammad and Jesus). (Ibn Khaldun, *Muqaddima* 3.51)
[IBN KHALDUN 1967: 2:193–194]

14. "A Man from My Family"

Thus, the Muslims' expectation of the End Time included the return of Jesus. What is new in the Islamic tradition is that he will come in the company of, or following upon, another messianic figure, the Mahdi, or "Guided One." There were in circulation a great many Prophetic traditions on the subject, the chief of which are reported and analyzed by Ibn Khaldun in his Prolegomenon to History. *Typical of the simplest and most direct of them are the two following, which occur in canonical collections of the traditions of the Prophet by al-Tirmidhi and Abu Dawud and are reported here by Ibn Khaldun.*

With their chain of transmitters going back to Ibn Mas'ud, al-Tirmidhi and Abu Dawud have published the following tradition . . . on the authority of the Prophet: "If no more than one day remained of the world . . . God would cause the day to last until there be sent a man from me—or: from my family—whose name will tally with my name, and the name of whose father will tally with the name of my father." . . . The version of al-Tirmidhi has: "The world will not be destroyed until the Arabs are ruled by a man from my family, whose name will tally with my name." . . . Al-Tirmidhi states in connection with both versions that it is a good and sound tradition. (Ibn Khaldun, *Muqaddima* 3.51)
[IBN KHALDUN 1967: 2:159–160]

Muhammad could not serve as his own messiah; he was a mortal man and he was dead. The Islamic focus on the messiah as restorer came to rest, then, on one of the Prophet's family. The messiah will be, the traditions begin to insist, a descendant of one of the offspring of Muhammad's daughter Fatima. This was a tribute not so much to Fatima as to her husband Ali, the cousin of the Prophet and the figure about whom the major schism in Islam, that between Sunnis and Shi'ites, had developed.

Abu Dawud published a tradition relating to Ali in his chapter on the Mahdi . . . on the authority of Abu al-Tufayl, on the authority of Ali, on the authority of the Prophet, who said: "If only one day in the whole duration of the world remained, God would send a man of my family who would fill the world with justice, as it has been filled with injustice." With a chain of transmitters going back to Ali, Abu Dawud also published the following tradition . . . on the authority of Abu Ishaq al-Sabi'i, who said that Ali, looking at his son al-Hasan, said, "This son of mine is a lord, as he was called by (his grandfather) the Messenger of God. From his spine there will come forth a man who will be called by the name of your prophet and who will resemble him physically, but will not resemble him in character. . . ."

The following tradition, furthermore, was published by Abu Dawud, as well as by Ibn Maja and al-Hakim through Ali ibn Nufayl . . . on the authority of Umm Salima, who said: I heard the Messenger of God say: "The Mahdi is one of my family, one of the descendants of Fatima." This is Abu Dawud's version. He did not make any critical remarks concerning it. Ibn Maja's version has: "The Mahdi is one of Fatima's descendants." Al-Hakim's version has: "I heard the Messenger of God mention the Mahdi. He said, 'Yes, he is a fact, and he will be one of the children of Fatima.'" (Ibn Khaldun, *Muqaddima* 3.51) [IBN KHALDUN 1967: 2:162–165]

Shiʿite speculation about the return of the Mahdi centered more and more on the return of their "concealed" Imam, but Sunni and Shiʿite alike devoted considerable time and energy to what Ibn Khaldun obviously considered a useless pursuit.

There are many similar such statements. The time, the man and the place (of the Mahdi's return) are clearly indicated in them. But the time passes, and there is not the slightest trace (of the prediction coming true). Then some new suggestion is adopted which, as one can see, is based upon linguistic equivocations, imaginary ideas, and astrological judgments. The life of every one of those people is spent on such things. (Ibn Khaldun, *Muqaddima* 3.51) [IBN KHALDUN 1967: 2:195]

15. The Resurrection of the Flesh

As we have read, Paul addressed the question of the Final Judgment in letters to his flock at Thessalonica. There he was chiefly concerned, because the Thessalonians were, with the imminence of the Second Coming of Jesus. But the new Christians elsewhere had different queries, regarding the resurrection of the dead, for example.

You may ask, how are the dead raised? In what kind of body? How foolish! The seed you sow does not come to life unless it has first died; and what you sow is not the body that shall be, but a naked grain, perhaps of wheat, or of some other kind; and God clothes it with the body of His choice, each seed with its own particular body. All flesh is not the same flesh: there is flesh of men, flesh of beasts, of birds and of fishes, all different. There are heavenly bodies and earthly bodies. . . . So it is with the resurrection of the dead. What is sown in the earth as a perishable thing is raised imperishable. Sown in humiliation, it is raised in glory; sown as an animal body, it is raised as a spiritual body. If there is such a thing as an animal body, there is also a spiritual body.

To explain this "spiritual body," Paul invokes one of his more familiar notions, the parallelism between Adam and Jesus.

If there is such a thing as an animal body, there is also a spiritual body. It is in this sense that Scripture says, "The first man, Adam, became an animate being," whereas the last Adam has become a life-giving spirit. Observe, the spiritual does not come first; the animal body comes first, and then the spiritual. The first man was made of the "dust of the earth"; the second man is from heaven. The man made of dust is the pattern of all men of dust, and the heavenly man is the pattern of all heavenly men. As we have all worn the likeness of the man made of dust, so we shall wear the likeness of the heavenly man.

What I mean, my brothers, is this: flesh and blood can never possess the kingdom of God, and the perishable cannot possess immortality. Listen, I will unfold a mystery: we shall not all die (before the return of Christ), but we shall all be changed in a flash, in the twinkling of an eye, at the last trumpet call. For the trumpet will sound, and the dead will rise immortal, and we shall be changed. This perishable being must be clothed with the imperishable, and what is mortal must be clothed with immortality. (Paul, *To the Corinthians* 1.15:35–53)

Paul's metaphor of the seed sown and reborn is taken up and elaborated by Gregory of Nyssa (ca. 335–394 C.E.), brother of Basil of Caesarea and himself a prominent theologian.

It seems to me that the argument of the Apostle (Paul) [that is, in the text just cited] is in perfect accord with our own idea of the resurrection, and manifests much the same notion as our definition, which asserted that the resurrection is nothing other than the reconstitution of our nature to its pristine state. For as we learn from Scripture, in the first cosmogony [that is, in Genesis], the earth first brought forth a green plant, and then a seed was produced from this plant, and this latter seed, once it had fallen to the ground, produced another plant in the same form as the original growth. Now the inspired Apostle says that this is what happens also at the resurrection. Thus we learn from him not only that human nature is changed into a far nobler state, but also what we are to hope for is just this: the return of human nature to its pristine condition. The original process was not that of an ear from the seed, but of the seed from the ear, the ear thereafter growing from the seed.

The order of events in this simile clearly shows that all the happiness which will be ours through the resurrection will be a return to our original state of grace. Originally we too were, in a sense, a full ear, but we were withered by the torrid heat of sin; and then on our dissolution by death the earth received us. But in the spring of the resurrection the earth will again display this naked grain of our body in an ear, tall, luxuriant and upright, reaching up as high as heaven, and, for stalk and beard, decked with incorruption and all the other godlike characteristics. . . . The first ear was the first man, Adam. But with the entrance of evil, human nature was divided into a plurality; and, as happens with ripened grain in the ear, each individual person was stripped of the beauty of the ear and mingled with the earth. But in the resurrection we are reborn in that pristine beauty, becoming the infinite number of harvest fields instead of that single original ear. (Gregory of Nyssa, *On the Soul and the Resurrection*)

Augustine too speaks to Paul's text, not to the seed simile but to the difficult notion of a "spiritual body."

When the spirit is subservient to the flesh it is appropriately called carnal, and when it is subject to the spirit it is rightly called spiritual, not because it has become spirit, as some have inferred from the text of Scripture that says "sown as an animal body, it is raised as a spiritual body," but rather because it will be subject to the spirit, readily offering total and wonderful obedience. And this will lead to the fulfillment of their [that is, the souls of the dead saints] desire, the secure attainment of assured immortality, the removal of all feeling of discomfort, all corruptibility and reluctance. (Augustine, *The City of God* 13.20)

16. Creation Restored

There were Christians whose expectations of a physical renewal in the End Time went beyond the mere resurrection of individuals' bodies. Ireneus (d. ca. 200 C.E.), for example, had this broad vision of "the restored creation of the righteous."

Some men hold beliefs which have been introduced from heretical discourses; they are ignorant of God's ways and of the mystery of the resurrection of the just and of their kingdom, the first of which is the beginning of immortality, while the kingdom is the means by which such as have proved worthy are gradually accustomed to receive God. For this reason we must say something on this subject and explain that in the restored creation the righteous must rise first at the appearance of God to receive the inheritance promised by God to the fathers, and to reign in it; then follows the Judgment. For it is only right that they should receive the reward of their endurance in that (same) created order in which they suffered trouble and pain and were much tested by sufferings. . . . Therefore this created order must be restored to its first condition and be made subject to the righteous without hindrance. (Ireneus, *Against the Heresies* 5.32.1)

This understanding that at the Judgment all of physical creation will be restored to a pristine glorified state casts light for Ireneus on a remark made by Jesus to his disciples at the Last Supper.

I tell you, never again shall I drink from the fruit of the vine until that day when I drink it new with you in the kingdom of my Father. (Matthew 26:29)

Jesus promised [Ireneus resumes] to "drink from the fruit of the vine" with his disciples and in so doing he indicated two things: the inheritance of the earth in which the new fruit of the vine will be drunk, and the physical resurrection of his disciples. For it is the body which arises anew which receives the new wine, and we cannot conceive of him drinking from the fruit of the vine once he has taken his place with his followers in the region above the heavens. And more, those who drink it are not disembodied, since to drink wine belongs to the body rather than to the spirit. (Ireneus, *Against the Heresies* 5.33.1)

17. A Millennial Kingdom

Ireneus' reflections on "the resurrection of the just and their kingdom," while they are presented as a simple, almost matter-of-fact extension of the belief in a return to life of the bodies and souls of the elect, are nourished by another New Testament text that had a profound influence on later Christian thinking and imagining about the Last Things. It comes from the apocalyptic Book of Revelation.

Then I saw an angel coming down from heaven with the key of the abyss and a great chain in his hands. He seized the dragon, that serpent of old, the Devil or Satan, and chained him up for a thousand years; he threw him into the abyss, shutting and sealing it over him, so that he might seduce the nations no more until the thousand years were over. After that he must be let loose for a short while.

Then I saw thrones, and upon them sat those to whom judgment was committed. I could see the souls of those who had been beheaded for the sake of God's word and their testimony to Jesus, those who had not worshiped the beast and its image or received its mark on their forehead or hand. These came to life again and reigned with Christ for a thousand years, though the rest of the dead did not come to life until the thousand years were over. This (raising of the martyrs) is the first resurrection. Happy indeed, and one of God's own people, is the man who shares in this first resurrection! Upon such the second death has no claim; but they shall be priests of God and of Christ, and shall reign with him for the thousand years.

After the millennium Satan is once again released, only to be defeated once again and consumed by fire sent down from heaven. There follows the Final Judgment.

Then I saw a great white throne, and the One who sat upon it; from His presence earth and heaven vanished away, and no place was left for them. I could see the dead, great and small, standing before the throne; and the books were opened. Then another book was opened, the roll of the living. From what was written in these books the dead were judged upon the record of their deeds. . . . Then Death and Hades were flung into the lake of fire. This lake of fire is the second death, and into it were flung any whose names were not to be found in the roll of the living. (Revelation 20:1–15)

The notion of a thousand-year reign of Christ's kingdom before the Final Judgment and the beginning of eternity took strong hold in certain Christian quarters. Here are Tertullian's reflections on the Millennium from about 207 C.E.

It is also our belief that a kingdom has been promised to us on earth, and before we attain heaven; but in a condition other than this, namely, in the (first) resurrection. That resurrection will last for a thousand years, in a city of God's making, a Jerusalem sent down from heaven, which the Apostle (Paul) also describes as "our mother from above" (Gal. 4:26); and when he proclaims that our . . . citizenship "is in heaven" (Phil. 3:20), he is surely ascribing it to a heavenly city. . . . We maintain that this is the city designed by God for the reception of the saints at the (first) resurrection, and for favoring them with abundance of all goods, spiritual goods to be sure, in compensation for the goods we have despised or lost in this present age. For indeed it is right and worthy of God that His servants should also rejoice in the same place where they suffered affliction in His name. This is the purpose of the kingdom; it will last a thousand years, during which the saints will arise sooner or later, according to their degrees of merit, and then, when the resurrection of the saints is completed, the destruction of the world and the just conflagration will be accomplished; we shall be "changed in a moment" into the angelic substance, by the "putting on of incorruption" (1 Cor. 15:52–53), and we shall be transferred to the celestial kingdom. (Tertullian, *Against Marcion* 3:24)

18. Paul in the Third Heaven

For the Christians, as for the Jews, what awaited both saint and sinner in the afterlife was justice, justice that would be meted out not merely in another time but in another place. For Paul, that "other place" was already located in the world above. Here in his letter to the flock at Corinth he speaks of himself, as often, in the third person.

I am obliged to boast. It does no good; but I shall go on to tell of visions and revelations granted by the Lord. I know a Christian man who fourteen years ago (whether in the body or out of it, I do not know—God knows) was caught up as far as the third heaven. And I know that this same man (whether in the body or out of it, I do not know—God knows) was caught up into Paradise and heard words so secret that human lips may not repeat them. (Paul, *To the Corinthians* 2.12:1–4)

This is oblique boasting at best, unmistakable as to the fact but with no revelation of what Paul saw in the third heaven. The early Christian tradition did not scruple to fill in the details. In the so-called Apocalypse of Paul we can see how fourth-century Christians combined Genesis' description of Adam's earthly garden with Greek features and moved the entire landscape to the world above. Paul's alleged account begins exactly where the letter to the Corinthians ends.

I peered up into the height and I saw there other angels whose faces shone like the sun. Their limbs were girt with girdles of gold, and they bore palms in their hands, and the sign of God; they were clothed in garments on which was written the name of the Son of God. (*Apocalypse of Paul* 12)

And he [that is, Paul's angel guide] took me away from where I had seen all these sights, and there before me was a river of white, whiter than the whiteness of milk. I said to the angel, "And what is this?" And he replied: "Before you is Lake Acherusia, where the City of Christ is located. But it is not permitted to every man to go into that city, since this is the way which leads to God. And so if anyone is a fornicator and ungodly but turns and repents and produces the appropriate fruits of repentance, then when first he leaves the body he is brought here and worships God and is then handed over at God's command to the angel Michael, who baptizes him in Lake Acherusia and leads him into the city with those who have not sinned." . . .

Then the angel said to me: "Follow me and I shall lead you into the city of Christ." He took his stand by Lake Acherusia and put me in a golden boat; then about three thousand angels sang hymns in my presence until I reached the city of Christ.

The city of Christ is surrounded by the same four rivers found in Eden (Gen. 2: 10–14), though they now flow, as they did for Enoch, in a more allegorical fashion.

And in the round of the city there were found twelve gates of great beauty, and four rivers which encircled it. . . . And I asked the angel: "What are these rivers which encircle this city?" And he replied: "These are the four rivers whose abundant flow is for those who are in this land of promise; as for their names, the river of honey is called Phison; and the river of milk, Euphrates; and the river of oil, Gihon; and the river of wine, the Tigris. Since the righteous, during their time in the world did not exert the power they had over these things and so went hungry without them and afflicted themselves for the name of the Lord God, so when they enter this city the Lord will bestow these same upon them beyond number or measure." (*Apocalypse of Paul* 22–23)

19. An Angelic Account of the Afterlife

Like Paul before him, and like many others in an even earlier Jewish tradition, Muhammad too was taken on a heavenly journey. The original intent of the account of his ascension, hinted at in Quran 17:1 and fleshed out in some detail in Ibn Ishaq's Life, *may have been to validate Muhammad's credentials as a prophet. But when that no longer seemed necessary, the heavenly journey could serve, as it had for any number of figures from Enoch to Paul, as an occasion to lay out both the geography and the demography of the afterlife. In this thirteenth-century example, however, it is not Muhammad who has the vision but his guide upon that journey, the angel Gabriel, a fact that makes it possible to give a view of Gehenna as well as of Heaven.*

Yazid al-Raqashi has related from Anas ibn Malik that Gabriel came to the Prophet, may God's blessing and peace be upon him, at an unwonted hour and with a changed countenance. The Prophet, God's blessing and peace be upon him, said: "How is it that I see your countenance changed?" He answered: "O Muhammad, I have come to you in that hour when God has given command that the bellows blow up the Fire. No man who knows that Gehenna is a reality, that the fire therein is a reality, that the torment of the tomb is a real thing, and that God's punishment is even greater (than thought) ought to be in tranquillity till he is secure therefrom." The Prophet, upon whom may God bestow His blessing and peace, said: "O Gabriel, describe Gehenna to me." He replied, "Very well. When God, may He be exalted, created Gehenna He had it stoked for a thousand years till it grew red. Then he had it stoked for another thousand years till it grew white. Then He had it stoked for another thousand years till it went black. So it is black as the darkest night, but its flames and burning coals may never be put out."

The physical description of Gehenna continues until Gabriel reaches the gates of the descending circles of Hell, where he has an opportunity of sorting out the Islamic hierarchy of sinners. "Are they like our gates?" Muhammad asks.

"No!" Gabriel said. "They open one below the other, gate after gate, between a seventy years' journey, and each gate is seventy times hotter than the gate that preceded it. God's enemies are driven to it, and as they reach its gate the Zabaniya [or infernal attendants] meet them with fetters and chains. The chain is inserted in the man's mouth and brought out his rectum. His left hand is fettered to his neck and his right hand is thrust through his heart and pulled out between his shoulders, where it is fastened with chains. Moreover, every human will be chained to a satan." . . .

The Prophet, upon whom be God's blessing and peace, said: "Who are the dwellers in those gates?" Gabriel answered: "The lowest section has in it the Hypocrites [that is, those Medinese who pretended to believe in the Prophet; Quran 4:145], those of the People of the Table who disbelieved [that is, disbelieved in Jesus' miracle; Quran 5:115], and the People of the Pharaoh's household [that is, those who disbelieved in Moses' miracle; Quran 40:46]. Its name is Hawiya (101:9). The second section (upward) has in it the polytheists. Its name is Jahim (69:30). The third in it has the Sabians. Its name is Saqar (74:26ff.). The fourth section has in it Iblis [that is, the Fallen Angel] and his followers, and the Magians [that is, the Zoroastrians]. Its name is Laza (70:15). The fifth section has the Jews in it. It is called Hutama (104:4). The sixth section has the Christians in it. Its name is Saʿir (4:10)."

At this point Gabriel held back out of respect for the Messenger of God, may God's blessing and peace be upon him, but he, may God's blessing and peace be upon him, said: "Are you not going to inform me about the dwellers in the seventh (or uppermost) section?" So he replied: "In it are those of your community who have committed grave sins and have died without having repented." At this the Prophet, may God's blessing and peace be upon him, fell down in a swoon, but Gabriel set his head on his own breast until he recovered. When he recovered he said: "O Gabriel, great is my affliction and violent is my grief. Can it be that any of my community will enter the Fire?" "Yes," he said, "those of your community who are guilty of grave sins." At that the Messenger of God, upon whom be God's blessing and peace, wept, and Gabriel also wept. (Samarqandi, *Arousing the Heedless*) [JEFFERY 1962: 233–235]

20. Hades and Hell

It is clear from the Jewish apocalypses of the second century B.C.E. onward that Jewish ideas of the afterlife, in details if not in substance, were being affected by Greek notions of the underworld. Orpheus in Greek mythology, Odysseus in the Odyssey, and finally Aeneas in Virgil's epic all made circumstantial trips into Hades, journeys that fixed in literary form both popular and learned ideas about the afterlife. Thus

the biblical Sheol passed into a punitive but still Jewish Gehinnom and then, from
1 Enoch onward, to a composite Gehenna-Hades.

The Gospels reflect a view that is still somewhat more Gehenna than Hades;
but once the Christian movement passed out of its native Jewish environment, more
and more elements of Greco-Roman eschatology began to appear in the Christians'
accounts. So close was the resemblance, in fact, that Tertullian had to defend himself
against the charge that the Christians had stolen their ideas of the afterlife from the
pagans.

We are also derided because we maintain that that God is going to
judge the world, just as the (pagan) poets and philosophers place a judgment seat in the underworld. And if we threaten Gehenna, which is a
store of hidden subterranean fire for purpose of punishment, we are
received with hoots of derision, though they too have a (fiery) river
Pyriphlegethon in the abode of the dead. And if we would mention Paradise, a place of divine delight appointed to receive the spirits of the saints
which is separated from the knowledge of this everyday world by a kind
of fire zone, then the Elysian Fields have anticipated the Faith. Whence,
I ask you, come these similarities to our teachings in the (pagan) philosophers and poets? They are simply taken from our holy teachings, which,
since they are earlier, are the more trustworthy and the more credible.
(Tertullian, *Apology* 47)

Tertullian is not terribly embarrassed by the resemblance, then; nor apparently were
the many other Christians who continued to elaborate on both the geography and
the theodicy of the underworld. The late-fourth-century Apocalypse of Paul *has*
already been cited on its revelations about the "city of Christ" that awaits the
virtuous in the next world; it is even more explicit on what awaits the damned.
"Come," says Paul's angel guide, "follow me and I shall show you the souls of the
godless and sinners that you may know what the place is like."

I saw a river boiling with fire, and in it was a great crowd of men and
women immersed up to their knees, while others were immersed up to
their navels, and others up to their lips and hair. I asked the angel: "Sir,
who are these people in the river of fire?" And the angel answered and
said to me: "These are they who are neither hot nor cold because they
were found neither among the number of the righteous nor among the
number of the godless. They spent the period of their sojourn on earth
by passing some days in prayer but other days in sin and fornication right
up to the moment of their deaths." And I asked him: "And who are the
ones who are immersed up to their knees in fire?" "These are those who,
after they have left the church spend their time indulging in strange dis-

courses. Those, however, who are immersed up to the navel are those who, after they have received the body and blood of Christ, go away off and fornicate and do not leave off sinning until they die. And those who are immersed up their lips are the ones who, on meeting in God's church, spend their time slandering one another. Those immersed up to the eyebrows are those who nod signs to each other and so secretly prepare evil against their neighbor." (*Apocalypse of Paul* 31)

These are relatively mild punishments compared to what follows.

   . . . I saw girls wearing black clothing and four fearsome angels with blazing chains in their hands. They placed the chains on the girls' necks and led them into the darkness. I tearfully asked the angel: "Who are these, sir?" And he said to me: "They are women who, though they were appointed as virgins, defiled their virginity before being given to their husbands, and that without the knowledge of their parents. And it is for that reason they continuously pay their own particular penalty." . . .

   And I saw other men and women suspended by their eyebrows and their hair, and they were dragged along by a river of fire. I asked: "Who are those, sir?" And he said to me: "They are those who did not give themselves to their own husbands and wives but rather to adulterers, and for that reason they continuously pay their own particular penalty."

   And I saw other men and women covered with dust, and their faces were like blood, and they were in a pit of tar and brimstone, and they were running along in a fiery river. And I asked: "Who are those, sir?" And he said to me: "These are the ones who have committed the iniquity of Sodom and Gomorrah, men with men, and for that reason they continuously pay the penalty." (*Apocalypse of Paul* 39)

Next Paul sees men and women being strangled in the fire. They are, he is told, those who killed their own children.

   But their children appealed to the Lord God and to the angels who oversee the punishments, saying: "Defend us from our parents, for they have defiled what God has fashioned; they bear the name of God but they do not keep His commandments, and they give us as food to dogs and to be trampled by pigs; and they threw others of us into the river." But those children were handed over to the angels of Tartarus who were in charge of the punishments, so that they might lead them to a spacious place of mercy. Their fathers and mothers were, however, strangled in an everlasting punishment.

Paul is aghast and breaks into tears.

The angel said to me. "Why are you weeping? Are you more compassionate than the Lord God, who is blessed forever, who has assigned judgment, and has allowed every man to choose good or evil and act as he wishes?" Again I wept even more vehemently, and he said to me: "You are weeping and you have not yet seen the greater punishments? Follow me and you will see some that are seven times greater than these."

And he brought me to the north, to the place of all punishments, and he placed me above a well, which I found was sealed with seven seals. . . . And when the well was opened, there instantly arose from it a foul and evil smell which was far worse than all the punishments. And I looked into the well and saw on all sides fiery masses burning. . . . The angel said to me: "If someone is sent down into this well of the abyss, and it is sealed above him, no reference is ever made to him in the presence of the Father and the Son and the Holy Spirit and the holy angels." And I said: "And who is it who is sent into this well?" And he said to me: "Here are all those who have not confessed that Christ entered into the flesh and that the Virgin Mary bore him, and who say that the bread of the Eucharist and the cup of the blessing are not the body and blood of Christ."

And I looked away from the north and toward the west, and there I saw the worm that never rests, and in that place there was gnashing of teeth. The worm was a cubit in length and had two heads. And I saw there men and women amidst the cold and gnashing of teeth. And I asked and said: "Sir, who are these people in this place?" And he said to me: "These are those who say that Christ has not risen from the dead and that this flesh does not rise." (*Apocalypse of Paul* 40–42)

21. The Harrowing of Hell

This graphic approach to the afterlife arises in part from a juridical and pastoral concern to have eschatological punishments seem to fit the offenses to which they are attached, simply as a matter of God's justice. It was this same concern, as we shall see, that caused some to think there was a place between Heaven/Paradise and Gehenna/Hell, which came to be called Purgatory, where God's justice might be fulfilled, or even perhaps tempered, through remedial rather than punitive punishments. On the same score, room had to be found for the Limbo of Children, that "spacious place of mercy" hinted at in the Apocalypse of Paul *as the final resting place of minors incapable of sin or virtue and so incapable of either meriting Heaven or deserving Hell. Finally, the Limbo of Patriarchs was reserved as the resting place of the souls of the righteous who died before the coming of Jesus and whose release was the object of Jesus' "harrowing of Hell." There is a prediction in the Gospels*

*that Jesus would descend into the underworld after his death, though with no details
as to how or why that might be accomplished.*

"I tell you this: there is not a thoughtless word that comes from
men's lips but that they will have to account for it on the day of judgment. For out of your own mouth you will be acquitted and out of your
own mouth condemned."

At this some of the doctors of the law and the Pharisees said, "Master, we should like you show us a sign." He answered, "It is a wicked,
godless generation that asks for a sign. The only sign that will be given it
is the sign of the prophet Jonah. Jonah was in the sea monster's belly for
three days and three nights, and in the same way the Son of Man will be
three days and three nights in the bowels of the earth." (Matthew 12:
36–40)

*By the turn from the second into the third Christian century there was no doubt—
indeed, there may have been none from the beginning—as to what this "sign"
meant.*

Among us the underworld is thought of as a bare cavity or some kind
of cesspool of the world open to the sky; rather, it is a vast space in a deep
pit beneath the earth, a hidden depth in the very bowels of the earth,
since we read that Christ spent three days "in the bowels of the earth"
(Matt. 12:40), that is, in the innermost recess which is concealed within
the earth itself, and hollowed out within it and lying atop the abysses
which stretch away underneath. Now Christ is God, because he both died
as man according to the Scriptures and was buried according to those
same Scriptures, and here too he fulfilled the law of humanity by comply-
ing with the condition of human death in the underworld; nor did he
"ascend to the heights" of heaven until he had previously "descended into
the depths" (Eph. 4:8–9) of the earth that he might make the prophets
and the patriarchs sharers of himself. (Tertullian, *On the Soul* 55)

22. The Bosom of Abraham

*Matthew's reference to Jesus' descent into the "bowels of the earth" was connected
with the place called the "Bosom of Abraham" in this celebrated parable in Luke.*

There was once a rich man who dressed in purple and the finest
linen and feasted in great magnificence every day. At his gate, covered
with sores, lay a poor man named Lazarus, who would have been glad to
satisfy his hunger from the scraps from the rich man's table. Even the
dogs used to come and lick his sores.

One day the poor man died and was carried away by the angels to
Abraham's bosom. The rich man also died and was buried, and in Hades,
where he was in torment, he looked up, and there far away was Abraham
and Lazarus at his side. "Abraham, my father," he called out, "take pity
on me. Send Lazarus to dip the tip of his finger in water, to cool my
tongue, for I am in agony in this fire." But Abraham said, "Remember,
my child, that all the good things fell to you while you were alive and all
the bad to Lazarus; now he has his consolation here and it is you who is
in agony. But that is not all: there is a great chasm between us; no one
from our side who wants to reach you can cross it, and none can pass
from your side to us." (Luke 16:19–26)

*Where Abraham and Lazarus lay, then, was in the Limbo of Patriarchs, patiently
awaiting the coming of Christ for their release; the rich man was begging some
assistance from another place, the remote ancestor of what would become in Western
Christianity Purgatory. How Abraham and others found their release is described
in the third- or fourth-century popular account of Jesus' trial and execution called
The Gospel of Nicodemus. In this apocryphal gospel Jesus' descent to Hell and the
substance of the Lazarus parable have been brought together into a single dramatic
narrative. The source for this account is said to be that Simeon who performed the
circumcision rite on Jesus (Luke 2:25–35); he had died and had been in the
underworld when Jesus arrived there. The time is midnight on the Friday of Jesus'
crucifixion.*

We were then in Hades with all who have died since the beginning
of the world. And at the hour of midnight there shone forth in the
darkness there a light like the light of the sun, and the light fell upon all
of us and now we saw one another. And immediately our father, Abraham, together with the patriarchs and the prophets, was filled with joy,
and they said to one another: "This shining comes from a great light."
The prophet Isaiah, who was present there, said: "This shining comes
from the Father and the Son and the Holy Spirit. I prophesied this when
I was still living, when I said 'The land of Zabulon and the land of Neph-
thalim, the people that sat in darkness saw a great light.' " Then there
came into our midst another figure, a hermit from the wilderness. The
patriarchs asked him: "Who are you?" He replied: "I am John, the last of
the prophets, who made straight the ways of the Son of God . . . the only
begotten Son of God comes here so that whoever believes in him should
be saved, and whoever does not believe in him should be condemned.
Therefore I say to you all: When you see him, do you all worship him. For
it is only now that you have an opportunity for repenting the fact that you

worshiped idols in the vain world above and sinned. At another time it will be impossible." (*Gospel of Nicodemus* 18–19)

Jesus at length appears at the entrance of Hades.

... [T]he gates of brass were shattered, and the gates of iron were crushed, and all the dead who were bound up were loosed from their chains, and we with them. And the King of Glory entered in like a man and all the dark places of Hades were filled with light. ... The King of Glory stretched forth his right hand and took hold of our forefather Adam and raised him up. Then he turned also to the rest and said: "Come with me, all you who have suffered death through the tree which this man [that is, Adam] touched. For behold, I raise you all up again through the tree of the cross." ... The Savior blessed Adam with the sign of the cross on his forehead. And he did likewise to the patriarchs and prophets and martyrs and all the forefathers, and he took them and leaped up from out of Hades. And as he went the holy fathers sang his praises, trailing behind him and saying: "Blessed be he who comes in the name of the Lord. Alleluia. To him be the glory of all the saints." (Ibid. 21–24)

They mount up to the heavenly Paradise. In their company is "a humble man carrying a cross on his shoulder."

The holy fathers asked him: "Who are you, you who have the appearance of a thief, and what is the cross you carry on your shoulder?" He answered; "I was, as you say, a robber and thief in the world, and therefore the Jews took me and delivered me to the death of the cross together with our Lord Jesus Christ. ... And he said to me, 'Truly, I say to you, today you shall be with me in Paradise' (Luke 23:43). So I came to Paradise carrying my cross and found Michael the Archangel. ... And when the flaming sword saw the sign of the cross, it opened to me and I entered in. Then the archangel said to me: 'Wait a short while. For Adam also, the forefather of the race of men, comes with the rest of the righteous that they also may enter here.' And now that I have seen you, I have come to meet you." When the saints heard this they all cried with a loud voice: "Great is our Lord and great is his power!" (Ibid. 26)

We stand here near the narrative and descriptive beginning of the Christian understanding of the punitive and purgatorial states of the afterlife. How they are shaped at the end of the process of their systematization appears in this theological handbook from 1268 C.E.

In order to know what Hell Christ descended to, we must remember that Hell has two meanings, and refers either to the punishment or the place of punishment. . . . If Hell designates the place of punishment, then a distinction must be drawn among four places. There is the Hell of the damned, in which one endures both the punishments of the senses and punishment of damnation [that is, deprivation of the divine presence] and in which there is both inner and outer darkness, i.e., absence of grace; it is eternal mourning. Above it is the Limbo of the Children, where one endures the punishment of damnation but not the punishment of the senses, and there is both inner and outer darkness.

Above this place is Purgatory, where there is the punishment of the senses and the punishment of damnation (but only) for a certain period, and there is outer darkness, but not inner darkness, for by grace one has inner light there, because one sees that one will be saved. The upper place is the Limbo of the Holy Fathers [that is, the Patriarchs] where there was the punishment of damnation but not of the senses, and there was outer darkness but not the darkness of the deprivation of grace. It is into this place that Christ descended and liberated his own and thus "swallowed up" Hell, for he completely destroyed death. . . . This place is also called the Bosom of Abraham; it is the heaven of the empyrean, for Abraham is there forevermore. Between these places there is no passage, except in the past from the third to the fourth, that is, from Purgatory to the Limbo of the Holy Fathers. (*Compendium of the True Theology* 4:22)

[Cited by LE GOFF 1984: 264–265]

23. Punishment as Purgation

The thirteenth-century Compendium *takes Purgatory as a given, as indeed it was in the Western Church at that point. The origins of the idea are much earlier, of course, and lay perhaps in that interval between the death of the individual Christian and the universal judgment of the Last Day. What occurred then, it seemed to many early Christians, was some purely temporary state of punishment for those who required it, punishment that was purgative rather than punitive. That Tertullian believed in such is certain.*

"Are all souls then," you ask, "in the realm of the underworld?" Yes, whether it pleases you or not. And there are (both) punishments and re-freshments there. . . . Why cannot you imagine that the soul experiences either punishment or comfort in the underworld, in the period while it is awaiting the judgment, whether punishment or reward, with a kind of anticipation? . . . Otherwise, what will happen in that interval? Shall we be sleeping? But souls cannot sleep. . . . Or do you think that nothing happens there? . . . Surely it would be the height of injustice if in that place the souls of the wicked continued to prosper and the good were still deprived of happiness. . . . And so, since we understand that "prison" indicated in the Gospel as the underworld and the expression "last penny" (Matt. 5:25) to refer to the fact that every small sin will be expiated there in the interval before the resurrection, no one will doubt that the soul in the underworld pays some price, without prejudice to the fulfillment of the process at the resurrection, which also will be effected through the medium of the flesh. (Tertullian, *On the Soul* 58)

Nor was the Latin Tertullian the only Christian Father who subscribed to the notion of remedial chastisement in the afterlife. The Christian Hellenists of Alexandria also viewed it that way.

All who are virtuous change to better dwellings, the reason for this change being the choice of knowledge. . . . But strict chastisements, through the goodness of the great judge, the overseer, compel (the wicked), through increasing suffering, to repent. The punishments are inflicted through the attending angels, through the various previous (individual) judgments and by the general judgment. (Clement of Alexandria, *Stromateis* 8.2)

If . . . they will not listen to the song . . . let them be disciplined by God's hand, suffering paternal correction before the judgment, until they are ashamed and repent and so do suffer the final condemnation by their stubborn unbelief. For these are only partial disciplinings, called chastisements, which most of us who have lapsed into sin incur, though we belong to the Lord's people. But our chastisement by Providence is like that of children by a teacher or a father. God does not take vengeance, which is the repayment of evil by evil; rather, He chastises for the benefit of the chastised. (Ibid. 7.16)

Clement's fellow Alexandrian, Origen (ca. 185–255 C.E.), likewise believed in the remedial nature of divine punishment.

Just as an excess of food causes fevers (in the body) . . . so the soul accumulates an abundance of sins, and in due time this buildup of evils comes to a boil for the sinner's punishment and catches fire for his retribution. This is when the mind itself, or the conscience, which through divine power keeps a record of all things . . . sees set out before its eyes the story of its misdeeds. . . . God acts in dealing with sinners like a physician . . . and the fury of His anger is useful for the purging of souls. Even that penalty which is said to be imposed by fire is understood as applied to a sinner to assist his health. (Origen, *On First Principles* 2.10.4, 6)

Moreover, Origen was willing to take the next step, though with a great deal of hesitation: if punishment after death is remedial rather than punitive, then one must think it will at some point end, when all the wicked among God's creatures will have been rehabilitated by their chastisements.

We speak very tentatively and uncertainly on this subject, more by way of promoting discussion than of drawing definite conclusions. . . . The end and consummation of the world will occur, and then each being will have to undergo the punishment which his sins have merited. God alone knows that time. . . . We suppose that the goodness of God will restore the unity of the whole creation in the end, through His Christ, when all His enemies have been subdued and overcome. . . . Whether any of those ranks who act under the devil's leadership will be able in some future time to be converted to goodness, inasmuch as they still have the power of free will; or whether a persistent and inveterate evil becomes their very nature from long habit, I leave to the reader's judgment. . . . Meanwhile both in time and in eternity all these matters will be dealt with in due order and proportion according to their deserts; so that some are restored in the first ages, some in later, some even in the last times; restored through greater and graver punishments, and long-term penalties that are endured, it may be, through many ages. (Origen, *On First Principles* 1.6.1–3)

Basil (330–379 C.E.), bishop of Caesarea in Anatolia, regarded such speculations as pernicious: hell is as eternal as heaven will be.

Many men have forgotten such important sayings and pronouncements of the Lord, and on their own initiative set a time limit to punishment, in order that they may sin with greater confidence. This is a result of the devil's trickery. But if there is any time limit for eternal punishment, it follows that there must be a time limit for eternal life itself. And since we cannot imagine this with regard to eternal life, what case can be made for ascribing a limit to eternal punishment? The adjective "eternal" applies equally to both. (Basil, *Shorter Rule* 267)

Augustine is equally opposed to this view. Although he is censuring pagan Platonists, his remarks would pertain with similar point to Origen's position.

Now the Platonists, while refusing to believe than any sins go unpunished, hold that all punishments are directed toward purification, whether they are punishments inflicted by human laws or those imposed by divine decree, and whether the latter are suffered in this life or after death, when someone is spared in this life or when his affliction does not result in his correction. . . . Those who hold this view will have it that the only punishments after death are those intended to purify, so that the soul may be cleansed from any infection contracted by contact with the earth. . . .

For our part, we acknowledge that even in this mortal life there are indeed some purificatory punishments; but penalties inflicted on those whose life is not improved thereby, or is even made worse, are not purificatory. Punishments are a means of purification only to those who are disciplined and corrected by them. All other punishments, whether temporal or eternal, are imposed on every person in accordance with the treatment he is to receive from God's providence; they are imposed either in retribution for sins, whether past sins or sins in which the person so chastised is still living, or else they serve to exercise and to display the virtues of the good; and they are administered through the agency of men or of angels, whether good or evil angels. . . . As for temporal pains, some people suffer them in this life only, others after death, others both in this life and the other; yet all this precedes that last and strictest judgment. However, not all men who endure temporal pains after death come into those eternal punishments which are to come after the judgment. Some in fact will receive forgiveness in the world to come for what is not forgiven in this. (Augustine, *City of God* 21.13)

Finally, Aquinas (d. 1277 C.E.) devotes an article of his Summa Theologica *to the question of the penalties of the afterlife and the possibility that they might be purely remedial, and so finite, in nature. First he responds directly to the issue of the eternity of punishment for sin.*

I answer that: Sin incurs a debt of punishment because it disturbs an order, and the effect remains for as long as the cause remains. Therefore as long as the disturbance of the order continues, so too must the debt of punishment. Now sometimes the disturbance of an order is reparable and sometimes it is irreparable because a defect which destroys the principle is irreparable, while, if the principle is saved, defects can be repaired by virtue of that principle. For instance, if the principle of sight is destroyed, sight cannot be restored except by divine power; whereas, if the principle of sight is preserved, while there might arise certain impediments to seeing, these can be remedied by nature or art.

Now in every order there is a principle by which one becomes a member of that order. Consequently, if a sin destroys the principle of the order by which man's will is subject to God, the disorder will be such as to be considered in itself irreparable, though it is possible to repair it by the power of God. Now the principle of this order is the last end, to which man adheres by charity. Therefore, whenever sin turns man away from God so as to destroy charity, considered in themselves, such sinners incur a debt of eternal punishment.

But in responding to the corollary issue of the possibility of penal rehabilitation in the afterlife, Aquinas prefers to invoke the example of human criminal justice.

Punishment is proportioned to sin in point of severity, both in divine and in human judgments. In no judgment, however, as Augustine says (*City of God* 21.11), is it requisite for the punishment to equal the fault in point of duration. For the fact that adultery or murder is committed in a moment does not call for a momentary punishment; in fact, they are punished sometimes by imprisonment or banishment for life—sometimes even by death. Now this does not take into account the time occupied in the homicide but aims at removing a murderer from the society of the living; so that this (capital) punishment represents, in its own way, the eternity of punishment inflicted by God. Now according to Gregory (*Moralia* 34.19), it is just that he who has sinned against God in his own eternity should be punished in God's eternity. A man is said to have sinned in his own eternity not only because he has sinned throughout his whole life, but also because, from the very fact that he fixes his end in sin, he has the will to sin everlastingly. . . .

Even the punishment that is inflicted according to human laws is not always intended as a remedy for the one who is punished, but sometimes only for others. Thus when a thief is hanged, this is not for his own amendment, but for the sake of others, who at least may be deterred from crime through fear of the punishment, according to Proverbs 19:25: "The wicked man being scourged, the fool shall be wiser." Accordingly, the eternal punishments inflicted by God on the reprobate are remedial punishments for those who refrain from sin through the thoughts of these punishments. (Aquinas, *Summa Theologica* I/2, ques. 87, art. 3)
[AQUINAS 1945: 2: 711–712]

24. Purgatory

The point being argued by both Augustine and Aquinas is that at least some of the punishments of the afterlife are eternal. Neither would deny that other punishments inflicted on men between their death and the Final Judgment are indeed remedial and so will come to an end, at that Judgment or possibly sooner. What had occurred between the writings of the two men was that the remedial punishment of the afterlife had been localized in a fixed place, Purgatory. At the Second Council of Lyons in 1274 C.E., which marked the reunion, however temporary, of the Western and Eastern branches of Christendom, the Western position on Purgatory was defined and explicated for Eastern acceptance.

Because of various errors that have been introduced by the ignorance of some and the malice of others, we state and publicly pronounce that those who lapse into sin after baptism ought not to be rebaptized but that they obtain pardon for theirs sins through a true penitence. That if, truly penitent, they die in charity before having, by worthy fruits of penance, rendered satisfaction for what they have done by commission or omission, their souls . . . are purged after their death, by purgatorial or purificatory penalties, and that, for the alleviation of these penalties they are served by the suffrages of the living faithful, to wit, the sacrifice of the mass, prayers, alms and other works of piety that the faithful customarily offer on behalf of others of the faithful according to the institutions of the Church. The souls of those who, after receiving baptism, have contracted absolutely no taint of sin, as well as those who, after contracting the taint of sin, have been purified either while they remained in their bodies, or after being stripped of their bodies, are, as we stated above, immediately received into heaven. The souls of those who die in mortal sin or only with original sin, soon descend into Hell, to be chastised with differing punishments, however. The same Roman Church nonetheless firmly believes and firmly asserts that on the day of judgment all men will appear in their bodies before the tribunal of Christ to give an account of their own deeds. (Profession of Faith of Michael Palaeologus)

25. The Preaching of God's Final Judgment

The very foundations of Islam are cast on eschatology, and the earliest suras of the Quran ring incessantly with the certainty of the Judgment and threats and promises of the future life.

Has news of the Overpowering Event reached you?
Many faces will be contrite on that day,
Laboring, wearied out,
Burning in scorching fire,
Given water from the boiling spring to drink.
They will have no food except bitter thorn,
Neither nourishing nor banishing hunger.
Well-pleased with their endeavor,

In the high empyrean,
Never hearing idle talk.

There is a stream of running water in it;
And within it are couches placed on high,
Goblets set,
Cushions arranged,
And rich carpets spread.
(Quran 88:1–16)

Surely for those who persecute believers, men and women, and do not repent afterwards, there is the punishment of Hell, and the punishment of burning.

Surely for those who believe and do the right there are gardens with rivers running by. That is the greatest success. (Quran 85:10–11)

Ah, the woe that day for those who deny,
Who call the Day of Judgment a lie!
None denies it but the sinful transgressors.
When Our revelations are recited before him,
    he says: "These are fables of long ago."
No. In fact what they have been doing has rusted their hearts.
Therefore they will be screened off from their Lord that day,
Then they will indeed burn in Hell.
They will then be told:
"This is what you had denied." . . .

Verily the pious will be in heaven,
On couches face to face.
On their faces you will see
    the glow of beatitude.
They will be served the choicest wine, sealed
With a sealing of musk.
(Quran 83:10–26)

Surely a time is fixed for the Day of Judgment.
The day the trumpet blast is sounded you will come in hordes;
The heavens will be opened wide and turn into so many doors.
The mountains put into motion turning into mirage.
Certainly Hell lies in wait,
The rebels' abode,
Where they will remain for aeons,
Finding neither sleep nor anything to drink there

Except boiling water and benumbing cold:
A fitting reward.
They were those who did not expect a reckoning,
And rejected our signs as lies.
We have kept an account of everything in a book.
So taste, for We shall add nothing but torment.

As for those who preserve themselves from evil and follow
        the straight path, there is achievement for them:
Orchards and vineyards,
And graceful maidens ever of the same age,
And flasks full and flowing.
They will hear no blasphemies there or disavowals:
A recompense from your Lord, a sufficient gift.
(Quran 78:17–36)

The whole of Sura 82 is in fact an early Muslim résumé of the Last Things.

THE CLEAVING

In the name of God, most benevolent, ever-merciful.

When the sky is split asunder.
When the stars dispersed,
When the oceans begin to flow,
When the graves are overturned,
Each soul will know what it had sent ahead and what it had left behind.
O man, what seduced you from your munificent Lord,
Who created you, then formed your symmetry, then gave you the
                right proportion,
Shaping you into any form He pleased?
Even then you deny the Judgment.
Surely there are guardians over you,
Illustrious scribes
Who know what you do.
The pious will surely be in heaven,
The wicked certainly in Hell:
They will burn in it on the Day of Judgment,
And will not be removed from it.
How then can you comprehend what the Day of Judgment is?
It is the day when no soul will have the power to do the least for a soul,
                and God's will alone will be done.

(Quran 82:1–19)

Yet, as Jesus himself had warned, no man knows the day or the hour.

They ask you about the Hour: When is its predetermined time? Say: "Only my Lord has the knowledge. No one can reveal it except Him. Oppressive for the heavens and the earth will it be. When it comes, it will come unawares." They ask you about it as if you knew. You tell them: "Only God has the knowledge." (Quran 7:187)

But there will be signs of its immediate approach. Those cited in Sura 82 were chiefly cosmological, but elsewhere in the Quran (e.g., 22:2) they are social as well. The graves will be emptied of the dead. There will be a judgment: every man's deeds have been recorded by angels, and each individual will be confronted with his own account. The righteous will henceforth lead a life of pleasure in what is elsewhere called "the Garden" or "the Garden of Eden"; the evildoers are condemned to a fiery Gehenna. God alone will be the judge.

When the single blast is sounded on the trumpet,
And the earth and the mountains heaved and crushed to powder with
　　　　　one leveling blow,
On that Day will come what is to come.
The sky will cleave asunder on that day and fall to pieces.
On its fringes will be angels, eight of them, bearing their Lord's
　　　　　throne aloft.
You will then be set before Him, and no one of you will remain
　　　　　unexposed.
He who is given his ledger in his right hand, will say: "Here, read
　　　　　my ledger.
I was certain I will be given my account."
So he shall have an agreeable life
In high empyrean
With fruits hanging low within reach;
"Eat and drink to your fill as a reward for deeds you have done in
　　　　　days of yore."
But whoever gets his ledger in his left hand, will say: "Would that I were
　　　　　never given my ledger,
And not known my account!
I wish death had put an end to me.
Of no use was even my wealth.
Vanished has my power from me."
"Seize him and manacle him,
Then cast him to be burnt into Hell;
And string him to a chain seventy cubits long.

He did not believe in God the supreme,
Nor urged others to feed the poor.
And that is why he has no friend today,
Nor food other than suppuration
Which none but the hellish eat."
(Quran 69:13–37)

And from the Sura called "The Inevitable":

When what is to happen comes to pass—
Which is bound to happen undoubtedly—
Degrading some and exalting others;
When the earth is shaken up convulsively,
The mountains bruised and crushed,
Turned to dust, floating in the air,
You will become three kinds:
Those of the right hand—how happy those of the right hand!
Then those of the left hand—how unhappy those of the left hand!
Then those who go before, how pre-excellent,
Who will be honored
In gardens of tranquillity;
A number of the earlier peoples,
But a few of later times,
On couches wrought of gold,
Reclining face to face.
Youths of never-ending bloom will pass round to them
Cups and decanters, beakers full of sparkling wine,
Unheady, unebriating;
And such fruits as they fancy
Bird meats that they relish,
And companions with big beautiful eyes
Like pearls within their shells,
As recompense for all they have done.
They will hear no nonsense there or talk of sin,
Other than "peace, peace," the salutation.

As for those on the right hand—how happy those on the right hand—
They will be in the shade of the thornless lote tree
And acacia covered with heaps of bloom,
Lengthened shadows,
Gushing water,
And fruits numberless,

Unending, unforbidden,
And maidens incomparable.
We have formed them in a distinctive fashion,
And made them virginal,
Loving companions matched in age,
For those of the right hand,
A crowd of earlier generations
And a crowd of the later.

But those of the left hand—how unhappy those of the left hand—
Will be in the scorching wind and boiling water,
Under the shadow of thick black smoke
Neither cool nor agreeable.
They were endowed with good things
But persisted in that greater sin,
And said "What! When we are dead and turned to dust and bones,
                shall we be raised again?
And so will our fathers?"
Say: "Indeed, the earlier and the later generations
Will be gathered together on a certain day which is predetermined.
Then you, the erring and the denyers,
Will eat of the tree of Zaqqum,
Fill your bellies with it,
And drink over it scalding water,
Lapping it up like female camels raging of thirst with disease."
Such will be their welcome on the Day of Judgment. . . .

If he is one of the honored,
There will be peace and plenty, and gardens of tranquillity for him.
And if he is one of those of the right hand,
There will be the salutation by those of the right hand: "Peace be
                upon you."
But if he is of the denyers and the errants,
The welcome will be boiling water
And the roasting in Hell.
This is indeed the ultimate truth.
Then praise your Lord, the most supreme.
(Quran 56:1–95)

*There is more than one problem of interpretation here. The first has to do with the
identity of the "three kinds" of men who will face judgment. They seem to corre-*

spond to those who stand on the right and on the left and "those who go before," but they do not appear to match three distinct types of punishment or reward. Zamakhshari (1134 C.E.) attempts to explain.

 . . . "Those on the right side . . . left side" . . . : It may be a question of those of high rank and those of low rank. . . . The right side constitutes a good sign and the left side constitutes a bad sign. . . . Others say that those on the right and those on the left are those who experience happiness and unhappiness: the blessed are happy with themselves because of their obedience, while the damned are unhappy with themselves because of their disobedience. Still others say that the inhabitants of Paradise come to stand on the right and those of hell fire on the left.

"Those who go before" (are) those with pious hearts who arrived there first, for God summoned them and they were not surpassed in striving as God's pleasure indicated. There are some who say that there are three classes of men: (1) the one who enters into the good early in his life and perseveres in it until he leaves this world. This is the one who "goes before" and stands near God. (2) Then there is the man who enters into sin early in his life and is remiss for a long time, but then turns in repentance toward God. This is the one on the right side. (3) Finally, there is the man who enters into evil early in life and who is thereafter incapable of refraining from it until his death. This is the one on the left side. (Zamakhshari, *The Unveiler of the Realities, ad loc.*)

The second problem has to do with the two apparently contradictory verses: "A number of the earlier peoples / But a few of later times" (13–14) and "A crowd of earlier generations / And a crowd of the later" (40). Zamakhshari's commentary on Sura 56 continues.

The word "number" designates a numerous community. . . . What is meant is: "those who go before" are numerous among the former generations. These are the communities from Adam's day to Muhammad. "But a few of later times" refers to the community of Muhammad. Others say that the former and later times refer to the older and younger members of the (Muslim) community.

This latter interpretation would seem to refer respectively to the Meccan and then the Medinese converts to Islam. That reading would lead naturally to the interpretation of verse 40 cited disapprovingly by Zamakhshari.

It is related that the Muslims were severely persecuted when this verse "But a few of later times" (verse 14) was revealed, and that for this reason the Messenger of God once again took counsel with his Lord until there was revealed (the later verse): "And a crowd of the later." To this I answer: This is not likely for two reasons. In the first place, the verse under discussion (verse 14) refers clearly to "those who go before," while the second verse (verse 40) refers to "those on the right side" . . . and second, because abrogation (of one verse by another) is possible (in the case of commands), but not in the case of simple information.

The following sura represents a somewhat more schematic, and considerably clearer, view of the afterlife as the place where God's justice will be fulfilled.

For those who fulfill their covenant with God and do not break
                    their agreement,
Who keep together what God has ordained held together, and fear their
                    Lord and dread the hardship of the Reckoning,
Who persevere in seeking the way of their Lord, who fulfill their
                    devotional obligations, and spend of what We have given
                    them, secretly and openly, who repel evil with good:
                    For them is the recompense of Paradise:
Perpetual gardens which they will enter with those of their fathers, wives
                    and children who are virtuous and at peace. . . .
    As for those who break God's covenant after validating it, and sever
relations which God enjoined cohered, and spread corruption in the land,
there is condemnation for them and an evil abode.
    God increases or decreases the fortunes of whosoever He will, and
they rejoice in the life of this world. Yet the life of this world is nothing
but a trifle as compared to the life of the next. (Quran 13:20–26)

In the passage just cited, the moral quality of the afterlife is stressed. There is no lack of passages, however, where the emphasis is on the physical details of both the punishments of the sinner and the rewards of the just. In the translation of this next graphic sura the refrain verse, "How many favors of your Lord will you then deny?" which is repeated after every verse, has been omitted after the first occurrence.

O society of demons and men, cross the bounds of heaven and the earth
                    if you have the ability, then pass beyond them; but
                    you cannot unless you acquire the law.
How many favors of your Lord will you then deny?
Let loose at you will be smokeless flames of fire so that you will not be
                    able to defend yourselves.
When the sky will split asunder, and turn rosy like the dregs of
                    anointing oil.

Neither men nor demons will be questioned on that day about his sin.
The sinners will be recognized by their marks and seized by the forelock
                    and their feet.
This is Hell the sinners called a lie.
They will go round and round between it and boiling water.
But for him who has lived in awe of the sublimity of his Lord,
                    there will be two gardens,
Full of overhanging branches,
With two springs of water flowing through them both.
In both of them will be every kind of fruit in pairs.
Reclining on carpets lined with brocade, fruits of the garden hanging
                    low within reach.
In them maidens with averted glances, undeflowered by men or demons
                    before them,
As though rubies and pearls.
Should the reward of goodness be anything but goodness?
And beside these are two other gardens,
Of darkest verdant green,
With two fountains gushing constantly,
With fruits in them,
And dates and pomegranates.
In them good and comely maidens,
Houris cloistered in pavilions,
Undeflowered by men or demons before them.
Reclining on green cushions and rich carpets excellent.
Blessed by your Lord, full of majesty and beneficence.
(Quran 55:33–76)
The tree of Zaqqum will indeed be the food of sinners.
It is like pitch. It will fume in the belly
As does boiling water.
"Seize him and drag him into the depths of Hell," (it will be said).
"Then pour over his head the torment of scalding water."
"Taste it, you were indeed the mighty and the noble!
This is certainly what you had denied."
Surely those who fear and follow the straight path will be in a place
                    of peace and security
In the midst of gardens and of springs,
Dressed in brocade and shot silk,
        facing one another.

Just like that. We shall pair them with companions with large black eyes.
They will call for every kind of fruit with satisfaction.
There they will not know any death apart from the first death they
              had died.
(Quran 44:43–56)

26. The End Defined

*These extended selections from the Quran reveal at once a highly developed and
central view of the Last Things: the Last Judgment, Heaven, and Hell all have a
vivid, if sometimes highly allusive, reality. The details were filled in, as they were
in Judaism and Christianity, by popular preaching and the collections of Prophetic
traditions, while the dogmatic issues began to emerge from the workshops of the
theologians in the eighth and ninth centuries. We join that latter tradition in the
mid-ninth century in a series of statements of what then passed as Islamic orthodoxy,
collectively called* The Testament of Abu Hanifah. *The eschatological articles,
buttressed with appropriate Quranic support, begin with number 17.*

Article 17: We confess that God ordered the pen to write. Then the
pen said, "What shall I write, my Lord?" God said: "Write what shall
happen every day till the Resurrection," as He says: "Everything that they
do is in the books kept by the guardian angel; every action, whether small
or great, is written down" (Quran 54:52ff.).

Article 18: We confess that the punishment in the tomb shall without fail take place.

Article 19: We confess that, in view of the traditions on the subject,
the interrogation by Munkar and Nakir is a reality.

Article 20: We confess that Paradise and Hell are a reality and that
they are created and existing at present, that neither they nor their inhabitants shall vanish, since the Scripture says regarding the Faithful: "It [that
is, Paradise] is prepared for the God-fearing" (Quran 3:127), and regarding the infidels: "It [that is, Hell] is prepared for the infidels" (Quran 2:22,
3:126). They were created with a view to reward and punishment respectively.

Article 21: We confess that the balance is a reality, since Scripture
says: "And we will appoint balances for the Day of Resurrection" (Quran
21:48).

Article 22: We confess that the reading of the book on the Day of
Resurrection is a reality, since the Scripture says: "Read your book, there
is needed none but yourself to make out an account against you this day"
(Quran 17:15).

Article 23: We confess that God will restore to life those souls after death, and cause them to rise, on a day of which the duration will be fifty thousand years, for retribution and reward and paying of duties, as Scripture says, "In truth God will wake up to life those who are in the tombs" (Quran 22:7).

Article 24: We confess that the meeting of God with the inhabitants of Paradise will be a reality, without description, comparison or modality.

Article 25: The intercession of our Prophet Muhammad, upon whom be God's blessing and peace, is a reality for all those who belong to the inhabitants of Paradise, even though they should be guilty of mortal sins. . . .

Article 27: We confess that the inhabitants of Paradise will dwell there forever, and that the inhabitants of Hell will dwell there forever, as the Scripture says regarding the Faithful: "They are the companions of Paradise, they shall dwell there forever" (Quran 2:76), and regarding the infidels: "They are the companions of the fire, they shall dwell there forever" (Quran 2:75, 214). (*Testament of Abu Hanifah*) [WENSINCK 1932: 129–131]

27. The Torments of the Grave

Each of these articles has its own background and history. Articles 18 and 19, for example, offered without Quranic support but with a generic reference to the Prophetic traditions, look like this in one of the traditions. It is highly wrought into a careful narrative, assembled by Abu'l-Layth al-Samarqandi (d. 983 C.E.) and reported with a full chain of authorities reaching back to al-Bara ibn Azib.

[Muhammad said, on the occasion of the funeral of one of his Medinese followers:] When a man who is a true believer is drawing near to the next world and is about to be cut off from this world, there descend to him angels whose faces are as white as the sun, bringing with them a shroud from Paradise and celestial aromatics, and take their seat just within his vision. Then the Angel of Death arrives, takes a seat at his head and says: "O you tranquil soul, come forth to God's favor and God's forgiveness." Then, said the Prophet, upon whom be God's blessing and peace, it [that is, the soul of the believer] comes forth, flowing as easily as a drop from a waterskin, whereupon those angels take it, not leaving it in his hand more than the twinkling of an eye before they take it, wrap it in the aforementioned shroud and aromatics so that the odor from it is more redolent than the finest musk to be found on the face of the earth, and mount up with it. . . . At last they come to the gate of the lowest heaven and ask that it be opened for it. It is opened to them and the chief personages in each heaven receive it and accompany it to that which lies beyond it, till at last they arrive with it at the seventh heaven. There God, exalted be He, says: "Write its record in Illiyun (Quran 83:18–21) and return it to the earth from which I created men, into which I make them return, and out of which I will bring them a second time" (Quran 20:55). The spirit is then returned to its body, whereupon two angels [that is, Munkar and Nakir, unmentioned in the Quran] come to it and ask: "Who is your Lord?" It replies: "God is my Lord." They ask: "What is your religion?" "Islam is my religion," it replies. Then they say: "And what say you about this man who was sent among you?" and it answers: "He is the Apostle of God, upon whom be God's blessing and peace." They ask: "What works have you?" and it answers: "I have read God's Book, believed it and in it put my trust." Then a herald will call: "He has believed My servant [that is, Muhammad]. Spread for him a bed from the Garden, clothe him in a celestial garment, open for him a door giving onto the Garden through which may come to him its breezes and its aroma and expand his grave for him as far as the eye can reach. . . ."

But when an unbeliever is drawing near to the next world and being cut off from this world, there descend to him from heaven angels whose faces are black, bringing with them haircloth, and take their seats just within his vision. Then the Angel of Death arrives, takes his seat at his head and says: "O you pernicious soul, come forth to God's discontent and wrath." Thereupon his soul is scattered all through his members and the angel drags it forth like the dragging of an iron spit through moist wool, tearing the veins and sinews. Thus he takes it, but it is not in his hand more than the twinkling of an eye before those angels take, put it in the haircloth where the odor from it is like the stench of a decomposing carcass. They mount up with it . . . and at last they come with it to the gate of the lowest heaven, and ask that it be opened for it, but it is not opened for it. . . . Then God will say: "Write his record in Sijjin (Quran 83:7–9), then let his spirit be thrown out." . . . So his spirit is returned to his body, whereupon two angels come and sit by him. They ask him, "Who is your Lord?" and he replies, "Alas, I know not." And they ask him: "What is your religion?" to which he again replies: "Alas, I know not." They ask: "Well, what do you say about this man who was sent among you?" but again he replies: "Alas, I know not." At which a herald cries from heaven: "He has given My servant (Muhammad) the lie. Spread him a bed from the Fire, clothe him in fire, open for him a door giving out on the Fire, through which its heat and smoke may enter to him, and contract his grave so his ribs pile one upon the other." Then there approaches him a man, ugly of countenance, ill-dressed and foul-smelling, who says to him: "Receive tidings of that which will grieve you. This is your day which you were promised." He will ask: "And who are you?" to which the man will reply: "I am your evil deeds," whereat he will say: "O Lord, let not the Hour arrive, let not the Hour arrive." (Samarqandi, *Arousing the Heedless*) [JEFFERY 1962: 208–210]

The narrative is smooth and reassuring, but there were doctrinal problems here, at least early on in Islam. They can still be heard echoing in this theological manual written by al-Nasafi (d. 1114 C.E.).

The Mu'tazilites, the Jahmites and the Najjarites [that is, the ninth-century rationalizing groups of theologians] teach that neither intelligence nor analogy can accept the reality of the torments of the tomb or the questioning of Munkar and Nakir. (Their argument is that) if He punishes man it must be either that He torments the flesh without the spirit or that He causes the spirit to re-enter the body (after death) and then torments it. Now it would be useless to punish the flesh without the spirit for (then) it would not feel the pain, yet it is not possible to think that He causes the spirit to re-enter the flesh and then torments it, for if He caused the spirit to re-enter the flesh, it would make necessary a second dying, which is not possible, for God has said, "Every soul shall taste death" (Quran 3:185), and this verse informs men that they will not taste of death more than once. Since these two possibilities are shown to be hopeless, there remains but the third, namely, that there is no torment in the tomb.

Having stated the objection, Nasafi now supplies the rejoinder.

There is a proof that the torment of the tomb is something which the intelligence can accept. Do you not see that a sleeper's spirit goes out from him (in sleep) and yet remains connected with the body, so that he may suffer pain in a dream, and both the pain and the relief (from it) reach him? Also conversations take place in dreams because the spirit is (still) connected with the body. It is related of the Prophet, upon whom be God's blessing and peace, that he was asked how the flesh suffers pain in the grave when there is no spirit in it, and he answered: "In the same way that your tooth suffers pain though there is no spirit in it." (Thus) the Prophet informed his (questioner) that the tooth may be subject to pain because it is connected with the flesh, even though there is no spirit in it, and so, in like manner after death, because a man's spirit is (still) connected with his body, the body may feel pain. (Nasafi, *The Sea of Discourse on the Science of Theology*) [JEFFERY 1962: 436–438]

28. The Resurrection of the Body Demonstrated

They say: "O Lord, twice You made us die, and twice You made us live. We admit our sins. Is there still a way out for us?" (Quran 40:11)

*The resurrection of the body, to which this Quranic verse was generally thought to refer, was as difficult a conceptual question for the Muslims as it was for the Christians. Al-Ash*ari (d. 935 C.E.), one of the first proponents of theology in Islam, attempted a demonstrative proof of its possibility with the new weapons of rational science. At the same time, to defend the usefulness and validity of that science, he made God the theologian in this instance.*

All dialectical theology which treats in detail of questions deriving from the basic dogmas of God's Oneness and Justice is simply taken from the Quran. Such is also the case with theological discourse on the possibility and impossibility of the resurrection (of the body). This question had been disputed by intelligent Arabs (of Muhammad's day) and by others before them until they were amazed by the possibility of that and said, "What! When we have died and become dust? That is an incredible return!" (Quran 50:3) . . . and "Who will quicken bones when they have decayed?" (Quran 36:78). . . . Apropos of such theological discussion of theirs God put into the Quran arguments designed to confirm, from the viewpoint of reason, the possibility of the resurrection after death. He taught and instructed His Prophet how to argue against their denial in two ways, according to the two groups of adversaries. For one group admitted the first creation but denied the second, while the second group denied both (creations) on the ground that the world is eternal [that is, both *a parte ante* and *a parte post*].

So against him who admitted the first creation, God argued by saying, "Answer: He will quicken them who produced them the first time" (Quran 36:79), and by saying, "It is He who gives life by a first creation and then restores it; and it is very easy for Him" (Quran 30:27), and by His words, "As He first made you, you will return" (Quran 7:29). By these verses He called their attention to the fact that he who was able to effect something [to wit, the original creation] without reference to a pre-existing exemplar is all the more able to effect something which has already been produced. Indeed, the latter is easier for him, as you know from your own experience. But in the case of the Creator, it is not "easier" for Him to create one thing than to create another. . . .

As for the group which denied both the first creation and the second [that is, the "re-creation" of the resurrection] and maintained the eternity of the world, a doubt entered their minds simply because they said: "It is our experience that life is wet and hot and death is cold and dry, akin to the nature of earth. How then can there be any combination of life and earth and decayed bones, resulting in a sound creation, since two contraries do not combine?" For this reason, then, they denied the resurrection.

It is certainly true that two contraries do not combine in one substratum, or in one direction, or in what (already) exists in the substratum. But they can exist in two substratums by way of propinquity. So God argued against them by saying: "He who makes fire for you from a green tree—for behold, you kindle fire from it" (Quran 38:80). In saying that, God was referring to their own knowledge and experience of the emergence of fire from green trees, notwithstanding the heat and dryness of the former and the coldness and wetness of the latter. Again, God made the possibility of the first production a proof of the possibility of the last production, because it is a proof of the possibility of the propinquity of life to earth and decayed bones and of making it a sound creation, for He said, "Just as We created man a first time, so We shall restore him" (Quran 21:104). (Ashʿari, *The Science of Dialectical Theology* 9–12)

[ASHʿARI 1953: 123–125]

29. The Resurrection of the Body Contested

Neither Ashʿari's attempted demonstration nor the later distinction of a spirit that is not in the flesh but somehow remains connected with it to a sufficient extent to allow the body to suffer the physical pains and enjoy the physical pleasures of the afterlife solved the problem. The early rationalizing sectarians may have denied the literal truth of the torment of the tomb, but once the full impact of Greek philosophy began to be felt in Islam, a far greater problem arose: the resurrection of the corruptible body and its reunion with the incorruptible soul. And if this seemed improbable, then equally improbable would be the body's share in either the physical pains of Hell or the physical pleasures of Paradise. Ibn Sina (d. 1038 C.E.), a thinker deeply imbued with Greek philosophy but a Muslim withal, here attempts to solve the problem in terms of Paradise. He is speaking of the fate of the middle range of souls, neither recognized saints nor inveterate sinners.

It may be true, as some theologians state, that when souls, supposing they are pure, leave the body, having firmly fixed within them some such beliefs concerning the future life as are appropriate to them, being the sort of picture that can properly be presented to the ordinary man, when souls such as these leave the body, lacking both the force to draw them upward to complete perfection . . . but all their spiritual dispositions are turned toward the lower world and drawn to the corporeal . . . these souls may well imagine all those afterlife circumstances in which they believed as actually taking place before them, the instrument reinforcing their imagination being some kind of celestial body.

It is then in the deceased soul's imaginative faculty that the physical pleasures of Paradise appear to occur, with an assist from a higher body, one of the immortal heavenly bodies. This is no ersatz pleasure, or ersatz pain, Ibn Sina continues.

In this way the pure souls will really be spectators of the events of the grave and the resurrection about which they were told in this world, and all the good things of the afterlife; while the wicked souls will similarly behold, and suffer, the punishment which was portrayed to them here below. Certainly the imaginative picture is no weaker than the sensual image; rather it is the stronger and clearer of the two. This may be observed in dreams: the vision seen in sleep is often of greater moment in its kind than the impression of the senses. . . . As you know, the image seen in dreams and that sensed in waking are alike simply impressed upon the soul; they differ only in this, that the former kind originates from within and descends into the soul, while the latter sort originates from without and mounts up to the soul. It is when the image has already been impressed that the act of contemplation is consummated. It is this impression, then, that in reality pleases or pains the soul, not any external object. (Ibn Sina, *The Book of Deliverance*) [AVICENNA 1951: 74–75]

30. The Incoherence of the Philosophers

Avicenna's argument was ingenious, but it was not very convincing to Ghazali, who pointed out in his Incoherence of the Philosophers, *as we have already seen in Chapter 5 above, that the issue of the literal resurrection of the body, and the literal truth of the pains of Gehenna and the pleasures of Paradise, was one of the irreconcilable issues that separated the philosophical from the Islamic tradition. And the chief offender in the Muslim camp was no less than Ibn Sina himself, who is here reflecting more generally on the question of the afterlife.*

The afterlife is a notion received from religious teaching; there is no way of establishing its truth save by way of religious dogma and acceptance of the prophets' reports as true; these refer to what will befall the body at the resurrection, and those corporeal delights or torments which are too well known to require restating here. The true religion brought into this world by our Prophet Muhammad has described in detail the state of happiness or misery awaiting us hereafter so far as the body is concerned. Some further support for the idea of the hereafter is attainable through reason and logical demonstration—and this is confirmed by prophetic teaching—namely, that happiness or misery posited by spiritual apprisement, though it is true that our conjecture falls short of realizing a full picture of them now, for reasons which we shall explain. Metaphysicians have a greater desire to achieve this spiritual happiness than the happiness which is purely physical; indeed, they scarcely heed the latter, and were they granted it would not consider it of great moment in comparison to the former kind, which is proximity to the First Truth, in a matter to be described presently. Let us therefore consider this (spiritual) state of happiness, and of contrasting misery; the physical sort is fully dealt with in the teachings of religion. (Ibn Sina, *Book of Deliverance*)

[AVICENNA 1951: 64]

If this seems innocuous enough, we should recall a text of the same work, where Avicenna remarks on the methods of the prophet-lawgiver.

The prophet's duty is to teach men to know the majesty and might of God by means of symbols and parables drawn from things which they regard as mighty and majestic, imparting to them simply this much, that God has no equal, no like and no partner. Similarly he must establish in them a belief in an afterlife in a manner that comes within the range of their imagination and will be satisfying to their souls; he will liken the happiness and misery to be experienced there in terms which they can understand and conceive. (Ibid.) [AVICENNA 1951: 44–45]

Ibn Rushd (d. 1198 C.E.), a Spanish philosopher who took his Muslim faith seriously, attempted to answer Ghazali. He too begins where Ibn Sina had, on the very nature of eschatological revelation, in a text cited in part at the very beginning of this chapter.

All religions agree on the fact that souls experience states of happiness or misery after death, but they disagree in the manner of symbolizing these states and explaining their existence to men. And it seems that the kind of symbolization that is found in this religion of ours is the most perfect means of explanation to the majority of men and provides the greatest stimulus to their souls to the life beyond; and the primary concern of religions is with the majority. . . . It seems that corporeal symbolization provides a stronger stimulus to the life beyond than the spiritual kind; the spiritual (kind) is more acceptable to the class of debating theologians, but they are the minority.

For this reason we find the people of Islam divided into three sects with regard to the understanding of the symbolization which is used in (the texts of) our religion referring to the states of the future life. One sect holds that existence is identical with this existence here with respect to bliss and pleasure, i.e., they hold that it is the same sort and that the two existences differ only in respect to permanence and limit of duration, i.e., the former is permanent and the latter is of limited duration. Another group holds that there is a difference in the kind of existence. This group has two subdivisions. One subgroup holds that existence symbolized by these sensible images is spiritual, and it has been symbolized thus [that is, in sensible material images] only for the purpose of exposition; these people are supported by many well-known arguments from Scripture, but there would be no point in enumerating them. Another subgroup thinks that it is corporeal, but think that the corporeality of the life beyond differs from the corporeality of this life in that the latter is perishable while the former is immortal. They too are supported by arguments from Scripture. . . .

It seems that this opinion is more suitable to the elite, for the admissibility of this opinion is founded on facts which are not discussed in front of everyone. One is that the soul is immortal. The other is that the return of the soul (after death) to other bodies does not involve the same absurdity as its return to these same (earthly) bodies. This is because it is apparent that the material of the bodies that exist here is successively transferred from one body to another. . . . Bodies like these cannot possibly all exist actually (at the same time), because their material is one. A man dies, for instance, his body is transformed into dust, that dust is transformed into a plant, another man feeds on that plant; then semen proceeds from him, from which another man is born. But if other bodies are supposed, this state of affairs does not follow as a consequence. (Ibn Rushd, *Unveiling of the Programs of Proof*) [AVERROES 1961: 76–77]

And this is in fact Ibn Rushd's own view, expressed when he takes Ghazali on directly, in his Incoherence of the Incoherence.

What Ghazali says against them [that is, the philosophers] is right, and in refuting them it must be admitted that the soul is immortal, as is proved by rational and religious proofs, and it must be assumed that what arises from the dead are simulacra of these earthly bodies, not these bodies themselves, for that which has perished does not return individually and a thing can only return as an image of that which has perished, not as a being identical with what has perished, as Ghazali declares. (Ibn Rushd, *Incoherence of the Incoherence* 586) [AVERROES 1954: 1:362]

31. An End to Hell?

Another trace of Purgatory in Islam, or at least a discussion of the premises—namely that punishment after death is (1) remedial in its intention, and hence (2) temporary and finite—occurs in Zamakhshari's treatment of Sura 11:103–110.

In this surely is a sign for him who fears the torment of the Hereafter, the day when mankind will be assembled together, which will be a day when all things would become evident. We are deferring it only for a time ordained. The day it comes no soul will dare say a word but by His leave; and some will be wretched and some will be blessed. And those who are doomed will be in Hell; for them there will be sighing and sobbing, where they will dwell so long as heaven and earth endure, unless your Lord wills otherwise. Surely, your Lord does as He wills. Those who are blessed will be in Paradise, where they will dwell so long as heaven and earth endure, unless your Lord wills otherwise: this will be a gift uninterrupted. (Quran 11:103–108)

Is it conceivable, then, as this sura seems to suggest, that Paradise and Gehenna will survive only so long as this finite heaven and earth of ours? Zamakhshari comments.

"So long as heaven and the earth endure": There are two possible meanings here. First, the heaven and the earth of the Hereafter are being referred to, since these endure forever. That the Hereafter does possess heaven and earth is shown by the words of God [14:48 and 39:74]. . . . Since it is essential for the inhabitants of the Hereafter that something exist that will bear and shelter them, then either there must exist a heaven or else the Throne (of God) must shelter them. Anything that shelters someone is, in effect, a kind of heaven. Or second, this ("so long as") is an expression for affirming (perduration) and for denying termination. Thus the Arabs say . . . "so long as a star shines" and other similar formulas affirming (perduration).

Could God end Paradise and Gehenna by His own will then? Zamakhshari continues.

Someone may now ask: What is the meaning of the exception referred to in God's words "unless your Lord wills otherwise"? For it is certain that the inhabitants of Paradise and those of hell fire will remain there forever without exception. My response is that the exception refers to eternal persistence in the punishment by fire and eternal stay in the blessing of the Garden. The inhabitants of the hell fire will not continue to be punished only by fire; rather, they will also be punished through severe frost and in other ways, and especially by a punishment which is stronger than all these kinds, namely, that God will be angry with them, will reject them, will regard them as contemptible. By the same token, the inhabitants of Paradise will enjoy, in addition to the Garden, something more important and more moving than that, namely the complaisance that God will have in them. Thus God says:

"God has promised men and women who believe gardens with streams of running water where they will abide forever, and beautiful mansions in the Garden of Eden, and the blessings of God above all. That will be happiness supreme" (Quran 9:72).

Thus, in addition to the reward of the Garden, they receive yet another gift of God, the nature of which no one knows but Him. This is what is meant by the exception.

But the exegesis of the passage is not yet complete. The phrase "verily, your Lord does as He wills" raises another possibility, the one that makes the Christian position on Purgatory possible. Zamakhshari dismisses it immediately, however.

The meaning of God's words "Surely, your Lord does as He wills" . . . is as follows: He allots whatever he wills as punishment to the inhabitants of hell fire, just as He grants his gifts unceasingly to the inhabitants of Paradise. One should reflect upon this, since one part of the Quran explains another. One should not be deceived here by the assertion of the Mujbira [that is, those who oppose the doctrine of free will], who maintain that the (first) exception means that the people of grave sins will be brought out of hell fire through intercession. For the second exception [that is, "Surely your Lord does as He wills"] clearly accuses them of falsehood and proves they lie.

There is also a Prophetic tradition much to the same point as the contention of the Mujbira—and earlier of Origen. Zamakhshari now turns to it.

But what are we to think of those who repudiate the Book of God on the basis of a Prophetic tradition which has come down to them from a non-expert like Abdullah ibn Amr ibn al-As? According to this tradition, a day will come when the gates of Gehenna will be closed and no longer will anyone be inside. And this is supposed to happen after the inhabitants have been there for a very long time. It has come to my attention that those who let themselves be misled by this tradition and believe that the unbelievers will not remain forever in hell fire have fallen prey to this error. This and similar views are clear deceptions, from which may God preserve us! . . . If this tradition according to Abdullah ibn Amr ibn al-As is sound, then its meaning can only be that the unbelievers will come out of the heat of the fire and into the cold of severe frost. Only in this sense would Gehenna be empty and its gates closed. (Zamakhshari, *The Unveiler of the Realities, ad loc.*)

32. The Vision of God

That the afterlife of the blessed consisted, in some degree and in some manner, of the vision of God does not seem to have been doubted by the first generation of Jesus' followers.

Now we see only puzzling reflections in a mirror, but then we shall see face to face. My knowledge now is partial; then it will be whole, like God's knowledge of me. (Paul, *To the Corinthians* 1.13:12)

How great is the love that the Father has shown us! We were called God's children, and such we are; and the reason why the godless world does not recognize us is that it has not known Him. Here and now, dear friends, we are God's children; what we shall be has not been disclosed, but we know that when it is disclosed, we shall be like Him because we shall see Him as He is. (John, *Letters* 1.3:1–3)

By the time of Ireneus, bishop of Lyons in the late second century C.E., the Mosaic experience on Sinai had to be addressed as part of the scriptural context of what the Christians called "the beatific vision."

Because of His greatness and His wonderful glory, "no mortal man may look upon God and live" (Exod. 33:30); for the Father is beyond comprehension. But because of His love and His compassion, and because all things are possible for Him, this too He granted to those who love themselves, that is, to see God. . . . Man of himself does not see God. It is He who is willingly seen by those whom he wishes, and when He wishes, and how He wishes. For God is powerful in all things: He is seen by the spirit of prophecy; He is seen by the Son by way of adoption; and

He will be seen in the kingdom of heaven paternally, while the Spirit prepares man in the Son of God, the Son brings him to the Father, and the Father gives incorruptible life for all eternity, which occurs to each in that he sees God. (Ireneus, *Against the Heresies* 4.20.5)

Augustine had somewhat greater difficulty with the ocular vision of God in the afterlife, and far less confidence in his ability to explain it. He begins with Paul's "now . . . puzzling reflections in a mirror . . . then face to face."

This [that is, face to face] is the way the holy angels now see, the ones called our angels. . . . The way they now see is the same way we will see; but not yet, so Paul says "now . . . puzzling reflections in a mirror. . . ." That vision is preserved for us as the reward of our faith, and it was of that John was speaking when he said "we shall see Him as He is." The face of God ought to be understood as His manifestation and not as some body part as such, like the one we have and call by that name. So when I am asked what the blessed will do in that spiritual body of theirs, I do not say that I see but rather that I believe. . . . And so I say that they will see God in that body, but whether with it, the way we now through our body see the sun, the moon, the stars and the earth and all the things in it, is no insignificant question. (Augustine, *City of God* 22.29.1)

The incorporeal God who rules all will be seen by us also by our bodies. Whether God will be seen by those eyes by reason of their possessing a degree of excellence like the mind's whereby they too might perceive incorporeal natures is difficult or impossible to show on the basis of examples or texts from the Sacred Scriptures; or, what is easier to understand, God will be known and obvious to us in such a way that He will be seen by the Spirit in and by each of us: He will be seen by one man in another, He will be seen in Himself, and He will be seen in the new heaven and the new earth, and in every creature that will then exist. (Ibid. 22.29.6)

The Quranic proof-text on the vision of God occurs in Sura 75.

> You love this transient life,
> And neglect the Hereafter.
> How many faces will be refulgent on that Day,
> Looking toward their Lord;
> And how many faces on that day will be woe-begone
> Thinking that some great disaster is about to fall upon them.
> (Quran 75:20–25)

The theologian Ash'ari (d. 935 C.E.) offers his direct and succinct exegesis of a text that already in his day had become the subject of controversy. He begins by rejecting the parallel to other Quranic uses of the same verb "looking toward" in contexts where it means "considering as an example" or "feeling sympathy for" or "expecting." "And so," Ash'ari concludes:

> . . . [I]t is certain that His words "looking toward their Lord" here mean "seeing" since they cannot refer to any of the other kinds of "looking toward." For if "looking" is limited to four kinds, and three are impossible in the present case, the fourth kind must be certain, namely, the "look" of the seeing of the eye which is in the face.

But there is a possible objection arising from the next phrase. Ash'ari's exegesis now takes the form of a scholastic disputation with an anonymous opponent.

> But has not God (also) said, "And on that day other faces will be despondent thinking that 'some great disaster will fall upon them'" (Quran 75:24–25)? But thinking is not done with the face, and so similarly His words ". . . looking toward their Lord" must mean the "look" of the heart.
>
> Your objection has no force [Ash'ari responds] because thinking is not done with the face but only with the heart [that is, with an interior faculty]. Hence, since God coupled thinking with a mention of the face, it must refer to the thinking of the heart because thinking is done only with the heart. And if "looking" were (likewise) restricted to the heart, His mentioning it in connection with the face would have to refer to the heart. But since "looking" may be done with the face and in others ways, in connecting it with a reference to the face, He must mean by it the "looking" of the face.

The anonymous objector brings another text into play.

> Question: Then what is the meaning of His words, "Eyes do not attain Him but He attains to eyes" (Quran 6:103)?
>
> Response [by Ash'ari]: They refer to this life and not the next. Hence, when God says in another verse that eyes *will* look at Him, we know that the time of which He says that eyes do not attain Him must be different from the time in which He has revealed that they will be looking at Him. (Ash'ari, *The Science of Dialectical Theology* 75–79)

[ASH'ARI 1953: 48–50]

Few were probably convinced by such highly wrought dialectic. The mystics knew they would see God in the Hereafter because some of their number had in fact seen

Him in this life. The theologians had to be content to struggle with the mere possibility, something that their metaphysical premises suggested was not beyond reach, no matter how little the Quran, the traditionists, and general Muslim sensibilities encouraged them to entertain that thought. For the Christian, the God-man Jesus provided an inviting bridge by which to cross over to the Godhead Itself. Most Muslims, like the great majority of Jews, paused gravely on the hither side, uncertain whether the enormous chasm that separated creature and Creator could ever be transcended, here or even hereafter.

Short Titles

ABOTH RABBI NATHAN 1955. *The Fathers According to Rabbi Nathan*. Translated by Judah Goldin. New Haven: Yale University Press.

ALEXANDER 1984. P. S. Alexander, *Textual Sources for the Study of Judaism*. New York: Barnes and Noble.

ANAWATI & GARDET 1961. G. C. Anawati and Louis Gardet, *Mystique musulmane*. Paris: Librairie philosophique J. Vrin.

AQUINAS 1945. *Basic Writings of Thomas Aquinas*. Edited and annotated by Anton Pegis. 2 vols. New York: Random House.

ARBERRY 1950. A. J. Arberry, *Sufism: An Account of the Mystics of Islam*. London: George Allen & Unwin, Ltd., 1950; rpt. New York: Harper & Row, 1970.

ARBERRY 1964. A. J. Arberry, *Aspects of Islamic Civilization, as Depicted in the Original Texts*. London: George Allen & Unwin, Ltd., 1964; pbk. Ann Arbor: University of Michigan Press, 1976.

ARNOLD 1928. T. Arnold, *Painting in Islam*. Oxford: Oxford University Press, 1928; rpt. New York: Dover Books, 1965.

ASHʿARI 1953. Richard J. McCarthy, S.J., *The Theology of al-Ashʿari*. Beirut: Imprimerie Catholique.

ATTAR 1966. *Muslim Saints and Mystics: Episodes from the Tadhkirat al-Awliya ("Memorials of the Saints") by Farid al-Din Attar*. Translated by A. J. Arberry. Chicago: University of Chicago Press.

ATTAR 1984. Farid ud-Din Attar, *The Conference of the Birds*. Translated by Afkham Darbandi and Dick Davis. Harmondsworth: Penguin.

AUGUSTINE 1947. *Writings of Saint Augustine*, vol. 4: *Christian Instruction*. Translated by J. J. Gavigan. New York: Cima Publishing Company.

AUGUSTINE 1948. *Basic Writings of Saint Augustine*. Edited by Whitney J. Oates. 2 vols. New York: Random House.

AVERROES 1954. *Averroes' Tahafut al-Tahafut (The Incoherence of the Incoherence)*. Translated by Simon van den Bergh. 2 vols. London: Luzac & Company.

AVERROES 1961. *Averroes on the Harmony of Religion and Philosophy*. Translated by G. F. Hourani. London: Luzac & Company.

AVICENNA 1951. A. J. Arberry, *Avicenna on Theology*. London: John Murray.

AYOUB 1984. M. Ayoub, *The Qurʾan and Its Interpreters*. Vol. 1. Albany: State University of New York Press.

BAYNES 1955. N. H. Baynes, "Idolatry and the Early Church." In N. H. Baynes, *Byzantine Studies and Other Essays*, pp. 116–143. London: Athlone Press.

BIRUNI 1879. Al-Biruni, *The Chronology of Ancient Nations*. . . . Translated and edited by C. E. Sachau. London: 1879; rpt. Frankfurt: Minerva, 1969.

BOKSER 1981. Ben Zion Bokser, *The Jewish Mystical Tradition*. New York: Pilgrim Press.

BURTON 1977. John Burton, *The Collection of the Qur'an*, Cambridge: Cambridge University Press.

(PSEUDO)-DIONYSIUS 1987. *Pseudo-Dionysius: The Complete Works*. Translated by Colm Luibheid with Paul Rorem. New York: Paulist Press.

FARABI 1961. Al-Farabi, *Fusul al-Madani: Aphorisms of the Statesman*. Edited and translated by D. M. Dunlop. Cambridge: Cambridge University Press.

GHAZALI 1953. W. Montgomery Watt, *The Faith and Practice of al-Ghazali*. London: George Allen & Unwin, Ltd.

GUILLAUME 1924. Alfred Guillaume, *The Traditions of Islam: An Introduction to the Study of the Hadith Literature*. Oxford: Clarendon Press, 1924; rpt. Lahore: Universal Books, 1977.

HALEVI 1905. Judah Halevi, *The Kuzari: An Argument for the Faith of Israel*. Translated by H. Hirschfeld. 1905; rpt. New York: Schocken Books, 1964.

HALPERIN 1984. D. J. Halperin, "A New Edition of the Hekhalot Literature." *Journal of the American Oriental Society* 104 (1984), 543–552.

HAUSHERR 1927. I. Hausherr, *Le méthode d'oraison hésychaste*. Rome: Orientalia Christiana.

HUJWIRI 1911. *The "Kashf al-Mahjub," the Oldest Persian Treatise on Sufism by al-Hujwiri*. Translated by Reynold A. Nicholson. London: Luzac & Company, 1911; rpt. London: Luzac, 1959.

IBN AL-ARABI 1980. Ibn al-Arabi, *The Bezels of Wisdom*. Translated and edited by R.W.J. Austin. New York: Paulist Press.

IBN BATTUTA 1959–1962. *The Travels of Ibn Battuta, A.D. 1325–1354*. Translated and edited by H.A.R. Gibb. 2 vols. Cambridge: Cambridge University Press.

IBN ISHAQ 1955. *The Life of Muhammad: A Translation of Ishaq's Sirat Rasul Allah*. Translated and edited by A. Guillaume. London: Oxford University Press.

IBN KHALDUN 1967. Ibn Khaldun, *The Muqaddimah: An Introduction to History*. Translated by Franz Rosenthal. 3 vols. 2nd corrected ed. Princeton: Princeton University Press.

IBN QUDAMA 1950. H. Laoust, *Le Précis de droit d'Ibn Qudama*. Beirut: Institut Français de Damas.

JEFFERY 1962. A. Jeffery, *A Reader on Islam: Passages from Standard Arabic Writings Illustrative of the Beliefs and Practices of Muslims*. 's-Gravenhage: Mouton and Company.

JOHN CLIMACUS 1982. *John Climacus, The Ladder of Divine Ascent*. Translated by Colm Luibheid and Norman Russell. New York: Paulist Press.

JUNAYD 1962. Ali Hassan Abdel-Kader, *The Life, Personality and Writings of al-Junayd*. London: Luzac & Company.

JUWAYNI 1968. M. Allard, *Textes apologétiques de Juwaini*. Beirut: Dar al-Machreq.

LANE 1836. Edward Lane, *Manners and Customs of the Modern Egyptians* (1836). 5th ed. rpt. New York: Dover Publications.

LAURENT 1873. J.C.M. Laurent, *Peregrinatores Medii Aevi Quattuor*. 2nd ed. Leipzig: J. C. Hinrichs.

LE GOFF 1984. Jacques Le Goff, *The Birth of Purgatory*. Chicago: University of Chicago Press.

LERNER & MAHDI 1972. R. Lerner and M. Mahdi (eds.), *Medieval Political Philosophy: A Sourcebook*. Glencoe, Ill.: Free Press, 1963; pbk. Ithaca: Cornell University Press, 1972.

LEWIS 1974. Bernard Lewis, *Islam from the Prophet Muhammad to the Capture of Constantinople*. 2 vols. New York: Harper & Row.

LEWIS 1976. Bernard Lewis, "On That Day: A Jewish Apocalyptic Poem on the Arab Conquests." In *Mélanges d'Islamologie . . . de Armand Abel*, pp. 197–200. Leiden: E. J. Brill, 1974. Reprinted in Bernard Lewis, *Studies in Classical and Ottoman Islam (7th–16th Centuries)*. London: Variorum Reprints, 1976.

MCNEILL & GAMER 1938. J. T. McNeill and H. M. Gamer, *Medieval Handbooks of Penance*. New York: Columbia University Press.

MAIMONIDES 1963. Moses Maimonides, *The Guide of the Perplexed*. Translated and edited by Shlomo Pines. Chicago: University of Chicago Press.

MAIMONIDES 1965. *The Code of Maimonides: Book XIV*. New Haven: Yale University Press.

MAIMONIDES 1968. *The Commentary to Mishneh Aboth*. Translated by Arthur David. New York: Bloch Publishing Company.

MANGO 1972. Cyril Mango, *The Art of the Byzantine Empire, 312–1453: Sources and Documents*. Englewood Cliffs, N.J.: Prentice-Hall.

MASSIGNON 1968. Louis Massignon, *Essai sur les origines du lexique technique de la mystique musulmane*. Paris: J. Vrin.

MASSIGNON 1982. Louis Massignon, *The Passion of al-Hallaj: Mystic and Martyr of Islam*. Translated by Herbert Mason. 4 vols. Princeton: Princeton University Press.

MIDRASH RABBAH 1977. *The Midrash Rabbah*. Translated by H. Freedman et al. 5 vols. London, Jerusalem, New York: Soncino Press.

NACHMANIDES 1971. Ramban (Nachmanides), *Commentary on the Torah: Genesis*. Translated by C. B. Chavel. New York: Shilo Publishing House.

NEMOY 1952. *Karaite Anthology: Excerpts from the Early Literature*. Translated by Leon Nemoy. New Haven: Yale University Press.

NICHOLSON 1921. Reynald A. Nicholson, *Studies in Islamic Mysticism*. Cambridge: Cambridge University Press.

PALAMAS 1983. Gregory Palamas, *The Triads*. Edited by John Meyendorff; translation by Nicholas Gendle. New York: Paulist Press.

PESIKTA RABBATI 1968. *Pesikta Rabbati*. Translated by William G. Braude. 2 vols. New Haven and London: Yale University Press.

PETER LOMBARD 1917. E. F. Rogers, "Peter Lombard and the Sacramental System." Ph.D. diss., Columbia University.

PHILO 1945. Philo, *Selections*. Edited and translated by H. Lewy. In *Three Jewish Philosophers*. Philadelphia: Jewish Publication Society, 1945; rpt. New York: Meridian Books, 1960.

PHILO 1981. Philo of Alexandria, *The Contemplative Life, The Giants, and Selections*. Translated by David Winston. New York: Paulist Press.

PINES 1971. S. Pines, *An Arabic Version of the Testimonium Flavianum and Its Implications*. Jerusalem: Israel Academy of Sciences and Humanities.

RAHMAN 1958. F. Rahman, *Prophecy in Islam: Philosophy and Orthodoxy*. London: George Allen & Unwin, Ltd.

RUMI 1925–1940. Jalal al-Din Rumi, *Mathnawi*. Edited, translated, and annotated by R. A. Nicholson. 8 vols. London: Luzac & Company.

SAADYA 1945. Saadya Gaon, *Book of Doctrines and Beliefs*. Abridged translation by A. Altman. In *Three Jewish Philosophers*. Philadelphia: Jewish Publication Society, 1945; rpt. New York: Meridian Books, 1960.

SAADYA 1948. Saadya Gaon, *The Book of Beliefs and Opinions*. Translated by S. Rosenblatt. New Haven: Yale University Press.

SACHEDINA 1981. A. Sachedina, *Islamic Messianism: The Idea of the Mahdi in Twelver Shiʿism*. Albany: State University of New York Press.

SAHAS 1972. D. J. Sahas, *John of Damascus on Islam: The "Heresy of the Ishmaelites."* Leiden: E. J. Brill.

SCHAEFER 1982. P. Schaefer, *Synopse zur Hekhalot-Literatur*. Tübingen: J.C.B. Mohr.

SHAFIʿI 1961. *Islamic Jurisprudence: Shafiʿi's Risala*. Translated by Majid Khadduri. Baltimore: Johns Hopkins University Press.

SMITH 1931. Margaret Smith, *Studies in Early Mysticism in the Near and Middle East*. London: Sheldon Press, 1931; rpt. Amsterdam: Philo Press, 1973.

SMITH 1950. Margaret Smith, *Readings in the Mystics of Islam*. London: Luzac & Company.

SOKOLOW 1981. M. Sokolow, "The Denial of Muslim Sovereignty over Eretz-Israel in Two 10th Century Karaite Bible Commentaries." In J. Hacker (ed.), *Shalem*, 3: 309–318. Jerusalem: Yad Izhak Ben-Zvi Institute.

STANIFORTH 1968. *Early Christian Writings: The Apostolic Fathers*. Translated by Maxwell Staniforth. Harmondsworth: Penguin.

SYMEON NEOTHEOLOGUS 1980. *Symeon the New Theologian: The Discourses*. Translated by C. J. Catanzaro. New York: Paulist Press.

TRIMINGHAM 1971. J. Spencer Trimingham, *The Sufi Orders in Islam*. London: Oxford University Press.

TWERSKY 1980. I. Twersky, *Introduction to the Code of Maimonides (Mishneh Torah)*. New Haven and London: Yale University Press.

VAN BERCHEM 1922. Max Van Berchem, *Corpus inscriptionum arabicarum. Syrie du Sud*, vol. 2: *Jerusalem, "Ville."* Cairo: Institut français d'archéologie orientale.

VERMES 1968. Geza Vermes, *The Dead Sea Scrolls in English*. Harmondsworth: Penguin

WENSINCK 1932. A. J. Wensinck, *The Muslim Creed: Its Genesis and Historical Development*. Cambridge: Cambridge University Press.

WILLIAMS 1971. J. A. Williams, *Themes of Islamic Civilization*. Berkeley: University of California Press.

WRIGHT 1848. T. Wright, *Early Travels in Palestine*. London: H. G. Bohn.

ZENKOVSKY 1963. Serge A. Zenkovsky, *Mediaeval Russia's Epics, Chronicles and Tales*. New York: E. P. Dutton.

ZERNOV 1945. N. Zernov, *The Russians and Their Church*. London and New York: Macmillan.

Index